MILITARY
AIRCRAFT
1919–1945

Other Titles in ABC-CLIO's
WEAPONS AND WARFARE SERIES

Aircraft Carriers, *Paul E. Fontenoy*
Air Defense, *Shannon A. Brown*
Ancient Weapons, *James T. Chambers*
Artillery, *Jeff Kinard*
Ballistic Missiles, *Kev Darling*
Battleships, *Stanley Sandler*
Cruisers and Battle Cruisers, *Eric W. Osborne*
Destroyers, *Eric. W. Osborne*
Helicopters, *Stanley S. McGowen*
Machine Guns, *James H. Willbanks*
Medieval Weapons, *Kelly DeVries, Robert D. Smith*
Military Aircraft in the Jet Age, *Justin D. Murphy, Matthew A. McNiece*
Military Aircraft, Origins to 1918, *Justin D. Murphy*
Pistols, *Jeff Kinard*
Rifles, *David Westwood*
Submarines, *Paul E. Fontenoy*
Tanks, *Spencer C. Tucker*

MILITARY AIRCRAFT 1919–1945

An Illustrated History of Their Impact

Justin D. Murphy

Matthew A. McNiece

A B C ⬥ C L I O

Santa Barbara, California   Denver, Colorado   Oxford, England

Copyright © 2009 by ABC-CLIO, Inc.

Cataloging-in-Publication Data is on file with the Library of Congress

ISBN 978-1-85109-498-1   eBook 978-1-85109-404-2

13 12 11 10 09   1 2 3 4 5 6 7 8 9 10

Editorial Manager: James P. Sherman
Submission Editor: Kim Kennedy-White
Production Manager: Don Schmidt
Media Editor: Ellen Rasmussen
Media Resources Manager: Caroline Price
File Management Coordinator: Paula Gerard

This book is also available on the World Wide Web as an eBook.
Visit www.abc-clio.com for details.

ABC-CLIO, Inc.
130 Cremona Drive, P.O. Box 1911
Santa Barbara, California 93116–1911

This book is printed on acid-free paper ∞
Manufactured in the United States of America

CONTENTS

Introduction to Weapons and Warfare Series,
Spencer C. Tucker   vii

Preface and Acknowledgments   ix

CHAPTER ONE

Military Aviation in the Interwar Years, 1919–1939   1

CHAPTER TWO

Military Aviation in World War II, 1939–1945   37

CHAPTER THREE

Fighter and Attack Aircraft   79

CHAPTER FOUR

Bomber Aircraft   123

CHAPTER FIVE

Reconnaissance and Auxiliary Aircraft   165

CHAPTER SIX

Naval Aircraft   195

Aircraft by Country   235

Aircraft in Alphabetical Order   238

Glossary of Terms   319

A Selective Bibliography of Military Aircraft, 1919–1945   323

Index   329

About the Authors   349

INTRODUCTION TO
WEAPONS AND WARFARE SERIES

WEAPONS BOTH FASCINATE AND REPEL. They are used to kill and maim individuals and to destroy states and societies, and occasionally whole civilizations, and with these the greatest of man's cultural and artistic accomplishments. Throughout history tools of war have been the instruments of conquest, invasion, and enslavement, but they have also been used to check evil and to maintain peace.

Weapons have evolved over time to become both more lethal and more complex. For the greater part of humanity's existence, combat was fought at the length of an arm or at such short range as to represent no real difference; battle was fought within line of sight and seldom lasted more than the hours of daylight of a single day. Thus, individual weapons that began with the rock and the club proceeded through the sling and boomerang, bow and arrow, sword and axe, to gunpowder weapons of the rifle and machine gun of the late nineteenth century. Study of the evolution of these weapons tells us much about human ingenuity, the technology of the time, and the societies that produced them. The greater part of technological development of weaponry has taken part in the last two centuries, especially the twentieth century. In this process, plowshares have been beaten into swords (e.g., the tank evolved from the agricultural caterpillar tractor). The process is occasionally reversed and military technology has impacted society in a positive way. Thus, modern civilian medicine has greatly benefited from advances to save soldiers' lives, and weapons technology has impacted such areas as civilian transportation and atomic power.

Weapons can have a profound impact on society. Gunpowder weapons, for example, were an important factor in ending the era of the armed knight and the Feudal Age. They installed a kind of rough democracy on the battlefield, making "all men alike tall." We can only wonder what effect weapons of mass destruction (WMD) might have on our own time and civilization.

This series will trace the evolution of a variety of key weapons systems, describe the major changes that occurred in each, and illustrate and identify the key types. Each volume begins with a description of the particular weapons system and traces its evolution, while discussing its historical, social, and political contexts. This is followed by a heavily illustrated section that is arranged more or less along chronological lines that provides more precise information on at least 80 key variants of that particular weapons system. Each volume contains a glossary of terms, a bibliography of leading books on that particular subject, and an index.

Individual volumes in the series, each written by a specialist in that particular area of expertise, are as follows:

Ancient Weapons
Medieval Weapons
Pistols
Rifles
Machine Guns
Artillery
Tanks
Battleships
Cruisers and Battle Cruisers
Aircraft Carriers
Submarines
Air Defense
Military Aircraft, Origins to 1918
Military Aircraft, 1919–1945
Military Aircraft in the Jet Age
Helicopters
Ballistic Missiles
Destroyers

We hope that this series will be of wide interest to specialists, researchers, and even general readers.

Spencer C. Tucker
Series Editor

PREFACE AND ACKNOWLEDGMENTS

THE LEGACY OF AIR POWER in the Second World War is often synonymous with place names: Pearl Harbor, London, Dresden,
Hiroshima, Nagasaki. Indeed, aircraft inflicted tremendous damage
throughout the war, from close air support against troops and tanks,
to strategic bombing of industrial centers, to terror bombing of civilian centers and the harnessing of the destructive power of both fire
and atomic fission. It is truly difficult to imagine the war without the
aircraft it made famous: Zeroes, Mustangs, Shturmoviks, Stukas, Spitfires, Superfortresses, and many, many others.

Air power unquestionably increased the destructiveness of war, especially with the introduction of heavy, long-range bombers that could
drop thousands of pounds of high explosives on areas previously considered safe from attack. Such infamous events as the fire-bombings of
Tokyo and Dresden certainly demonstrated this, although citizens of
both London and Berlin—to say nothing of those in countless other
cities—bore the brunt of more "conventional" bombings. Even the military experienced this kind of awakening to the ways aircraft would
change combat forever. The incredibly successful Japanese torpedo
bombing of the U.S. Fleet stationed at Pearl Harbor demonstrated, quite
conclusively, that oceans no longer provided walls of separation from
belligerents. In just a few hours, Japanese naval aircraft inflicted more
damage on American warcraft than the Imperial Fleet could have hoped
to do in days of pitched battle in the open waters. Of course, the American use of atomic bombs against Hiroshima and Nagasaki demonstrated that aircraft could be used—quite effectively, if ruthlessly—to
deliver the most frighteningly potent of new weapons, one so immensely
powerful that it forced a nation into immediate capitulation and which,
many historians argue, has since kept the many nations of the world
from foolishly lurching into a Third World War.

Often unnoticed by many students and scholars alike, however, is the fact that aircraft also increased the speed of modern war, and they did so by an order of magnitude. They could both inflict previously unthought-of levels of destruction and could do so with previously unthought-of immediacy. As will be seen in the following chapters, even many heavy bombers of the World War II era eclipsed the speeds generated by the most advanced aircraft of World War I. Tremendous advances in this area continued throughout the war, culminating in the introduction of jet-powered aircraft capable of speeds and airborne feats likely never conceived of by the air power theorists of the inter-war era.

Despite these rapid advances in technology, the famous theorists and air power proponents of the preceding generation—especially Giulio Douhet, William "Billy" Mitchell, and Hugh Trenchard—accurately predicted that aircraft would lead future wars. Even though they turned out to be wrong in certain respects, as detailed in the following chapters, air power did in fact play a decisive role in many battles and campaigns throughout the war. Their theories led many nations to expand their air arms even during the interwar years (i.e., when no new "great" war seemed imminent, and even when the worldwide economic depression made government funds scarce). Civilian aviation contributed many great innovations and improvements to the industry, however, especially as the early battles of the war proved time and again that those with air supremacy generally carried the day, so the great powers proceeded through World War II with the impetus to develop what one might consider "modern" air forces.

This definition of modern means more than mere technological innovation in aircraft design, or simple improvement in aircraft performance. Even though these are certainly part of the equation, one must also recognize that the Second World War witnessed the trend of highly specialized aircraft for highly specific tactical missions. There were certainly multipurpose aircraft, and others that saw most of their service in a role different than that which their designers envisioned; however, the bulk of World War II aircraft were committed to a single category from the design stages onward. Smaller, lighter, more maneuverable, and faster fighter and attack aircraft became responsible for establishing air superiority and assisting ground troops with tactical strikes on the enemy's front lines. Moreover, they became responsible for escorting heavy strategic bombers on long-range missions deep into enemy territory—establishing something of a flying zone of air superiority. This was vital because bombers, too, had become far more specialized. Although highly adept at carrying great payloads across great distances, most heavy bombers were very vulnerable to enemy fighters. Even those with the heaviest defensive armament could not operate with impunity in enemy airspace unless friendly fighters provided escort. There were also light bombers and torpedo bombers, however, that performed roles that simply could not be performed by heavy bombers. Naval variants of these types flourished, especially in the Pacific Theater, and especially with the proliferation of aircraft carriers. Indeed, World War II aircraft continued performing the invaluable reconnaissance and auxiliary roles for which air power had been originally adopted by the world's armies.

The chapters following this brief introduction will, it is hoped, give the reader a better understanding of the development of these more specialized uses of military aircraft. Chapter One discusses the tremendous growth of the aviation industry and vast technological advances of the interwar years, as well as the impact these developments had upon the integration of aviation into the militaries of the major powers. Chapter Two offers an overview of the role of military air power during the various campaigns of World War II. These chapters are clearly not exhaustive. Neither are the chapters that follow, which detail the most important aircraft in the following categories: Fighters and Attack Aircraft (Chapter Three); Bombers (Chapter Four); Auxiliary Aircraft (Chapter Five); Naval Aircraft (Chapter Six). They represent, however, the authors' best efforts at producing an efficient, well-organized, and, above all else, easily accessible reference work. In the process we faced the daunting task of deciding which aircraft should be included and the even more difficult challenge of deciding which aircraft had to be excluded to stay within the space limitations of this volume. We ultimately focused on those that marked an important transition in technology during the interwar years and those that played the most important role in warfare, which is the purpose of the Weapons and Warfare series. One can safely assume we will have left out some detail or model that another scholar considers vital, and for that we apologize. Nevertheless, we are confident readers will find this work quite informative; of course, we hope they find it quite enjoyable, too.

Dr. Justin D. Murphy wishes to thank first his co-author without whom this volume would not have been written. Equally important, the understanding of my wife, Jessica, who endured far too much time without me and took on far more responsibilities that should have been shared, enabled me to devote the time that made this book possible. Special consideration also needs to be given to my two sons, Jonathan and Jason, who put up with a sometimes irritable father and accepted my absence. My mentor, Dr. Spencer C. Tucker, the editor of this series, deserved special consideration for his support, encouragement, and understanding when things did not proceed as quickly as planned. The same is true of the publication staff. Words cannot adequately express my gratitude. Finally, my faithful companion Snickers must be mentioned, for he spent many a long day on his bed under my desk. Granted he enjoyed the long naps, but he was there to wag his tail and offer affection when it was needed most.

Mr. Matthew McNiece reflects on the great and exciting changes in his personal and professional life since he began researching World War II aircraft for this book. He has married Jennifer, whom he wishes to thank above anyone else because, after all, she knows where he lives. He has completed the coursework toward a Ph.D. in American History at Texas Christian University, where professors and colleagues alike gave him great encouragement in his growth as a scholar and in his pursuit of a position at his alma mater, Howard Payne University, where he has the honor of teaching some of the same courses as his own mentors. He hopes he lives up to their legacies. Finally, he wishes to thank his friends, his family, and those precious few (they know who they are) whom he is honored to count as both.

CHAPTER ONE

Military Aviation in the Interwar Years, 1919–1939

As the guns fell silent on November 11, 1918, the European powers were exhausted after four years of carnage on a level never experienced before in history. Approximately 10 million people had been killed and another 20 million were wounded, taken prisoner, or missing. Those who survived, whether combatants or noncombatants, were forever changed by the horror they had endured and by the gap left within an entire generation. This would be indelibly etched into the living memory by the monuments erected to honor those who had fought and died. Although most images of the First World War—the mud and mire of the trenches, the moonscape appearance of No Man's Land, poison gas and gas masks, film of soldiers suffering from shell shock—evoke this sense of horror, this is not true when it comes to the role of aircraft in the war.

With the exception of the German bombing campaign over England, the air war has tended to be glamorized and as a consequence its true impact has often been distorted. Numerous factors have contributed to this. First, the desire to find something noble in the carnage of the war led to a glorification of fighter pilots, who were depicted as medieval knights engaged in personal combat. The reality was far different because pilots flew and fought in squadrons and only rarely engaged in individual conflict. Second, the media provided popular culture with a glamorized version of aerial combat through film, magazines, and books.

Third, the proponents of air power greatly exaggerated the impact of strategic bombing during the war in order to advance and justify the expansion of air power afterwards.

In contrast to the media and air power proponents, most postwar military officials and military historians downplayed the impact of military aircraft on the war, granting it only an auxiliary role in effecting the war's outcome. Although military aircraft fulfilled the prewar expectations of providing surveillance, the technological limitations of military aircraft prevented them from living up to the prewar expectations of aviation enthusiasts and journalists who believed that air power would have a decisive impact upon warfare, despite the tremendous breakthroughs that did occur during the war. Strategic bombers produced only minimal physical damage and never created the psychological devastation that many had predicted. Likewise, fighters played primarily a defensive role, protecting surveillance aircraft and denying airspace over their own lines. Bombers and fighters were used in close cooperation with ground forces, assisting in attack and in defense, only toward the end of the war. Throughout the war, therefore, reconnaissance and observation duties were the most important role played by military aircraft.

Although military aircraft did not have a decisive impart in determining the outcome of the First World War, the war did have a decisive impact upon military aviation. First and foremost, military necessity accelerated the pace of aviation technology. By the war's end, aircraft had little in common with their prewar predecessors. Second, military commanders, such as General Eric Ludendorff and Field Marshal Ferdinand Foch, and military historians, such as Sir Basil H. Liddell-Hart, had seen enough promise in the performance of military aircraft during the war that they boldly predicted that aircraft would have a tremendous impact on future wars. This in part explains the Versailles Treaty's ban on a German air force. Third, military aviation gained an identity of its own, eventually leading to its separation from the army and navy as an independent branch of service. For instance, the Royal Air Force became the world's first independent air force in April 1918. Fourth, despite the limited impact of strategic bombing, military theorists Giulio Douhet, Hugh Trenchard, and William "Billy" Mitchell accumulated enough evidence—albeit sometimes imagined and sometimes exaggerated—to promote the use of air power as a war-winning strategy in the postwar years. In the process their theories influenced the organization of air power in the interwar years as well as its use in the Second World War.

Air Power Theory during the Interwar Years

Giulio Douhet

Prior to the First World War, Giulio Douhet emerged as one of the earliest air power theorists. Douhet, who was born on May 30, 1869, in Caserta, entered the Italian army as an artillery officer at age twenty-three in 1892. With the advent of aircraft and airships in the early twentieth century, he became the foremost enthusiast of air power in the Italian army and clashed with his superiors, criticizing their preference for airships and demanding an independent air force. In the aftermath of Italy's victorious campaign against the Turks in the Tripolitan War in 1911–1912, Douhet parlayed his official report on the use of airships and aircraft in that conflict into command of an aviation battalion stationed at Turin. He also published *Rules for the Use of Aircraft in War*, the world's first manual for the use of air power. Douhet predicted that the line between civilians and combatants would be erased as belligerents would use aircraft to bomb their enemy's centers of armament production. In so doing civilians would inevitably suffer from aerial bombardment and become casualties of war. Although almost all of his contemporaries dismissed him as a fanatical theorist and barbarian, Douhet received a lot of attention and won a few admirers. But his combative criticism of his superiors undermined his influence within the Italian army. Indeed, when Douhet ordered several three-engine bombers from his close friend, Gianni Caproni, without the authorization of his superiors, he was "kicked upstairs" by being reassigned in 1914 as chief of staff to an army division.

Although his superiors might have hoped that his "promotion" would keep Douhet quiet, they were to be sorely disappointed. When Italy entered the First World War in April 1915 on the side of the Allies, Douhet wrote articles that were increasingly critical of how his superiors were waging the war as Italian losses and casualties mounted. Rather than continue foolhardy infantry attacks, Douhet argued that Italy's resources should be used to build a huge bomber force capable of bombing enemy cities on a daily basis. His stinging indictments against his superiors led to his court-martial in September 1916. He continued writing on behalf of air power while in prison over the next year. Italy's disastrous defeat at Caporetto in the fall of 1917 validated Douhet's criticisms and led to the reorganization of the Italian air service as a General Commissariat within the War Office. Douhet was appointed director of aviation in January 1918 after his release from prison in December 1917. Despite this exoneration, he remained frustrated and retired from the army in June 1918. After the war he appealed his court-martial conviction, which was overturned in 1920. Although promoted to brigadier general in 1921, Douhet chose not to return to active service. Instead, he published *Command of the Air* later in the year to promote his theories on air power.[1]

Firm in his belief that air power had permanently altered warfare and that future wars would be won in the air, Douhet set out to demonstrate how air power must be used in the future. Although securing command of the air was the first priority, Douhet argued that this was to be achieved through destroying the enemy's ground installations and aircraft industry rather than through direct air battles against the enemy's air force. For this reason, Douhet asserted that a nation must devote its resources for offensive weapons (a multipurpose battle aircraft capable of carrying out long-range bombing attacks with massive force, while defending itself against enemy fighters) rather than for defensive weapons (fighters or anti-aircraft artillery). The Boeing B-17 "Flying Fortress," developed by the United States in the 1930s, epitomized Douhet's ideal aircraft. Long-range reconnaissance would be necessary only to assess damage and plan follow-up attacks. Douhet based his philosophy on the premise that the bomber would always get through and that future wars must be initiated by an overwhelming assault on an enemy's communication systems, government buildings, industrial infrastructure, transportation network, and will of the populace. The last of these priorities was perhaps the most notorious and controversial aspect, yet Douhet did not shrink from the harsh realities of modern warfare ushered in by air power. Indeed, he advocated the use of chemical weapons as absolutely necessary because he believed that the resulting horror of such an attack on civilians would force the enemy's government to surrender. It should be emphasized that Douhet considered the end result (a short war with fewer overall casualties) far preferable to the long, drawn out war that Europeans had just experienced.

Historians have long debated the impact of Douhet's theories. Whereas other theorists were influenced by his ideals, it is important to note that *Command of the Air* was not fully translated into English until the early 1940s. Its international impact was therefore fairly limited, and other theorists developed their own ideas in light of the conditions within their own countries. In addition, several points of debate remain about the merit of Douhet's theories. First, the technology of the time did not make the implementation of his theories very practical. Second, the political realities of the interwar years made it impossible for governments to shift resources away from the armies and navies to the extent that Douhet demanded. Third, the financial devastation left by the First World War did not leave governments with the means to invest in the air power, particularly more expensive bombers, to the levels needed to implement his theories. Fourth, Douhet's premise that the bomber would always get through did not take into consideration that technological advances in other areas might change that equation, as later demonstrated in the Battle of Britain. Fifth, Douhet, as well as other air power theorists, greatly overestimated the damage that bombing would have on an enemy's infrastructure and, more importantly, on the civilian population. As the Second World War would demonstrate, civilians were far more resilient than Douhet and others assumed. Indeed, at the height of the Allied bombing campaign, Allied bombers were dropping more than 3,000 times as many bombs per day as Douhet had calculated would be necessary to defeat an enemy in a week. Nevertheless, Douhet deserves credit for being the first to articulate a systematic vision for the use of air power.

William "Billy" Mitchell

Although Douhet's influence is open to debate, in part because Italy lacked the resources to implement his ideas, his American counterpart, Brigadier General William "Billy" Mitchell, had by far the greater impact upon air power theory and practice during the interwar years and beyond. Mitchell was born into a wealthy and prominent family on December 28, 1879, in Nice, France. He launched his military career upon the outbreak of the Spanish-American War in 1898, enlisting as a private in the First Wisconsin Volunteer Infantry. His father, then a U.S. senator from Wisconsin, used his influence to secure Mitchell a commission in the Signal Corps, the most scientific branch of the army. Mitchell quickly demonstrated a gift for organization during tours in Cuba, the Philippines, and Alaska that resulted in rapid promotion based on his own merit. A captain by age thirty-three, Mitchell graduated from the Army Staff College in 1909 and became the youngest officer on the Army General Staff in 1912. Mitchell saw the potential of aviation early on and paid for his own flying lessons in 1916, and briefly served as Deputy Chief of the Signal Corps Aviation Section. He also flew in the First Aero Squadron during the Punitive Expedition into Mexico in 1916–1917.

As U.S. entry into the First World War became increasingly likely in 1917, Mitchell, by then a major, was dispatched to France as a military observer, primarily because he was fluent in French. The timing could not have been better for Mitchell's future because the United States declared war on Germany just four days before his arrival in Paris on April 10. As one of the senior American aviators in France, Mitchell proved to be an excellent networker, interviewing Allied aviators and observing Allied aviation organization and operations as he took charge of American preparations for air units that were scheduled to arrive in France. Of equal importance, Mitchell succeeded in winning the confidence and friendship of the Royal Flying Corps commander, Major General Hugh Trenchard, from whom he gained an appreciation of the role of aircraft as offensive weapons and the necessity of air supremacy. It should be emphasized, however, that Mitchell's ideas were ultimately shaped by numerous sources, including Douhet, whom he met after the war, and members of his own staff, especially Major Edgar Gorrell, who served as chief of the technical section, air services, of the American Expedition Force (AEF).

Mitchell was promoted to colonel in June 1917 and had a detailed plan ready for organizing American air power by the time Major General John J. Pershing arrived in Europe with the first units of the AEF. Mitchell called for developing two distinct types of air forces: fighter squadrons to attack enemy aircraft and bomber squadrons to conduct a strategic campaign against enemy targets. Although Pershing refused to give the air service the degree of independence that Mitchell desired, he assigned Mitchell with the task of organizing the 1,500 Allied aircraft that Supreme Allied Commander Field Marshal Ferdinand Foch had put at the AEF's disposal for the Saint-Mihiel Offensive in September 1918. There, Mitchell developed an aerial battle plan unparalleled in the war. He assigned approximately one third of his force to support ground operations and divided the remaining two thirds into two brigades of 500 planes each, which were used in a variety of strategic missions unprecedented in the war: achieving air superiority; attacking German troops, supply depots, and communication centers; and bombing enemy air bases to force them into the open. Mitchell was promoted to brigadier general after Saint-Mihiel and next organized aircraft for the Meuse-Argonne Offensive that was launched on September 26 and would continue until the Armistice on November 11.

During the course of the war Mitchell wrote numerous articles that pressed for a major expansion of American air power. By war's end he was recognized as America's top airman, in part because of his undeniable achievements and in part because of his public charisma. Mitchell's outspokenness, however, clearly rankled many of his superiors. Although he retained his rank of brigadier general after the war, he was denied his goal of being chief of the air service in the postwar army and was appointed chief of training and operations instead. In an effort to keep him out of Washington, Mitchell's superiors dispatched him on several inspection trips to Europe and Asia. This backfired, however, as Mitchell returned with fresh ideas about aircraft and their use as well as a conviction that Japan, then a U.S. ally, would be the U.S.'s future enemy.

Realizing that he could not achieve his ideas through military channels, Mitchell did not hesitate to go over the heads of his superiors by testifying at congressional hearings, writing articles, and giving speeches on the necessity of air power. In order to keep military aviation in the public's mind, Mitchell ordered the air service to aid in fighting forest fires and encouraged army pilots to challenge any and all aviation records. Mitchell took matters a step further by openly criticizing both the army and navy for neglecting air power, which he believed was crucial to national security. Mitchell argued that aircraft had transformed the nature of warfare because the army and navy would not be able to conduct campaigns in the future until an air force had gained air superiority over the enemy. It was therefore vital that the United States maintain a strong air force in peacetime in order to be prepared upon the outbreak of war. More important, Mitchell asserted that air power must be an independent branch of service separate from the army and navy. Unlike Douhet, who emphasized the all-purpose battle plane, Mitchell's training as a military pilot meant he understood that specialized aircraft were needed to perform the specific roles an air war would require. In contrast to Douhet, Mitchell maintained that the bulk of the air service should consist of pursuit aircraft because these would be needed to destroy the enemy in the air. He also saw the need for close support attack aircraft and observation aircraft, in addition to bombers and pursuit aircraft, and called for organizing the air service along these four separate roles: Pursuit, Bombardment, Attack, and Observation.

Mitchell became increasingly outspoken in leading his campaign for an independent air force. In particular, Mitchell came to see the navy as the chief obstacle to achieving his ideas and in the process repeatedly painted the navy as antiquated in its ideas, when in fact there were naval officers (William Sims, W. F. Fullam, Bradley Fiske, and William Moffatt) who recognized the importance of naval aviation, but were not as outspoken as he was. More important, Mitchell claimed that air-based aircraft could intercept enemy warships on the high seas and sink surface ships without any aid from the fleet. He even boasted that he could prove this if given the chance to bomb captured German battleships. In July 1921, Mitchell's bomber squadrons, using 2,000 pound bombs, successfully sank several ships, including the German prize dreadnaught *Ostfriesland*. The Navy correctly pointed out that the ships had been stationary and undefended, but this did not stop Mitchell from asserting that the test offered conclusive proof that air power was now the primary defense force, thus making the navy surface fleet obsolete. The tests ironically resulted in the navy establishing the Bureau of Aeronautics under Rear Admiral William A. Moffett and converting two battle cruiser hulls into aircraft carriers (*Lexington* and *Saratoga*).

In the aftermath of the 1921 tests, Mitchell became more vociferous in his campaign for an independent air force, even though such close associates as Henry "Hap" Arnold urged him to be more circumspect. Given the declining military budgets of the 1920s and competition between the army and navy for what funds Congress was willing to appropriate, it is not surprising that Mitchell's superiors turned a deaf ear to his increasingly strident demands. In attempts to get him off the front page Mitchell had been reassigned to Hawaii by 1924, and then to Asia. Upon his return, he submitted a 324-page report predicting war with Japan. An outline and time line detailing how the Japanese would launch surprise air attacks on Pearl Harbor and the Philippines were included in the document. In 1925 Mitchell found himself reassigned from the air service to Fort Sam Houston, Texas, and demoted to his permanent rank of colonel. Although demotions from temporary rank to one's permanent rank were not unusual, in this case the move was seen as punishment and exile; however, Mitchell would not go quietly. While in Texas, he published one of his first books, *Winged Defense: The Development and Possibilities of Modern Air Power—Economic and Military*, which was clearly intended to sway public opinion. More important, when the navy dirigible USS *Shenandoah* crashed in a storm on September 3, 1925, killing most of the crew, Mitchell called a press conference and accused the senior leaders of the army and navy of incompetence and criminal administration of the nation's defenses.

In response to Mitchell's charges, President Calvin Coolidge adroitly appointed an advisory board under Dwight Morrow to examine American aviation, while at the same time ordering court-martial proceedings against Mitchell. Because Mitchell was called to testify before the Morrow Board, this avoided making him a martyr. Even though the Morrow Board did not support the creation of an independent air force as Mitchell had demanded, its recommendations did support some of Mitchell's ideas and ultimately led to the creation of the U.S. Army Air Corps in 1926. This would not save Mitchell at his court-martial. After a seven-week trial in which Mitchell floundered under withering cross-examination, he was found guilty of insubordination and suspended from duty for five years without pay. Although Coolidge lessened the sentence to half-pay, Mitchell resigned on February 1, 1926. He continued to speak out for air power until his death in New York City on February 19, 1936.

Although Mitchell's fall from grace was swift, his influence upon American air power proved to be immense and long-lasting. His emphasis upon research and development contributed to technological breakthroughs (pressurized air cabins, improved navigation instruments, bomb sights, self-sealing tanks, and the supercharger) that were vital to American air power in World War II. More important, he inspired such subordinates as Henry H. "Hap" Arnold, Ira Eaker, and Carl A. Spaatz, who firmly believed Mitchell's claim that air power alone could bring victory through strategic bombing and who would attempt to carry that out during World War II. Although this belief ultimately proved to be incorrect, the establishment of the United States as the supreme air power of the world by the end of the war is indeed a reflection of Mitchell's achievement. Likewise, Mitchell's stature was enhanced by the Japanese surprise attack on Pearl Harbor, which happened just as he had predicted.[2] During World War II, the North American B-25 was named the "Mitchell" in his honor. In 1946, Mitchell posthumously received a special medal in recognition of his foresight in aviation and promotion to major general. This was followed by the voiding of his court-martial in 1955 by the U.S. Air Force.

Hugh Trenchard

In sharp contrast to Douhet and Mitchell, the leading British postwar air power theorist, Hugh Trenchard, proved far more flexible and effective in applying his theories as commander of the Royal Air Force after the First World War. Trenchard, who was born at Trauton on February 3, 1873, entered the army in 1893 and served in the Boer War. He obtained his pilot's license while on leave in 1912 and became commandant of the Central Flying School in 1913. Upon taking command of the Royal Flying Corps in France on August 19, 1915, Trenchard emphasized the need for aggressive offensive action in the air by concentrating Allied fighters into fighter squadrons rather than scattering them piecemeal among squadrons. Unlike Douhet and Mitchell, Trenchard saw aviation's role as an extension of the army's efforts on the ground and for this reason stubbornly persisted in his relentless offensive strategy despite heavy losses, believing it would ultimately result in victory over the Germans. As a result, pilots of the Royal Flying Corps endured a similar level (comparative in scope) of fruitless attrition suffered by the infantry under Field Marshal Sir Douglas Haig's command.

Irony fills Trenchard's tenure as commander of the Royal Flying Corps during the First World War. When German bombing attacks on London in 1917 led the public and Prime Minister David Lloyd George to call for a similar response, Trenchard adamantly opposed strategic bombing as a waste of resources. Trenchard's resistance contributed to the merger of the Royal Flying Corps and Royal Naval Air Service on April 1, 1918, into the Royal Air Force (RAF), the first independent air service in history. This move also resulted in Sir Frederick Sykes replacing Trenchard as chief of the air staff and Trenchard's reassignment as commander of the Independent Bombing Force, which had been created to carry out strategic bombing campaigns against Germany (the very thing Trenchard had opposed in the first place). Nevertheless, Trenchard, unlike Douhet and Mitchell, consistently valued military duty above personal feelings and devoted himself to this new directive with his usual single-mindedness. Although the Armistice came before its impact could be proven conclusively, Trenchard became a convert to the doctrine of strategic bombing. The intensive raids he directed against German railways, airfields, and industrial centers, which were designed to force Germany to the bargaining table, deeply influenced Trenchard's postwar theories.

Although Trenchard had been demoted in favor of Sykes upon the creation of the RAF, he remained popular among RAF airmen and, more importantly, with Winston Churchill, who was named minister of war and air in 1919 and charged with postwar demobilization. Churchill, who despised Sykes, turned to Trenchard, with whom he had served in India years before, and asked Trenchard to prepare a report on the role of the postwar RAF. Trenchard's 800-word report so impressed Churchill that it helped preserve the RAF as an independent force and resulted in Trenchard returning to command the RAF from 1919 to 1929.

As chief of the air service, Trenchard proved both flexible and pragmatic, adjusting his theories to meet the circumstances he confronted. As commander of the Royal Flying Corps during the First World War, he had dismissed strategic bombing in favor of a relentless offensive against German military targets because he viewed the RFC's role as supporting the army's effort on the ground. Later, however, as commander of the Independent Bombing Force, he conducted a rigorous strategic bombing campaign because that was the purpose of his force. Now, as commander of the RAF, Trenchard created an air power doctrine that called for an independent, strategic weapon, arguing that the RAF could defend Britain at the beginning of any future war by launching its massive striking power against any threat from France or Germany. In addition, he stressed that aircraft would provide a more cost-effective means of policing the empire. Like Douhet, Trenchard emphasized the psychological impact that strategic bombing would have upon civilian populations, arguing that its effect upon morale would be twenty times greater than the actual physical damage inflicted. Unlike Douhet, however, Trenchard did not advocate targeting civilians per se. Rather, he recognized that civilian deaths would be collateral damage in any bombing campaign. He also pointed out that in an age of total war there was not much difference in killing munitions workers when bombing a factory than killing enemy soldiers when bombing a military installation.

The first major battle that Trenchard had to fight was the battle of the budget. With the RAF having shrunk from 250 squadrons at war's end to 25 squadrons in 1919, Trenchard feared that further losses of aircraft and crews to the navy for aircraft carriers or the army for close support missions would spell the end of the RAF itself. His advocacy of strategic bombing, therefore, was in part designed to secure funds for the RAF, but the budgetary constraints of the 1920s and 1930s provided neither Trenchard nor his successors the means to implement his theories. Indeed, the RAF received only about 15 percent of the total military budget throughout most of the interwar years. It should also be emphasized that British military spending as a whole was greatly reduced from 1919 to 1933 as economy-minded government officials imposed the Ten Year Rule, which based annual military appropriations on the premise that there would not be another war in Europe for ten years. In characteristic fashion, Trenchard adjusted accordingly. Although he continued to focus on strategic bombers, Trenchard spent the majority of the RAF's funds on air bases and pilot training. Equally important, he maintained a logistical base by spreading out aircraft contracts among multiple contractors, thereby keeping companies in business. In addition, since Trenchard considered France to be the main threat to Britain during the 1920s, he established numerous fighter bases in southeastern Great Britain. This later proved critical to victory in the Battle of Britain.

Although Trenchard lacks the reputation of Douhet and Mitchell, in part because he was virtually incapable of expressing his views coherently, he was perhaps more effective than Douhet and Mitchell. Above all else, Trenchard followed military protocol and avoided the public confrontations that proved the undoing of both Douhet and Mitchell. He also had an uncanny ability to make do with what he had, and to do it well. Despite tight budgets, he maintained the RAF as a viable organization that attracted highly qualified officers whose leadership proved vital during the next war. Trenchard was promoted to air marshal in 1927, and after retiring in 1929, he served as commissioner of the Metropolitan Police from 1931 to 1935. He was elevated to the House of Lords in 1936 and died in London on February 10, 1956.

Technological Improvements in Aviation during the Interwar Years

The great advances in air power theory brought on by those like Douhet, Mitchell, and Trenchard demanded similar advances in the science of aviation technology. Although the First World War had witnessed tremendous improvements in aircraft performance, these had been brought about primarily by improved engines. With few exceptions, aircraft at the close of the war were rather fragile, using wooden structures, wire bracing, and fabric or plywood covering. Designers favored biplanes because the short wing spans and low-wing loading improved climbing and maneuverability. Even though the biplane remained a favored design during the interwar years, there were clear limits on its performance. By the end of the 1920s the development of more powerful engines increased the speed of biplane fighters by 30 percent, but this was not true of bombers and other support aircraft, which were not much faster than their World War I ancestors. Even though military innovations stalled during the 1920s, as governments drastically reduced wartime spending levels, civilian aviation and aircraft competitions yielded several technological breakthroughs. For instance, Charles Lindbergh's solo flight across the Atlantic in 1927 made him an international celebrity and stimulated private investment in aviation.

The increasing use of aircraft for transporting passengers and freight brought about more innovation in aircraft design than perhaps any other aspect of civil aviation. In the immediate aftermath of the First World War, governments sold surplus military aircraft, primarily bombers and large reconnaissance airplanes, at substantial discounts. Civilian companies purchased and adapted these military aircraft for civil use as mail carriers and passenger liners. This military-civilian cooperation also took the form of government subsidies to struggling airline companies. This proved critical in the case of Germany to maintaining an aircraft industry that could be reconverted to military production. Nevertheless, commercial airline companies recognized that bargain prices on surplus military aircraft were only part of the equation. Requiring passengers to bundle up like arctic explorers in open air cockpits when faster, more comfortable means of transportation were available on the ground was a losing proposition. The industry required safer, faster, and more comfortable aircraft.

One of the first designers to respond to this new market was Anthony Fokker, the famed designer who had developed numerous German fighters during World War I. Fokker returned to his native Netherlands after the war and introduced the F.VII high-wing monoplane in 1924. Capable of carrying eight to ten passengers and designed to accept a variety of engines in either a single or trimotor configuration, it would be licensed-built in several European counties, the United States, and Japan. It was quickly followed in 1925 by the Ford Trimotor, a high-wing all-metal monoplane that could accommodate up to sixteen passengers.

Although flying boats dominated passenger service in the Mediterranean and across the oceans, the all-metal monoplane design represented the wave of the future, particularly as advances in aerodynamics improved performance. Realizing that reducing drag during flight would increase cruising speed and the distance that could be traveled, designers sought to develop more streamlined aircraft with smoother lines and smooth skins for improved air flow. One step in this direction was to cover the wheels (trousers), but the most important development was completely retractable undercarriages. The only practical way to achieve this was using a low-wing configuration, so that the wheels could be retracted into the wings after takeoff. Although this could be done manually, it made far more sense to use the engine to power a hydraulic system. Another important step was the addition of cowlings around the engines to minimize drag. To their surprise, designers found that the cowlings increased speed and resulted in improved cooling by allowing for air ducts to provide a more efficient stream of air around the engine. This was first demonstrated in November 1928 when a Lockheed Vega set a new transcontinental record, crossing the United States in 18 hours and 13 minutes. The addition of the cowling alone increased its cruising speed from 157 mph to 177 mph.

Despite the Great Depression, the demand for passenger service increased in the 1930s. In an effort to increase profitability, airlines sought aircraft capable of carrying more passengers while still reducing the consumption of fuel. The result was three remarkable aircraft, the Boeing 247, the Douglas DC-3, and the Boeing 347 Stratoliner, that transformed passenger service. The Boeing 247, introduced in February 1933, incorporated numerous improvements in aerodynamic design. Constructed of a lightweight aluminum alloy with stressed metal skin and retractable undercarriages, the Boeing 247 was powered by just two 550 hp Wasp engines, yet its streamlined design made it 50 percent faster than the Ford Trimotor. Even more significant was the Douglas DC-3, which was introduced in 1935. Whereas the Boeing 247 could carry just ten passengers, the massive twin-engine DC-3, which boasted a 95-foot wing span, could carry up to 28 passengers. It would soon dominate the market with 10,654 being built by Douglas and several thousand being licensed-built around the world. Numerous military versions used for transporting troops and supplies would later be built. By the end of the 1930s, Boeing responded with the Boeing 307 Stratoliner, the world's first pressurized airliner, which could carry 33 passengers. The 307 was powered by four 900 hp Wright Cyclone engines providing a 220 mph cruising speed at ceiling of 26,000 feet, which generally placed it above adverse weather conditions.

In order to develop aircraft of such size (the Boeing 307 Stratoliner had a wing span of 107 ft 3 in. and loaded weight of 42,000 lbs), increasing the power and efficiency of engines was vital. World War I aircraft had relied upon three primary engine types: a rotary engine, in which the engine revolved around a stationary crankshaft, a liquid-cooled inline or V-configuration engine, or an air-cooled radial engine in which the cylinders were configured in a star pattern. Because of the immense torque produced by rotary engines, they had reached the limits of their use by war's end. Even though the merits of air-cooled or liquid-cooled engines generated much debate throughout the interwar years, two important innovations of the 1920s (the supercharger and variable pitch propellers) would boost engine performance and efficiency. The supercharger increased power by forcing air and fuel into the engine, thereby increasing its capacity and power, which is especially critical at higher altitudes. Developed by General Electric in the 1920s, the supercharger could be driven either mechanically by a gear powered by the engine itself or by a turbine powered by the exhaust gases. Since the single wooden propeller used on World War I–era aircraft became increasingly inefficient after taking off and climbing, switching to separate, metal-bladed variable pitch propellers made it possible to adjust the pitch or bite of the propeller at higher altitudes to grab more air, thereby resulting in improved engine efficiency and higher cruising speeds.

In addition to increasing the power and efficiency of engines, manufacturers incorporated other technologies to accommodate the increased size and weight of aircraft and make landing safer. World War I aircraft had landed at relatively fast speeds, which presented dangers that commercial passenger lines could not risk. In addition, flying at high speed with varying winds could result in a very rough flight. Several innovations were designed to resolve these difficulties. The installation of flaps on the back edge of wings, which had been introduced on some World War I aircraft, became a standard feature on aircraft in the interwar years. Extending the flaps downward before takeoff increased lift and allowed for a quicker ascent and extending the flaps downward while landing similarly increased drag, which allowed for a slower, more controlled, and safer landing. This had the added benefit of minimizing the need to expand runways as aircraft became larger and heavier, and it was absolutely essential for naval aircraft to land on aircraft carriers. The addition of leading edge slats on the front of wings helped reduce turbulence and prevent stalls by forcing air over the upper surface of the wings. The addition of trim tabs on the rudder and elevator allowed the pilot to make adjustments during flight to provide greater stability without the pilot having to maintain constant pressure on the controls. The addition of hydraulic systems was also essential in helping the pilot control and maneuver aircraft during all stages of flight, but most especially on takeoff and landing, and in the case of military aircraft, when acrobatic maneuvers were necessary.

Concerns for safety in adverse weather conditions resulted in numerous innovations that made aircraft far more complex. The First World War had seen the addition of wireless transmitters and receivers on reconnaissance and observation aircraft in order to provide immediate intelligence to commanders on the ground and to direct artillery fire. As radio communications expanded during the 1920s, radios were incorporated into aircraft to assist in navigation. Much in the way that ships had for centuries relied upon lighthouses to guide them to a harbor, radio signals emitted from a tower assisted pilots in locating their position in adverse weather conditions by allowing them to tune into the frequency range of a particular tower and then plot a course from tower to tower without relying upon visual observation. By 1940, VHF technology allowed direct verbal communication without using Morse code. This later proved vital to the RAF during the Battle of Britain because it allowed Fighter Command to direct RAF fighter pilots to approaching German aircraft that had been detected by radar. The use of gyroscope systems, pioneered by Lawrence Sperry in the United States, helped the pilot maintain the equilibrium of the aircraft during flight and in combination with radio technology allowed instrumental flight. In addition, gyroscope systems provided a means of autopilot, which relieved the constant strain a pilot would otherwise expend on a long flight. These sophisticated systems not only required an onboard electrical system but also made pilot training far more complex. Indeed, larger aircraft required an entire trained flight crew: the pilot, a copilot with a duplicate system of controls, a navigator to plot the course, and a radio operator for the onboard communications system.

When applied to military aircraft, these technological innovations had a revolutionary impact on aircraft design in the 1930s, raising the possibility of aircraft fulfilling the roles advocated by air power theorists. The remaining chapters in this volume provide much greater detail on specific military aircraft and their roles, but a brief overview of the key military aircraft that incorporated these innovations is necessary to appreciate the dramatic transformation of military aviation during the 1930s, a decade when changing international conditions brought about renewed military spending in general and for new military aircraft in particular.

As indicated previously, air power theorists had emphasized the importance of the bomber as the chief offensive weapon of their air forces for many years. Bomber design throughout the 1920s did not significantly differ from the large, lumbering bombers of World War I. By the 1930s, however, designers began applying the lessons learned from improved civilian passenger and transport aircraft to bombers. In early 1932 the U.S. Army Air Corps began the first test flights of the twin-engine Martin B-10 bomber, which entered production in 1934. Its low-wing design, internal bomb storage, transparent enclosed canopies, and retractable undercarriage enabled it to reach a maximum speed of 207 mph, faster than almost any existing biplane fighter. In addition, the Martin B-10 incorporated an enclosed turret in the nose for the front gunner. These truly revolutionary features were quickly adopted in other bomber designs.

One of the issues that remained hotly debated in bomber design was the best means for delivering bombs accurately. Although rudimentary bombsights had been developed during the First World War, hitting a target successfully had more to do with luck than anything else. In trials conducted in the late 1920s the U.S. Navy found that dive bombers provided far greater accuracy than a high-flying aircraft whose bombs were affected by varying winds after being released. In addition, the dive bomber could adjust its course to hit a moving target, but the heavy stress placed upon a dive bomber's wings when it pulled out of its steep descent meant dive bombers required much stronger wing support systems. Although biplanes could provide this and many were produced for dive bombing roles (the Vought SBU Scout and the Curtiss SBC Helldiver), the biplane configuration resulted in greater drag and lower performance than a monoplane design. As a result, a low-wing cantilever design in which a single large beam (spar) runs through the wing and affixes it solidly to the fuselage offered a better design, especially because the undercarriage could be retracted. In 1936, Junkers, which had pioneered this design type with the all-metal Junkers C-1 and D-1 in World War I, introduced the Junkers Ju 87 Stuka. After the Ju 87 proved its accuracy with great success in the Spanish Civil War and the opening blitzkrieg attacks of the Second World War, Ernst Udet, the Luftwaffe's head of procurement, insisted upon dive bombing capabilities for all German bombers. Udet's policy effectively killed the development of a four-engine bomber and ultimately placed serious limitations on the strategic power of the Luftwaffe throughout World War II.

Although dive bombers are accurate with bomb delivery, they are vulnerable to anti-aircraft fire during their descent, a fact the Germans discovered during the Battle of Britain. In addition, dive bombers had a more limited bomb-carrying capacity than what was needed to conduct the strategic bombing campaigns envisioned by Douhet, Mitchell, and Trenchard. As mentioned earlier, the Martin B-10 provided a revolutionary change in bomber design that was adopted by other powers because it offered the possibility of flying as fast as fighters. In 1936 Italy introduced the twin-engine Fiat Br 20 Cignona and Germany introduced the Heinkel He 111, both of which featured a low-wing cantilever design, a retractable undercarriage, and speeds of up to 260 mph. Although these two bombers relied primarily upon their speed to avoid enemy fighters, other powers looked to large, high-altitude bombers. The four-engine Boeing B-17 Flying Fortress came equipped with a Norden bombsight that under ideal conditions allowed the bombardier to calculate speed and altitude and drop bombs within 200 feet of the intended target. The Norden bombsight was also integrated with the B-17's autopilot system, which allowed the bombardier to control the B-17 during its approach over the target and improve the chances of bombs hitting the target. In addition, the B-17 featured hydraulically powered gun turrets that American air power advocates argued would make it invulnerable to enemy fighters. Although experiences during World War II showed otherwise, it is important to note that the bomber revolution of the 1930s reinforced the belief, stated by British Prime Minister Stanley Baldwin, that the bomber would always get through. Without evidence to the contrary, this belief, and fear of the Luftwaffe, contributed to British and French appeasement of Hitler during the 1930s.

Fighters underwent a similar technological revolution during the interwar years. Improvements in engines alone increased fighter speeds by approximately 30 percent between 1919 and 1930. Although production of high-performance biplane fighters continued in the 1930s (Italy introduced the Fiat CR 42 biplane fighter in 1938), the most significant trend of the 1930s was toward all-metal mono-planes with streamlined fuselages and high-performance super-charged engines. Poland, which introduced the all-metal PZL.P.7 high-wing gulled fighter in 1932, ironically was the first country to have an air force equipped solely with all-metal monoplane fighters. In 1934 the Soviet Union introduced the Polikarpov I-16 low-wing fighter, which combined a wooden fuselage with metal wings, as the first fighter equipped with a retractable undercarriage. It was the world's fastest fighter for a two-year period (1935–1936) with a top speed of 283 mph. Japan introduced an equally fast low-wing can-tilever monoplane fighter in 1937 with the Nakajima Ki-27, the army version of the Mitsubishi A5M. Its speed of 286 mph came at the sac-rifice of defensive armor, however, and this would prove to be a weak-ness during the Second World War. The Messerschmitt BF-109, a low-wing cantilever monoplane introduced in 1937 at the Interna-tional Flying Meet in Zurich, Switzerland, was far more important. Capable of a top speed of 350 mph, it was the fastest fighter in the world and proved itself in the Spanish Civil War. It was fortunate for Great Britain that the British introduced the Supermarine Spitfire, whose first versions entered service in 1939. Although it was slightly slower than the BF-109, it proved to be more maneuverable.

In addition to improvements in speed and design, the new genera-tion of fighters was far better armed than its World War I ancestors. For the most part, World War I fighters had been equipped with rifle-caliber machine guns. The Fokker Eindecker, introduced in the fall of 1915, had been the first to provide a synchronization gear to allow the gun to fire through the propeller, which in essence enabled the fighter pilot to use the aircraft to aim the gun. Rifle-caliber machine guns were more than sufficient to shoot down wooden-framed aircraft, but heavier armaments became necessary as more rugged, all-metal aircraft began to be introduced. Although fighters would continue to be equipped with rifle-caliber machine guns into World War II, designers began adding cannon (ammunition in excess of 20 mm) to fighters in the 1930s. At first, cannon were fitted to fire through a hollow tube that passed through the engine block and propeller, something that the French had actually introduced in the SPAD XIII during World War I. The advent of low-wing cantilever monoplane fighters allowed for placement of cannon in the wing, which provided for far greater firepower. In addition to cannon, experiments were also made with air-to-air rocket missiles. Although a few attempts had been made with rockets during World War I without much success, the Soviet Union would catch the Japanese by surprise in 1939 when it equipped some of its Polikarpov I-16 fighters with air-to-air rocket missiles mounted under the wings.

The 1930s would also see the introduction of twin-engine fighter-bomber aircraft that were designed to play a role similar to the specially designed close-support aircraft of World War I. The twin-engine Messerschmitt BF-110, which was introduced in 1936, was designed to be a long-range destroyer that would clear a path through enemy fighters so that bombers could reach their target. Although the Bf-110 had a top speed of 336 mph, the Battle of Britain would demonstrate that it was no match for the RAF's more maneuverable single-engine Spitfires and Hurricanes.

As military aircraft became more advanced during the interwar years, two important consequences followed. First, the time required to design, produce, and introduce new aircraft became much longer. During the First World War, new generations of aircraft could be designed and put into service in just a matter of months. By the 1930s this process could take up to four years and the timing of when a nation entered the production wave made a tremendous difference in whether its aircraft would be obsolete or front-line. Second, it was necessary to provide far more rigorous training of pilots. Whereas British pilots generally had received no more than five hours of training in 1914 and no more than fifty hours of training in 1918 before earning their wings and entering service, the British standard had risen to 200–300 hours of training by the start of World War II. Pilots advanced through a series of training aircraft before being turned loose in combat aircraft. In the case of bombers, an entire crew (pilots, co-pilots, navigators, radio operators, bombardiers, and gunners) had to be trained before missions could be undertaken. As will be demonstrated in the next chapter, maintaining a pool of pilots and crewmen would have just as important an impact on the conduct of the air war as would the ability to produce aircraft.

The Major Powers and the Organization of Air Power in the Interwar Years

The First World War transformed the nature of air power as aircraft developed new roles and gained greater importance in the overall scheme of the war itself. When the European powers entered the First World War, their air services were divided between their armies and their navies, as in the case of the British Royal Flying Corps and the Royal Navy Air Service. This often resulted in interservice rivalries over the procurement and allocation of new aircraft, and over the missions that each was to pursue. During the course of the war the various powers gave aviation increased presence within the respective high commands so that intelligence gathered from the air could be communicated to top commanders faster and aircraft could be used in conjunction with ground campaigns. More important, the use of bombers raised the possibility of conducting a strategic campaign independent of the army or navy, and this led Great Britain to establish the Royal Air Force as an independent branch of service in April 1918. After aircraft proved their value in the First World War, postwar air power theorists provided a rationale for their use, and technological innovations improved the capabilities of military aircraft, the interwar years witnessed important changes in the organization of air power.

Italy

As the home of Douhet, the leading theorist of the interwar years, Italy was regarded as one of the world's leading air powers during most of the interwar years, as demonstrated by ninety-six international aviation awards won by Italian aircraft in the period. Its commercial air fleet was surpassed only by Germany and Great Britain. Although fascist dictator Benito Mussolini was an aviation enthusiast who learned to fly and saw the propaganda benefit of aircraft, three primary factors prevented the organization of the Regia Aeronautica along the lines envisioned by Douhet. First, Italy lacked the resources to build a strategic air force large enough to implement Douhet's principles and maintain its army and navy at the same time. Second, Douhet had burned far too many bridges with his bristling attacks upon Italian military leaders, who naturally resented him and even blocked funding for his ideas long after Douhet had departed the scene. Third, unlike Mitchell and Trenchard, Douhet had not cultivated a core of young officers to carry out his theories. As a result, the Regia Aeronautica was led by men who did not have a strategic mission in mind for its use.

Italo Balbo, appointed minister of aviation in 1929 and promoted to air marshal in 1933, presided over the Regia Aeronautica during the crucial decade of the 1930s. An able administrator, Balbo recognized that Italy's limited resources made the implementation of Douhet's strategic force impractical and therefore concentrated on providing a force capable of providing support to ground and naval forces. Although the Regia Aeronautica was an independent force that retained control over all pilots, its command structure was spread out over three air zones, which were in turn divided into regional commands. This resulted in a lack of effective overall direction and coordination with army and naval forces. The Regia Aeronautica was also a victim of its success in the conquest of Ethiopia and in supporting Franco's Nationalist forces in the Spanish Civil War. Although Italian aircraft performed their roles well, this created the illusion that everything was fine and led the Regia Aeronautica to continue producing biplane fighters that were clearly becoming obsolete. The end result was that the Regia Aeronautica entered the Second World War with an ineffective organizational structure and inadequate aircraft.

United States

Although Mitchell's bombastic campaign for an independent air force ended with his court-martial, Mitchell nevertheless succeeded in winning the support of a cadre of airmen who were dedicated to implementing his ideas. The Morrow Board, appointed by President Coolidge in response to Mitchell's charges that the military was neglecting air power to the detriment of national security, endorsed many of Mitchell's recommendations. On July 2, 1926, Congress reconstituted the Army Air Service as the U.S. Army Air Corps. Although this was not the independent force that Mitchell had advocated, it did result in the establishment of the Air Corps Tactical School (ACTS), which promoted and expanded upon Mitchell's ideas while training a number of officers who would lead American air power in the Second World War.

From its inception the ACTS promoted strategic bombing as the raison d'être of the Army Air Corps. It is not surprising that this resulted in the belief that the bomber, not the fighter, was the essential offensive weapon in the Air Corps' arsenal. The Martin B-10 bomber was faster than almost all fighters when it was introduced in 1934, reinforcing the ACTS's doctrine. The development of the Boeing B-17 bomber, which was equipped with the Norden bombsight and hydraulic powered defensive gun turrets, further convinced American airmen that a bomber force could strike with precision and fight its way through enemy fighters. Although the B-17 was clearly intended as an offensive weapon, it should be emphasized that it was officially presented to an isolationist Congress as a long-range coastal defense weapon. The reality, however, was that the Army Air Corps was preparing itself to conduct a strategic bombing campaign. Because the Atlantic and Pacific separated and thereby protected the United States from potential enemies, the Army Air Corps believed that its bombers would be able to target vital centers of industry and so disrupt an enemy's economy that victory could be attained by air power alone. It conveniently overlooked its lack of transcontinental bombers and the obvious need for foreign bases to attack potential enemies. Regardless, strategic bombing became the article of faith upon which the Army Air Corps entered the Second World War.

Although Rear Admiral William Moffett, named head of the U.S. Navy's Bureau of Aeronautics in 1921, had led the navy's fight against Mitchell's campaign for an independent air force, this stemmed from Moffett's belief in air power, not his opposition to it. Indeed, Moffett recognized that aircraft would transform naval warfare and wanted to insure that the U.S. Navy would be able to develop its own air power without interference from the army or an independent air force. Compared with the British Navy, the U.S. Navy did indeed have an easier time developing its maritime aviation for that very reason. Until his death aboard the naval airship *Akron*, which went down off the coast of New Jersey in 1933, Moffett promoted the development of carrier-based aircraft because he was convinced that Japan would most likely be the U.S. Navy's opponent in the future and that the navy would have to operate against land-based aircraft. Naval aviators conducted numerous experiments with dive bombers and torpedo bombers. In addition, the navy came to favor air-cooled radial engines over liquid-cooled engines. More important, the navy placed a heavier emphasis upon fighters than did the Army Air Corps, and this proved critical in the air war over the Pacific.

Great Britain

Established in April 1918 as the world's first independent air service, the Royal Air Force (RAF) developed a strategic bombing doctrine based in part on the need to have a strategic mission to justify its independence. This was absolutely vital in light of the financial hardships that Great Britain faced in the aftermath of the First World War. Although tight military budgets based on the Ten Year Rule prevented the RAF from building the strategic bombing force that Trenchard had envisioned, Trenchard and his successors did succeed in maintaining the vitality of the RAF with the resources they had. Trenchard's belief that France posed the primary threat to Great Britain during the 1920s proved ill-founded, but his decision to establish fighter bases throughout southeastern England proved vital during the Battle of Britain. He also helped keep British aircraft manufacturers afloat by spreading out contracts among multiple suppliers. This helped maintain the infrastructure ultimately needed for rearmament when the Ten Year Rule was finally abandoned in 1933. At the time the RAF had only 833 front line aircraft. It can be argued that the RAF ironically was ultimately better off because when it did begin rearming it was able to take advantage of the technological advances made during the interwar years from the beginning.

After Hitler's remilitarization of the Rhineland in March 1936, the British recognized that war was a distinct possibility and began planning accordingly. This impacted the RAF in three important ways. First, the RAF vigorously pursued a radar detection system as proposed the prior year by the RAF's aeronautical committee, which was chaired by Henry Tizard. This later proved critical to the RAF's success in the Battle of Britain. Second, in July 1936 the RAF was reorganized with the establishment of Bomber Command, Fighter Command, Coastal Command, and Training Command. Third, production of fighters became the RAF's primary focus. It should be emphasized, however, that this had more to do with economics than a change of air power doctrine because Thomas Inskip, appointed minister for the coordination of defense in 1937, recognized that three fighters could be built for the same cost of one bomber. It is extremely ironic that Great Britain's survival in the early years of the Second World War resulted primarily from Inskip's emphasis upon fighters rather than the RAF's official doctrine of strategic bombing.

Although the Royal Navy had recognized the importance of aviation in the First World War, several factors prevented it from developing air power to the same levels as the navies of the United States and Japan. To a certain extent the Royal Navy languished because of the RAF. Despite the establishment of the Fleet Air Arm in 1924, the RAF was more interested in pursuing Trenchard's doctrine of strategic bombing and therefore neglected naval aviation. Thus, the Royal Navy lacked aircraft comparable to those of the United States or Japan. Tight budgets also limited the construction of new aircraft carriers. Of the seven aircraft carriers in the fleet at the start of the Second World War, only one could be called modern. Although Inskip restored the Fleet Air Arm to the Royal Navy's control in 1937, the Second World War began before the navy had a chance to build up its air power. As will be seen in the next chapter, the navy's lack of long-range observation aircraft would almost be its undoing during the Battle of the Atlantic.

Germany

Although Germany lacked an air power theorist of the stature of Douhet, Mitchell, or Trenchard, its military leaders studied the lessons of its defeat in the First World War, considered the theories of Douhet, and slowly (and secretly) initiated plans that eventually resulted in Germany's reemergence as a major air power prior to the Second World War. Germany's achievement is monumental when one considers that the Treaty of Versailles resulted in the confiscation of 20,000 aircraft and 27,000 engines by the Allies, forbade a German air force altogether, and placed restrictions on its development of civilian aircraft. Credit must first be given to Generaloberst Hans von Seeckt, who served as the chief of staff of the Reichswehr from 1919 to 1926. Although the Treaty of Versailles limited the Reichswehr to just 100,000 men, this enabled Seeckt to be highly selective. Recognizing the importance of air power and determined that Germany would eventually have an air force, Seeckt assigned 180 officers under Lieutenant Colonel Helmuth Wilberg, who was charged with studying air power and developing plans for the future German air force. In addition, after Weimar Germany recognized the Soviet Union in the Treaty of Rapollo (1922), Seeckt worked secretly with his Soviet counterparts to circumvent the restrictions imposed by the Treaty of Versailles by establishing secret air bases in the Soviet Union in exchange for providing much-needed technical assistance to the Russians. Although Seeckt was dismissed in 1926 for his outspoken monarchist views (he had refused to intervene in the Kapp Putsch of 1920 and had offered a military post to ex–Crown Prince Wilhelm in 1926) his efforts laid the groundwork for the resurrection of German air power.

The development of German air power doctrine directly resulted from Wilberg's study of Germany's use of air power in the First World War. Wilberg's conclusions shaped German air doctrine in three important ways. First, Wilberg concluded that Germany's defensive strategy of denying airspace to its enemies had been fundamentally flawed. Although Germany succeeded in shooting down enemy aircraft, it was ultimately overwhelmed by the sheer numbers of allied aircraft and lost control of the air. In the future, Wilberg asserted that fighters must be used to gain and maintain air superiority. Second, Wilberg concluded that Germany's strategic bombing campaign against Great Britain had failed in its objectives. Although he did not discount the importance of strategic bombing and recognized the need to have a strategic bombing force, Wilberg disagreed sharply with the assertions of air power theorists like Douhet, Mitchell, and Trenchard in their belief that strategic bombing alone was a winning strategy. Third, Wilberg concluded that the most effective use of German air power in the First World War had been in providing close support to the German army, and he asserted that this would become more important in the future. In 1926 Wilberg's *Guidelines for the Conduct of the Operational Air War* formalized German air doctrine. It is important to note that his use of the term *operational* was intended to emphasize a flexible, nondoctrinaire approach to war, and that he did not commit the future Luftwaffe to being merely a support arm of the army.

Hitler's coming to power as chancellor on January 30, 1933, also influenced German air doctrine. Although Hitler placed former World War I ace and Nazi party leader Hermann Göring in charge of civil aviation and Germany's secret air force, Göring was preoccupied with his other political duties, including direction of Germany's Four Year Plan. Göring consequently left the development of German air power to such subordinates as Dr. Robert Knauss. Knauss, who was a former combat pilot who later worked at Lufthansa, adapted World War I Admiral Alfred von Tirpitz's "risk fleet" theory to air power, arguing that a strategic bombing force would defend Germany against Britain and France because they would be unwilling to risk a confrontation with Germany. Erhard Milch, the former head of Lufthansa, became secretary of state for aviation and placed a heavy emphasis upon building air bases and navigational and communication technology. General Walther Wever, named chief of the air command office in September 1933, joined Wilberg in writing *Air Force Regulation on the Conduct of the Air War* (1935), which governed the employment of the Luftwaffe throughout World War II. Wever and Wilberg emphasized the need for air supremacy, calling for the Luftwaffe to attack and destroy the enemy air force, which would secure German air space from enemy attacks. The Luftwaffe would then shift its focus to supporting the army against the enemy's ground forces. Wever shared Trenchard's and Douhet's belief that strategic bombing of an enemy's industrial structure was essential to winning a war and advocated the development of four-engine strategic bombers. He was killed in a airplane crash in June 1936. Wever's successor, Lieutenant General Albert von Kesselring, unfortunately for Germany, recommended canceling the development of four-engine bombers in favor of fighters and tactical bombers, a decision that appeared wise in light of German success in the Spanish Civil War. Although one can argue Germany made better use of its limited resources by developing an air force that was essentially a ground support arm (a role in which it would succeed brilliantly), the lack of a strategic bomber would prove a serious weakness during the Second World War.

France

Although France eagerly developed aircraft prior to the First World War and remained one of the leading air powers during the war, the French failed to develop a coherent air power theory after the war. In large measure this was because French military leaders learned the wrong lessons from the First World War. Having attempted some strategic bombing without enjoying much success, French airmen dismissed the arguments that Douhet, Mitchell, and Trenchard advanced for strategic bombing. The most important factor that affected French air doctrine, however, was that French military commanders believed that the next war would be a continuation of the trench warfare of World War I. Traumatized by their repeated offensive failures (the Nivelle Offensive of 1917 had resulted in a widespread Army mutiny) French commanders, with few exceptions, clung to a defensive strategy throughout the interwar years. This attitude was best symbolized by the construction of the infamous Maginot Line and the military's reluctance to respond offensively to Hitler's remilitarization of the Rhineland in March 1936. Needless to say, this had a determining impact upon the French view of air power. As German military thinkers were developing a doctrine that emphasized the role of aircraft in providing close air support for offensive purposes (the tactics of blitzkrieg), the French saw aircraft as providing support for defensive purposes (the tactics of sitzkrieg).

Political turmoil also hampered French efforts to develop a coherent air power doctrine. An Air Ministry was not created until 1928 and the Armée de l'Air was not established until 1934. Budgetary restrictions also led the French to neglect specialized aircraft in favor of multipurpose B.C.R. (Bombing, Combat, Reconnaissance) aircraft that could provide cover from enemy air attack, conduct reconnaissance and observation missions, and carry out bombing attacks on the enemy. The resulting aircraft, such as the Amoit 143 and Potez 540, proved inadequate to fulfill any of these roles particularly well. French Air Minister Pierre Cot, who served from January 1933 to February 1934 and January 1936 to December 1938, sought to change this by pushing through a bold production plan in 1933 that called for building 350 bombers, 350 fighters, and 310 reconnaissance aircraft. This would enable France to carry out strategic bombing and obtain air superiority, but political turmoil and bureaucratic stagnation delayed implementation of the plan. Part of the problem was that French nationalization of the aircraft industry under the Popular Front, which had come to power in 1936, disrupted production. It should be emphasized that the French military never adopted Cot's vision for an offensive strategy. When Cot fell along with the Popular Front in December 1938, the French reverted back to assigning aircraft for defensive roles in supporting army units. As will be demonstrated in the next chapter, the failure to develop a coherent air power doctrine contributed to the paralysis of the French response upon the outbreak of the Second World War.

Soviet Union

Although Imperial Russia failed to develop an adequate air service during the First World War, aircraft played an important role in helping the Bolsheviks win the Russian Civil War and fight Poland to a draw in the Russo-Polish War of 1918–1920. This success led several Soviet military commanders to make air power an integral part of the Red Army. General Mikhail Frunze, who succeeded Leon Trotsky as chief of staff of the Red Army in January 1925, recognized the importance of aircraft in making the Red Army a mobile fighting force, which was vital given Russia's vast landscape. Although Frunze died in October 1925, his emphasis upon air power was continued by his successor Marshal Mikhail Tukhachevski.[3] Known for his concept of *deep battle*, Tukhachevski pioneered the use of airborne forces to be dropped behind enemy lines by parachute or gliders in order to disrupt the enemy, something that both Germany and the United States would effectively incorporate in their militaries. General Yakov Alksnis, named commander of the Red Air Forces in June 1931, promoted the development of the Tupolev TB-3, the world's first four-engine monoplane heavy bomber. It should be emphasized, however, that Alksnis intended for these to be used in support of the Red Army rather than as a strategic bombing force as advocated by Douhet, Mitchell, and Douhet. General Yakov Smuchkevich commanded Soviet air units during the Spanish Civil War in successful air-ground operations in 1937, and he soundly defeated the Japanese in air conflicts over Manchuria in 1939. Smuchkevich's successes confirmed the Soviet Union's emphasis upon using aircraft for close air support. In addition, his efforts in Manchuria contributed to Japan's decision to expand into Indochina, a course of action that saved the Soviet Union from later having to fight a two-front war and ultimately resulted in war between Japan and the United States.

Although Soviet military leaders developed an effective strategy for using air power in support of its ground forces, their efforts were effectively undone by Joseph Stalin. Suspicious to the point of paranoia, Stalin deeply distrusted the Soviet military leadership and carried out a thorough purge of the Red Army prior to the Second World War. Using intelligence planted by the Germans, Stalin had Tukhachevski arrested and executed in 1937 after a public show trial. Alksnis was arrested for treason in December 1937 and executed in 1940. Although Smushkevich survived the purge, he was held responsible for the Red Army's collapse after the Nazi invasion of June 22, 1941, and shot on Stalin's orders on October 28, 1941. Nevertheless, the Red Army's doctrine of using air power as an integral part of its ground forces had been firmly established and would ultimately prove effective in defeating Germany on the Eastern Front.

Japan

Although a deep-seated rivalry between the Imperial Japanese Army and Imperial Japanese Navy prevented the establishment of an independent air force with a strategic mission, both services saw the need for air power and established their own air forces (the Japanese Army Air Force and the Japanese Navy Air Force) to support their respective missions. More important, the Japanese committed the necessary resources to build up their own aircraft industry to avoid foreign dependence. As a result, Japanese aircraft production expanded ten times during the 1930s from 445 aircraft in 1930 to 4,467 aircraft in 1939. Although the Japanese had to make some technological concessions (less armor and firepower) because of limited raw materials, they proved adept in designing specialized aircraft to fulfill their intended missions.

Although army commanders viewed aircraft primarily in terms of providing ground support, navy commanders developed a more strategic view for air power. Indeed, Admiral Shigeyoshi Inoue, the only major leader to advocate an independent air force, argued that the navy should avoid dependence upon aircraft carriers by using long-range bombers and flying boats that could operate from islands in the Pacific and carry out strategic bombing missions independent of the fleet. Although Admiral Isoruku Yamamoto was not prepared to go that far, he recognized that aircraft had transformed naval warfare and shifted Japanese spending from battleships to aircraft carriers despite some opposition from naval traditionalists. Yamamoto also implemented Admiral Jisaboro Ozawa's proposal to concentrate on aircraft carriers in order to increase their offensive power. This brought about a reorganization of the Japanese Naval Air Force in early 1941 into air fleets that combined carrier-based aircraft and land-based aircraft into a combined strike force. Vice-Admiral Chuichi Nagumo, named commander of the First Air Fleet in April 1941, later demonstrated the effectiveness of this reorganization in the attack on Pearl Harbor.

Two other Japanese admirals deserve mention for their contributions to the navy's emphasis upon air power. Admiral Takijiro Onishi, himself an ace in Japan's takeover of China, argued that aircraft had made the battleship obsolete and condemned battleship construction as a waste of precious resources. Although Onishi supported Yamamoto, he believed that Yamamoto conceded too much to the battleship admirals. Admiral Matome Ugaki initially viewed Yamamoto's emphasis on air power with great skepticism, but would undergo what amounted to a conversion experience after Japanese aircraft sank the HMS *Prince of Wales* and HMS *Repulse* and carried out the successful attack on Pearl Harbor in December 1941. From that point on, he was one of Yamamoto's most ardent supporters within the navy.

The Use of Air Power in the Interwar Years

Although the major air powers would have to wait until the Second World War to test their theories and doctrines, the interwar years did provide a few opportunities to demonstrate the power of military aircraft. In particular, air power offered a more cost-effective means of policing the empires. For example, in 1919 the British used a Handley Page V/1000 bomber, developed too late for use against Berlin, to drop bombs on Kabul in order to quell an Afghan uprising. Trenchard and the RAF seized upon this success to help justify the RAF's existence and throughout the 1920s used aircraft to suppress rebellious tribesmen and to provide support to ground forces. In 1920 the RAF successfully suppressed an uprising in Somalia led by Sayyid Muhammad Ibn Abdulla Hassan by dropping bombs on rebel strongholds and supporting British ground troops in a three-week campaign that cost £77,000. Winston Churchill estimated that a conventional ground campaign without aircraft would have cost £5,000,000. The British also successfully used transport aircraft to evacuate forces tied down in Sulaimaniya, Iraq, in 1922, and to carry reinforcements to its garrison in Kirkuk, Iraq, in 1923. During a civil war in Afghanistan in 1928, British aircraft evacuated King Amanullah and 500 British subjects from Kabul. At first, the RAF had relied upon such World War I bombers as the Airco D.H.9 for these types of operations, but the early 1920s witnessed the introduction of such bomber-transport aircraft as the Vickers Vernon and Vickers Victoria that were designed with precisely such missions in mind. Italy and France used aircraft in a similar fashion to police their empires, and the United States Marine Corps relied upon aircraft to evacuate wounded Marines during its intervention in Nicaragua between 1925 and 1929.

From the inception of its takeover of Manchuria in 1931 to its invasion of mainland China in 1937, air power played an important role in Japanese aggression. To support its forces, the Japanese developed long-range bombers (the Mitsubishi G3M and G4M) and outstanding fighters (the Mitsubishi A5M and A6M). These were used to support Japanese ground forces and to conduct what amounted to a terror campaign by bombing defenseless cities. This set the tone for the Army's brutal massacre of as many as 300,000 civilians and soldiers in Nanjing between December 13, 1937, and January 22, 1938. Just prior to the "Rape of Nanjing," Japanese naval aircraft sank an American gunboat, the U.S.S. *Panay*, in the Yangtze River as it was evacuating American civilians from Nanjing, killing three passengers and injuring twelve. Although the American flag was clearly visible during the attack, the Japanese claimed it was an accident, apologized, and paid an indemnity of $2.2 million.

Despite overwhelming international condemnation of Japan's actions, the Soviet Union would be the only power to offer significant assistance to China, which included ground forces commanded by Lieutenant General Georgi Zhukov. Supported by Red Air Force units employing Polikarpov I-15 and I-16 fighters and Tupolev SB-2 bombers, Zhukov fought the Japanese in Manchuria to a bloody standstill. The most significant development of the air campaign over Manchuria was the Red Air Force's use of air-to-air RS-82 rockets, which caught the Japanese by surprise. Given the exaggerated claims on both sides (the Russians claimed they had destroyed 676 Japanese aircraft while losing 207 and the Japanese claimed they had downed 1,269 Russian aircraft while losing 168) the exact toll of this air war will never be known, but one outcome is certain. Because of its setbacks against the Soviet Union, Japan shifted its imperial ambitions to Indochina and the Pacific. This resulted in Japan fighting a war with the United States and prevented the Soviet Union from having to fight a two-front war when Germany invaded it in 1941.

As the Japanese expanded in Asia, Germany began openly rearming after Hitler's appointment as chancellor on January 30, 1933, and consolidation of executive authority after President Paul von Hindenburg's death on August 2, 1934. By then Hitler had concluded a nonaggression pact with Poland (a move that shocked France) and supported a botched coup attempt by Austrian Nazis in which Austrian Chancellor Engelbert Dollfuss was mortally wounded. When Mussolini threatened to dispatch air and ground units to the Austrian border, Hitler renounced any involvement in the coup attempt. Although Mussolini's gesture was really a bluff, it led Hitler to escalate the pace of Germany's rearmament, which was formally announced on March 16, 1935. Even though this was a direct violation of the Treaty of Versailles, the British and French failed to take any steps to stop Germany. Indeed, the British even concluded a naval treaty with Germany on June 18, 1935, in which they recognized the right of Germany to build a surface fleet and submarine fleet.[4] This decision caught France by surprise and put it at a tremendous disadvantage. France had neglected naval aviation throughout the interwar years in large measure because Germany had not presented a naval threat to France.

Although British and French acquiescence to German rearmament undoubtedly caused Mussolini to reconsider Italy's relationship with Germany, one of the key turning points in European diplomacy during the interwar years came from Mussolini's decision to invade Ethiopia on October 3, 1935. This had more to do with Mussolini's failed domestic policies than anything else because he realized that redressing the humiliating defeat Italy had suffered at Adowa when it invaded Ethiopia in 1896 would provide a useful diversion. Unlike 1896, the Italians invaded with an army supported by air power. The Regia Aeronautica distinguished itself by attacking Ethiopian forces and by keeping Italian forces on the ground supplied. In addition, the Italians used their aircraft to drop poison gas, which broke the will of Ethiopian forces to resist. The conquest was complete within seven months.

Although the Italian invasion of Ethiopia was not as significant from an air power standpoint as the Japanese invasion of Manchuria, it had many important consequences. First, the use of aircraft to drop poison gas had a psychological impact upon European diplomacy because it raised the specter of a similar deadly assault upon European cities in the event of war. Second, the success of the Regia Aeronautica contributed to Italy's belief that its aircraft were more than sufficient, when in fact they were becoming obsolete. Third, the opposition of Great Britain and France to the invasion of Ethiopia created an open rift in their relationship with Italy. Fourth and most important, Hitler took advantage of the Ethiopian crisis by ordering the remilitarization of the Rhineland. With Italian forces tied down in Ethiopia, Mussolini could do nothing more than protest even though Italy was a guarantor of the Locarno Treaties of 1925 that had forbade remilitarization.

The failure of France and Great Britain to take any action against Germany's remilitarization of the Rhineland was without a doubt one of the greatest blunders in history. An unfounded fear that the Luftwaffe would strike Paris and London contributed to French and British inaction. The fact is that the Luftwaffe was in no position to carry out an attack. Only one of its three fighter units was even fitted with machine guns, and these guns did not work. Although its Junker Ju 52/3 bombers theoretically could have bombed Paris, they were incapable of reaching London while loaded with bombs. Hitler's generals had adamantly opposed the operation and most likely would have overthrown him had the French and British acted. Simply put, Hitler gambled and won. The mentality that the bomber would always get through paralyzed policy makers in Paris and London. This was a lesson in blackmail that Hitler would not forget. But policy makers were not the only ones at fault. French generals had inexplicably made no contingency plans other than all-out war and that was something they did not want to fight, especially if they could not count on British support.

The outbreak of the Spanish Civil War on July 18, 1936, in the immediate aftermath of the Italian conquest of Ethiopia and Hitler's remilitarization of the Rhineland presented a new challenge to international peace, and this time air power would prove decisive. Hitler jumped at the opportunity to aid General Francisco Franco in his rebellion against the Spanish Popular Front government by dispatching Junker Ju 52/3 transports to carry approximately 13,000 of Franco's troops and their equipment from Spanish Morocco to Cadiz between July and October 1936. Without German assistance, Franco's nationalist forces would almost certainly have been defeated at the inception of the rebellion. More important, Hitler's support for Franco convinced Mussolini to intervene as well and would lead Hitler and Mussolini to create the Rome-Berlin Axis on October 25, 1936.

The Spanish Civil War had a profound impact upon air power. Although the German Kondor Legion had no more than 6,000 men and 100 aircraft in Spain at any one time, the German military rotated some 19,000 men and 350 aircraft into Spain during the conflict. Whereas Germany used the Spanish Civil War as a training exercise, Italy actually made a major commitment of forces, maintaining three divisions and 750 aircraft in Spain, for most of the war. With France and Great Britain imposing an arms embargo, the Republican forces had little alternative but to accept Stalin's demands for Spanish gold reserves in exchange for Soviet assistance, which came primarily in the form of aircraft. From an air power standpoint, the most significant event of the Spanish Civil War was the bombing of Guernica on April 16, 1937, by German and Italian aircraft supporting a nationalist force of 40,000 men. The resulting destruction was immortalized in paint by Pablo Picasso and reinforced the fear of bombing. From a tactical standpoint, the Luftwaffe gained valuable experience that would be applied in the opening campaigns of the Second World War. From a strategic standpoint, however, the impact of the air war on Germany and Italy had negative consequences because it convinced the Germans that the Heinkel He 111 was sufficient as a strategic bomber, confirmed the Germans in the necessity for strategic bombers to have a dive-bombing capacity, and led the Italians to continue producing outmoded biplane fighters.

The success of the German and Italian air forces in the Spanish Civil War had its most telling impact upon European diplomacy. Although Great Britain began a rearmament program that provided the RAF with the Hawker Hurricane and Supermarine Spitfire, the British were not prepared for war. Since France was unprepared to challenge Germany without British assistance, Hitler was in the position of being able to blackmail both French and British policymakers by the threat of war, which they expected would be accompanied by the bombing of British and French cities. Emboldened by French and British acquiescence to his annexation of Austria in March 1938, Hitler turned his attention to Czechoslovakia in September of that year, demanding that the Sudetenland be handed over to Germany. Although Czechoslovakia was prepared to fight, British Prime Minister Neville Chamberlain and French Premier Edouard Daladier succumbed to Hitler's demands at the Munich Conference on September 30, 1938, and forced Czechoslovakia to comply. Chamberlain's claim that he had secured peace for our time upon his return to London proved to be peace for a year. In March 1939 Hitler sent forces into Czechoslovakia, annexing Bohemia and Moravia and creating a puppet state of Slovakia. With the British and French failing to act, Hitler had no reason to believe their warnings that they would intervene when he turned his attention to Poland in the summer of 1939, especially after Germany concluded a non-aggression pact with the Soviet Union on August 23. This time Hitler was mistaken, for his invasion of Poland on September 1 resulted in a British and French declaration of war on September 3.

Although some have argued that Great Britain gained valuable time to mobilize by agreeing to Hitler's demands and sacrificing Czechoslovakia at the Munich Conference, this is really more of a revisionist attempt to rationalize Chamberlain's appeasement of Hitler. One can just as easily argue that the gains the British made in aircraft production between September 1938 and September 1939 were offset by similar gains in German aircraft production and their acquisition of Czech aircraft. Had Great Britain and France called Hitler's bluff at Munich, if in fact he was bluffing, they would have found that Germany was ill-prepared for war. The Luftwaffe had only 600 first-line bombers and 400 first-line fighters and these were hardly sufficient for a campaign against Czechoslovakia, Great Britain, and France, especially when one considers the strong likelihood that the Soviet Union would have entered the war in September 1938. British and French betrayal of Czechoslovakia served only to convince Stalin that the West could not be trusted and resulted in his non-aggression pact with Hitler. As the next chapter will indicate, Great Britain and France paid a heavy price for the time gained at Munich.

The interwar years, overall, witnessed major strides in the technological development of both military and commercial aviation. When coupled with the air power theories that emerged during the period, these advancements enabled military leaders to test those theories in reality upon the outbreak of World War II. While the results did not quite fulfill the expectations, as the next chapter will demonstrate air power played a decisive role in the war.

Endnotes

1. After Benito Mussolini came to power in 1922, he placed Douhet in charge of aircraft development, a role he would continue to play until his death in Rome on February 15, 1940.

2. It should be pointed out, however, that Mitchell's claim that land-based aircraft would always be superior to naval aircraft, because the latter would have to be lighter to operate from carriers, proved to be untrue as did his claim that aircraft would make it unnecessary for the U.S. to transport as many troops to Europe as it had in the First World War.

3. Although officials reported that Frunze died from complications of stomach surgery, there is a strong possibility that he was assassinated on Stalin's orders.

4. The German surface fleet was to be limited to 35 percent of the Royal Navy's, and the German submarine fleet was to be limited to 45 percent of the Royal Navy's.

CHAPTER TWO

Military Aviation in World War II, 1939–1945

FROM GERMAN STUKA SUPPORT OF the blitzkrieg to the Allied fire-bombing of Dresden, and from Japanese torpedo bombers at Pearl Harbor to American B-29s over Hiroshima and Nagasaki, military air power played a memorable and arguably a decisive role in both the European and Pacific Theaters of World War II. Although sometimes exaggerated and oftentimes romanticized—then and now—one might say that airpower predicted the outcome of the war. Those powers that continually produced technologically advanced aircraft gained an advantage; those that developed the most diverse air forces—equally capable of maintaining air superiority as inflicting massive damage through strategic bombing—proved the victors.

The European Air War

Upon the outbreak of the Second World War, Germany and its three opponents (Great Britain, France, and Poland) were fairly evenly matched from a quantitative standpoint, with Germany having approximately 3,000 aircraft[1] compared with 1,466 British aircraft, 1,076 French aircraft, and approximately 397 Polish aircraft. From a qualitative standpoint, however, the Luftwaffe had a decisive advantage because the bulk of its aircraft were front-line, including the Messerschmitt BF-109 fighter, the excellent Heinkel He 111 medium bomber, and the Junkers Ju 87 Stuka dive bomber, all of which had proven themselves while serving with the Kondor Legion in the Spanish Civil War. In contrast, the British had no more than 1,000 front-line aircraft, France had just 282 modern fighters and 8 modern bombers, and Poland's aircraft, with the exception of 75 PZL P 37 Los twin-engine bombers, were clearly obsolete. More important, Germany developed a proactive strategy for using its air power to support its ground forces, whereas the British and French simply played a waiting game.

The Role of Air Power in the Opening Campaigns of the War

Germany invaded Poland on September 1, 1939, with overwhelming force: 1.25 million men in 60 divisions and 1,600 aircraft. Against this force, Poland had 800,000 men organized in six different army groups supported by 400 aircraft. When one considers that Germany left just 30 divisions in the West, where France had 94 divisions, it is hard to believe that France did not press this advantage. Yet the French remained ensconced behind the Maginot Line, leaving the Poles to go it alone. The French did not even follow through on their promise to fly shuttle-bombing missions (bombing German cities, landing in Poland, rearming, and flying back to France).

Aircraft played a prominent role in the Polish Campaign, opening the attack on September 1 at 4:34 a.m. when three Stuka dive bombers attempted to destroy the detonating wires that Polish engineers had placed on two railroad bridges spanning the Vistula River near Dirschau. One of the big myths of the Polish Campaign is that the Luftwaffe destroyed the Polish Air Force on the ground in the first days of the campaign. Instead, the Polish Air Force had taken the precaution of redistributing its aircraft to 43 secret airfields just days before the German attack. As a result the Polish Air Force was able to disrupt German bombing attacks carried out against Warsaw on September 1. With the Luftwaffe holding a four to one numerical advantage, however, the Polish Air Force had little chance. Although its gull-wing PZL P 11 fighters could outmaneuver the Messerschmitt BF-109 and BF-110 in a dogfight, the Messerschmitts could rely upon their 100 mph speed advantage to strike and evade the Poles. More important, the rapid advance of German ground forces quickly overran Polish airbases, contracting the space in which the Poles could operate. After the first week, the Polish Air Force offered only token resistance. This lack of air support doomed to failure the army's advance on the German Army Group South near Poznan on September 9. By contrast, the Luftwaffe bought enough time for the German Army to regroup by carrying out almost 1,700 sorties against the Poles.

By September 14 the Germans had succeeded in surrounding Warsaw. Three days later the Soviet Union moved into eastern Poland as provided in the nonaggression pact that had been signed with Germany on August 23. Although the Poles put up a valiant defense of their capital, their efforts were futile as German artillery began pounding the city. Beginning on September 25, the Luftwaffe under General Wolfram von Richthofen, cousin of the famed Red Baron, unleashed German bombers on the defenseless city. Warsaw was reduced to rubble by almost 600 tons of bombs; the army began its assault on September 26, and Warsaw fell on September 27.

In a mere four weeks the Germany Army had defeated Poland with the Luftwaffe playing a leading role in the process. Its success in achieving air superiority, disrupting Poland's communication system, and providing close support to the German Army, overwhelmed and demoralized the Polish Army. Its bombing of Warsaw helped prevent a protracted siege and allowed the German Army to shift forces back to the West. The Polish Air Force was virtually wiped out, losing 83 percent of its aircraft and 30 percent of its pilots.[2] The Luftwaffe had suffered some significant losses of its own, however. The campaign cost at least 285 of its 1,600 aircraft, 60 percent of its bombs, and most of its fuel reserves. This should have clearly indicated that Germany was not prepared for a long war, but the quick victory in Poland gave German leaders false confidence. As a result, German aircraft factories continued to operate as they had in peacetime (one shift for five or six days per week) producing just less than 700 aircraft per month, whereas the British began multiple shifts and were producing more than 1,000 aircraft per month by April 1940.

When Great Britain and France rejected Hitler's offer of peace after the Polish Campaign, Hitler wanted to attack France almost immediately, despite the protests of his generals that the army was not prepared. Poor weather resulted in repeated delays of a German offensive, leading to the so-called Phony War or "Sitzkrieg" between September 1939 and April 1940. Several isolated incidents involved aircraft during this period, with the French losing 63 aircraft, the British losing 11, and the Germans losing 80. The RAF limited its actions primarily to attacking German naval targets. One of its largest raids occurred on December 18, 1939, when the RAF dispatched 24 Vickers Wellingtons on a daylight raid of Wilhelmshaven. Although air power advocates had asserted for two decades that bombers could fight their way to the target, the Wilhelmshaven raid proved otherwise. Messerschmitt BF-109s and BF-110s shot down 12 of the 22 British bombers that made it to Wilhelmshaven; five British bombers were so badly damaged that they crashed on their return flight. Only five returned safely. The raid proved deeply significant as it convinced Bomber Command that because of modern fighter aircraft, daylight bombing campaigns only invited disaster. As a result, night bombing became its modus operandi during the war.

Perhaps the most significant aspect of the Phony War is how different it appeared than the air power theorists said it would. During the interwar years theorists had predicted sudden and overwhelming air assaults and used these claims to justify government spending on aircraft. This did not happen for two reasons. First, none of the powers had the capacity for such an attack. Second, each feared that launching one would invite a retaliatory strike that they could not defend. Indeed, this had been Britain's and France's rationale for appeasing Hitler at Munich, and it certainly appears groundless in hindsight.

With German plans for an invasion of France on hold, Hitler shifted his attention to Scandinavia, launching an attack on Denmark and Norway on April 9, 1940. Several factors contributed to this decision. First, the Soviet Union had invaded Finland on November 30, 1939, threatening Germany's supply of iron ore and other materials from Sweden. Establishing a German presence in Scandinavia would keep Stalin in check. Second, Hitler was infuriated by the British Navy's seizure of a German ship, the *Altmark*, in neutral Norwegian waters on February 16, 1940.[3] Third, Grand Admiral Erich Raeder convinced Hitler that occupying Norway and Denmark would limit the Royal Navy's ability to interfere with German shipping and provide bases from which Germany could more effectively conduct its U-boat campaign against the British. Although the Germans did not know it, Churchill, who had long advocating mining Norwegian waters and had been placed in charge of Great Britain's overall defense on April 4, issued orders for the mining operation to begin on April 8 and was initiating plans to occupy Norway. Germany acted first, unfortunately for the British.

Operation Weser swung into action on April 9. As the German navy landed troops at key ports, the Luftwaffe mobilized 1,098 aircraft that bombed Danish and Norwegian cities and dropped paratroopers to seize air fields, which Junker Ju 52/3 and G 38 transports quickly reinforced with troops and supplies. Denmark surrendered by the evening of April 9. Operations in Norway took longer because the Norwegians put up a fierce resistance and the British dispatched three aircraft carriers as well as bombers and reconnaissance aircraft from Scotland to

Norway. For the British and Norwegians, unfortunately, their Gloster Sea Gladiator biplanes were easily swept from the air by German Messerschmitts as the Luftwaffe proved the difference in the campaign. The lone Allied success came at Narvik, which was beyond the Luftwaffe's reach. The Royal Navy sank 18 German ships while losing just 2 destroyers and landed 12,000 troops that seized the city. It proved to be a short-lived victory, however, because the British abandoned Narvik after the Germans launched the long-awaited invasion of France on May 10.

The Role of Air Power in the Battle of France

France and Great Britain took advantage of the so-called Phony War to build up their air forces. Where the French had only 232 modern fighters in September 1939, on May 10 the Armée de l'Air was equipped with 637 fighters, including the excellent Dewoitine 520, out of a total of approximately 2,900 front-line aircraft organized into 67 fighter squadrons, 66 bomber squadrons, and 30 observation squadrons. Although additional aircraft were being built (a total of 851 between May 10 and June 15) and American-built Curtiss Hawk 75A fighters were being delivered, the French lacked trained pilots to put them into service. More important, in February 1940 Armée de l'Air commander General Joseph Vuillemin had given in to General Alphonse Georges's demands that the fighter and observation squadrons be placed under the command of his army group commanders. As a result, only about half of the Armée de l'Air's aircraft were in the critical northeastern frontier when the Germans attacked. Moreover, French commanders proved to be unwilling to release units even though they were desperately needed in other sectors. Although the British had formed the British Air Force in France (BAFF) in January 1940 to support the British Expeditionary Force, its 10 squadrons included only 160 Hawker Hurricanes. The bulk of BAFF's aircraft were more mediocre models, including outmoded Fairey Battles, Bristol Blenheim bombers, Westland Lysanders, and Glouster Gladiators. The RAF dispatched two additional squadrons during the Battle of France, but Fighter Command leader Hugh Dowding vigorously opposed sending more to what he considered a lost cause when they were vital to Great Britain's defense.

The Luftwaffe had also taken advantage of the lull to replace the losses it suffered in Poland and Norway. By May 10 it had approximately 4,000 first-line aircraft, of which about 2,750 were committed to the offensive in the West. Nevertheless, overconfidence and hubris following success in Poland led Göring to a fatal error with enormous long-term consequences. Convinced that the Luftwaffe was already equipped with the type of aircraft it needed and that the war would be concluded quickly, he ended all work on projects that could not be completed in time for the coming campaign in February 1940. This directive halted work on Junker jet engines and the Messerschmitt Me 262. Although it was later reversed, the delay meant that jet fighters would not be available until much later in the war, when they came too few and too late to change the course of the war.

From a quantitative standpoint the balance of forces was relatively even on May 10. Germany had 136 divisions and 2,700 tanks compared with the Allies' 135 divisions and 3,000 tanks. From a qualitative standpoint, however, the advantage lay with the Germans for several reasons. First, the German army was battle tested from the Spanish Civil War and campaigns in Poland and Scandinavia. Second, German morale was generally strong, and especially so compared with the British and the defeatist French. Third, the Germans concentrated their tanks into armored divisions, whereas the Allies, many of whose tanks were superior, dispersed their tanks among their units thereby reducing their overall fighting power. Fourth, the Luftwaffe was better equipped and better organized, a crucial advantage during the ensuing campaign.

Although the Germans had originally planned a repeat of the 1914 Schlieffen Plan with a concentrated attack on the Right through the Netherlands and Belgium—something the British and French expected—the delays during the winter and spring led Hitler to approve General Erich von Manstein's plan to concentrate their attack on the center of the Allied position. Because Manstein's plan included General Feodor von Bock's Army Group B attacking the Netherlands and Belgium with 28 divisions, the British and French assumed that their expectations were correct and rushed into Belgium. The Germans allowed them to do so without contest. While General Wilhelm von Leeb's Army Group C tied down French forces by feinting an assault on the Maginot Line, General Gerd von Rundstedt's Army Group A carried out the brunt of the German attack through the Ardennes with 44 divisions and 7 armored divisions. Because the French considered the Ardennes impassable for tanks, they had just nine divisions stationed at the point of the German attack.

Aircraft played a critical role in the success of the German offensive. Bombing attacks on major cities and air strikes against the Dutch and Belgian air forces initiated Army Group B's attack on the Netherlands and Belgium. German aircraft destroyed approximately half of the 400 aircraft in the Dutch Air Force on the ground. More important, the campaign witnessed the first large-scale airborne attack in history. Following an attack plan designed by General Kurt Student, German paratroopers dropped by Junkers Ju 52/3 transports seized key bridges and airfields in the Netherlands, while paratroopers borne by 41 DFS 230A gliders that had been towed by Junkers Ju 52/3 transports seized key points in Belgium, including the fortress of Eban Emael. Although the Dutch Air Force put up a fierce resistance, claiming 53 victories, Queen Wilhelmina and the Dutch government fled to England on May 13 and General Henri Gerad Winkelman surrendered in face of German bombing attacks on Rotterdam on May 14.[4]

Although British and French troops stopped Army Group B's advance in Belgium on May 14, the tide was already turning in the south where the 1,800 tanks of Army Group A had broken through the Ardennes and reached the Meuse River on May 12. With Stuka dive bombers providing close support and Messerschmitt Me 109 and Me 110 fighters clearing Allied aircraft from the sky (71 Allied aircraft were shot down on May 14 alone) General Erwin Rommel's Seventh Panzer Division crossed the Meuse, establishing a bridgehead that allowed the Germans to cross in force. By May 16 Germans took Sedan, the site of the great German victory over Napoleon III in 1870. Armored divisions next raced to the English Channel. The Luftwaffe effectively disrupted French attempts to halt the German breakthrough, sending Heinkel He 111, Dornier Do 17, and Junkers Ju 88 bombers to attack bridges, railroads, and communication centers, while Stuka dive bombers provided close support to German panzers. The Germans reached the English Channel by May 21, essentially ending the Battle of France.

Despite the German army's overwhelming success, largely enabled by the Luftwaffe, Germany foolishly allowed the evacuation of 338,000 British, French, and Belgian forces from Dunkirk. Rundstedt, fearful that German panzers would get bogged down on the coast, requested a halt on May 26, which Hitler approved in part because Göring convinced him that the Luftwaffe could destroy the remaining Allied forces from the air. By then, Churchill, who had replaced Chamberlain as prime minister on May 10, had amassed some 850 ships, ranging from destroyers to small private boats, which began extracting Allied forces on May 26. Over the next nine days, the RAF scored its first victory over the Luftwaffe, shooting down 240 German aircraft while losing 177. One of the keys to this success was the introduction of the Supermarine Spitfire, which proved a match for the previously untouchable Messerschmitt BF-109.

In the aftermath of Dunkirk, the Germans shifted their attention to the south to finish off France. Although the French still possessed more guns and tanks than the Germans, the Armée de l'Air had effectively ceased to exist before the Germans began their drive on Paris on June 5. Hoping to keep France in the war at all costs, Churchill overrode Dowding's objections and dispatched two squadrons of Hurricanes to France, even though the British were already losing 25 aircraft per day. The sacrifices proved to be in vain. On June 10 Mussolini brought Italy into the war against the Allies, creating a new front in the south for the French to fight. On June 12 Rundstedt's armored divisions broke through at Châlons, leaving an open road to Paris, which the French government abandoned on the same day. In order to avoid Paris suffering the same fate that befell Warsaw and Rotterdam, the French declared it an open city on June 13 and the Germans marched in on June 14. Meanwhile, the Germans had wheeled behind the Maginot Line, preventing the French forces there from retreating to the south where they might have been able to regroup and continue the fight. By June 16 the French were prepared to capitulate and appointed Marshal Henri Philippe Pétain, hero of the epic World War I battle of Verdun, as premier to negotiate the surrender, which Hitler insisted be signed on June 20 in Compiègne in the same railway car in which Germany had signed the armistice ending World War I on November 11, 1918. In total the French suffered an overwhelming defeat, with 90,000 troops killed, 200,000 wounded, and 1.9 million captured or missing, compared with German losses of just 30,000 killed and 165,000 wounded since May 10. The losses in the air campaign were not as lopsided, however. The Luftwaffe lost almost 1,300 aircraft, including 500 bombers and 300 fighters, whereas the French lost 757 aircraft and the British lost 950 aircraft, including 386 Hurricanes and 67 Spitfires.

The Battle of Britain

Although General Erhard Milch argued that Germany should launch an immediate invasion of Great Britain while the British were in disarray, he was virtually alone in this sentiment. Bloodied by the Royal Navy during its campaign in Norway, the German Navy was extremely reluctant to face it again. Grand Admiral Erich Raeder further insisted that the Luftwaffe must first secure complete superiority over the English Channel. Germany's lack of sufficient landing craft to convey the army and its armored divisions also provided an argument against Milch. Perhaps the key factor was Hitler, who foolishly believed that the British would agree to the peace terms he extended in a speech to the Reichstag on July 19. Hitler completely misjudged the British, who on July 3 demonstrated their resolve by destroying the French Fleet at Mers-el-Kebir to prevent it from falling into the hands of the Germans. As a result a full month passed, from the fall of France on June 20 to the British rejection of Hitler's peace overtures on July 19, before the Germans began serious preparations for Operation Sea Lion, which Hitler approved on July 16. Whether the plan could be implemented, however, would depend upon the outcome of the Battle of Britain, the first battle in world history to be decided entirely in the air.

The delay provided both the RAF and Luftwaffe with an opportunity to rebuild their forces. The RAF had paid a heavy toll in France, especially with the loss of 515 pilots. Whereas Fighter Command had only 1,094 pilots of the 1,456 it needed, by mid-August the British nearly doubled the number of its fighter aircraft since Dunkirk to 704, of which 620 were Hurricanes and Spitfires. Of equal importance, Lord Beaverbrook, who had been placed in charge of British aircraft production in May 1940, pushed a 250 percent increase in aircraft production; in 1940, Great Britain produced 4,283 fighters to Germany's 3,000. The Luftwaffe had also paid a heavy price during the spring of 1940, losing approximately 28 percent of its aircraft since the start of the Scandinavian campaign. Another 8 percent had been damaged, resulting in a total reduction of 1,916 aircraft. These losses included 257 Messerschmitt BF-109 fighters, 110 Messerschmitt BF-110 twin-engine fighters, 112 Junkers Ju 87 dive bombers, and 213 Junkers Ju 52/3 transports. Nevertheless, the Luftwaffe still possessed a tremendous quantitative advantage at the start of the Battle of Britain with 2,550 aircraft, including 805 Messerschmitt BF-109s, 224 Messerschmitt BF-110s, 261 Junker Ju 87s, and 998 bombers of all types.

Although the Luftwaffe commenced small-scale attacks on July 10, bombing British targets at night and sinking approximately 40,000 tons of British shipping in the English Channel, the Battle of Britain did not begin in earnest until August 8 when newly promoted Reichsmarschall Göring issued orders for Operation Adler. With the destruction of the RAF as its object, Operation Adler called for attacks from Field Marshal Albert Kesselring's Luftflotte 2, stationed in Belgium and northern France, Field Marshal Hugo Sperrle's Luftflotte 3, stationed in Normandy, and General Hans-Jürgen Stumpf's Luftflotte 5, stationed in Norway. Since the Germans lacked a single-seat fighter with the range to accompany Stumpf's bombers from Norway, this resulted in heavy losses during the first and only daylight raid conducted by Luftflotte 5. The Luftwaffe's campaign would therefore be conducted primarily by Luftflotte 2 and Luftflotte 3.

In preparation for the German attacks, Dowding divided Great Britain into four defensive zones, with Air Vice Marshal Keith Park's No. 11 Group stationed along the English Channel, Air Vice Marshal Trafford Leigh-Mallory's No. 12 Group stationed in the midlands, Air Vice Marshall Richard Saul's No. 13 Group stationed north of Manchester, and Air Vice Marshal Sir Christopher Brand's No. 10 Group stationed in southeastern England. Sharp differences of opinion divided Fighter Command itself. Leigh-Mallory resented being charged with providing support to Park's No. 11 Group and advocated a concentration of fighters to take the battle directly to the Luftwaffe. Dowding and Park disagreed, preferring instead to rely upon its network of radar stations and ground observers to identify approaching German formations and then scramble fighter squadrons to attack them. In addition, British cryptographers at Bletchley Park used the Ultra code-breaking system, supplied by the Poles, to decode German transmissions and give Fighter Command advance notice of the Luftwaffe's intended targets. Whereas Dowding's primary objective was to minimize the number of German bombers that got through to their targets, his strategy more importantly minimized the loss of pilots over the English Channel or in enemy territory. To put it simply, Dowding could replace aircraft; he could not replace pilots. For every aircraft lost over Great Britain, there was a good possibility that the pilot could parachute to safety and rejoin his squadron to fight again.

Although poor weather delayed Adlertag until August 13, the Luftwaffe conducted a successful raid on August 12 against RAF radar stations in Dover and Portsmouth, temporarily disabling some of them. The Luftwaffe's commanders, including Göring, failed to recognize how vital these were to the RAF. Throughout the campaign, they shifted their focus elsewhere, allowing the British to put radar installations quickly back into service. On August 13 Altertag commenced with three waves of attacks by Luftflotte 3 against British airbases in southeastern England, shooting down 15 RAF aircraft while losing 39, most of which were Junkers Ju 87s. The Luftwaffe's chief of military intelligence, Colonel Josef Schmid, however, grossly overestimated British losses and damage to British airfields, a pattern that would be repeated throughout the campaign as German intelligence repeatedly overestimated the damage caused by their bombs.

Believing that the RAF was on the verge of collapse, Göring ordered a massive assault for Thursday, August 15, from all three Luftflotten, hoping to crush the RAF with one fatal blow. In the north, the RAF intercepted a flight of 65 Heinkel He 111s and 20 Messerschmitt BF-110s from Luftflotte 5, shooting down eight of the former and seven of the latter without losing a single fighter of their own. This effectively ended Luftflotte 5's role in the campaign. In the south, RAF Spitfires tied up Messerschmitt BF-109 fighters while Hurricanes attacked Messerschmitt BF-110s and German bombers. In total, the Luftwaffe flew 1,786 sorties, losing 76 aircraft. Although the RAF lost 34 aircraft, only 17 of its pilots were killed, proving the effectiveness of Dowding's strategy. Several factors contributed to the RAF's initial success. First, the Messerschmitt BF-109's limited range gave it only about 20 to 30 minutes flying time over England. Second, the Spitfire could outturn the Messerschmitt BF-109, which compensated for the Messerschmitt's superior climbing ability. Third, the twin-engine Messerschmitt BF-110 proved totally inadequate against the Hurricane, which actually carried the brunt of Fighter Command's defense. As a result, Göring would order that the Messerschmitt Bf 109s stay in close support of German bombers and even the Messerschmitt BF-110, effectively surrendering the BF-109's advantages in combat ceiling and speed and working instead to the advantage of the RAF fighters.

Although German losses continued mounting after August 15 (reaching 403 aircraft, half of which were fighters) by August 24 the attacks on RAF air bases were succeeding, costing the British 175 aircraft, primarily fighters, in the same period. Beginning on August 24 the Luftwaffe transferred Luftflotte 3's Messerschmitt BF-109 fighters to Luftflotte 2, where the shorter distance across the Pas de Calais maximized their time over England. Göring also concentrated bombing attacks on southern and southeastern England. Over the next two weeks, the RAF lost 295 aircraft, with another 171 lost to repairs. More important, Fighter Command lost 240 pilots, stretching its reserves precariously thin. Dowding responded by organizing two Polish and two Czech squadrons to help alleviate the pressure. The Poles in Squadron 303 proved highly skilled, earning a kill-to-loss ratio of 14-to-1, the highest in Fighter Campaign. It was at this point, however, that Hitler ordered the Luftwaffe to commence the terror bombing of London. Although this resulted in widespread destruction and heavy civilian casualties, it actually relieved the pressure on Fighter Command, enabling it to recover and ultimately win the Battle of Britain.

The decision to switch targets stemmed from the events of the night of August 24, when German bombers bound for Rochester got off course and mistakenly dropped their bombs on London. Churchill had already ordered Bomber Campaign to plan a night raid on Berlin if such an attack occurred, and this was carried out immediately with 81 bombers. Outraged, Hitler ordered the Luftwaffe to shift its focus to London, initiating the so-called Blitz on September 7. The first attack involved almost 1,000 aircraft, including 350 bombers, and resulted in the deaths of more than 300 civilians. Although the RAF lost 28 fighters while shooting down 34 German aircraft, the focus on London removed pressure on its airfields and aircraft companies. On September 15 the Luftwaffe mounted what it believed would be the winning blow, attacking with 277 bombers in three separate waves. To their surprise, RAF fighters shot down 35 bombers and 20 fighters, providing convincing evidence that German intelligence reports were wrong; indeed, the RAF remained more than capable of defending its airspace. More important, the delay caused Hitler to miss a window of opportunity for a cross-channel invasion, forcing the indefinite postponing of Operation Sea Lion. Unable to sustain the heavy losses incurred during daytime raids, the Luftwaffe shifted to more limited nighttime attacks. This effectively closed the Battle of Britain.

The performance of the RAF provided a much-needed victory for the British. Although they lost 1,017 fighters and 537 pilots, the RAF downed 1,733 German aircraft and cost the Luftwaffe 3,000 of its best-trained crewmen. This more than anything else shattered the myth of the untouchable bomber—the air power theorists of the preceding generation were indefensibly wrong about this. The Battle of Britain caused attentive nations to alter their plans for strategic bombing dramatically, and demonstrated the need for effective long-range fighter escorts for heavy bombers. Although the U.S. Army Air Force would later engage in daylight bombing campaigns against Germany, it paid a notoriously high price for this tactic. The campaign also showed quite conclusively that air power would not replace conventional ground forces in a modern war. The Royal Navy remained a serious impediment to German strategy, even in an air war. Finally, the RAF's success in establishing and maintaining air superiority during and after the Battle of Britain made the isle a key point in the Allied counterattack that was to come. Indeed, it is difficult to overstate the legacy of the RAF following this campaign. Churchill famously eulogized Fighter Command thusly: "Never in the field of human conflict was so much owed by so many to so few."

Although the opportunity to invade Great Britain had been lost, at least temporarily, Hitler ordered the Luftwaffe to continue pounding Great Britain in a night bombing campaign that the British came to call the Blitz. Stretching from October 1940 to May 1941, the Blitz would see attacks involving an average of 200 German bombers dropping bombs on English cities and industrial centers, including the spectacular November 14–15 raid that destroyed much of Coventry. By the time the Blitz came to an end in May, German bombers had succeeded in killing approximately 40,000 civilians, injuring another

46,000, and destroying approximately 1 million homes. Nevertheless Germany gained little else, as the Blitz had in essence extended a battle that Germany had in fact already lost and that even Hitler probably realized could not be won. Indeed, even though Hitler certainly did not want to give the British a respite, it can be argued that the Blitz filled his psychological need to punish a foe who failed to submit and to escape the reality that he had been defeated. Nevertheless, the Blitz did have three important consequences. First, the Blitz steeled British resolve to resist, demonstrating that Douhet and Trenchard had miscalculated the capacity of civilians to endure devastating hardship, something that the Allies should have realized Germans would also demonstrate. Second, the Blitz fueled the British desire for revenge, which Bomber Command would carry out against German cities. Indeed, more Germans would die in one night in the firestorm unleashed on Hamburg than the British lost in the entire Blitz. Third, and more important from a strategic standpoint, the newsreel accounts of the Blitz that Americans viewed provided the public support that President Franklin Delano Roosevelt needed to push Lend-Lease through Congress, taking a very reluctant nation closer to war.

In the end the Battle of Britain is probably most significant in that it reinforced Hitler's desire to attack the Soviet Union because much like Napoleon a century and a half before, Hitler believed that defeating Russia would bring Great Britain to the negotiating table, a view he had expressed to his generals on July 31, 1940. Besides, as he had spelled out in *Mein Kampf*, the Soviet Union, not Great Britain, was Germany's true enemy because the Soviet Union possessed the *lebensraum* (living space) that Germans needed to secure the future of the master race. The Soviet Union's poor performance against Finland further convinced him that it would collapse under the pressure of a German attack. On July 21, 1940, well before Altertag, Hitler had ordered his general staff to initiate plans for an invasion, which he approved on December 18, 1940. Before Operation Barbarossa was launched, however, Germany would be diverted to the Mediterranean in order to save Mussolini from an embarrassing defeat. The result was a four-year campaign that, while little more than a sideshow, provided another testing ground for air power.

The Role of Air Power in the Mediterranean Campaigns

Without consulting Hitler, Mussolini invaded Greece on October 28, 1940, in an attempt to establish Italian supremacy in the Mediterranean. Mussolini calculated that Greece could be easily taken, in part because he believed his advance of 200,000 men from Libya into Egypt would keep the British from interfering in Greece; ultimately, Mussolini completely overestimated the will of his own soldiers to fight and underestimated both the tenacity of the Greek army and the resolve of the British. When he sent seven of his best divisions into Greece from Albania, which Italy had occupied in April 1939, three Greek divisions promptly drove them back into Albania. More important, on November 11, 1940, the Royal Navy carried out a stunning attack on the principal Italian naval base at Taranto, in which Fairey Swordfish torpedo biplanes launched from the HMS *Illustrious* sank the battleship *Duilio* and damaged the battleships *Cavour* and *Littorio*. One month later the British followed up with an overwhelming victory on December 10 at Sidi Barrani, where 31,000 British troops routed the Italian army in Egypt, capturing 38,000 prisoners and the bulk of its equipment. In January 1941 the Greek government accepted a British offer for assistance, and in early March 1941 an Imperial Expeditionary Force of 53,000 men, supported by approximately 80 RAF aircraft, arrived in Greece.

Because the Italian debacle and British intervention posed a potential threat to the German Army's southern flank, Hitler decided to intervene, a decision that ultimately delayed the invasion of Russia by one month. Another factor leading to German intervention in the Balkans and the Mediterranean was the Yugoslav Army's coup against Prince Regent Paul, who had been pressured into an alliance with Germany and Italy on March 25, 1941. In a monumental effort, the Luftwaffe transferred approximately 1,000 aircraft in just a few days before commencing the campaign on April 6 with a two-day bombardment of Belgrade that killed as many as 17,000 civilians. Meanwhile, German armored divisions supported by aircraft poured into Yugoslavia and Greece from Bulgaria, destroying the Greek and Yugoslav armies and forcing the British to evacuate their forces from Greece.

Enthused by this success, Göring convinced Hitler to implement General Kurt Student's suggestion that paratroopers be used to seize Crete, which could then be used as a staging area for attacks on Cyprus and the Suez Canal. With the Luftwaffe securing air supremacy over Crete and the sea lanes around it, on May 20, 1941, Junkers Ju 52/3 transports began dropping paratroopers and glider-borne troops onto Crete. Although the German paratroopers lacked the support of ground units—as they had in their successes in the Netherlands and Belgium—the lack of sufficient air support doomed the Allied resistance. By June 1, Student's forces secured Crete, but at the heavy price of 5,670 elite troops who could have been put to more effective use on the Russian front.

Meanwhile, the British followed up their victory at Sidi Barrani by pushing into Libya. The campaign quickly demonstrated the vulnerability of the Regia Aeronautica. Although it had approximately 1,800 front-line aircraft, more than half of which were bombers, its fighters were obsolete and undergunned compared with the RAF's Hurricanes. Indeed, Italy continued producing outmoded Fiat CR 42 biplane fighters. Despite these deficiencies, air power was not responsible for Italy's failure in North Africa. To state it bluntly, the Italian Army was poorly led and did not want to fight. In two months of combat, culminating with the surrender of the Tenth Army on February 7, the British captured 130,000 prisoners, 380 tanks, 845 artillery pieces, and hundreds of aircraft, while losing just 500 killed and 1,400 wounded. The RAF lost 26 aircraft, while downing 58 Italian aircraft.

Even though he had already sent the Luftwaffe's X Fliegerkorps to Sicily in early January 1941 to support Mussolini's bombing campaign against Malta, Hitler dispatched Lieutenant General Erwin Rommel and two divisions to Libya in mid-February. Although Rommel had little air support, he launched a counteroffensive on March 31, 1941, placing the British garrison at Tobruk under siege on April 10 and reaching the border of Egypt by April 14. During the summer and fall of 1941, the British counterattacked in an effort to lift the siege of Tobruk. The withdrawal of Luftwaffe units for the Russian Campaign, which was launched on June 22, 1941, aided the British by making it easier for the RAF and naval aircraft to disrupt Rommel's supply lines in the Mediterranean. By November 1941 Rommel was down to 414 tanks, 320 aircraft, and 9 divisions, 3 of which were German, whereas the British had approximately 700 tanks, 1,000 aircraft, and 8 divisions. The British efforts in building up the RAF in North Africa were monumental because aircraft were either sent by ship around the Cape of Good Hope and up the Red Sea or flown in excess of 3,700 miles from West Africa to Egypt. These strenuous efforts paid off, however, because on November 29, the British Eighth Army lifted the 240-day siege of Tobruk. Of equal importance, RAF attacks claimed 62 percent of Axis shipping in the Mediterranean, forcing Hitler to transfer Luftflotte 2 from Russia to Sicily. Combined with the British transfer of forces from North Africa to Singapore and India after the Japanese attack on Pearl Harbor, the arrival of the Luftflotte 2 improved Rommel's flow of supplies and enabled him to resume offensive operations on January 21, 1942.

Both sides launched a series of attacks and counterattacks throughout 1942 in which air power played an important role. After driving the

British Eighth Army back 300 miles in his initial attack on January 21, 1942, Rommel continued to Gazala, where he halted to regroup on February 4. Over the next three months, the RAF's Western Desert Force and a combined Luftwaffe–Regia Aeronautica force conducted a vigorous air campaign against each other in the skies of North Africa, with the former having approximately 600 aircraft to the latter's 530. Despite the RAF's slight numerical advantage, the Luftwaffe's force included 120 Messerschmitt BF-109F fighters. The British consequently lost approximately 300 aircraft between February and May. Rommel launched a new offensive on May 26 that resulted in the capture of Tobruk on June 21 and pushed the British back to within 120 miles of El Alamein by the end of June. Rommel's successes led Churchill to name General Sir Harold Alexander as commander-in-chief of the Middle East and Lieutenant General Sir Bernard Montgomery as commander of the Eighth Army.

On August 30 Rommel launched a new offensive at Alam Halfa, hoping to bypass El Alamein and drive straight to the Nile River. Unbeknownst to Rommel, the British had learned about his plans in advance through the Ultra secret and began a nonstop bombing campaign on August 21 that would drop more than 1,000 tons of bombs on his forces by September 2. More important, the RAF had been reinforced by a United States Army Air Corps squadron equipped with the North American B-25 Mitchell. With Rommel forced to halt his attack on September 3, Montgomery began plans for an offensive of his own. By late October Montgomery had amassed a force three times larger than Rommel's and initiated the Battle of El Alamein on October 23 with a massive artillery barrage. Despite suffering approximately 10,000 casualties in the first five days, Montgomery pressed on with his attacks, relying upon the RAF for close ground support. By November 4 Rommel had no choice but to begin a 1,400-mile retreat to Tunisia with Montgomery in hot pursuit.

While Rommel retreated into Tripoli, the United States and Great Britain carried out the Operation Torch landing at Casablanca, Oran, and Algiers on November 8, 1942. Hitler responded immediately by occupying the rest of France[5] and began sending reinforcements to Rommel that would increase the size of the Afrika Korps to 250,000 men. Although Rommel succeeded in defeating the United States at Kasserine Pass on February 14–15, 1943, it was only a matter of time before the superior numbers of the Allies launched attacks from the east and the west. Allied air superiority also made a key difference as newly introduced Spitfires and Lockheed P-38 fighters countered the Luftwaffe's Messerschmitt BF-109s, and the new Hurricane IID, which was equipped with two 40-mm cannon, finally gave the Allies a weapon that could knock out Rommel's tanks. In addition, Douglas C-47s proved critical in keeping Allied forces supplied. Allied fighters downed a total of 435 Axis transport aircraft between April 5 and April 17, depriving the Afrika Korps of much needed fuel and supplies. On March 9, Hitler recalled Rommel to Germany, leaving command of the Afrika Korps to General Hans Jürgen Dieter von Arnim. By May 13 Arnim had no choice but to surrender his 250,000-man army, 150,000 of whom were German.

Following their victory in North Africa, the Allies launched invasions of Sicily and southern Italy later in 1943 with Allied aircraft playing important roles in their success. The Germans would lose approximately 1,000 aircraft in the two months that followed the invasion of Sicily. For the remainder of the Italian campaign, the Luftwaffe provided only token resistance. Even though this gave the Allies command of the air, the Germans proved adept at hunkering down on the ground during Allied air attacks, then emerging to put up a stiff resistance. Because of the strategic bombing campaign, which involved the United States' Fifteenth Air Force operating out of southern Italy, and the preparations for the Normandy invasion, Allied forces in Italy lacked the level of air support needed for decisive results within the theater, although the bombing of Rome contributed to Mussolini's overthrow in September 1943. The two most noteworthy events involving aircraft in Italy came with the Luftwaffe's rescue of Mussolini (an audacious glider assault led by Otto Skorzeny on September 12, 1943, against the Campo Imperatore Hotel at Gran Sasso) and the Allied bombing of the monastery at Monte Cassino (on February 15, 1944).

The Role of Air Power on the Eastern Front

Although Hitler dispatched units to the Mediterranean in the spring of 1941, this did not prevent him from assembling a massive force of 3 million men organized in 162 divisions and supported by 2,770 aircraft for Operation Barbarossa. Although the number of aircraft was similar to that used in the Battle of France, the scope of the campaign was far greater with a vast front stretching 1,000 miles when the invasion was launched on June 22, 1941. General Alfred Keller's Luftflotte 1 supported Army Group North's drive through the Baltic states, Field Marshal Albert Kesselring's Luftflotte 2 supported Army Group Center's advance to Smolensk and Moscow, and General Alexander Löhr's Luftflotte 4 supported Army Group South's attack toward Kiev.

Despite more than 500 long-range observation flights deep into Russia in the months leading up to the attack, Stalin ignored all warnings and refused to take defensive measures lest this provoke the Germans. As a result, when the Luftwaffe attacked 66 Soviet airfields on the first day, they destroyed 1,811 Soviet aircraft, all but 322 of which were on the ground, while losing just 32 aircraft of their own. Over the next four days the Luftwaffe destroyed an additional 2,008 Soviet aircraft. As was the case with the Red Army, the Red Air Force paid a heavy price for Stalin's purges prior to the war because their pilots generally proved woefully ill-prepared for their battle-tested opponents.

By October 5 Soviet losses totaled more than 5,000 aircraft as Stalin ordered inexperienced Russian airmen flying Polikarpov I-15 and I-16 fighters and obsolete bombers to attack the Germans no matter the cost. German aces racked up victories that made the Red Baron's 80 kills in World War I pale in comparison (Major Erich Hartmann would earn 352 victories and 106 other Luftwaffe aces would surpass 100 victories by the end of the war). Despite the relentless German air attacks and rapid advance of the German army, the Soviet Union managed to move more than 15,000 factories and 10 million workers from western Russia to areas beyond the Urals. Although this disrupted aircraft production by about 30 percent for approximately three months, it was a monumental feat that ultimately saved the Soviet Union. By October production levels surpassed prewar levels. More important, the Soviet Union began introducing better aircraft, including the Yakovlev Yak 9, Mikoyan and Guryevich MiG-3, Petlayakov Pe-2, and Illyushin Il-2 Shturmovik. To a certain extent the Luftwaffe's success in 1941 was deceptive because it had come at the expense of aircraft the Red Air Force could afford to lose.

Meanwhile, three German army groups had advanced so far by mid-August (the front extended an incredible 1,800 miles in length) they had stretched their supply lines to the limit, forcing a halt for the next six weeks. On October 1 Hitler ordered a concentrated assault on Moscow. Although the advance initially enjoyed great success, by November torrential rains turned Russia's primitive roads into quagmires and the German army quite literally began to bog down. In addition, the Red Army began transferring forces from Manchuria after Soviet spies learned that the Japanese had decided to attack the United States. Desperate to save Moscow, Stalin ordered vicious counter-assaults on German forces. By the end of November, the Soviet Union had lost 3 million men whereas the Germans had lost 800,000 men. Had Hitler not transferred Luftflotte 2 to Sicily in support of Rommel's Afrika Korps, thereby depriving Army Group Center of effective air support, the Germans might have taken Moscow. Instead the U.S.S.R.'s Marshal Georgi Zhukov called upon the Red Air Force to conduct more than 51,300 sorties against German forces in front of Moscow. These attacks included increased numbers of Ilyushin Il-2 Shturmoviks anti-tank aircraft, which turned the tide in favor of the Soviets. The German offensive ground to a halt just 19 miles from the city.

In the aftermath of the failed German drive on Moscow, the Soviet Union launched a massive counteroffensive on December 5 along a 560-mile front. As one of the coldest winters in Russian history left German forces freezing in their summer uniforms, the Russians advanced up to 150 miles during January and February. Whereas the Luftwaffe's available aircraft declined to no more than 500 planes, the Red Air Force fielded more than 1,000 aircraft around Moscow. Having assumed personal command of the army, Hitler forbade any retreat. Even though this resulted in heavy casualties, it did prevent what otherwise would have been a Russian breakthrough. The Luftwaffe was unable to conduct effective offensive operations, but it did succeed in airlifting supplies to 100,000 German troops surrounded at Demyansk in February, enabling them to hold out until German reinforcements reached them on May 20, 1942. Even though it was successful, the Demyansk operation ironically contributed to the German debacle at Stalingrad later in the year by convincing Hitler that aircraft could sustain the beleaguered Sixth Army.

Despite losing almost 50 percent of his original invasion force, Hitler ignored his generals' advice that the German Army pull back to a defensive position and decided instead to continue the German siege of Leningrad and launch a new campaign into southern Russia. Shifting forces from other fronts and mobilizing 51 divisions from their allies, the Germans began advancing toward Stalingrad on June 22, 1942. By then the Luftwaffe had been restored to preinvasion levels and once again enjoyed success against the Red Air Force. Having learned from its mistakes the prior year, the Red Army pulled back, allowing General Friedrich von Paulus's Sixth Army to reach Stalingrad by August 10. Although the Luftwaffe committed approximately 1,000 aircraft to the Stalingrad sector, their efforts were wasted by bombing the city itself instead of concentrating against Soviet supply lines. As the Sixth Army became entangled in vicious street-to-street fighting inside Stalingrad, Zhukov amassed 500,000 troops and 900 T-34 tanks for a counterattack that was launched on November 19 against the Romanian Army on Paulus's northern flank. Zhukov followed this easy victory with a similar attack on Paulus's southern flank the following day. By November 24 the Sixth Army was surrounded.

Göring's vow that the Luftwaffe could duplicate the Demyansk air-lift proved an empty boast, as the distance involved and the amount of supplies required outstripped its capabilities, especially with the onset of winter. More important, the Red Air Force had grown in strength and quality as more than 41,000 aircraft had entered service since June 22, 1941. As a result, the Red Air Force flew more than twice as many sorties (35,929) as the Luftwaffe between November 19, 1942, and February 2, 1943. Although Paulus might have been able to fight his way out, Hitler forbade it and even promoted him to field marshal. With the Luftwaffe averaging 113 tons of supplies dropped per day, far below the 250 tons required for survival, Paulus was forced to surren-der his starving army on January 31, 1943. No more than 5,000 of the 151,000 German prisoners who had been captured during the course of the battle would survive to return to Germany after the war.

With the debacle at Stalingrad accompanied by losses in the Mediterranean and increasing commitments against the American and British strategic bombing campaigns, the Luftwaffe was unable to regain air supremacy on the Eastern Front, where it committed no more than 2,500 aircraft in 1943. In vicious fighting on the Kuban Peninsula between April 17 and June 7, 1943, where ground forces fought to a stalemate, the Red Air Force lost 2,800 aircraft to the Luft-waffe's 800, but these were losses it could replace, especially with the addition of Lend-Lease aircraft from the United States and Great Britain. The turning point on the Eastern Front came in July 1943 with Germany's offensive in the Kursk salient—the last it would mount in the East. The Luftwaffe amassed more than 2,000 aircraft for the offensive, but only 600 were fighters. Despite initial success on the ground and in the air, the German attack was stopped on July 11 after the greatest tank battle in history, which pitted 600 German tanks against 600 Soviet tanks. Supported by its Ilyushin Il-2 Shturmovik antitank aircraft, Soviet tanks carried the day. Although Manstein, who had originally opposed the offensive, urged Hitler to continue the bat-tle in hopes that the German Army could achieve a breakthrough, the German losses combined with news of the Allied invasion of Sicily caused Hitler to lose his nerve and cancel the offensive.

Although Stalin had long demanded that the United States and Great Britain launch a cross-channel invasion to relieve pressure on the Soviet Union—he considered the campaigns in the Mediterranean a mere diversion—the fact of the matter was that the Red Army was well on its way to winning the war on the Eastern Front. In the after-math of Kursk the Red Army maintained its momentum, launching one offensive after another and pushing the German Army steadily back. Although the Normandy Invasion on June 6, 1944, created the second front Stalin had demanded, Russia continued to carry the brunt of the fighting because Germany kept approximately 75 percent of its forces on the Eastern Front. Even though the Luftwaffe gained local air superiority on a few occasions well into late 1944, the Red Air Force eventually wore it down. By the time the Red Army began its drive on Berlin in April 1945, the Red Air Force boasted more than 7,500 aircraft, whereas the Luftwaffe could muster no more than 400. To put it simply, Hitler's decision to attack the Soviet Union doomed Germany to defeat.

Air Power in the Battle of the Atlantic

Although Stalin's frustration with the British and American failure to open a second front until 1944 is understandable, especially given the tremendous sacrifices the Soviet Union was making, creating an invasion force in Great Britain was a monumental undertaking that could not be achieved until the Allies first won the Battle of the Atlantic. This was no easy task. Although the Germans entered the war with just 36 oceangoing U-boats, which enabled Grand Admiral Karl Dönitz to keep as few as six U-boats at sea in late 1941, the escalation of U-boat construction increased the number of U-boats operating in the Atlantic to almost 100 by 1943. At the height of the German U-boat campaign between November 1942 and March 1943, the Germans were sinking close to 800,000 tons of Allied shipping per month, which exceeded their building capacity.

Air power ironically played a leading role in both the German Navy's early successes and in the Allied Navy's ultimate victory in the Battle of the Atlantic. After the fall of France, the Luftwaffe deployed the four-engine Focke Wulf Fw 200 Condor, a commercial liner that had been converted for military use. With a range of almost 2,800 miles, the Condor proved an ideal long-range antishipping bomber and indeed the model accounted for 85 ships between August 1940 and April 1941 alone. More important, the Condor provided a useful reconnaissance role, locating Allied convoys and relaying that information to U-boat wolf packs. Although the Allies had long-range four-engine bombers that could have been used against U-boats, Bomber Command reserved these for its strategic bombing campaign against Germany. As a result, the Allies relied upon such relatively short-range aircraft as the Consolidated PBY Catalina and Short Sunderland, leaving a vast air gap south of Greenland in which U-boat wolfpacks could operate relatively safely. As Allied losses mounted in late 1942 and early 1943, they finally began using long-range Consolidated B-24 Liberators armed with depth charges to eliminate the air gap. Combined with an increased naval presence, B-24s reversed the Battle of the Atlantic, as more than 100 U-boats were destroyed by the Allies between April 1 and June 30, 1943.

By August 1943, Dönitz realized the Battle of the Atlantic had been lost as U-boat losses greatly exceeded the construction of new U-boats. Nevertheless, Hitler insisted that U-boat attacks continue; they did, but with disastrous results. By the end of the war, 784 of 1,116 U-boats had been destroyed and almost 80 percent of its 40,900 submariners had been lost at sea or taken prisoner. Even though they had taken a heavy toll on Allied shipping, sinking 2,840 Allied merchant vessels totaling 14.3 million tons, it was not enough to starve the British into submission. Neither did it prevent the United States from building up the forces it needed in Great Britain to carry out the strategic bombing campaign against Germany and the cross-channel invasion that helped bring the war to a close.

The Strategic Bombing Campaign against Germany

Throughout the interwar years air power theorists argued that bombing would be a war-winning strategy by destroying an enemy's economic infrastructure and reducing the population's will to fight. Indeed, Trenchard firmly believed that the psychological damage inflicted by bombing would be twenty times greater than the actual physical damage it produced. The Allies would persist in this view, even though the Battle of Britain and the Blitz had demonstrated that German bombing campaigns failed to break the will of British civilians and, if anything, actually strengthened their resolve. In addition, air power theorists had asserted that well-armed battle planes could fight their way through enemy fighters, and nations had responded by building such aircraft. Although RAF experiences at Wilhelmshaven and during the Battle of Britain had disproved this, leading Bomber Command to switch to safer nighttime bombing raids, the belief in the value of strategic bombing remained an article of faith. Indeed, when the United States entered the war Army Air Force commanders were convinced that its more heavily armed bombers could successfully carry out daylight raids against Germany without fighter escorts. As will be seen, American airmen would pay a heavy price for this misplaced belief. In the end, it was the long-range fighter, not the bomber, that produced decisive results. Indeed, of the 2.79 million tons of bombs dropped by Bomber Command and the United States Strategic Air Forces on Germany, its allies, and its occupied territories during the war, 85 percent were dropped after June 1, 1944, when long-range fighters were available to escort bombers.

After its failed daylight raid on Wilhelmshaven on December 18, 1939, Bomber Command switched to nighttime attacks, including the retaliatory attack on Berlin during the Battle of Britain. Throughout 1940 and into 1941, the British persisted with attacks that Bomber Command believed were inflicting significant damage to strategic targets. In August 1941, however, the Butts Report revealed that only one third of British bombers came within five miles of their intended target. Despite this evidence, which Bomber Command vigorously disputed, the British persisted in their attacks primarily because it remained their only viable means for waging war directly against Germany.

Moreover, Air Chief Marshal Sir Arthur Harris, who was placed in charge of Bomber Command in February 1942, remained convinced that Germany's population was the proper target. He therefore gave up all pretense of striking strategic targets and shifted Bomber Command's focus to killing as many Germans as possible. Toward that end, Harris slowly built up Bomber Command's force, incorporating such new bombers as the Avro Lancaster, which could carry a bomb load of 14,000 lbs. On the night of May 30–31, 1942, Harris launched his first 1,000 aircraft raid, striking Cologne in a devastating attack that destroyed 18,000 buildings, damaged 39,000 others, and killed 500 Germans. The following months witnessed similar, albeit smaller, raids on other German cities. The most devastating assault was carried out on Hamburg a year later, on the night of July 27–28, 1943. A combination of unusually heavy incendiary bombs and unique atmospheric conditions caused a firestorm that produced temperatures of 1,000 degrees Celsius and tornado force winds that killed at least 50,000 Germans.

Despite the widespread destruction of these attacks, they had little strategic value. The German will to fight was not diminished and German production was generally disrupted by no more than three days. More important, the Germans developed vastly improved defensive measures, including the introduction of radar-equipped Heinkel He 219 night fighters. As a result, when Harris launched a four-month-long campaign against Berlin beginning on November 18–19, 1943, the Germans downed 1,047 British aircraft and heavily damaged another 1,600, leading to serious divisions within the RAF leadership about the effectiveness of Harris's methods. In any event, by the end of March 1944, Bomber Command ceased its campaign against Berlin so its bombers could help prepare the way for the Normandy Invasion.

Meanwhile, the U.S. Army Air Forces (USAAF) established the Eighth Air Force in February 1942 to conduct its strategic bombing campaign against Germany. Although the British tried to convince Americans to follow their nighttime strategy, the USAAF was committed to a precision bombing campaign that necessitated daylight raids. This had been recommended prior to the U.S. entry in the war by its Air War Plans Division (AWPD), which was composed of Air Corps Tactical School alumni who firmly believed that heavily armed bombers like the Boeing B-17 Flying Fortress could successfully overcome fighter resistance and use their Norden bombsights to hit strategic targets. The AWPD calculated that a successful campaign of this nature would require a total operation force of 63,500 aircraft of all types and 2.16 million men, numbers the United States would indeed come close to reaching by the end of the war. A subsequent AWPD report issued in September 1942 added the necessity of destroying the Luftwaffe in order to obtain the air supremacy required for successful ground operations.

Implementing the AWPD's recommendations was no easy task for Eighth Air Force commander Brigadier General Ira Eaker. It was not enough simply to amass aircraft. It took time to train crews for instrument flying, bombing, and gunnery. In addition, a large reserve of spare parts had to be available to keep aircraft operational. With the exception of summer, adverse weather limited the Eighth Air Force to an average of five bombing days per month. Compounding Eaker's problems was that aircraft from the Eighth Air Force were transferred to meet the needs of Allied forces in the Mediterranean theater. This included sending two bomber groups to support the Ninth Air Force's costly raids against the Ploesti oil fields in Romania on August 1, 1943. Although President Franklin D. Roosevelt, Chief of Staff General George C. Marshall, and USAAF commander General Henry "Hap" Arnold made the decisions that caused these transfers, they still complained about the Eighth Air Force's lack of success and ultimately, perhaps unfairly, held Eaker accountable.

The Eighth Air Force launched its first heavy bomber raid on August 17, 1942, with Eaker leading the way to Rouen in the *Yankee Doodle*, although its attacks on Germany did not commence until January 1943. At the Casablanca Conference, held January 14–24, 1943, FDR and Churchill had announced that around-the-clock bombing of Germany would commence, primarily to placate Stalin. On January 27 Eaker dispatched 91 bombers against the German naval base at Wilhelmshaven.

Although 55 bombers reached their targets, they inflicted only minimal damage, while shooting down seven German fighters and losing just three of their bombers. As the Eighth Air Force increased the number of bombers in its raids during the course of 1943, the Luftwaffe, now equipped with Focke-Wulf Fw 190 fighters and anti-aircraft artillery, began inflicting heavy losses, especially because the Allied fighters available at the time lacked sufficient range to escort bombers beyond Aachen. With the Eighth Air Force's average losses approaching 8 percent per mission, American bomber crews could not expect to survive more than 13 missions, which was well below the 25-mission standard tour of duty. Colonel Curtis E. LeMay, commander of the 305th Bombardment Group, attempted to rectify the situation by implementing combat wings consisting of three combat box formations of 18–21 bombers flying in tight echelon formations separated by 1,000 foot differences in altitude to maximize the combined firepower of their defensive guns. This meant German fighters faced up to 540 machine guns per American bomber group.

LeMay's tactics improved bomber accuracy but did not significantly alter the percentage of losses the Eighth Air Force was suffering. Raids on August 17, 1943, against the Messerschmitt factory at Regensburg and ball-bearing factories at Schweinfurt dramatically proved this point. LeMay, newly promoted to brigadier general, led the Fourth Bombardment Wing's 146 bombers against Regensburg. Facing heavy German fighter resistance from Belgium all the way to the target, LeMay's force lost nineteen aircraft before dropping their bombs and lost another five before escaping across the Alps and landing in North Africa. Although the damage disrupted the production of Messerschmitt BF-109 fighters for five months and delayed the introduction of Messerschmitt Me 262 jet fighters by several months, it came at the price of 24 lost aircraft and crews. Meanwhile, Brigadier General Robert B. Williams's First Bombardment Wing lost 36 of its 230 aircraft in the attack on Schweinfurt. Although production of ball-bearings was reduced by about two thirds over the next few months, the Germans were able to purchase sufficient replacements from Sweden. With a loss of 60 bombers and another 30 being so heavily damaged they had to be scrapped, the raids on Regensburg and Schweinfurt resulted in an attrition rate of 23 percent. A follow-up attack against Schweinfurt on October 14 with 229 aircraft resulted in the loss of 60 bombers and an additional 17 that had to be scrapped, resulting in a net reduction of one third of the attacking force.

Although Eaker performed as well as should have been expected given the lack of long-range fighters to escort his bombers, he nevertheless received the blame for the Eighth Air Force's losses and limited results. As a result, when Arnold reorganized the USAAF in Europe in January, he transferred Eaker to command of the Mediterranean Allied Air Forces and placed Major General James H. "Jimmy" Doolittle, previously the commander of the Fifteenth Air Force, in charge of the Eighth Air Force. In addition, Arnold established the United States Strategic Air Forces under Lieutenant General Carl A. Spaatz. Perhaps most important was the arrival of the P-51B Mustang to the Eighth Air Force. The P-51 originally entered service with the RAF in April 1942, but its nonsupercharged Allison engine made it ineffective at high altitudes. When the British outfitted it with the supercharged Rolls-Royce Merlin engine, however, the Mustang could outperform all German fighters. More important, the addition of external drop tanks enabled it to escort Allied bombers all the way to Berlin. Instead of simply using bombers to attack strategic targets, Doolittle employed them to draw Luftwaffe fighters into traps set by the Eighth Air Force's Mustangs. Rather than achieving mere air superiority, the Allies now had the means of establishing air supremacy.

By January 1944 the Luftwaffe had amassed approximately 1,650 fighters to combat the Allied strategic bombing campaign. On February 19 the Allies launched Operation Argument, using the combined strength of the Eighth Air Force's 1,046 serviceable bombers and the Fifteenth Air Forces's 570 and dispatching them across the Alps for daylight attacks, while Bomber Command continued its night campaign against Berlin. The primary objective was to force German fighters into the open so that Allied long-range fighters could destroy them. This resulted in an overwhelming defeat of the Luftwaffe in what the USAAF appropriately called Big Week. By February 25, the Eighth and Fifteenth Air Forces had lost 226 bombers (a loss rate of almost 6 percent) while flying more than 3,800 missions and dropping almost 10,000 tons of bombs on German targets. Only American 28 fighters had been lost. More important, the Luftwaffe lost 2,121 aircraft during the month of February. Attacks continued in March with similar results. Although the United States lost 69 of 660 aircraft in a daylight raid against Berlin on March 6, the Luftwaffe lost another 2,115 aircraft during March. Unable to sustain such losses, the Luftwaffe provided less resistance from that point forward, even though its fighter production was increasing and included Messerschmitt Me 262 jet fighters beginning in August 1944. Despite the production of approximately 1,400 Me 262s, however, only 315 saw combat. The Allied bombing campaign destroyed the rest.

Once air supremacy was established with the introduction of the long-range fighters, the Allied strategic bombing campaign escalated in dramatic fashion. Of the 1.9 million tons of bombs dropped on Germany during the Second World War, 76 percent (1.45 million) were dropped after January 1, 1944. Equally important, these results were accompanied by lower loss rates. By September 1944 Bomber Command's loss rate fell to 1.34 percent. For all the damage inflicted and lives lost, however, including Bomber Command's apocalyptic fire-bombing of Dresden that claimed approximately 45,000 lives on the night of February 13, 1945, the Allied strategic bombing campaign did not destroy the German will to fight. Nevertheless, it was a crucial part of the ultimate Allied victory in three important ways. First, when one considers the gains in production that Germany made as a result of Albert Speer's dispersal program, it is clear that German production would have been significantly higher had the strategic bombing campaign not occurred. Second, the strategic bombing campaign forced Germany to retain aircraft for combat against it and thereby diverted much-needed resources from beleaguered German units along the Eastern Front. Third, the destruction of the Luftwaffe as an effective fighting force helped clear the way for the Normandy landing and subsequent invasion of Germany, which did force Germany to surrender.

Air Power from the Normandy Invasion
to the German Surrender

By the time Supreme Commander of Allied Expeditionary Forces General Dwight D. Eisenhower launched the D-Day Invasion in Normandy on June 6, 1944, the RAF and USAAF had established true air supremacy. Whereas the Luftwaffe conducted several hundred sporadic sorties between June 6 and September 1, 1944, the Allies flew almost 500,000. In addition, the invasion was preceded by dropping 23,000 airborne troops of the British 6th and American 82nd and 101st airborne divisions via parachute, British General Aircraft Hamilar and Horsa gliders, and U.S. Waco C6–4A Hadrian gliders. Although many of these forces landed in the wrong locations, this actually contributed to German confusion regarding the invasion point. In addition, the Hamilar was large enough to carry a British Tetrarch Mark Mk.IV tank, and these were put to good use behind German lines. It is also important to note that Hitler rejected Rommel's advice to keep German forces forward, in part because the German High Command expected an invasion at the Pas de Calais—the narrowest point across the Channel—by Lieutenant General George Patton's phantom First Army, one of the most successful deceptions of the Second World War. As a result the Allied Invasion succeeded in establishing its bridgehead and landed

1 million men by the end of June. By the time Hitler released the Fifteenth Panzer Army from the Pas de Calais in late July, the Allies were poised to break out of Normandy, as American and British aircraft disrupted German efforts to rush in supplies and reinforcements. Rommel was killed in a strafing attack on July 17, 1944.

With fighters and fighter-bombers providing close air support using direct radio communication with American tanks, newly promoted General George Patton, commander of the U.S. Third Army, led the breakout in early August. Allied aircraft had a field day in mid-August, destroying German tanks, troops, vehicles, and artillery that had been forced into the Falaise-Argentan pocket after a failed counterattack by the German Fifth Panzer Army and Seventh Army. By August 24 Allied Forces had liberated Paris and began driving the Germans out of France, although the logistical difficulties of maintaining fuel and supplies eventually forced Eisenhower to order a halt. Although the Luftwaffe managed to mobilize 800 aircraft for Operation Bodenplatte on January 1, 1945, this attempt to support the German Army's Ardennes Offensive achieved only tactical surprise when it struck Allied airfields in Holland and Belgium. The Allies could easily replace the 134 aircraft lost, whereas the Luftwaffe could not easily replace the 220 aircraft it lost.

By March 1945 the combination of continued strategic bombing, the Russian drive to Berlin from the East, and the Allied advance across the Rhine had removed the Luftwaffe's ability to resist, although Jagdgeschwader 7 did have some 60 Me 262 jet fighters. As the noose tightened on a prostrate Germany, Bomber Command ended its operations on April 16, 1945, in part because of the public backlash to the fire-bombing of Dresden. The Eighth Air Force carried out its last major raid on April 25, 1945, striking the Skoda works in Czechoslovakia. For all practical purposes, the British and Americans had run out of targets. A week after Hitler's suicide on April 30, General Alfred Jodl surrendered at Eisenhower's headquarters in Reims, on May 7, 1945. Europe's long nightmare was over, and the United States was now able to shift resources, including the Eighth Air Force, to the Pacific. There it would unleash a nightmare of its own over Japan.

The Pacific Air War

While sheer numbers may indicate that the air war over Europe was more widespread, in the Pacific Theatre air power was far more central to the strategies of both sides. Indeed, the Pacific Theatre is unique in that it opened and closed with air strikes, first at Pearl Harbor and ending with the atomic bombings of Hiroshima and Nagasaki. This theatre was the proving ground for many modern-era air power tactics, including and especially those of long-range bombing, the strategic importance of power-projection through the use of aircraft carrier groups, and of the marriage of atomic weaponry to the tactics of strategic bombing. Combined, these dramatically altered the manner by which nations would assert and project their military strength in the future.

This longue dureé traces its roots to the beginnings of air power, but more directly to the influence of Japanese Admiral Isoroku Yamamoto. After assuming command of the Imperial Japanese Navy (IJN) in the midst of the Empire's expansion in the Pacific, Yamamoto recognized that the primary threat to continued Japanese expansion was the American Pacific fleet based in Pearl Harbor, Hawaii. He promulgated a plan, equal parts innovation and daring, to employ air power as a first-strike force that would, ideally, cripple the entire U.S. Navy presence in the Pacific. Planning for this historic raid began in early 1940, with mock attacks taking place in Kagoshima Bay. The rehearsals afforded the opportunity to refine the battle plan, and even the equipment itself. The torpedoes used in the attack were most famously fitted with wooden fins and the propellers were modified in order to be more effective in Pearl Harbor's shallow waters and to counter the torpedo-netting countermeasures likely to be in place. Yamamoto's original plan similarly called for a more limited strike force comprised primarily of torpedo bombers, but at the urgings of his subordinates (especially Commander Genda Minoru) it was expanded to employ the elite of virtually the entire roster of IJN aircraft, including the most advanced fighters and level-bombers in the inventory. On November 26, 1941, the Carrier Task Force, comprised of 31 vessels including six carriers and more than 400 aircraft, set sail across the Pacific. By December 2 the group neared the launch point, and the infamous order, "Niitaka Yama Ni Nabore—Climb Mount Niitaka," was radioed.

The first wave of the surprise Japanese assault on Pearl Harbor began with 183 aircraft launching from their decks at 6:00 a.m. on December 7, 1941. An hour and fifty minutes later, the attack force reached its targets in Pearl Harbor and surrounding air bases. A6M Zero fighters provided cover for D3A and B5N bombers, which proved relatively unnecessary as the Japanese planes encountered virtually no resistance from the stunned American forces. As this first wave inflicted heavy damage on American ships, and even more on the American aircraft at Hickam Field, Ford Island, and Wheeler Field, the Japanese second wave was launching. Perfectly executed timing provided relentless assault on the U.S. forces, from seemingly all directions at once. Separate flights of B5N "Kate" torpedo bombers dropped their deadly cargoes simultaneously from both east and west on the unsuspecting ships docked along "Battleship Row." The second wave, arriving approximately an hour after the first (8:50 a.m.), encountered slightly more organized resistance. A majority of the 29 Japanese planes lost in the attack were downed during this wave, including 14 D3A "Val" bombers. Yamamoto's plan had nonetheless been a resounding success. At the cost of 29 Japanese planes, five midget submarines and one fleet submarine lost in the operation, 11 American ships were sunk (including four battleships), all battleships were either lost or badly damaged, and nearly 300 aircraft damaged—including 188 completely destroyed, the vast majority while still on the ground. An estimated 100 Japanese crewmen lost their lives, compared with 2,280 American dead and an additional 1,100 wounded. Within four hours, from the launch of the first aircraft to the recovery of the last, the Japanese attack on Pearl Harbor succeeded in severely crippling the American presence in the Pacific. Although it accomplished everything Yamamoto had hoped, and likely in a far more efficient manner than he dared estimate, it ultimately served to galvanize the American spirit in a manner in which neither he nor any of his superiors had envisioned.

For the moment, however, the Japanese war machine was virtually unfettered in the Pacific. Following the attack on Pearl Harbor, Japanese air, ground, and sea forces moved on Allied positions throughout Southeast Asia and east to the Solomon Islands. In the march from island to island, the Japanese air forces were generally used as the proverbial tip of the spear for bombings in advance of naval bombardments and ground assaults. Japanese aircraft remained unchallenged in the skies for the next several months. Japan, it seems, became both complacent and overextended with these quick and massive gains. At the outset of this action it is estimated that Japan enjoyed a 10 to 1 ratio of combat-capable aircraft as compared with the U.S. forces (roughly 4,000 to roughly 400), most of which were far more maneuverable and better-performing than their Allied counterparts. Within a year, however, Allied forces turned the tide thanks to improved technology and vastly increased production.

As early as February 1, 1942, the Americans struck back against Japan, with a bombing raid of the Marshall Islands by carrier-launched Dauntlesses, Devastators, and F4F Wildcats. A few days later, on February 19, the Japanese air forces struck at Darwin, Australia, with the most extensive bombing raids conducted since Pearl Harbor. Far more important to both sides, especially in terms of symbolism and morale, were the "Doolittle Raids" of April 18. With Japan seemingly at the peak of its power in the Pacific, Lieutenant Colonel James Doolittle led a flight of 16 B-25 Mitchells off the deck of the carrier *Hornet* and more than 600 miles on a one-way bombing raid of Tokyo. Most of the crews were forced to ditch their planes shy of the Chinese airfields they had hoped to reach. One crew landed in Vladivostok and was held for the remainder of the war by the Soviets; eight U.S. airmen were captured by Japanese forces, who then executed three of them. The positive effects on Allied morale and the negative impact on Japanese strategy were far greater than the actual physical damage caused by the raid itself; where it spurred on the Allied counteroffensive effort and provided invaluable propaganda material, it caused Admiral Yamamoto to charge far too aggressively after the U.S. Navy's aircraft carriers.

This new strategy led to the first carrier-on-carrier battle, in which neither surface fleet actually sighted the other, in history. In early May 1942, the American carriers *Lexington* and *Yorktown* threatened Japanese moves on Port Moresby, New Guinea, with each launching a number of harassment strikes. The IJN thus directed the light carrier *Shoho* and fleet carriers *Shokaku* and *Zuikaku* to support the invasion force and interdict the American carrier groups. By May 7, the opposing carrier groups were within a mere 70 miles of one another, leading both sides to launch air strikes. Two American vessels were lost, the *Sims* sank completely, whereas the *Neosho* was badly damaged and incapacitated; more than 90 USN aircraft attacked the *Shoho* group, sinking the light carrier. The following morning, scout planes from each side once again made contact with the enemy, and a fresh round of full strikes proceeded. The *Shokaku*'s aircraft launching capabilities were damaged, effectively removing her from combat, whereas the *Lexington* and *Yorktown* were heavily damaged. The former remained afloat for several hours before being abandoned due to a series of uncontrollable fires, and was scuttled; the latter withdrew to Pearl Harbor for repairs. Approximately 99 Japanese aircraft were lost, compared with 77 American planes, but this does not reflect the damage done to the two American carriers. Nevertheless, even though the Americans sustained heavier losses, this was far from an unequivocal victory for the Japanese. Even though they perhaps "won" the Battle of the Coral Sea, they "lost" their invasion of Port Moresby, and the remainder of the Pacific War would see the IJN in retreat.

This is much more starkly represented in and after the Battle of Midway, June 4–5, 1942, in which Yamamoto's overzealousness with regard to destroying the American carriers led the Japanese Navy to a staggering defeat. It is important to note that the U.S. Navy was able to repair the *Yorktown* in under a month's time, whereas both the *Shokaku* (still in repair) and *Zuikaku* (due to a lack of available aircraft) were noncombatants when the dueling air forces next clashed. Yamamoto hoped to seize Midway Island first as the keystone to Japan's Pacific defense perimeter, and secondarily as the staging base for an eventual invasion of the Hawaiian Islands. He considered Midway so strategically critical that he dedicated virtually the whole of the IJN to the campaign, more than 100 vessels (including eight carriers) and more than 600 aircraft of various types. Although Yamamoto's strategy was not necessarily flawed, his intelligence certainly was; contrary to reports, the Americans had at least three carrier groups in the area, where none were expected, including the *Yorktown*, which Yamamoto believed had been sunk during the Battle of the Coral Sea. Furthermore, American code-breakers delivered critical information to the U.S. Navy about Yamamoto's master-plan, undercutting the effectiveness of diversionary attacks in the Aleutian Islands. Instead of springing a trap on the responding U.S. Navy, it was Yamamoto's force that stumbled into an ambush.

On June 3, a flight of B-17 Flying Fortresses launched from Midway and attacked the Japanese force; naval aircraft followed with a nighttime torpedo attack by four Consolidated PBY bombers, although neither raid did serious damage to the Japanese fleet. The Japanese Navy responded the next morning, with carriers launching a 100-plane raid, consisting mostly of D3A and B5N bombers, against Midway. Yamamoto's plan recalled the Pearl Harbor raid (a second wave would reach Midway just as the first was leaving to refuel and rearm): however, in the interim the American carriers had launched their aircraft, with Devastator torpedo-bombers attacking the Japanese fleet. Nevertheless, the IJN initially responded with aplomb, downing all but four of the 50 American planes in the first strike. Much like after Pearl Harbor and Coral Sea, however, the Japanese forces underestimated the resolve of the U.S. Navy. The Japanese aircraft returned to their carriers to rearm with torpedoes for a decisive strike against the much-prized American carriers; as they sat on the decks, surrounded by fuel drums and munitions, the second wave of 37 American Dauntless bombers struck with devastating effectiveness. The Japanese carriers *Akagi*, *Kaga*, and *Soryu* were immediately engulfed in flames, as B5Ns and D3As from the as-yet unscathed *Hiryu* attacked and crippled the *Yorktown*. By the end of the day, however, the *Hiryu* was also taken out of the fight, incapacitated by Dauntlesses from the *Enterprise*.

Both sides repositioned the next day, the Japanese trying to consolidate their forces, and the American Task Force 16, under the command of Rear Admiral Raymond Spruance, stalking them to the east. On June 6, the final assault during the Battle of Midway commenced with an American dive-bombing of the IJN fleet, resulting in the sinking of the cruiser *Mikuma*, and the damaging of three other vessels. As the Japanese surface fleet began a limping withdrawal westward, a submarine torpedoed and sank the U.S.S. *Yorktown*. This was the lone American carrier lost, compared with the four Japanese carriers, which incidentally were those used in the attack on Pearl Harbor. In terms of aircraft, the U.S. lost 147 and the Japanese a staggering 330. Japan proved incapable of replacing the power-projecting carriers, and—perhaps more immediately consequential—the more than 100 well-trained pilots lost in the battle.

The tactic first formulated by Yamamoto and used so effectively at Pearl Harbor, using aircraft carriers to project air power rather than relying on battleship-focused grand naval strategy, was expertly employed against him at Midway. The loss at Midway led indirectly to the loss of Guadalcanal (for lack of Japanese air support), and it was from Guadalcanal that a flight of P-38 Lightnings launched, intercepting and downing Yamamoto's G4M transport near Bougainville on April 18, 1943. This was, ironically, one year to the day after the Doolittle Raids led Yamamoto to overaggressively target the American carriers.

U.S. forces seized the airfield at Guadalcanal on August 8, 1942, and for the next several weeks Japanese bombers stationed at Rabaul engaged in regular raids on the island. With the ground battle for control of Guadalcanal well underway, U.S. Naval Intelligence indicated Japanese fleet movements out of Rabaul and heading toward the eastern Solomon Islands. On August 24, the two air forces engaged in the Battle of the Eastern Solomons, pitting Japanese A6M Zero fighters, D3A Val bombers, and American F4F Wildcats against one another. The Wildcats and anti-aircraft fire from both the U.S.S. *Enterprise* carrier and her destroyer escorts took a heavy toll on the Japanese planes, which were able to inflict a good deal of damage on the *Enterprise* but could not sink her. The Japanese navy lost the light carrier *Ryujo* to SBD Dauntless bombers from the carrier *Saratoga*, and more than 70 aircraft. On September 15, however, Japanese torpedoes sank the carrier *Wasp*, and during the Battle of Santa Cruz on October 26, 1942, incapacitated the *Hornet*, which was later scuttled. American aircraft severely damaged the Japanese carrier *Shokaku*. In the end, the Japanese lost nearly 100 Japanese aircraft in the battle, compared with 80

American, and, as after Midway, the most costly consequence to the Japanese was the loss of skilled air crews. Yet another of Yamamoto's plans for tightening Japan's grip on the Pacific had turned against him; even though Japanese forces succeeded in damaging or sinking several American carriers, this came at far too high a cost in both material and human terms.

From this point through the end of the war, American aircraft asserted their dominance of the skies over the Pacific. First, it was easier for the United States to replace machine- and manpower than it was for the Japanese. Second, with each new territorial gain, it was easier for the American air forces to launch strikes from ground bases in addition to aircraft carriers. Bombing raids led the way to American gains at Guadalcanal, at Bougainville (November 1943), the Marshall Islands (January 1944), the Mariana Islands (February 1944), and throughout the Pacific Theater. American B-29s bombed Japanese forces at Bangkok, Thailand, on June 5, 1944, and just ten days later a group of B-29s launched from China engaged in the first raids of the Japanese Home Islands since Doolittle's raid.

In response, the IJN concentrated on challenging the American invasion of Saipan. In what was likely the most extensive carrier battle in history, nine Japanese and fifteen American carriers, and hundreds of aircraft, engaged in the Battle of the Philippine Sea, on June 19–20, 1944. American training and technology had by this time surpassed that of the Japanese forces. Where the Japanese design bureaus saw great initial success by sacrificing armor and armament for increased speed and maneuverability (making the A6M Zero a superior weapon in the hands of a well-trained pilot when in battle against slower and less-agile Allied aircraft), the Allied aircraft plants had succeeded in the early 1940s in improving power, speed, and maneuverability, all while improving armor and armament. Combined with the hemorrhaging of trained pilots from their ranks due to losses at Midway and subsequent battles, Japanese forces were ill-equipped in the face of a stronger, faster, better-equipped and better-trained American navy and air force. The first Japanese strike of approximately 70 aircraft sustained more than 60 percent losses as A6M Zeroes and D3A Vals proved little competition for the F4F Hellcats flying combat air-patrols over the American carriers. The second strike of approximately 130 aircraft fared even worse, with approximately 75 percent going down to American fighters and anti-aircraft fire from the carrier groups. A third assault of 90 planes was diverted to Guam, unwittingly flying into an American trap there with almost 80 percent being lost to American fighters, anti-aircraft fire, or to the sea as the Japanese pilots searched in vain for a safe place to land aircraft running out of fuel. On the nineteenth alone, Americans lost just one plane for every eight Japanese aircraft downed. Overall, the Japanese lost three fleet carriers and more than 450 aircraft, with American losses totaling approximately 130 aircraft and only light damage to a couple of surface vessels. The merciless effectiveness of the American forces in this engagement led to its more descriptive moniker, the Marianas "Turkey Shoot."

Following this, the Japanese carrier fleet essentially ceased to exist as an operational component. American aircraft operated virtually unchallenged in support roles during the Battle of Okinawa. Although the Battle of Leyte Gulf (October 23–26, 1944) was a more traditional ship-on-ship naval battle, it involved significant air power as well. Perhaps most importantly, Japanese aircraft based out of the Philippines sank the carrier *Princeton* by using the newly authorized kamikaze suicide tactics. American aircraft sank the battleships *Musashi* and *Yamato*. American planes later finished off the Japanese carriers *Chitose*, *Chiyoda*, *Zuikaku*, and *Zuiho*, in what was a bloody but decisive naval victory for the Allies. The introduction and increasing use of kamikaze tactics show in stark relief the desperation of the Japanese military leadership; by the war's end, more than 2,200 Japanese aircraft were employed in suicide attacks.

To many observers the American use of incendiary bombs on civilian areas was equally as frightening as the Japanese kamikaze corps. With the seizing of the Marianas Islands, long-range B-29 bombers had yet another base from which to launch air strikes on the heart of Japan. Under the command of General Curtis LeMay, the Twenty-First Bomber Command began using fire-bombs in raids on Kobe, Japan, on February 3, 1945. On February 23–24, a total of 174 B-29s raided Tokyo. On May 9–10, a strike force of twice that size (334) struck with more than 1,700 tons of payload that set more than 15 square miles of the city ablaze and killed an estimated 100,000 people, more than in any other strike in the entire war. Just twenty of the roughly 2,000 American aircraft used in raids against the Home Islands were lost to enemy fire. Conventional bombing of Japan increased substantially as well, and was planned to involve more than 100,000 tons of bombs per month by the close of 1945.

A primary reason for the scant American losses in these raids was the hard-fought campaign to take Iwo Jima (February 19–March 12, 1945). The first series of B-29 raids on the Home Islands made treacherous roundtrips to and from Saipan. From three air fields on Iwo Jima, Japanese fighters could harass the American bombers in the air, and Japanese bombers could threaten the B-29s on the ground; indeed, approximately 30 Saipan-based B-29s were damaged or destroyed by Japanese bomber raids launched from Iwo Jima. LeMay pressured the Pacific command to take the island, correctly assuming that it was the last main stronghold of Japanese air defenses. Bases at Iwo Jima provided refuge for damaged B-29s that could not return to their bases at Saipan (more than 2,000 would do so), and perhaps most importantly, provided a staging point for P-51 Mustang fighter escorts all the way to the Home Islands. In the battle most famous for the heavy toll inflicted on, and by, the U.S. Marines, American aircraft offered primarily support roles. In addition to an extensive, but rather ineffectual, initial bombardment campaign, carrier-launched planes offered close air support to the ground troops and combat air patrols to protect the surface fleet from the Japanese bombing and kamikaze sorties. More than 40,000 combined casualties were suffered in the contest. U.S. military planners came to the conclusion that they must either prepare for an even bloodier invasion of the Home Islands, one that they assumed would dwarf even the number of casualties suffered during the Normandy Invasion, or they must force Japan to surrender by other means.

These other means came as the United States ushered the world into the atomic age, unleashing against the Japanese a weapon more terrifying than either incendiary bombs or kamikaze sorties. In late December 1944, U.S. military command created the 509th Composite Group; in late July 1945, they were tasked with delivering atomic bombs on a selection of Japanese cities. Chosen specifically because they had sustained comparatively light damage during the bombing raids of the Home Islands, the cities of Hiroshima, Nagasaki, Kokura, and Niigata would provide the United States—and the world—with an indication of the power of this new bomb. On July 26, President Harry S Truman authorized the use of the atomic weapon, and the B-29 *Enola Gay* was slated to carry the bomb and drop it over Hiroshima. On August 6, 1945, at 8:15 a.m., the "Little Boy" atomic bomb detonated, toppling almost everything for a two-mile radius, and killing 71,000 in its immediate blast.

After a message of warning by Truman was ignored by the Japanese military command, the B-29 named *Bockscar* from the Twentieth Air Force in Guam was ordered to deliver the second atomic bomb, called "Fat Man," on Kokura. Launching a few minutes before 4:00 a.m. on August 9, *Bockscar* found Kokura obscured by cloud cover; switching their target to Nagasaki, the flight crew dropped the bomb at 11:02 a.m. When it exploded, it immolated everything within 1,000 yards, and immediately killed 74,000 people, with countless thousands more dying in the months and years afterward.

By August 14, Japanese Emperor Hirohito agreed to an unconditional surrender, and on September 2 the formal surrender ceremony took place on the deck of the U.S.S. *Missouri*, anchored in Tokyo Bay. A symbolic final statement of the nature and consequence of the Pacific War can be taken from the numerous carrier-launched aircraft flying protective combat air patrols overhead. The air war over the Pacific changed the nature of military power, proving the usefulness and importance of both air and atomic power—arguably the two most important features of post–World War II national power.

The Mobilization of Air Power during the War

Even though Germany and Japan entered the war with advantages of aircraft and other war materiel because they had begun military production much earlier than did the Allies, the combined industrial potential of the latter far exceeded that of the former. Even though German, Japanese, and Italian (up through 1941) aircraft production would increase during the course of the war, it paled in comparison to that of the Allies, especially that of the United States. To the extent that WWII was a total war that depended upon industrial output, the Allied advantage in man and industrial power ultimately proved decisive. Aircraft production is a key indicator of that advantage, as demonstrated in the following chart.

AIRCRAFT PRODUCTION IN WORLD WAR II[6]

AXIS POWERS

	Germany	Japan	Italy	Axis Totals
1939	8,295	4,467	1,692	**14,454**
1940	10,826	4,768	2,142	**17,736**
1941	11,776	5,088	3,503	**20,367**
1942	15,556	8,861	2,818	**27,235**
1943	25,527	16,693	967	**43,187**
1944	39,807	28,180	x	**67,987**
1945	7,544	8,263	x	**15,807**
Axis Totals	**119,331**	**76,320**	**11,122**	**206,773**

ALLIED POWERS

	Great Britain	Soviet Union	United States	Allied Totals
1939	7,940	10,382	5,856	**24,178**
1940	15,049	10,565	12,804	**38,418**
1941	20,094	17,735	26,277	**64,106**
1942	23,673	25,436	47,836	**96,945**
1943	26,263	34,845	85,898	**147,006**
1944	26,461	40,246	96,318	**163,025**
1945	12,070	20,052	49,761	**81,883**
Allied Totals	**131,550**	**159,261**	**324,750**	**615,561**

The Axis Powers

Although Germany entered the war in September 1939 as the world's leading air power, with 4,840 front-line aircraft and with an aircraft industry that was producing 1,000 airplanes per month, there were serious defects in the Luftwaffe's arsenal. For instance, Germany had never developed a satisfactory long-range bomber in part because the German military's focus on Blitzkrieg emphasized production of medium-range bombers and ground-attack aircraft; indeed, this proved quite successful in the Spanish Civil War. Germany's defeat in the Battle of Britain, however, revealed the strategic flaw of this policy because such aircraft as the Heinkel He 111, Dornier Do 17, and Junkers Ju 87 proved ineffective against a technologically well-equipped enemy. Likewise, Germany's lack of a long-range bomber prevented it from striking Soviet manufacturing centers once they relocated deep within Russia. Overall German production was healthy, however, despite the damage inflicted by the Allied air campaign. Ably led by Fritz Todt and Albert Speer, the German armaments industry still managed to increase production from 8,295 aircraft in 1939 to 39,807 in 1944 and to introduce the world's first jet fighter, the Messerschmitt Me.262, in the second half of 1944. These successes, however, proved to be too little and too late to make a difference, and the Allies possessed air supremacy in the last two years of the war. It should also be emphasized that Germany, unlike the Allies, did not implement multi-shift production until late in the war.

Like Germany, Japan entered the war with a powerful air force, which included 2,900 combat-ready aircraft on December 7, 1941. Its attack on Pearl Harbor, however, was in part a desperate gamble designed to cripple the United States before its industrial might reached heights that Japan knew it could never reach. Indeed, Japanese industry produced just 5,088 aircraft in 1941 compared with 26,277 for the United States. Failure to destroy the American carriers in the surprise attack on Pearl Harbor ranks as a clear strategic defeat for Japan. Once it lost the Battle of Midway in early June 1942, it faced a defensive war in which it could not compete with the American war machine. It is a testament to the perseverance of its workers on the homefront that Japan still managed to produce 28,180 aircraft in 1944 despite Allied attacks that crippled its shipping industry and weakened its industrial infrastructure; however, it is also a testament to the futility of Japan's challenge of American industrial might that the United States produced 96,318 during the same year.

Although Benito Mussolini built a powerful Italian Air Force in the late 1920s and early 1930s, Italy's air force was largely obsolete by the time World War II broke out in 1939. This in part reflected Italy's false confidence from its campaigns in Ethiopia and Spain, which led to continued production of biplane fighters. When Italy joined the war on June 10, 1940, barely half of its 3,296 aircraft were combat-quality. Italy's weak economy prevented it from matching production rates of the Allies, although assistance from Germany, particularly in supplying aircraft engines, allowed the Italian aircraft industry to make modest increases from 2,142 aircraft produced in 1940 to 3,503 aircraft in 1941. Nevertheless, Italy's weak industrial sector could not withstand the impact of the Allied bombing campaign. Italy produced only 2,818 aircraft in 1942 and just 967 aircraft by the time it surrendered in September 1943.

The Allied Powers

Although Germany enjoyed a great lead in the number of its combat-ready aircraft at the start of the war, Great Britain had an advantage in timing. Its industry was then introducing aircraft (e.g., the Hawker Hurricane and Supermarine Spitfire) that incorporated technological advances over their German counterparts. This qualitative advantage proved to be a critical success in the Battle of Britain. Secure from the threat of German invasion, British industry succeeded in increasing productive capacity with each passing year of the war, and in introducing such aircraft as the Handley Page Halifax and Avro Lancaster that played a crucial role in the Allied bombing campaign against Germany. Although Great Britain's highest annual production total reached 26,461 aircraft in 1944 compared with 39,807 aircraft for

Germany in 1944, its overall production of 131,550 aircraft during the war exceeded that of Germany's 119,331 aircraft.

The Soviet Union faced a position somewhat similar to that of Italy, possessing large numbers of aircraft at the outbreak of the war; however, most of these were inferior to their German counterparts. Making matters worse, when Nazi Germany launched its invasion of the Soviet Union on June 22, 1941, it destroyed 1,200 Soviet aircraft in the first nine hours of the attack. The Soviet Union's ability to sustain this loss and to recover stems from its monumental efforts to transfer industries eastward beyond the reach of the German Army and Luftwaffe. In the first three months after the Nazi invasion, the Soviet Union transplanted a total of 1,523 factories. The primary production line for the Yakovlev Yak-1, for example, was moved more than 1,000 miles and returned to production in less than six weeks. The success of these efforts allowed the Soviet Union to exceed German production for each year of the war, including 1941, for a total of 159,261 Soviet aircraft.

Although the American economy was still suffering from the Great Depression in 1939, with a total of 8.9 million registered unemployed workers, the success of the German blitzkrieg in 1940 spurred the American war machine into action. The Burke-Wadsworth Act introduced peacetime conscription for the first time in American history, and massive military spending jumpstarted the American economy. Unlike Germany and Japan, the United States had both a large population base and virtually unlimited natural resources that could be mobilized for production, and it enjoyed an industrial infrastructure that was far removed from its enemies. By 1944 a total of 18.7 million Americans, approximately 50 percent of whom were women, had entered the American workforce. Of all of their industrial achievements, none were more spectacular than aircraft production. From just 5,856 aircraft produced in 1939, the United States reached the staggering total of 96,318 produced in 1944, which was almost one third more than that produced by Germany and Japan combined. For the war years as a whole, the United States produced a total of 324,750 aircraft compared with a total of 206,773 for the combined Axis powers. When combined with the production of the British and the Soviet Union, this gave the Allies an advantage of more than three to one, with 615,561 aircraft. With such an advantage, it is little wonder that the Allies won the air war.

Endnotes

1. Estimates of the number of aircraft in the Luftwaffe vary from as many as 3,750 to 2,650, depending upon serviceability.

2. A number of Polish pilots managed to escape to fight again with the RAF.

3. Churchill had ordered the seizure of the *Altmark* to free British prisoners who had been captured by the *Graf Spee*.

4. Although the Luftwaffe attempted to halt the attack on Rotterdam, the orders did not get through in time. Despite Allied claims that 30,000 innocent civilians had been killed, the actual number was approximately 1,000.

5. Under the surrender terms of June 20, 1940, the Germans had occupied northern France, while Pétain's government, which was based in Vichy, was left in charge of southern France. When Hitler ordered the occupation of the rest of France on November 9, the French responded by scuttling the remainder of its fleet in Toulon rather than let it fall into German hands.

6. *The Encyclopedia of World War II: A Political, Social, and Military History*, ed. Spencer C. Tucker (Santa Barbara, CA: ABC-CLIO, Inc., 2005), s.vv. "Aircraft, Production of."

CHAPTER THREE

Fighter and Attack Aircraft

A WAR THAT BEGAN WITH an almost universal belief in the claims of air power theorists that "the bomber [would] always get through" ended with hundreds of fighter aircraft circling above the deck of the U.S.S. *Missouri,* keeping watch over the signing of the Japanese instrument of surrender on September 2, 1945. Although bombing achieved many notable successes during World War II, it was arguably the introduction of advanced fighter aircraft that proved to be the difference. Advantages first went to the Japanese and Germans, and the Axis powers pushed ahead during the first phases of the war; next, British fighters turned the Battle of Britain in their favor, and American fighters and fighter-bombers helped break the Japanese Navy's hold across the Pacific. In the end, the Allies proved most successful at generating the most numbers of the most advanced fighter aircraft, and they won the air war as a result.

American Fighter and Attack Aircraft

American fighter development in the 1920s and 1930s was spurred by a number of factors. First, the United States was heavily reliant on French and British designs during World War I, and in the postwar period pushed for self-sufficiency. In addition, a useful rivalry between the army and navy further stimulated the industry. This was a period of rapid growth for the American air forces, as well as one of rapid technological advancement. What began as the height of the biplane era quickly gave way to monoplanes, just as piston-engine fighters eventually bowed to the onset of the jet age.

The first army fighter of the postwar period was the Thomas-Morse MB-3. It is most notable for being the first step toward American-designed, American-built aircraft filling the ranks of the American air forces. Although the military proved dependent on European manufacturers and designers throughout World War I, the Thomas-Morse Company of Ithaca, New York, was developing an American-bred fighter as early as 1918. Their prototype flew in 1919, and featured a wingspan of 26 ft, length of 20 ft, and height of 7 ft 8 in. It was an all-wood, fabric-covered biplane with clean lines, boasting a favorable power-to-weight ratio—although it weighed 2,539 lbs loaded, it maintained a maximum speed of 140 mph, with a service ceiling of 21,200 ft and range of 270 miles. The MB-3 was not without its problems, however; it offered a cramped canopy and limited sight-lines for the pilot, and suffered nearly continual maintenance problems. Nevertheless, the army was sufficiently impressed with its performance (and its American design) to order 200 copies. The competitive-bid production contract ironically went to Boeing rather than the designers.

Although it continued in front-line service through 1927, the MB-3 was gradually replaced by the PW-9 and PW-8 in the early 1920s. The latter was a Curtiss design favored by American airpower proponent General Billy Mitchell; just 25 were ordered, but one recorded the first dawn-to-dusk flight across the United States on June 23, 1924. The PW-9 was a Boeing biplane most notable for its impressive endurance rating of 2 hours 35 minutes. Another Curtiss design, the P-1 Hawk, replaced these two models beginning in 1925. Approximately 148 of the fast-moving P-1s were ordered, but they are most notable for leading to the design for the Curtiss P-6E Hawk.

The P-6E appeared in U.S. Army Air Corps (USAAC) inventories beginning in 1931, and they served through 1937. They were built specifically for competitive flying in the mid-1920s, and the model in fact won the National Air Races in 1927. When brought into USAAC service, the P-6E featured a more powerful, 600 hp Curtiss V-1570 twelve cylinder radial engine. An attractively designed biplane, it spanned 31 ft 6 in, with length of 23 ft 2 in, and height of 8 ft 10 in. Weighing 3,392 lbs, the Hawk featured a maximum speed of 198 mph with a service ceiling of 24,700 ft and range of 285 miles. It carried a single pilot, and was armed with two .30 caliber machine guns, although the model never faced combat. Curtiss produced fewer than 50 copies of the impressive P-6E, due in no small part to the depths of the Great Depression.

The Boeing P-12E served at approximately the same time as the P-6E. First developed for the navy (as the F4B), the model's prototype flew on June 25, 1928. Pleased with its performance, the U.S. Navy purchased 27 for use aboard the USS *Lexington* and USS *Langley*. The Army Air Corps soon warmed to the aircraft, and placed the first of a series of orders that would amount to more than 300 aircraft. The P-12 had a wingspan of 30 ft, length of 20 ft 3 in, and height of 9 ft. The model was powered by a 500 hp Pratt & Whitney Wasp nine cylinder radial engine, and it possessed a maximum speed of 189 mph at 7,000 ft, with a service ceiling of 26,300 ft and range of 585 miles. Like the P-6E, the P-12 accommodated a single pilot and was armed with two .30 caliber machine guns; together, the two models represented the culmination of the biplane era in American aviation.

The move to monoplane fighters was a story of success and failure. Two monoplanes entered service in 1934 (the Boeing P-26 Peashooter and the Consolidated PB-2A). Although the PB-2A (Pursuit, Bi-place) is notable as the only monoplane fighter adopted by the USAAC to feature a tail gunner, in addition to featuring a hand-cranked, retractable landing gear, constant speed propeller, and super-charged engine, it was completely overshadowed by the Boeing P-26.

The Peashooter actually preceded the PB-2A by a few months, thus earning the distinction of being the first all-metal monoplane in USAAC inventories. Completing its first flight on March 20, 1932, the P-26 spanned 27 ft 11 in, with length of 23 ft 7 in, and height of approximately 10 ft. The Peashooter featured a Pratt & Whitney Wasp nine cylinder radial producing 600 hp and possessed a top speed of 234 mph, service ceiling of 27,400 ft, and range of 620 miles. It was armed with twin .30 caliber machine guns and could carry up to 110 lbs of bombs. Total production numbered 125, with the first P-26 entering service in 1934. The Peashooter was the last USAAC aircraft with an open cockpit, a concession to the older aviators within the War Department, and it continued in front-line service through 1939.

By the mid-1930s, the USAAC decided to solicit a replacement for the P-26. In open competition, a redesigned, single-seat Consolidated PB-2A faced off against the Seversky P-35. In winning the competitive trials, the P-35 established itself as the army's first truly modern fighter. The P-35 was equipped with a 1,050 hp Pratt & Whitney Twin Wasp radial engine, and could achieve a maximum speed of 290 mph, which was quite an impressive performance when combined with a service ceiling of 31,400 ft and range approaching 950 miles. It was armed with a single .50 caliber and single .30 caliber machine gun mounted on the fuselage, and could carry a maximum bomb load in excess of 300 lbs; however, the model served during a time of rapid technological advances, and was disastrously underpowered, under-armed, and underarmored by the time it faced superior Japanese fight-ers during the opening days of the Pacific War; of the approximately 60 copies tasked to the Philippines, only eight survived the opening thrusts of the Japanese advance. More important than its poor com-bat record is that the model served as the basis for a far more combat-capable aircraft, the Republic P-47 Thunderbolt.

The Curtiss P-36 Hawk faced a similar fate as the P-35; while it would be a popular and impressive aircraft when first introduced in the late 1930s, by the outbreak of war it would prove its obsolescence. The Hawk featured a 1,050 hp Pratt & Whitney Twin Wasp radials and possessed a maximum speed in excess of 310 mph, with a service ceil-ing of 32,700 ft and range of approximately 830 miles. Its wingspan was 37 ft 4 in, with length of 28 ft 6 in, and height of 8 ft 5 in. It also featured a pair of .30 caliber or .50 caliber machine guns. The P-36 was ordered in greater quantity than any American fighter since 1922, with 210 copies purchased initially. There were approximately 500 additional copies exported to various nations, including France and China. The Nazis essentially recycled the captured Hawks, and in an ironic twist a number of French Hawks actually engaged American F4Fs during the Allied invasion of North Africa in November 1942. In the Pacific theater, P-36s were among the few American aircraft to engage their Japanese foes on December 7, 1941, at Pearl Harbor. Although a Hawk was credited with downing the first Japanese air-craft of the war, it was obvious to the USAAC that the model was sim-ply outclassed by its enemies. The remaining P-36s saw service throughout the war as trainers, and perhaps more importantly, the model's airframe served as the basis for the far more successful P-40 Warhawk design.

The most numerous aircraft in USAAC inventories at the time of the Japanese attack on Pearl Harbor was the Bell P-39 Airacobra. It sported a wingspan of 34 ft, length of 30 ft 2 in, and height of 12 ft 5 in, and could reach a maximum speed of 382 mph and operate at a ceiling of 35,000 ft. The Airacobra carried a 37 mm cannon and two 0.50 caliber machine guns in her nose, with four additional .30 caliber machine guns in the wings, and was an unusually well-armed fighter for its time. It featured other innovative design elements, including a tricycle landing gear and its 1,200 hp Allison 12 cylinder vee-type engine mounted behind the pilot. The prototype, first flown in 1939, performed even better with a supercharged engine; however, produc-tion models did not feature this element, confining the P-39 to low-altitude missions for the duration of its service. Although no fewer than 600 were in service by the end of 1941, the Airacobra would not see service until April 1942, where it took heavy losses over New Guinea. As a result, many were retasked to close air support, a role for which they proved far more adept. Of the 9,558 copies produced, approximately 4,773 were received by the Soviet Union through the Lend-Lease program.

The Curtiss P-40 Warhawk was more important in the immediate aftermath of Pearl Harbor. Developed from the P-36 Hawk, the Warhawk was immediately put into quantity production at the outbreak of war. By the end of its production run in 1944, an estimated 13,738 were constructed. It possessed a wingspan of 37 ft 4 in, length of 31 ft 9 in, and height of 12 ft 4 in. Thanks to its 1,150 hp Allison V-1710 12 cylinder vee-type engine, the P-40 could fly in excess of 360 mph, with a range of 850 miles and service ceiling of approximately 30,000 ft. Armed with six .50 caliber machine guns, the Warhawk could also carry up to 600 lbs of bombs attached to external hardpoints. Although it was relatively fast, reasonably well-armed, and able to sustain a good bit of damage, the P-40 proved ill-suited to combat against more modern German and Japanese fighters. It nevertheless remains one of the more famous American designs of the war thanks to the exploits of the Flying Tigers, the China-based American Volunteer Group led by Major Claire L. Chennault (USAAC, retired). Most, as with the P-39, were reassigned for use as ground support or ground attack fighter-bombers as the war progressed.

In 1937 the USAAC solicited designs for a long-range interceptor. The Lockheed Aircraft Company had never produced a military aircraft before, but nevertheless submitted one of the most radical designs in American aviation. The design team was led by Kelly Johnson, whose later designs included the similarly radical SR-71 Blackbird. Their model, the P-38, was a twin-engine, twin-boom fuselage design that placed the pilot in an armored central pod. With these features and a wingspan of 52 ft, length of 37 ft 10 in, and height of 12 ft, the P-38 was an extraordinarily large fighter aircraft, and it possessed one of the most unique silhouettes of its era. The model established a transcontinental speed record of 420 mph shortly after its first flight in February 1938. It was initially dubbed "Atlanta," but the RAF nicknamed it "Lightning"; although the British were uninterested in an underperforming model tested without supercharged engines, the moniker stuck. The Lightning carried four .50 caliber machine guns, a 20 mm cannon, and up to 4,000 lbs of bombs—a true measure of its versatility. Thanks to its speed, provided by a set of 1,475 hp Allison

V-1710 vee-type engines, and its range (1,100 miles) and service ceiling (40,000 ft), the P-38 overcame its lack of agility to prove a quite capable foe. The Germans dubbed it the "Fork-Tailed Devil," and it was a flight of P-38s that downed Japanese Admiral Isoroku Yamamoto's G4M transport over Bougainville. Its remarkable range and heavy armament made the model an ideal combatant in the Pacific Theater. Indeed, two of the USAAC's highest-scoring aces of the war, Richard Bong and Tom McGuire, flew many missions against the Japanese air forces in P-38s; Charles Lindbergh is also recorded as earning "kills" of Japanese aircraft in a Lightning.

Despite its impressive performance, the P-38 was far outclassed by the North American P-51 Mustang. In this regard the P-38 is far from alone; indeed, the Truman Senate War Investigating Committee reported the Mustang to be "aerodynamically perfect." Developed in only 122 days, the P-51 answered an urgent call from the RAF for a replacement for the P-40 Warhawk. It was immediately adopted by the British for production following its first test flight on October 26, 1940, but American interest lagged behind until the Japanese attack on Pearl Harbor. From then, production eventually totaled 15,576 of all models. Although it was initially powered by an Allison engine, its performance was greatly improved with the RAF modification of a Rolls-Royce Merlin engine of 1,595 hp. This produced a top speed in excess of 440 mph. Packard secured a license to produce the engine, which became the standard power plant for production-model P-51s. These aircraft spanned 37 ft, with length of 32 ft 2 in, and height of 13 ft 8 in, with a service ceiling approaching 42,000 ft. Later improvements netted a maximum speed of 487 mph, and extended range of 1,160 miles thanks to externally mounted drop tanks. Carrying up to six .50 caliber machine guns as well as a maximum of 2,000 lbs of bombs (or, alternatively, ten 5-inch rockets), the Mustang became the prototypical fighter of the entire war, and was in fact the only World War II–era fighter to continue in service with the U.S. Air Force into the 1950s.

The other great American fighter of the war was the Republic P-47 Thunderbolt, the largest single-engine aircraft built during the Second World War. Based on the earlier P-35 and P-43, which had proven to be inadequate, the P-47 featured a more powerful 2,000 hp Pratt & Whitney Double Wasp radial. This gave the 17,500 lb aircraft a maximum speed of up to 433 mph, service ceiling of 42,000 ft, and range of 1,030 ft. The large fighter spanned 40 ft 9 in, with length of 36 ft 2 in, and height of 14 ft 8 in, and was armed with six to eight .50 caliber machine guns. It could also be fitted with up to 2,500 lbs of bombs or ten 5-inch rockets. Production began approximately a year after its first test flight on May 6, 1941, although the P-47 did not enter active service until January 1943. When it did, it was an unpleasant surprise for its German foes in the European Theater.

Upon its arrival to bases in England, the pudgy aircraft was derisively nicknamed "The Jug." Its critics were soon quieted as the model proved to be an impressive combat performer. Thanks primarily to its weight, the fighter could outdive virtually any German enemy; it also proved capable of sustaining a great deal of damage while still returning safely to base. Only the P-51's greater range made it a more ideal escort for long-range bombing raids. Instead, the P-47 became one of the finest fighter-bombers in the American arsenal. A total of 15,579 were produced, with the –D model accounting for more than 80 percent. In service in both European and Pacific Theaters, P-47s engaged in more than 546,000 combat sorties, losing on average less than one aircraft per sortie. At the hands of the Air National Guard, the Thunderbolt remained in active service through 1955.

Caught unprepared by the attack on Pearl Harbor, in the coming months the USAAC was forced to turn to a number of stop-gap measures for specialized roles such as night-fighters. One of the first such aircraft was the Douglas P-70 Night Havoc, designed from the A-20 Havoc. Outfitted with radar developed at the Massachusetts Institute of Technology (MIT), and armed with four 20 mm cannon in an underbelly pod, approximately 269 copies were produced. Although notable for this use of radar—it was the first American fighter so equipped— the model proved substantially under-powered because its two Pratt & Whitney R-2600 radials were incapable of sustaining acceptable performance above 25,000 ft.

By early 1944, the P-70 Night Havoc was completely replaced by the Northrop P-61 Black Widow, the first American night-fighter specifically designed for this role. The model's prototype first flew on May 26, 1942, the direct result of lessons learned from the combat experience of British pilots facing German bombers in the night skies over London. With a wingspan of 66 ft, length of 48 ft 11 in, and height of 14 ft 2 in, the P-61 was powered by twin 2,100 hp Pratt & Whitney Double Wasp radials. This power plant produced a maximum speed of 369 mph, and afforded a range of 1,200 miles and service ceiling of 46,200 ft. The Black Widow acquired its nickname from both its black paint and its heavy armament (four .50 caliber machine guns, four 20 mm cannons, and a maximum bomb load of 6,400 lbs). The P-70 made its combat debut in the Pacific in July 1944, and served as the United States's primary night-fighter through the final year of the war. Total production numbered 706, some of which continued in service as night-fighters and trainers through 1952.

In addition to dedicated fighters, the USAAC developed a series of domestically designed attack aircraft. Among the first of such models was the Curtiss A-3/O-1, an attack and observation plane. This was the first American aircraft distinguished as a dedicated "A" ("attack") series plane. The Falcon, which first flew in 1927, was a two-seat biplane, powered by a single 435 hp Curtiss V-1150 engine. Spanning 38 ft, with length of 27 ft 2 in, and height of 10 ft 6 in, the aircraft could achieve a top speed approaching 140 mph. It possessed a service ceiling of 14,100 ft and maximum range of 600 miles. Designed as an observation and light bomber, the A-3/O-1 was instead most memorable for its retrofitting with six .30 caliber machine guns for use as a ground-attack aircraft.

Both Curtiss and General Aviation/Fokker entered designs to replace the A-3; in open competition, the Curtiss A-8 Shrike proved to be the superior model. In winning the 1932 production contract for 46 copies, the A-8 became the USAAC's first monoplane attack bomber. It also featured several other notable design innovations, such as all-metal construction and enclosed, separate cockpits for its two crewmembers. The model was constructed with wingspan of 44 ft, length of 32 ft 2 in, and height of 9 ft 4 in. Its 690 hp Wright Cyclone R-1820 radial power plant afforded a top speed of 175 mph, maximum range of 140 miles, and service ceiling in excess of 15,000 ft. The Shrike was armed with five .30 caliber machine guns, and could carry a 400 lb maximum bomb load. When it was fitted with a more powerful engine, the model was called the A-12.

The Northrop A-17 Nomad, which first appeared in the USAAC inventory in 1936, represented a tremendous technological advance in American attack aircraft. Based on Northrop's commercial Gamma and Delta designs, the A-17 spanned 47 ft 8 in, with length of 32 ft 5 in, height of 9 ft 9 in. With a 1,200 hp Wright Cyclone GR-1820 radial engine, the model could reach 32,000 ft, and it possessed a range of 910 miles and maximum speed of 265 mph. Armed like its predecessors, with five .30 caliber machine guns, the A-17 showed design advancement in its dramatically increased payload (1,800 lbs, up from the A-8/A-12's 400 lbs). It served as the front-line attack aircraft in the USAAC inventory until 1939, when it was outclassed by the Douglas A-20 Havoc; thereafter, a number of A-17s were exported to several nations.

The A-20 Havoc was Douglas's entry into the twin-engine light-bomber class. Following its first test flight in 1938, the model was ordered into quantity production for export to France; however, the

USAAC did not place an order for more than 200 A-20s until 1940. There were ultimately more than 7,300 Havocs of varying types produced, with well more than 3,000 shipped to the Soviet Union. The aircraft possessed a wingspan of 61 ft 4 in, length of 45 ft 11 in, and height of 17 ft 7 in. Its power plant, a dual set of 1,700 hp Wright Double Cyclone GR-2600 radials, afforded an impressive top speed of 350 mph, service ceiling in excess of 25,000 ft. The A-20 featured a 1,000 mile maximum range, and was armed with up to eight .50 caliber machine guns; in addition, it could carry up to 4,000 lbs of ordnance in an internal bay. They served well as light bombers, but were even better suited to the ground-attack role. For this purpose, the –G model was specifically designed to house six additional .30 caliber machine guns in the nose. As mentioned previously, the P-70 night-fighter was a direct descendant of A-20s adapted to that task.

Another attack aircraft in the USAAC inventory during World War II was the North American A-36 Apache, a derivative of the company's most famous model, the P-51 Mustang. Thanks in part to a British request for a dive-bombing version of the P-51, the Apache became the USAAC's premier attack aircraft. It spanned 37 ft, with length of 32 ft 3 in, height of 12 ft 2 in, and was powered by a single 1,325 hp Allison V-1710 engine. This was a lesser power plant than that featured by the A-36's fighter plane cousin, and high-end performance was thus reduced. Still, the Apache possessed impressive in-flight characteristics, including a top speed in excess of 360 mph, in addition to a service ceiling of 25,000 ft, and range of 550 miles. With six .50 caliber machine guns and a 1,000 lb bomb capacity, the A-36 was extremely well suited for close air support. The Apache achieved notable combat successes and recorded more than 8,000 tons of ordnance dropped on targets in fewer than three years of service; in that same time frame, fewer than 200 planes were lost in combat. As fighter technology improved, the need for a dedicated attack aircraft was reduced; A-36s were ultimately replaced by fighter-bomber variants of her P-51 muse.

British Fighter and Attack Aircraft

Although Great Britain had produced some of the best fighters of the First World War, among which was the Sopwith Camel, immortalized by Charles Schultz as Snoopy's preferred fighter in his Sunday morning cartoon battles against the dreaded Red Baron, the British neglected fighters throughout the 1920s and well into the 1930s.

Although budgetary pressures contributed to this, the primary factor was that Trenchard and his successors emphasized the bomber as the proper focus of the RAF. It was ironically the fighter, specifically the Hurricane and the Spitfire, that would help turn Great Britain's darkest days of World War II into its finest hour.

The financial restrictions that the RAF faced after World War I forced it to rely upon World War I–era fighters until 1927, when it introduced the Armstrong-Whitworth Siskin IIIA. The first British fighter with an all-metal structure, the Siskin featured a sesquiplane design with a wingspan of 33 ft 2 in, length of 25 ft 4 in, and loaded weight of 3,012. Its 450 hp Armstrong-Siddeley Jaguar IV radial engine provided a top speed of 156 mph and range of 150 miles. The Siskin was highly aerobatic and was armed with two .303 caliber synchronized machine guns. A total of 385 entered service between 1927 and 1932, when it was replaced by the Bristol Bulldog.

The venerable Bristol Bulldog served as the RAF's primary fighter from its introduction in 1929 until its replacement by the Gloster Gladiator in 1937. Designed as a response to high-speed bombers, the Bulldog offered a combination of speed and maneuverability that separated it from its predecessors. Although it still relied on fabric covering, the Bulldog was a rugged aircraft because of the stainless steel strips used to strengthen its wings and fuselage. It had a wingspan of 33 ft 10 in, length of 25 ft 2 in, and loaded weight of 3,660 lbs. Its 490 hp Bristol Jupiter VIIF radial provided a top speed of 174 mph, service ceiling of 29,300 ft, and range of 300 miles. It was armed with two .303 caliber synchronized machine guns. A total of 247 Bulldogs entered service, providing up to 70 percent of the RAF's fighters during the early 1930s. The Bulldog was exported to numerous countries and was used by Finland during the Russo-Finnish War.

In addition to the Bulldog, the RAF also had the Hawker Fury biplane as a front-line fighter in the early 1930s. With a wingspan of 30 ft, length of 26 ft 9 in, and loaded weight of 3,609 lbs, the Fury was just as maneuverable as the Bulldog. More important, the Fury's 640 hp Rolls-Royce Kestrel VI water-cooled engine provided a top speed of 223 mph (almost 50 mph faster than the Bulldog), a service ceiling of 29,500 ft, and a range of 270 miles. It was armed with two .303 caliber synchronized machine guns. Approximately 300 were built in two versions, about 50 of which were exported aboard.

Introduced in 1934, the Gloster Gauntlet was the last open cockpit biplane fighter produced by the British. It was originally rejected for service in favor of the Bristol Bulldog, but design modifications that provided greater streamlining and reduced drag gave it a 40 mph advantage over the Bulldog. It had a wingspan of 32 ft 9 in, length of 26 ft 2 in, and a loaded weight of 3,970 lb. Its 645 hp Bristol Mercury radial engine provided a maximum speed of 230 mph, service ceiling of 33,500 ft, and range of 460 miles. It was armed with two .303 caliber synchronized machine guns.

In 1937, the British introduced their last biplane fighter, the Gloster Gladiator, which featured a shoulder-mounted upper wing and enclosed canopy. It had a wingspan of 32 ft 3 in, a length of 27 ft 5 in, and a loaded weight of 4,864 lbs. Its 830 hp Bristol Mercury IX radial engine provided a top speed of 257 mph, service ceiling of 33,500 ft, and range of 440 miles. With four .303 caliber machine guns, the Gladiator had twice the fire power as the Gauntlet and Bulldog it replaced. Although a total of 747 were produced, the Gladiator proved to be obsolete when World War II erupted and it had to face low-wing monoplane fighters.

The introduction of the Hawker Hurricane in 1938 provided Fighter Command with a vastly improved fighter over the Gladiators it replaced and represented a remarkable achievement for British production because it would already comprise 60 percent of Fighter Command's strength in 1939. Although the Spitfire generally garners more attention, it was the Hawker Hurricane that carried the brunt of Fighter Command's attack on the Luftwaffe during the Battle of Britain. Employing a metal tube structure and fabric covering, the Hurricane was surprisingly strong and it was armed with eight .303 caliber machine guns. It had a wingspan of 40 ft, length of 32 ft, and loaded weight of 8,110 lbs. Its 1,280 hp Rolls Royce Merlin XX liquid-cooled engine provided a top speed of 336 mph, service ceiling of 35,600 ft, and range of 460 miles. Although it was outperformed by the Messerschmitt BF-109, it had a devastating impact on the Messerschmitt BF-110 and German bombers. A naval version, the Sea Hurricane, was introduced in 1942, and the Hurricane II was modified with two 40 mm cannon to become an effective antitank aircraft. A total of 14,449 of all varieties were built by 1945.

Although the Hurricane carried the main burden during the Battle of Britain, the Spitfire is generally considered to be the fighter responsible for British victory because of its success against the Messerschmitt BF-109, which was owed primarily to the Spitfire's superior turning ability. In addition, it served in a front-line capacity for a long period as more powerful engines were ever-increasingly added to it, increasing its maximum speed from 355 mph when it was first introduced to 448 mph by war's end. With a wingspan of 36 ft 10 in, a length of 32 ft 2 in, and a loaded weight of 8,500 lbs, it was the RAF's first all-metal fighter. When powered by the 2,050 hp Rolls-Royce Griffon liquid-cooled engine, the Mark XIV version had a maximum speed of 448 mph, a service ceiling of 44,500 ft, and a range of 460 miles. The Spitfire fielded two 20 mm cannon and four .303 caliber machine guns in its wings and could be fitted with 500 lbs of bombs. More than 20,000 of all versions were built, including 941 naval versions known as the Seafire.

The Boulton-Paul Defiant, which began entering service in early 1940, was a unique two-seat fighter that featured a four gun (.303 caliber) dorsal turret to the rear of the pilot but lacked forward-firing weaponry. It had a wingspan of 39 ft 4 in, length of 35 ft, and loaded weight of 8,600 lbs, and its 1,030 hp Rolls-Royce Merlin III liquid-cooled engine gave it a maximum speed of 303 mph and range of 480 miles. Although heavier and slower than single-seat fighters, the RAF believed that it would be effective because the pilot could concentrate on flying and leave the fighting to the gunner. It enjoyed initial success over Dunkirk, shooting down 65 German fighters in a single week, because the Germans initially mistook it for Hawker Hurricanes and attacked from the rear. From that point forward German pilots learned to attack it head on or from below. Shot down in large numbers, the Defiant was soon relegated to night-fighter duties.

The Bristol Beaufighter provided the RAF with one of its most versatile and rugged fighters of World War II. Using the same tail and rear fuselage as the Bristol Beaufort torpedo bomber, it had a wingspan of 57 ft 10 in, length of 41 ft 8 in, and loaded weight of 21,600 lbs. Its two 1,670 hp Bristol Hercules XVI radial engines gave it a top speed of 333 mph, range of 1,480 miles, and service ceiling of 26,500 ft. The Beaufighter's four 20 mm cannons and six .303 caliber machine guns gave it tremendous fire power. It was introduced in October 1940 and proved its worth as a night-fighter during the Blitz. Although supplanted by the De Havilland Mosquito in 1942, the Beaufighter gained a new lease on life when modified to serve as a torpedo bomber. It provided Coastal Command with a powerful weapon against German surface vessels and U-boats. A total of 5,562 were produced in Great Britain and Australia.

The Hawker Typhoon, introduced in 1942, became one of the most successful ground-attack aircraft of the Second World War, devastating German armor after the Normandy Landing. A low-wing monoplane with retractable undercarriage and stressed skin covering, the Typhoon had difficulty at first because of faulty engines. By 1943, however, it was fitted with the 2,180 hp Napier Sabre II liquid-cooled engine, which produced a maximum speed of 405 mph (the first

British aircraft to achieve this), service ceiling of 34,000 ft, and range of 510 miles. With a wingspan of 41 ft 7 in, length of 31 ft 11 in, and loaded weight of 13,980, the Typhoon was compact, yet powerful, with its four 20 mm cannon and 2,000 lb bomb or rocket load. Typhoons proved to be the bane of German tanks on the Western Front, destroying 137 in a single day after the German Army got trapped in the Falaise pocket.

Although the Gloster Meteor I-III was the only Allied jet to enter service during the Second World War, it was used primarily as a means of shooting down V-1 flying bombs and as a possible defense against the Luftwaffe's Me 262 jet fighter. While it shot down 13 of the former, it did not face the latter. The Meteor fired four 20 mm cannon mounted in the nose. It had a wingspan of 43 ft, a length of 41 ft 3 in, and a loaded weight of 13,920 lbs. The Meteor was powered by two 1700 lb thrust Rolls-Royce Welland I turbojets and had a maximum speed of 415 mph, which was actually slower than the Allies' fastest piston-driven fighters, but it could climb 2,155 ft in a minute. Even though only 230 were built by the end of the war, an additional 3600 were ultimately produced.

French Fighter and Attack Aircraft

French fighter development during the interwar years is reminiscent of Dickens's *Tale of Two Cities* with the 1920s being the best of times and the 1930s being the worst of times. Two factors help account for this. First, discounting the importance of strategic bombing and recognizing that fighters were cheaper to produce than bombers, the French spent their resources developing fighters and would in fact produce the best the world had to offer in the 1920s. Second, when Pierre Cot served as minister of air during much of the 1930s he pushed the development of bombers for their deterrent effect. Although Cot did not intend to neglect fighters—in fact, he recognized that they were equally important to bombers—the financial burdens France faced in the Great Depression, which hit it last and persisted longer, prevented it from doing both well. As a result, French fighter development suffered during the 1930s. Although it made belated efforts to correct this, the war came before new fighters, like the Dewoitine D 520, came in sufficient numbers to make up for lost time.

One of the primary French fighters throughout the 1920s was the Nieuport-Delage Ni-D 29, which had been intended for service in World

War I, but the armistice came before it entered production. Unlike previous Nieuports, which had used a sesquiplane layout and rotary motors, the Nieuport 29 featured a standard biplane configuration with a wingspan of 31 ft 10 in, a length of 21 ft 3 in, and a loaded weight of 2,535 lbs. Powered by a 300 hp Hispano-Suiza 8Fb water-cooled engine, the Nieuport 29 had a maximum speed of 146 mph, a service ceiling of 27,887 ft, and a range of 300 miles. The prototype was demonstrated in June 1918 and received rave reviews, but with the end of the war on November 11, 1918, production was delayed until 1921. It was armed with two 7.7 mm synchronized machine guns. Approximately 1,250 Ni-D 29s were produced, and it served as France's main fighter until 1928. It would also be licensed-produced in Italy and Japan for their air forces.

Although France relied primarily upon the Ni-D 29, it produced numerous other fighters during the 1920s, including the Blériot-Spad 51 biplane, the Potez 25 A2 sesquiplane, the Wilbault 72 C1, and the Loire-Gourdou-Leseurre LGL 32 C1. Of these the latter two are unique because they were high-wing monoplanes. The Wibault 72 C1 entered service in1926. It was of all metal construction and had a wingspan of 35 ft 11 in, a length of 24 ft 9 in, and a loaded weight of 3,351 lbs. Powered by a 420 hp Gnome-Rhone Jupiter 9AC radial, it had a maximum speed of 138 mph, a service ceiling of 27,887 ft, and a range of 373 miles. The Wibault proved to be an excellent climber, able to reach 13,000 ft in just 11 minutes. It was also highly maneuverable. Armed with two 7.7 mm machine guns in its wings and two 7.7 machine guns on the fuselage, the Wibault had more firepower than most other fighters of the period. Approximately 60 entered French service, with others being exported to Brazil and Chile, and Poland building at least 50. The LGL 32 C1, which was introduced in 1927 and was similar in design to the Wibault, used a more standard metal frame and fabric construction. It had a wingspan of 40 ft, a length of 24 ft 9 in, and a loaded weight of 3,033 lbs. Using the same engine as the Wibault, the LGL 32 C1 had a top speed of 155 mph, a service ceiling of 31,824 ft, and range of 410 miles. It also fielded the same armament. A total of 350 were produced between 1925 and 1936. A few were secretly supplied to the Popular Front forces in Spain, but they were no match for the fighters supplied by Italy and Germany.

As the last biplane fighter to enter French service, the Bleriot-Spad S 510 provides a perfect example of the failures of the French Air Ministry. With a wingspan of 29 ft, length of 24 ft 5 in, and loaded weight of 3,638 lb, the S 510 featured an all-metal airframe that was fabric-covered and had an open cockpit. Armed with two 7.7 mm machine guns, it was powered by a 690 hp Hispanso-Suiza 12Xbrs water-cooled engine that gave it a top speed of 201 mph. It was unfortunately based on 1930 specifications and did not enter production until 1936, by which time it was clearly obsolete. The French built 60 anyway, utilizing both money and resources that could have been used for developing low-wing monoplane fighters. Within a year of entering service the Bleriot-Spad S 510 was relegated to reserve squadrons.

Entering service in 1933, the Dewoitine D 500 provided France with one of its first all-metal, cantilever low-wing fighters. An improved version, the D 510, entered service in 1935. It had a wingspan of 39 ft 8 in, length of 26 ft, and loaded weight of 4,235 lbs. The D 510's 860 hp Hispano-Suiza 12Ycrs liquid-cooled engine provided a top speed of 250 mph, service ceiling of 34,500 ft, and range of 435 miles. It came armed with two 7.7 mm machine guns and one 20 mm cannon. Although it did not have an enclosed cockpit or retractable undercarriage, it was important as a transitional aircraft design that would lead the way to the more advanced Dewoitine D 520. There were approximately 325 D 500s and D 510s produced. They were still serving in front-line units in 1940 and provided easy targets for the Luftwaffe's Messerschmitt BF-109.

The Bloch MB 152 was a product of France's long search for an all-metal, low-wing monoplane fighter. Problems with the MB 150 prototype in the mid-1930s forced a complete redesign that delayed the introduction of the MB 151 until 1939. A total of 140 of this version were built before the French discovered they were unfit for service as fighters. Further modifications to its wing design and the introduction of the 1,080 hp Gnome-Rhone 14N-25 radial engine resulted in the final MB 152 version. With a wingspan of 34 ft 7 in, length of 29 ft 10 in, loaded weight of 5,908 lbs, and top speed of 320 mph it proved to be an effective fighter that could outdive any other in French service. It was armed with two 7.5 mm machine guns and two 20 mm cannon. A total of 383 MB 152's had been produced by September 1939, but the majority of these lacked gunsights and propellers. Nevertheless, as they became operational, the MB 152 served valiantly against the Luftwaffe, shooting down 170 German aircraft.

Having produced the successful D 500 and D 510, Dewoitine introduced the D 520 prototype in October 1938 in an effort to meet government specifications for an all-metal, low-wing monoplane capable of challenging the Messerschmitt BF-109. It had a wingspan of 33 ft 5 in, length of 28 ft 8 in, and loaded weight of 5,897. Its 930 hp Hispano-Suiza 12Y45 liquid-cooled engine produced a top speed of

332 mph and provided a service ceiling of 33,620 ft with a range of 553 miles. It was armed with four 7.5 mm machine guns and one 20 mm cannon. Impressed by its performance and firepower, the French government issued orders to put it into production. It proved unfortunate for France, however, that it came too late and in too few numbers to make a difference. Only one fighter group possessed D 520s upon the German invasion. These would shoot down 147 German aircraft, while suffering just 44 losses. It is a testament to their worth that the Germans continued production of the D 520 after the fall of France.

Although the Dewoitine D 520 fighter design was available, the French made the critical error of trying to develop several low-wing monoplane types at the same time, rather than choosing one and concentrating on it as Germany did with the Messerschmitt BF-109. As a result, the Morane-Saulnier MS 406, its worst performing monoplane fighter of World War II, also happened to be its most numerous. Using steel tube construction and a composite plywood, aluminum, and fabric covering, the MS 406 had a wingspan of 34 ft 9 in, length of 26 ft 9 in, and loaded weight of 5,445 lbs. Its underpowered 860 hp Hispano-Suiza 12Y-21 liquid-cooled engine provided a top speed of 302 mph, a service ceiling of 30,840 ft, and a range of 497 miles. In addition to being underpowered, it had only two wing-mounted 7.5 mm machine guns and one 20 mm cannon that fired through the propeller hub. A total of 1,080 MS 406s were produced before France fell. Of this number, at least 400 had been shot down by the Luftwaffe, compared with just 175 aircraft shot down by its aircraft.

German Fighter and Attack Aircraft

Subject to the provisions of the Treaty of Versailles, the German Air Force ceased to exist following the First World War. Beginning in 1922, the Treaty of Rapallo provided cover for continued German innovation under the guise of Soviet production. Restrictions were further loosened on Germany with the signing of the Locarno Treaties and Germany's admission into the League of Nations in 1926. Approval soon came for Germany to build multi-engine commercial planes, and, largely in the form of Lufthansa, German aviation technology resumed full-force. Upon Hitler's rise to power, the Luftwaffe was introduced to the world once more.

The Messerschmitt BF-109 series was both one of the first and most important fighters developed in Germany on the eve of World War II.

During the war it saw action on every front, and was manufactured in such quantity (approximately 35,000) that only the Soviet Ilyushin Il-2 equaled its production run. The model was clearly a workhorse for the Luftwaffe. Its prototype first flew in 1935, the answer to a 1934 specification calling for a small, light-weight fighter. With a wingspan of 32 ft 4.5 in, length of 28 ft, and a height of 8 ft 0.5 in, the BF-109 was armed with dual 7.9 mm machine guns in the nose, and three 20 mm cannons. The most numerous model in the run, the BF-109G series, was fitted with a powerful, 1,475 hp Daimler-Benz DB605 engine; this produced a top speed in excess of 380 mph, along with a service ceiling of 37,890 ft and range of 350 miles. Drop tanks could extend the aircraft's range by nearly 300 additional miles. There were approximately 200 BF-109s that led the assault on Poland in 1939, and they were still among the front-line fighters at the time of the Battle of Britain.

A concurrent development from Messerschmitt was a twin-engine, long-range fighter, the BF-110. After its May 1936 maiden flight, the BF-110 entered production powered by two 1,200 hp Daimler-Benz DB600 engines. The model possessed a top speed of 294 mph, service ceiling of 32,000 ft, and range of 565 miles. It spanned 53 ft 4.75 in, with length of 39 ft 8.5 in, and height of 11 ft 6 in. Carrying a crew of two, the BF-110 was armed with two 20 mm cannons and four 7.9 mm machine guns in the nose, and a 7.9 mm rear-firing machine gun. Later models, converted for use as fighter-bombers, could carry an external bomb load of 1,102–2,205 lbs. Production of the model peaked at 6,050 copies. Although the Luftwaffe had grander plans for the BF-110, the aircraft proved vastly inferior in combat over Great Britain in 1941. After losing more than 200 Bf 110s in the Battle of Britain, the model was relegated to secondary use as a light bomber, reconnaissance, and night-fighter.

Conceived as a successor to the BF-110, the Messerschmitt Me 210 was intended to be a multipurpose fighter-bomber; however, the development of the design proved one of the Luftwaffe's most agonizing, and utterly disappointing, chapters. Despite guarded reviews by its test pilot following the prototype's 1939 debut, a 1,000-copy production order was immediately placed. The aircraft suffered from terrible in-flight stability issues, and featured so many design flaws that only a few hundred of the order were ever delivered to combat units.

Although radically overhauled, the model did serve as the basis for the far more successful Me 410 Hornisse (Hornet). Powered by twin 1,750 hp Daimler-Benz DB603 inverted V-12 engines, the Hornet could achieve a maximum speed of 390 mph, and possessed a service ceiling of 32,810 ft and range of 1,450 miles. It was heavily armed in any of its 100-plus weapons configurations, but it most typically carried two 20 mm cannons and two 7.92 mm machine guns in the nose, along with two additional 13 mm remotely controlled machine guns mounted on the fuselage; it could also carry a maximum bomb load of 2,205 lbs. The Me 410 spanned 53 ft 7.75 in, with length of 40 ft 11.5 in, and height of 14 ft. Although it was considerably more successful than its predecessor, the "Destroyer" ("Zerstörer") concept of heavy-fighters proved to be one of the greater technological miscalculations of the war. More than 1,100 copies of this model were produced, but the type as a whole offered little in contribution to the war effort.

A similar dual-use model was the Henschel Hs 123. Conceived as a light- and dive-bomber, the Luftwaffe employed the Hs 123 as a ground-attack aircraft on both fronts throughout the war despite its increasing obsolescence. First flown in early 1935, the biplane spanned 34 ft 5 in, with length of 27 ft 4 in, and height of 10 ft 7 in. Its power plant was a single 880 hp BMW nine cylinder radial engine, which produced a top speed of 210 mph, service ceiling in excess of 29,500 ft, and maximum range of 534 miles. It was armed with two 7.9 mm machine guns, and could carry up to 992 lbs of bombs on under-wing racks; some models replaced the bomb racks with two 20 mm cannons. The Hs 123 was notable neither for its combat record nor for any major design innovations, but instead stands as an example of the Luftwaffe's willingness to keep an obsolete aircraft in front-line service so long as it was believed to fill a role. In the case of the Hs 123, its precision bombing capabilities led to its retainer in service as a ground-attack vehicle despite being intended solely as a prewar stopgap until the development of the Junkers Ju 87 Stuka dive-bomber. There were approximately 600 built from 1938 through 1944.

The Focke-Wulf Fw 190 series was far more important and is widely considered as the best German fighter, and one of the most capable of any service, of World War II. After first being flown in June 1939, designer Kurt Tank's Fw 190 appeared in combat over France in 1941; then, and for some time thereafter, it was the superior fighter in the European Theater. The model spanned 34 ft 5.25 in, with length of 29 ft and height of 13 ft. Most were equipped with a single 1,700 hp BMW 801D 14 cylinder air-cooled radial engine, which afforded a superlative top speed exceeding 400 mph, in addition to a service ceiling of 34,775 ft and range of nearly 500 miles. The model was aptly nicknamed Würger ("Butcher Bird"), and was armed with twin 7.9 mm machine guns and four 20 mm cannon. Prior to the introduction of the Spitfire IX series, the Fw 190 was virtually unchallenged over

England. A defecting pilot's Fw 190, however, would serve as the design impetus for the superior Hawker Fury. The model was, in a sense, therefore part of its own undoing. It was nevertheless an important part of the German ascendancy in Europe, and was produced in quantity numbering more than 20,000.

Whereas BF-109s, 110s, and Fw 190s were all modified for use as night-fighters, the Luftwaffe also employed several other models in this way. The most successful of this group were the Dornier Do 217 and the Junkers Ju 88 medium bombers, which will both be discussed in greater detail in Chapter Five, and the Heinkel He 219 Uhu (Owl). The Owl was a two-seat aircraft built in small numbers (just 294 of all models), but is notable for being designed specifically for use as a night-fighter. Along with a wingspan of 60 ft 8 in, length of 50 ft 11.75 in, and height of 13 ft 5.5 in, the He 219 featured dual Daimler-Benz DB603 inverted V-12 liquid-cooled engines. The power plant provided a top speed of approximately 415 mph, with operational ceiling of 41,667 ft. When combined with a range in excess of 1,200 miles, a radar set, and its heavy armament, these features made the Owl a deadly night-fighter. It typically carried two 20 mm cannons mounted in wing pods, along with two 30 mm cannons in ventral mounts and two upward-firing 30 mm cannon in the rear fuselage. The prototype so impressed the Luftwaffe commanders with its speed and agility that quantity production was ordered immediately after its November 1942 test flight. One of the lasting mysteries of the Nazi leadership was why valuable production resources were directed away from this relatively successful aircraft and instead spent on such lesser designs as the ill-fated Focke Wulf Ta 154 and Junkers Ju 388.

The introduction of the Messerschmitt Me 262 Schwalbe (Swallow), the world's first combat operational jet fighter, was far more famous; indeed, this was arguably the most lasting and significant of the Luftwaffe's contributions to military aviation. The model's design genesis began in 1938, with the prototype first flying in April 1941; however, this prototype featured a piston-driven, Jumo 210 power plant rather than turbojet engines. History's first jet-powered flight occurred on July 18, 1942, by which time testing with conventional engines generated other design refinements (the inclusion of a retractable tricycle landing gear). This flight was no great success, however, further delaying the aircraft's deployment by several months. It would not see combat until late June 1944, by which point the war was all but lost for Germany. Despite its limited combat record and the even more limited availability of experienced Luftwaffe pilots, the Me 262 was a successful fighter, recording more than 100 Allied kills before the end of the war. It was produced in

both fighter and night-fighter variations, the latter including a radar officer as a second crewmember. The model spanned 40 ft 11 in, with
length of 34 ft 8 in, and height of 12 ft 7 in. Its two Junkers Jumo 004B
turbojets produced 3,968 lbs of thrust, affording a top speed of over 540
mph, climb rate of more than 3,900 ft per minute, a service ceiling of
37,565 ft, and range of up to 650 miles. Even though 11,400-plus copies
were produced, fewer than 200 were deployed to combat units before
the end of the war.

One of the more unique fighters introduced by the Luftwaffe during the war was the Messerschmitt Me 163 Komet (Comet), a single-
seat rocket-powered interceptor. Designed by Alexander Lippisch, the
Me 163's frame was matched with a hydrogen peroxide–fueled motor
designed by Hellmuth Walter. Producing 3,750 lbs of thrust, the Walter HWK 509A-2 rocket motor propelled the prototype to a top speed
of 623 mph in a 1941 test flight. Sustained maximum speed for the Me
163 was 596 mph, with a service ceiling of 39,000 ft. The model
spanned 30 ft 7.25 in, with a length of 19 ft 2.25 in, and a height of 9
ft 1 in. It was armed with two wing-mounted 20 or 30 mm cannons.
The aircraft's shortcoming was its extremely limited range (60 miles)
and endurance (approximately 8 minutes). Although promising, the
355 copies produced for combat units failed to alter the course of the
war substantially. The odd aircraft was simply too difficult for increasingly inexperienced Luftwaffe pilots to man safely; subsequently,
losses in the model were high.

Italian Fighter and Attack Aircraft

Although Italy had been successful in producing bombers during the
First World War, with Caproni specializing in trimotor bombers, it had
not developed a successful fighter. This was a trend that continued
into the 1920s. This was partly a reflection of Douhet's emphasis upon
the bomber and Italy's failure to produce high-performance engines,
something that would plague all of its aircraft during the Second
World War. Nevertheless, Italy did develop two biplane fighters during
the 1920s (the Fiat CR 1 and Fiat CR 20) that would lead to the development in the 1930s of two of the best biplane fighters ever produced
in the Fiat CR 32 and the Fiat CR 42. By the time these came along,
however, other countries had recognized that the low-wing monoplane
provided a far better fighter, something that Italy was slow to realize to
its own detriment.

The Fiat CR 1 was introduced in 1924 and was similar in design to World War I biplane fighters. Using a wooden frame, fabric construction, it had a wingspan of 29 ft 4 in, a length of 20 ft 5 in, and a loaded weight of 2,546 lbs. It was powered by a 320 hp Isotta-Faschini Asso liquid-cooled engine that gave it a top speed of 168 mph, a service ceiling of 24,442 ft, and a range of 405 miles. It was armed with two 7.7 mm synchronized machine guns. There were approximately 100 produced before it was replaced by the Fiat CR 20. The CR 20 was slightly larger with a wingspan of 32 ft 1 in, a length of 22 ft, and a loaded weight of 3,278 lbs. It was also a much sturdier aircraft because it used a metal structure. It was unfortunately also slower as its 450 hp Isotta-Fraschini Asso liquid-cooled engine provided a top speed of 155 mph, a service ceiling of 16,404 ft, and a range of 311miles. A total of 450 were produced, including two-seat reconnaissance versions and floatplane versions. The CR 20 was used successfully in Italy's invasion of Ethiopia, where of course it encountered virtually no resistance.

An improved version of the earlier CR 20, the Fiat CR 32 Chirri, provided the Regia Aeronautica one of the best biplane fighters ever produced. It had a wingspan of 31 ft 1 in, length of 24 ft 5 in, and loaded weight of 4,343 lbs. Its 800 hp Fiat RA liquid-cooled engine provided a top speed of 205 mph, service ceiling of 26,245 ft, and range of 485 miles. Using a metal framed, fabric construction, its wings were well supported, making it one of the most acrobatic fighters to enter service in any air force. Armed with two 7.7 mm machine guns and two 12.5 mm machine guns, the CR 32 enjoyed success against the Soviet Polikarpov I-16 monoplane during the Spanish Civil War, which convinced Italy to continue production of the CR 32 (ultimately 1,212 were produced) and to introduce the CR 42 Falco (Falcon) in 1939. The Falco was the last major biplane to enter military service and it represented the technological zenith of that design type. It had a wingspan of 31 ft 10 in, length of 27 ft 1 in, and loaded weight of 5,060. Its 840 hp Fiat A.74 RC.38 radial engine provided a maximum speed of 267 mph, service ceiling of 33,465, and range of 482 miles. Although armed with just two 12.7 mm machine guns, the CR 42 was such a delight to fly that many Italian pilots preferred it over more modern monoplane types.

The Fiat G 50 Freccia provided the Regia Aeronautica with its first all-metal, low-wing monoplane fighter with a retractable undercarriage when it entered service in 1938. It had a wingspan of 36 ft 1 in, length of 27 ft 2 in, and loaded weight of 5,511 lbs. Its 840 hp Fiat A.74 RC.38 radial engine provided a maximum speed of 302 mph, service ceiling of 35,269 ft, and range of 621 miles. Armed with just two 12.7 mm machine guns, the G 50 was underarmed compared with the Messerschmitt BF-109, Hawker Hurricane, and Supermarine Spitfire. Its closed canopy also provided such a low field of vision that many pilots refused to fly it, preferring instead the CR 42 biplane. There were approximately 1500 built.

The Macchi MC 200 Saetta (Lightning Bolt) and MC 202 Folgore (Thunderbolt) entered service a year after the G 50 Freccia and would be the most numerous World War II Italian fighters. Featuring a low-wing design, fully enclosed canopy, and stressed-skin all-metal con-struction, the MC 200 had a wingspan of 34 ft 8 in, a length of 26 ft 10 in, and a loaded weight of 5,710 lbs. Its 870 hp Fiat A.74 RC.38 radial engine was unfortunately underpowered, giving it a maximum speed of just 312 mph, a service ceiling of 29,200 ft, and a range of 540 miles. Compounding matters, the MC 200 was underarmed, being equipped with just two 12.7 mm machine guns. Although Ital-ian pilots flying it fought bravely, the odds became increasingly stacked against them as the British were able to introduce better fighters (the Hurricane) into the Mediterranean Theater. Although only 156 were available for the Regia Aeronautica when it entered the war in June 1940, a total of 1,153 were ultimately produced and would be used by both sides until the war's end. Although the MC 200 had been a dis-appointment, Macchi began importing the 1,175 hp Daimler-Benz DB 601A liquid-cooled engine in early 1941, which increased its maxi-mum speed to 372 mph and its service ceiling to 37,730 ft. Those fit-ted with the Daimler Benz became known as the MC 202 Folgore (Thunderbolt), the best World War II Italian fighter. It also sported two additional 7.7 mm machine guns. A total of 1,200 of this variety were built and several served on the Russian front.

Perhaps the best fighter to enter the Regia Aeronautica in World War II was the Reggiane Re 2000 Falco (Falcon). Although it shared the same nickname as the Fiat CR 42 biplane fighter, the Re 2000 was a streamlined, low-wing monoplane with a retractable undercarriage and enclosed canopy. It was a compact fighter with a wingspan of 36 ft 1 in, a length of 27 ft 5 in, and a loaded weight of 6,989 lbs. It had been originally underpowered with Italian radial engines, but it pro-vided a maximum speed of 339 mph, a service ceiling of 39,205 ft, and a range of 646 miles when fitted with a 1,175 hp Daimler-Benz DB 601A liquid-cooled engine after Italy entered World War II. Although underarmed with just two 7.7 mm machine guns and two 12.7 mm machine guns—a flaw with all of Italy's fighters—it was fast and highly maneuverable. Only 285 were built, and all 48 of the final Re 2005 version were seized by the Luftwaffe.

Japanese Fighter and Attack Aircraft

The air wings of the Japanese military rose to preeminence on a ballistic arc, only to find themselves overtaken by Allied technological advances as the Japanese war machine ground to a halt. For a brief time, however, Japanese aircraft enjoyed virtually unchallenged reign in the air over the Pacific. It is quite likely that this result would never have come about if Japan's leadership were not quite so bent on technological and materiel self-sufficiency. Within a decade, Japan's military transitioned from near total dependence to complete independence from—and in some cases unquestioned superiority to—their rivals in the air.

The first step in this relatively brief but arduous process was taken in 1927. Seeking a replacement for its Type Ko 4 Fighter (a license-built copy of the French Nieuport), the Japanese Army Air Force (JAAF) issued a set of specifications to Nakajima, Mitsubishi, and Kawasaki, thus setting off the first open competition for a Japanese-designed aircraft. Within a few years, the Japanese military would solicit only Japanese designs. Nakajima's Shigejiro Ohwada and Yasushi Koyama, under the supervision of French designers André Marie and Maxime Robin, set about designing a parasol-winged prototype with an air-cooled radial engine; it had the French Nieuport-Delage as its model. Completed in May 1928 and first flown a short time later, the Nakajima entry proved vastly superior to her competitors. In late 1931 the JAAF ordered it in quantity production. More than 450 of this Army Type 91 Fighter were produced, and they quickly became the gold standard among the aircraft flown by the Japanese. The success of the design, which was fairly easy to fly and maintain, thrilled the army all the more because it was Japanese. The aircraft spanned 36 ft 1 in, with length of 23 ft 10 in, height of 9 ft 2 in, and wing area of slightly over 215 sq ft. It could achieve a top speed in excess of 187 mph, and possessed a climb rate of 9,845 ft in approximately four minutes, with a service ceiling of 29,527 ft and a 2 hour endurance rating. The Type 91 was an all-metal design with fabric covering over the metallic frame wings. It carried a single pilot in an open cockpit, and featured dual forward-firing 7.7 mm machine guns mounted in the fuselage. The first 320 produced of the model were powered by a 450–520 hp Nakajima Jupiter VII nine cylinder air-cooled radial engine, whereas the remaining production models (Type 91–2) incorporated the slightly more powerful Nakajima Kotobuki 2 radial engine. Although it was quite obsolete by the outset of the war, it was a model that propelled Japan toward the forefront of military aviation.

In September 1934, the JAAF determined that they lacked a fighter comparable to the Boeing P-26A or the Hawker Fury. To remedy this situation, they issued specifications to Kawasaki and Nakajima. The two companies took radically different approaches. Kawasaki's Takeo Doi led a design team that focused on the maneuverability and dog-fighting capabilities of a technologically advanced biplane; Nakajima's designers, on the other hand, opted for the improved speed and power afforded by a monoplane design. Shortly after Kawasaki's Ki-10 pro-totype rolled off the assembly line in March 1935, the JAAF pitted it against Nakajima's Ki-11 in competitive trials. The results were pre-dictable: The latter proved faster, but the former more agile. In a deci-sion that came to define the tactical thinking of Japanese designers for years to come, the JAAF favored the Ki-10, especially after a series of slight modifications, including replacing the two-bladed propeller with a three-bladed model, improving its speed without sacrificing much agility. In December 1935, Kawasaki won the army's contract and began building the first combat models of the Ki-10's 588-copy pro-duction run. The aircraft was an all-metal frame with fabric coverings, piloted by a single crewmember, and powered by a Kawasaki Ha-9-IIa 12 cylinder liquid-cooled engine. Dual 7.7 mm Type 89 machine guns served as the plane's offensive armament and were fixed in the fuse-lage above the engine mounting. The Ki-10-I (about 300 of the total produced) spanned 31 ft 3 in, was 23 ft 7 in long, with a height of 9 ft 10 in, and wing area of 215 sq ft. Later models, Ki-10-IIs (about 280 of the total produced), were slightly larger; the increased length and wingspan improved the aircraft's in-flight stability without significantly altering its performance. Both models could achieve a maximum speed of more than 248 mph, climb to 16,405 ft in approximately five min-utes, possessed a combat range of 684 miles, and could operate at alti-tudes of up to 32,810 ft. The model saw considerable action over China in the 1930s, but was relegated to the rear guard by the onset of World War II. Despite being rarely observed by Allied servicemen, the model was dubbed "Perry" during the war.

Continuing their trend, in 1934 the JAAF also solicited designs for a model to replace the Kawasaki KDA-5 (Type 92 Fighter). Nakajima's Ki-27, under the guidance of lead designer Koyama, resulted from this effort. The design process was troublesome, largely the result of many revisions and experimentations on the model by the Nakajima team. Finally, on October 15, 1936, the Ki-27 took to the air for its first flight. In competitive trials held in early 1937, the Nakajima model outclassed its competitors—the Mitsubishi Ki-33 and the Kawasaki Ki-28—and was ordered for production in late 1937. It was a single-seat fighter of monoplane design, featuring a pilot in an enclosed cockpit. Production models were powered by the 650 hp Army Type 97 (Nakajima's Ha-1a) nine cylinder air-cooled radial engine, and could achieve a top speed in excess of 290 mph. It spanned 37 ft 1 in, had a length of 24 ft 8 in, height of 10 ft 8 in, and wing area slightly under 200 sq ft. The Ki-27 featured dual synchronized 7.7 mm Type 89 machine guns, and could carry four 55 lb bombs or two 28 gal external drop tanks. With the latter configuration, the plane's normal range of 390 miles could be extended to 1,060 miles. As with the Ki-10, the Ki-27 (nicknamed "Abdul" by the Allies) saw most of its combat time over China, and was obsolescent by the onset of the war in the Pacific.

By the mid-1930s the modernization program rapidly propelled Japanese air forces toward parity with Western powers. Twin-engine fighters were becoming the status quo in Europe and America, so the JAAF solicited designs for a similar Japanese model; however, the army could not agree on any single set of specifications, and instead issued a very broad order for a twin-engine fighter in March 1937. Nakajima submitted the Ki-37, Kawasaki the Ki-38, and Mitsubishi the Ki-39, but the army still had not issued formal specifications. Based on these designs, however, the JAAF issued specifications in December 1937 for an aircraft capable of reaching a top speed of 335 mph, with a 4 hour 40 minute patrol endurance, and a 30 minute combat endurance. Kawasaki's Takeo Doi completed a prototype in January 1939, but various mechanical and design problems plagued its test flights. By April 1940, with no answer yet to the initial design specifications, the JAAF issued a new series of orders. Kawasaki's design would undergo a vast array of modifications over the next several months before being adopted for production in late 1941. The Ki-45 Toryu ("Dragon Killer") was built strong, with heavily armored body and fuel tanks. Despite the numerous trials and tribulations of its lengthy design phase it proved to be quite a capable and pilot-friendly aircraft. It was so easy to fly that it came to be tasked as a night-fighter, which is one example of a recurring theme in Japanese military aviation because as the war progressed aircraft were increasingly tasked to roles for which they had never been designed or intended to fulfill. Its use as a night-fighter brought the Ki-45 (code-named "Nick" by the Allies) into combat against B-24s and, late in the war, it served as one of the primary defenses against American B-29 raids on the Home Islands.

Slightly more than 1,700 copies of the Ki-45 were produced through the end of the war, each being of an all-metal construction and housing a crew of two. Most featured twin 950 hp Nakajima

Ha-25 radial engines, while a later modification replaced these with the more powerful Mitsubishi Ha-102 engines. The aircraft spanned 47 ft 6 in, was 33 ft 8 in long, with a height of 11 ft 8 in, and wing area of slightly more than 312 sq feet. Later models (including the Ki-45 KAIa and KAIc) were slightly larger in all respects. Early models achieved a top speed approaching 300 mph, with later models besting that figure by 40 mph. Later models similarly cut the climb rate of the first Ki-45s by one third, which could climb to 16,405 ft in a little more than 10 minutes. Ki-45s also featured a range of between 1,000 and 1,400 miles. In addition to their armored fuselages, the aircraft were defended by an array of machine guns and cannons. The most common assembly featured twin 12.7 mm Type 1 machine guns in the nose, a 20 mm Ho-3 cannon mounted on the right side of the body, and a single flexible, rear-firing 7.92 mm Type 98 machine gun. Those modified specifically for use as night-fighters (Ki-45 KAIc) featured dual 20 mm Ho-3 cannons mounted obliquely on the fuselage in place of nose-mounted machine guns.

The Nakajima Ki-43 Hayabusa ("Peregrine Falcon") faced a similarly trying developmental phase, but it overcame initial setbacks to become one of the most important planes in the entire Japanese air fleet in a couple of different ways. It was initially solicited as a more powerful, but equally maneuverable, replacement for the Ki-27; the JAAF's December 1937 specifications called for maximum speeds in excess of 310 mph, with a 16,000 ft in five minutes climb rate, a range in excess of 500 miles, and, innovatively, retractable undercarriage. Nakajima's Hideo Itokawa set about producing just such an aircraft, and his prototype flew in January 1939; however, the army was supremely disappointed with its lack of agility and rejected the model. Some sources report that it was at this time that the Imperial Japanese Navy used similar specifications, and the same engine, as in Itokawa's initial prototype when soliciting the design of the famous A6M "Zero." Indeed, the production version of the Ki-43, finally adopted in November 1942, was often mistaken by Allied servicemen as being a "Zero." Both planes shared a low-slung wing design, bubble canopy, and were of extraordinarily similar dimensions. The most numerous models of Ki-43 (–II and –III revisions) housed a single crewmember in an aircraft that spanned 35 ft 7 in, with length of 29 ft 3 in, height of 10 ft 9 in, and wing area of 230 sq feet. These same models featured the 1,150 hp Nakajima Ha-115 engine, enabling a maximum speed in excess of 330 mph, a 36,000-plus ft service ceiling, and range of between 1,000 and 1,990 miles. The Ki-43 sacrificed armor for maneuverability, and relied on its speed and agility (including a tighter turn radius than the A6M "Zero" and a climb rate of 16,405 ft in approximately 5 minutes 30 seconds) for defense. Most models did feature dual 12.7 mm Ho-103 machine guns, and could carry two external bombs (or drop tanks for extended range), but the aircraft was ultimately underdefended in the face of enemy fire. Still, and despite its exceedingly long developmental period, the Hayabusa became the most widely produced aircraft in the Japanese inventory, with 5,919 copies eventually made. The "Oscar," as it came to be known to Allied servicemen, served in every theater in which Japanese forces participated, and was arguably the most technologically advanced aircraft in the entire Pacific Theatre on its combat intro-duction. As would also be a recurring theme for the Japanese war machine, however, the Ki-43 remained in production far beyond its era; Allied technology eventually produced superior aircraft, but the Ki-43 continued to serve as a front-line fighter despite being outmoded at the end of the war.

As production of the Ki-43 more than adequately began to fulfill the JAAF's need for a front-line heavy fighter, the army solicited designs for an interceptor. The Ki-44 Shoki ("Devil-Queller"), designed by Kawasaki's Koyama, immediately became the JAAF's fastest and fastest-climbing fighter, although it sacrificed agility in pursuit of this straight-line power. The Ki-44, which was a single-seat aircraft, first flew in August 1940, and underwent various modifications (especially experi-mentations with different types of power plants) before being adopted for full-scale production in September 1942. It was produced through late 1944, when it was replaced by the Ki-84, by which time more than 1,200 copies were made. Most featured the 1,450 hp Nakajima Ha-109 14 cylinder air-cooled radial, although later models incorporated the more powerful 2,000 hp Nakajima Ha-145 18 cylinder radial. This enabled top speeds exceeding 360 mph, with cruising speeds of approx-imately 250 mph, and superlative climb rates as impressive as 16,405 ft in 4 minutes 17 seconds. The aircraft possessed a span of 31 ft, length of 28 ft 8 in, height of 10 ft 8 in, and wing area of approximately 161 sq feet. In general, its armament consisted of four 12.7 mm Ho-103 machine guns, two along the fuselage and one more mounted on each wing. Some replaced the wing-mounted machine guns with wing-mounted 37 mm or 40 mm cannons. External drop tanks could be fit-ted to the aircraft to increase range to more than 1,000 miles, almost double its normal range. After impressive performance in combat over China in May 1942, the JAAF eagerly awaited delivery of the produc-tion model Ki-44s, which came to be called "Tojo" by Allied servicemen in the China–Burma–India Theatre, where the Shoki defended the oilfields at Palembang against Allied bombing raids. It was a cantankerous aircraft, however, both in maintenance and in flight, and its performance never quite compensated for these difficulties.

In February 1940, the JAAF took a slightly different track in its production scheme by soliciting not completely new designs, but rather designs based on specific concepts that seemed to be successful in combat operations. For instance, the German Messerschmitt BF-109 and the British Spitfire featured liquid-cooled engines, a design the Japanese bureaus had virtually abandoned in favor of the seemingly more reliable (and definitely easier to maintain) air-cooled radials. The combat successes of the liquid-cooled engines over Europe convinced the JAAF that the design still had merit, and would be a useful component in its own air fleet. In February 1940, thererfore, the JAAF directed Kawasaki to design two different aircraft around liquid-cooled engines; the only other specific direction given Kawasaki by the army was to incorporate some sort of self-sealing mechanism on the fuel tanks, a safety innovation proving its merit in the European air wars. Kawasaki's designs were the Ki-60, a heavy interceptor, and the Ki-61 Hien ("Swallow"), which was more of an all-purpose fighter. It strongly resembled its Messerschmitt muse, and featured many of the same defining features in the construction and shape of the plane's nose and wings. Several historians report that Allied intelligence services suspected the Ki-61 to be a licensed copy of an Italian aircraft of some sort; hence, the plane's Allied code name, "Tony." Regardless of the impetus for the design produced by Kawasaki's Takeo Doi and Shin Owada, the Ki-61 proved to possess superior performance capabilities in competitive trials against multiple opponents. In its 1942 trials, it defeated prototypes from rival design firm Nakajima, as well as rival Western aircraft, including a Messerschmitt BF-109E and an American Curtiss P-40E. It thus entered production in late 1942, and saw its first combat in April 1943 over New Guinea.

Approximately 3,078 copies of the Ki-61 were eventually produced through the end of the war, most featuring the 1,100 hp Kawasaki Ha-40 12 cylinder liquid-cooled engine that delivered impressive performance (including a top speed in excess of 365 mph and a climb rate of 16,405 ft in 7 minutes or fewer) but proved incredibly difficult to maintain in the field. The model spanned 39 ft 4 in, with length of 28 ft 8 in, height of 12 ft 2 in, and wing area of more than 215 sq ft, and carried two 12.7 mm machine guns along the fuselage, and two more on the wings. When in service, the Hien proved on par with most of its rival Allied fighters, and could, in the hands of an experienced pilot, hold its own against American P-51 Mustangs; however, it was not up to the task of defending the Home Islands against B-29 raids, a task that the state of the war eventually thrust upon the Ki-61. The liquid-cooled engine, a licensed copy of the Daimler-Benz DB 601A, proved so problematic to the Japanese service crews as to render the plane a disappointment simply because it proved to be too difficult to maintain, and too unreliable, under combat conditions, and not because of its performance when in the air (indeed, it was superior to most of the aircraft it came up against).

About the same time as the Ki-61 was undergoing its flight tests and entering into production, the JAAF began soliciting designs for a modern long-range fighter to supplant the Ki-44. The Ki-84 Hayate ("Gale") was designed by Nakajima's Koyama and first flew in April 1943. The low-wing monoplane design so readily impressed the army that it was almost immediately ordered into quantity production. The army had requested a fighter capable of a top speed in excess of 400 mph, and even though the Ki-84 never achieved that mark, it did approach it. The failure to reach 400 mph was likely due to the meeting of various other specifications, including the inclusion of self-sealing technology on fuel tanks, which along with armor plating made the Ki-84 one of the safest aircraft for its pilots in the JAAF inventory. Despite the ideal top-end speed requested, the aircraft did deliver superior agility and impressive overall performance in both flight testing and eventually in combat, even as the exigencies of war forced the increasing use of wood in the production of originally all-metal airframes. The plane spanned 36 ft 10 in, with length of 32 ft 6 in, height of 11 ft 2 in, and wing area of 226 sq feet. The single crewmember sat in an enclosed cockpit, and possessed a total of four fuselage- and wing-mounted 20 mm Ho-5 cannons for weaponry. Some models featured external fixtures for dual drop tanks or two 551 lb bombs. Its 1,900 hp Nakajima Ha-45 18 cylinder air-cooled radial engine enabled the plane to climb to 16,405 ft in less than 6 minutes. Thanks to its power-plant and its airframe design, the aircraft featured an enviable turn radius and the superior agility characteristic of most Japanese fighters. There were approximately 3,514 Ki-84s produced through the end of the war, and like the Ki-61 it proved superior to many of its Allied opponents (when in the air). On the ground, however, the Ki-84 shared the same vexing maintenance problems that dramatically limited its contributions to the Japanese war effort.

As the war progressed, designer Takeo Doi (whose credits include the Ki-10, the Ki-45, and the Ki-61) suggested that the army solicit a design for a ground-attack fighter for close air support as well as for general purpose duties. In August 1943, Kawasaki began work on such a design, and in March 1944 produced the first flying prototype of the Ki-102. The Ki-102, which was code-named "Randy" by the Allies, saw only limited combat action, mostly over Okinawa, in various configurations as a close air-support, high-altitude, and night- fighter. The Ki-102 is notable for a few specific design innovations much more than for its combat record. For instance, the high-altitude fighter Ki-108, a derivative of the -102, incorporated a pressurized cabin for the pilot and radio operator; however, this model was still in preproduction stages at the war's end. The more useful innovation was the use of supercharged engines, which enabled a maximum speed approaching 375 mph, a climb rate of up to 32,000 ft in approximately 18 minutes, and a service ceiling in excess of 44,200 ft (Ki-102c models, powered by twin 1,500 hp Mitsubishi Ha-112-II Ru 14 cylinder air-cooled radial engines). Most models featured impressive offensive and defensive armament, including a 57 mm Ho-401 cannon in the nose, dual ventral-mounted 20 mm Ho-5 cannons, and a flexible 12.7 mm Ho-103 machine gun mounted in the rear. The aircraft's 1,200 mile range could be extended by using dual external drop tanks. The Ki-102 was 51 ft in span, 37 ft 7 in long, with a height of 12 ft 2 in, and wing area of approximately 366 sq ft. Only 238 of these aircraft were produced, including just two modified as -102c aircraft with increased range and performance.

The final JAAF aircraft to make its combat debut during the Second World War was the Kawasaki Ki-100, a dedicated high-altitude interceptor tasked with disrupting the devastating American B-29 bombing raids on the Japanese Home Islands. Beginning in June 1944, a batch of Ki-61s were refitted and redesigned for this task, but they still proved incapable of meeting the demands of high-altitude interception. In November 1944, Kawasaki redesigned the model around a different power-plant, and the resulting Ki-100 prototype took to the air in February 1945. It saw combat as soon as production could be ordered. Although born of a rather abrupt design period, the Ki-100 quickly became a favorite among pilots and service crews alike for its ease of flight and maintenance. It was capable of downing B-29s and staving off American F6F Hellcats with equal aplomb, but the Japanese war machine proved capable of producing neither enough aircraft (fewer than 400 Ki-100s were manufactured) nor pilots to turn back the tide of the war. The key difference between the troublesome Ki-61 and the ever-more reliable Ki-100 lay in the designers' choice of power-plant. The Ki-100 featured the 1,500 hp Mitsubishi Ha-112-II 14 cylinder air-cooled radial, rather than the difficult-to-obtain and even more difficult-to-maintain liquid-cooled engines of the Ki-61. In dimensions, the two were virtually identical. The Ki-100 spanned 39 ft 4 in, was 28 ft 11 in long, with a wing area of slightly over 215 sq ft. It could climb to 16,405 ft in 6 minutes, and more than 32,000 ft in 20 minutes, possessed a range of between 870 and 1,367 miles, with a maximum speed of 360 mph and service ceiling in excess of 36,000 ft. With its speed, maneuverability, and other performance characteristics, and being armed with two 20 mm Ho-5 cannons on the fuselage and a single 12.7 mm machine gun on each wing, the Ki-100 was technologically one of the best aircraft in the skies at the end of the Pacific War; however, its introduction came far too late to make any substantive difference for the JAAF.

The Imperial Japanese Navy concentrated the bulk of their efforts on developing carrier- or sea-based aircraft, although they proved quite willing to learn from combat experiences. After the second flare-up in China, the navy decided to solicit designs for long-range heavy bombers. The new bombers were far more technologically advanced than any available escort, so in 1938 a set of specifications went to Nakajima and Mitsubishi for a three-man, twin-engine aircraft capable of a 2,300-plus mile range, and the agility of a dedicated air-superiority fighter. Nakajima's Katsuji Nakamura employed a low-wing monoplane design, with powerful new 1,100 hp Nakajima engines spinning their propellers in opposite directions. Although this unique innovation improved the plane's lateral stability, it both limited other aspects of its performance and made maintenance much more difficult. First flown in May 1941, the J1N Gekko ("Moonlight") was extremely impressive, but was defeated nonetheless in competitive trials by the superlative A6M2. The fighter model was stripped down, and its engines replaced with a more normal matched pair and in July 1942 it was adopted for production as a long-range reconnaissance aircraft. After only a few months of combat service, a field commander named Yasuna Kozono determined that the aircraft's still-impressive agility, speed, and range would make it an ideal night-fighter with the proper modifications to its armament. After servicemen at Rabaul installed obliquely mounted cannons on a J1N, which was subsequently credited with two "kills" of American B-24 Liberators, the navy reissued orders to Nakajima to accommodate this design change. Of the 479 total J1Ns produced through December 1944, approximately 420 were of this type (designated J1N1-S). In this configuration, the "Irving" (as the Allies called it) carried a two-man crew in tandem enclosed seating, was powered by twin 1,130 hp Nakajima NK1F Sakae 21 radials, and featured twin 20 mm Type 99 Model 1 obliquely mounted, upward-firing cannons, as well twin cannons mounted on the belly, which were downward-firing. It spanned 55 ft 8 in, with length of 39 ft 11 in, height of 14 ft 11 in, and wing area of 430.5 sq ft. The Gekko was capable of a top speed in excess of 315 mph, and featured a climb rate of 16,405 ft in approximately 9 minutes 30 seconds and range of between 1,600 and 2,300 miles. As with many Japanese aircraft, the J1N in all its various configurations ended the war as a kamikaze suicide vessel, for which purpose it was loaded with two 551 lb bombs that were rigged to detonate on impact.

There were a number of highly innovative Japanese designs in the closing months of the war. These designs included among many others the long-range escort Ki-83 (Mitsubishi), the rocket-powered high-altitude interceptor J8M Shusui ("Sword Stroke," Mitsubishi), and the extremely "modern" looking J7W Shinden ("Magnificent Lighting," Kyushu) with its dramatically swept wings, canard configuration, and plans for a turbojet power plant. None of these impacted the course of the war, however, as they came too late and suffered crippling production delays and technology losses as Allied bombing took its ruthlessly effective toll on the Japanese Home Islands.

Soviet Fighter and Attack Aircraft

Although the Treaty of Rapallo provided Germany with a means for bypassing the arms limitations of the Treaty of Versailles, it gave much needed technological expertise to the Soviet Union as they rebuilt an air force that had been physically and intellectually decimated by the Civil War and various Communist-directed purges. Throughout the interwar period, however, Soviet projects gradually achieved parity with German and other foreign aircraft, thanks in large part to the efforts of a collection of supremely talented designers. Under the leadership and vision of design bureaus from Polikarpov's to the Mikoyan-Gurevich partnership, the interwar and World War II years saw the VVS rise from a virtual nonentity (possessing only several hundred operable aircraft in the early 1920s) to an unquestioned world power by the close of the 1940s.

One of the early geniuses of Soviet design was Nikolai Polikarpov, who produced a model in the early 1930s that signaled the apex of the biplane era in Russian aviation history. Just the third prototype produced out of the Central Design Bureau (TsKB), Polikarpov's model featured a prominent, gull-shaped upper wing that gave rise to the aircraft's nickname, "Chaika" (Seagull). Test pilot V.P. Chkalov took the biplane through its first flight tests in October 1933, with production of the I-15 beginning the following year. Throughout the production period, from 1934 to 1937, I-15s featured a number of different power plant configurations. This was not at all uncommon for Soviet designs of this era, and indicates both the industrial disruption within the Soviet Union (the result of the First World War, followed by the Civil War) and the pace of technological advances in the 1930s. It was routine to employ them in a production series of aircraft as new engines became available, usually with mixed results. The first series of I-15s featured a single 480 hp M-22 (i.e., a license copy of the Wright Cyclone), and spanned nearly 32 ft, with length of 20 ft, and wing area of 235.74 sq ft. They could achieve a top speed approaching 200 mph, with a service ceiling of 24,500 ft, and were armed with twin 7.62 mm PV-1 in the nose along with underwing mounts for up to 88 lbs of bombs. There were approximately 1,020 of this type produced.

The next version, the I-15*bis*, featured the 750 hp M-25 V (also a license copy of the Wright Cyclone), was slightly longer, wider by a foot, and with seven more square feet of wing area. Although heavier by almost 400 lbs, the I-15*bis* possessed improved performance, notably a top speed of 230 mph, increased climb rate, and a service ceiling up to 29,500 ft. Early models of this variant were armed similarly to the I-15 standard type, whereas later production aircraft featured a complement of four 7.62 mm ShKAS machine guns mounted in the nose. The I-15*bis* was also equipped to carry roughly 330 lbs in external weapons, generally a pair of 110 lb bombs. After initial deliveries in 1935, production of this model reached an estimated 2,700 copies.

A whole series of other revisions took place, mostly distinguished by engine type. There were approximately 3,450 I-15*ter* (also designated I-153) models delivered, and they differed from the previous models primarily by a more powerful engine. Total production of the I-15 line approximated 7,175 copies. The lasting allure of biplane fighters was due to their extreme maneuverability in dogfights, and in this regard the I-15 did not disappoint, seeing extensive combat action in the Spanish Civil War, over China during the second Sino-Japanese conflict, and during the Winter War phase of World War II. By the time of the German invasion, the technology of monoplane fighters had advanced to the point to where even an advanced and extremely agile biplane like the I-15 simply stood little chance against single-wing attackers. Losses quickly mounted, and I-15s that survived the initial German assault were retasked to close air support duties. Upon the arrival of the famed Il-2 "tank-killer," the I-15s were relegated to rear guard and training missions.

Even as modification and experimentation on his I-15 continued, Polikarpov turned his efforts toward designing a monoplane fighter; where the I-15 represented the apex of the biplane era in Russia, the Polikarpov I-16 represented the first Soviet foray into the modern fighter-plane era. This was the first movement in a collective effort in aviation innovation, and by the end of the Second World War these efforts would establish the Soviet Union as a world superpower whose air forces were challenged solely by those of the United States. The I-16 was initially produced of a mixed construction, a mostly wooden fuselage essentially built around the engine, with metal employed in fabricating the cantilevered single wing. The prototype featured a 480 hp M-22 engine, and successfully completed its first flight on December 31, 1933. Further testing generated a top speed of more than 270 mph. On the basis of such impressive performance characteristics the I-16 was ordered into production, making its public debut during the annual May Day flyover in 1935. No fewer than 30 different types of the I-16 were produced, distinguished by power plant and various more minor modifications. Approximately 278 I-16s participated in the Spanish Civil War, and the model saw far more extensive use at the hands of Soviet pilots facing Japanese invaders in China. The performances of these aircraft were so impressive that the I-16 became one of the most widely produced in the Soviet inventory; it is estimated that as many as six of every 10 Soviet fighters in 1941 were I-16s.

The two most numerous versions of the I-16 were types Type 10 and Type 24. The I-16 Type 10 was powered by the 750 hp Shvetsov M-25V radial engine, which afforded a top speed of nearly 280 mph and climb rate of 16,405 ft in 8 minutes 12 seconds, and possessed a service ceiling approaching 27,000 ft. It housed a single pilot in an enclosed cockpit, and spanned 29 ft 6 in, with length of 19 ft 2 in, height of 8 ft 5 in, and wing area of 156.51 sq ft. The Type 10 was armed with four 7.62 mm ShKAS machine guns, two in the nose and one mounted in each wing. The Type 24 featured a 1,100 hp Shvetsov M-63 radial, increasing maximum speed to more than 300 mph, service ceiling to 35,500 ft, and reducing the time to 16,405 ft by half; physical dimensions of the types were virtually identical. The Type 24 was better armed, often with two 20 mm ShVAK cannons replacing the wing-mounted machine guns, or alternately the inclusion of a 12.7 mm Beresin BS machine gun in the nose. This model was also fitted for up to 1,100 lbs of bombs, up to six RS-82 rockets for close air support missions, or both. An estimated 9,000 copies of the I-16 in all its various configurations were produced into the early 1940s. Although the initial production run ended prior to the Second World War, the

German invasion in 1941 led to the resumption of its production. Even though the design was rather obsolete by that time, it was easy to produce (especially due to its nonreliance on strategic materials) and served as a stop-gap for the VVS during the worst days of the war. In symbolic value, the I-16 is far more important to the history of Soviet aviation than its war record might otherwise suggest; indeed, it was in a Polikarpov I-16 that the famous Alexander Ivanovich Pokryshkin cut his combat teeth. Pokryshkin was the only figure thrice awarded Hero of the Soviet Union during the Great Patriotic War, and was their second leading combat ace of the war, with 59 confirmed kills in various aircraft, including I-16s, Mikoyan-Gurevich MiG-3s, Lavochkin La-5s and −7s, and American-provided P-39 Airacobras. Pokryshkin's dogfighting strategies heavily influenced a generation of Soviet pilots and tacticians.

The LaGG-1 followed a similar course in terms of its development and production as the I-16. Like Ilyushin's, the cooperative project of Semyon Lavochkin, Vladimir Gorbunov, and Mikhail Gudkov was designed of a mixed wood-metal composition, and its fuselage was built around its engine (in this case, the 1,240 hp Klimov M-105 12 cylinder liquid-cooled engine). The LaGG-1 spanned 32 ft 1 in, with length of 28 ft 10 in, height of 14 ft 5 in, and wing area of approximately 188 sq ft. Its first test flight took place on March 30, 1939, and after positive reviews a group of LaGG-1s were produced and sent to combat units for evaluation. The aircraft was rated for 377 mph, though crews reported that they seldom achieved that speed, and its range was severely limited at less than 350 miles. It was sluggish in the air, and difficult to maintain on the ground. Those who flew it, and survived it, claimed that the LaGG acronym actually stood for "Lakirovannii Garantirovannii Grob," or, "Varnished Guaranteed Coffin."

Following these rather ignominious reviews, the LaGG design team systematically overhauled the aircraft's design. Within a few months they produced the LaGG-3, which entered production in 1940 and was first delivered to combat units in early 1941. It differed from its predecessor by several weight-reducing features, saving more than 600 lbs and thereby increasing the aircraft's in-flight handling and agility. Although its top speed was slightly less than what had been initially promised of the LaGG-1, the LaGG-3 was far more reliable. It also featured increased range (more than 400 miles) and an increased service ceiling (31,500 ft). In addition, the LaGG-3 featured improved armament, including a 20 mm ShVAK cannon and two 7.62 mm ShKAS machine guns. The aircraft could also be fitted to carry up to 440 lbs of bombs or six RS-82 rockets. Despite these enhancements, the

LaGG-3 was draped with the same disparaging acronym as its predecessor and was also referred to as the "mortician's mate." Some
sources blame shoddy and unreliable workmanship on the part of
Soviet production facilities, whereas others blame inadequate pilot
training. Between these factors, the LaGG-3 had few positive traits in
the opinions of its operators. The aircraft did prove capable of sustaining considerable abuse from ground crews and enemy fighters
alike while still remaining airworthy. Its most valuable trait, however,
was likely that it could be rather easily mass produced, and at least in
part, of nonstrategic materials. A total of 6,258 LaGG-3s were built
through mid-1942, although it would prove to be the least successful
of the trio of new fighters to enter the Soviet arsenal in 1940 (along-
side the Yak-1 and MiG-1).

The LaGG-3, Yakovlev Yak-1 and Yak-3, and high-speed bomber
Petlyakov Pe.2 all employed the Klimov M-105 engine, which was in
increasingly short supply as these new designs entered mass production. Thus, in 1941 the VVS requested in its new specifications that
design bureaus accommodate different power plants. This proved well-
timed for Lavochkin, who was still struggling at that time to solve the
problems common to the LaGG-3 design. It was determined that a
more powerful engine would likely solve most of these issues, and the
new M-82 14 cylinder air-cooled radial was chosen for this purpose.
Lavochkin married the engine to the LaGG-3 airframe, resulting in an
oddly shaped aircraft with an oversized nose (necessary for the larger
engine). It appeared as if the too-large M-82 had been force-fed into a
LaGG-3. Despite its somewhat misshapen appearance, the La-5 with
its 1,480 hp engine was a far more capable combat aircraft than was the
LaGG-3. Once the aircraft was adopted into production following its
March 1942 flight testing, the airframe was very slightly modified from
that of the LaGG-1 and LaGG-3 line. The La-5 spanned 32 ft 1 in,
with length of 28 ft 2 in, height of 8 ft 4 in, and wing area of 188 sq ft.
Although slightly heavier, the La-5 featured improved performance in
virtually all categories. Its top speed exceeded 405 mph, with a climb
rate of 3,280 ft per minute, and a service ceiling of 36,000 ft. These performance characteristics only improved upon the introduction of the
fuel-injected, 1,850 hp M-82FN power plant, leading to the production
of a variant designated La-5FN. The aircraft was armed with dual 20
mm ShVAK cannons in the nose, and could be fitted with four RS-82
rockets or two 220 lb bombs on external hardpoints. Far from the reputation of the LaGG-1 and LaGG-3, Lavochkin's La-5 earned him little but unabashed praise. Indeed, the La-5 was immediately the class
of the Soviet fighter contingent. In battle against the German work-

horse Messerschmitt BF-109, the La-5 (and especially the La-5FN) proved more than equal, and their introduction into the Eastern Front helped stem the tide of the German advance. It is estimated that more than 10,000 La-5s entered the Soviet arsenal by late 1944.

The final wartime product of Lavochkin's bureau was the high-altitude, high-speed interceptor La-7 and La-7UTI. This was a direct development of the La-5 series that adapted the model to dedicated high-altitude interception; however, it required a number of design modifications. For the La-7, Lavochkin chose much more metal alloy in construction (a luxury not afforded to designers earlier in the war). This lighter, stronger airframe proved far more aerodynamic than its predecessors, and although it was of essentially the same dimensions and powered by the exact same engine as the La-5FN, the La-7 was faster, with greater agility, range, and overall performance at high altitudes. Another important tactical decision involved replacing the dual 20 mm ShVAK cannons of the La-5FN with a trio of Beresin B-20 cannons, which actually decreased weight (and thus improved performance) while making the aircraft better armed. There were approximately 5,753 La-7s built in the relatively short period from early 1944 through the end of the war.

The combat capabilities of the La-7 were unmatched by any other Soviet aircraft of the World War II era. Ivan Kozhedub, the leading Soviet World War II fighter ace with 62 confirmed kills and twice Hero of the Soviet Union, was an ardent patron of Lavochkin aircraft of all types. A majority of his kills came at the controls of La-5s, but roughly one third came thanks to what he considered to be the superlative performance of the La-7. Indeed, he succeeded in downing a German Messerschmitt Me-262 jet-powered fighter on February 19, 1945, in a La-7. One squadron recorded more than 50 kills with La-7s in their first month of service. Some Soviet records claim for the La-7 a staggering 30 to 1 kill-to-loss ratio throughout the war. The La-7 was arguably the most technologically advanced prop-driven aircraft in the Soviet arsenal, perhaps in the world, and was only made obsolete by the onset of the jet age.

Alexander Yakovlev followed his fellow designer Semyon Lavochkin's lead and began a project to develop an air-superiority fighter in the late 1930s. The Yak-1 prototype first flew on January 13, 1940. Despite an accident that resulted in the destruction of the prototype during testing, the model entered production that same year. The Yak-1 endured many modifications over its production lifetime, with the two most numerous variants bearing the designation Yak-1B and Yak-1M. When pilots of Yak-1s began to complain of hampered sightlines, ground crews modified the cockpit canopy and reduced the height of the rear portion of the fuselage. These modifications were standardized into the Yak-1B. In the Yak-1 and Yak-1B the power plant consisted of a 1,050 hp Klimov M-105PA 12 cylinder liquid-cooled engine, which allowed for a maximum speed in excess of 335 mph, a service ceiling exceeding 32,800 ft, and standard range of 435 miles. The model spanned 32 ft 10 in, with length of 27 ft 9 in, height of 8 ft 8 in, and wing area of approximately 184.61 sq feet. The single pilot sat in an enclosed cockpit, and controlled a single 20 mm ShVAK cannon in a nose mount and a 12.7 mm UBS machine gun mounted in the fuselage; additional weaponry occasionally consisted of up to 440 lbs of bombs or six RS-82 rockets on underwing mounts. All models featured retractable landing gear. The Yak-1M featured slightly modified, more tapered wings, and was powered by the 1,260 hp M-105PF engine. The overall weight was reduced by more than 500 lbs, allowing for a maximum speed in excess of 360 mph and increased range. This model also made use of self-sealing technology with fuel tanks, greatly increasing its capacity for absorbing damage without being lost.

The Yak-1 model remained in production through the end of the war, with the total of all variants numbering approximately 8,721. In battle, the Yak-1 earned high praise for its performance and reliability, garnering Yakovlev himself a great deal of respect and admiration. Its speed, endurance, and resiliency made it an ideal fighter escort for Il-2 Shturmovik "tank-busters," and its wide use in this role meant that it necessarily saw a great deal of combat action as an air-superiority fighter. It seldom disappointed, and was considered by many German pilots to be worth avoiding in a dogfight. A Yak-1 scored the first "kill" over Moscow, and was the aircraft of a number of Soviet fighter-pilot legends. Included among this group are two very noteworthy female pilots. Lilya Vladimirovna Litvyak flew a Yak-1, with a white lily painted on her cockpit window, to 12 confirmed kills. Misapprehension of the flower led to her nickname, "The White Rose of Stalingrad." The Yak-1 was also flown by Valeria Ivanova Khomyakova, who, on September 3, 1942, downed a German Junkers Ju-88, thus becoming the first woman with a confirmed combat kill. In the early years of the Great Patriotic War, before the La-5 was made available, the Yak-1 served as the stalwart of the Soviet fighter forces. It is estimated that perhaps as many as 20 percent of all aircraft engaged in the defense of Moscow were Yak-1s.

Despite the success of his first production model, Yakovlev almost immediately turned his attention to developing better, even more modern aircraft. His next design in numeric sequence (the Yak-3) suffered numerous technological setbacks, and did not appear in the field until 1943. Considering these aircraft in a more chronological order, Yakovlev's next entry into the Soviet VVS was the Yak-7. It was intended to fill a need for a two-seat cooperation trainer and auxiliary aircraft. After highly successful flight testing in early 1941, however, it was determined that the design would better serve Soviet needs by being converted to a single-seat fighter. In a three-year production run, ending in late 1943, approximately 6,400 Yak-7s were delivered to combat units. Approximately 1,400 of this number were two-seat versions used for liaison, training, and light transport duties, especially because they could be modified to land in remote regions of the northern Soviet Union via adapted, ski-type landing gear. The vast majority, however, were of the Yak-1B fighter variant. It was powered by the popular M-105 engine, which thanks to the aircraft's relatively light weight afforded a top speed in excess of 400 mph and service ceiling of more than 35,000 ft, with range of approximately 560 miles. The model spanned 33 ft 7 in, with length of 27 ft 10 in, height of 7 ft 11 in, and wing area of 159.53 sq feet. Most were armed with a single 20 mm ShVAK cannon and two 12.7 mm UBS machine guns. It was often mistaken in combat by attackers for being a Yak-1, usually resulting in an unpleasant dogfight with the superior-performing Yak-7.

The ultimate development of the Yak-1 series came in mid-1942 with the introduction of the Yak-9. Although it was otherwise similar to the Yak-7, the Yak-9 employed metal alloy construction of the wing spars, and shifted the cockpit a few inches aft. These and other more minor modifications decreased the aircraft's weight, improved its balance during flight, and streamlined its aerodynamic profile. Yak-9s were of slightly varying dimension than their predecessors, spanning 32 ft 10 in, with length of 24 ft 11 in, height of 9 ft 10 in, and wing area of approximately 184 sq feet. Like the other Yakovlev aircraft in this series, they were powered by the Klimov M-105 engine, which provided a top speed of approximately 370 mph, service ceiling of 33,00 ft, and standard range of 825 miles. The Yak-9 was armed with a single 20 mm ShVAK cannon and twin 12.7 mm UBS machine guns. It also possessed external hardpoints for two 220 lb bombs, and a variant was produced in small numbers that employed an internal bomb bay with the capacity for accommodating 880 lbs of payload. More Yak-9s were built in the latter stages of the war than any other VVS fighter. An estimated 14,579 were produced through 1945, although production continued through the remainder of the decade. Several Soviet-bloc countries used Yak-9s in their air forces in the postwar era, bringing the total produced during its production run to approximately 16,769 copies.

Yakovlev's final entrant into the VVS during the Second World War was the Yak-3. Although this project originated in 1941 as part of the Soviet push for weaning design bureaus off the M-105 power plant, various production delays and the lack of a suitable substitute engine meant that the Yak-3 did not fly for the first time until 1943, and was not delivered to combat units until late 1943 and early 1944. It was extremely lightweight, with an empty weight of just 4,960 lbs; this translated to exceptional agility in flight. High-end performance was expected with the use of the VK-107 engine, but designers eventually employed the venerable -105 instead. With the aircraft's slim profile, spanning 30 ft 2 in, with length of 27 ft 10 in, height of 7 ft 10 in, and wing area of 159.53 ft, and slight weight, the power plant produced some impressive performance figures. The Yak-3 possessed a top speed in excess of 400 mph, along with a service ceiling exceeding 35,400 ft, and range of 500-plus miles. The model was armed with what came to be the standard Yakovlev consignment of a single 20 mm ShVAK cannon, and dual 12.7 mm UBS machine guns. It excelled in low-level combat, reportedly leading to a Luftwaffe tactical doctrine of retreat, rather than engagement, if a Yak-3 was encountered at altitudes less than 13,000 ft. It proved a formidable fighter-plane, although it was produced in relatively few numbers (4,848). If it had not experienced frustrating delays in production schedule and the lack of availability of the power plant intended for it, the Yak-3 would likely have been an integral part of the Soviet airwar effort.

As part of the move away from overreliance on the Klimov M-105 engine, as also seen in the development of the Lavochkin La-5 and the proposed design of the Yak-3, the VVS called for competitive trials for an interceptor fighter designed around the 1,350 hp Mikulin AM-37 12 cylinder liquid-cooled engine. Nikolai Polikarpov, with his vast experience in the field, looked to be the certain winner until Stalin had him thrown into the gulag. This shocking development opened the field for a partnership between two relatively inexperienced designers, whose cooperation forged a designation soon synonymous with Soviet air power (Artem Mikoyan and Mikhail Gurevich, or, MiG). Their first design, the MiG-1, completed its maiden test flight on April 5, 1940, albeit with the AM-35 engine due to the unavailability of the more powerful AM-37. Undeterred, the design team produced a machine that was the very picture of a modern, low-wing monoplane fighter, one that fell short of hoped-for performance characteristics, yet still reportedly shattered Soviet speed records. It possessed a maximum speed of more than 400 mph, range of 360 miles, and service ceiling of 39,000 ft. These were impressive numbers, but less than expected. The MiG-1 spanned 33 ft 5 in, with length of 26 ft 9 in, height of 8 ft 7 in, and wing area of approximately 188 sq feet. Its size and weight produced sluggish turn rates, and pilots found spins and stalls were too easily induced by the aircraft's in-flight characteristics. Lacking much anything notably beyond its speed (even its armament was a rather standard setup of a single 12.7 mm UBS and dual 7.62 ShKAS machine guns), and with concerns about the aircraft's handling mounting with each passing flight of the approximately 100 MiG-1s produced, its creators decided to engage in a complete and radical overhaul of the model.

The promise of the MiG-1 netted Mikoyan and Gurevich their own design bureau, which they put to work in 1941 redesigning their seminal work. Out of this effort came the MiG-3, which in some ways was a variant of the MiG-1, yet was so dramatically renovated as to be designated separately. Structural modifications included a substantial increase in the dihedral curvature of the wings, and a redistribution of weight along the fuselage so as to improve the aircraft's in-flight stability and increase its agility. The MiG-3 shared the same wingspan and wing area as its predecessor, with slightly less length (27 ft 1 in) and greater height (11 ft 6 in). Powered by the same engine, the MiG-3 also shared similar performance characteristics (top speed, service ceiling, and range), as well as standard armament as the MiG-1; however, the structural modifications greatly improved the MiG-3's performance at high altitudes; unfortunately, it saw most of its combat at lower levels, which constrained its capabilities and usefulness, especially against enemy fighters specifically designed for low-level dogfighting. Aside from being easily mass-produced, a great necessity as the German invasion began to take its toll on Soviet production capacity, the MiG-1 and MiG-3 were themselves of little consequence in Soviet aviation history; however, both models helped propel the VVS into the modern fighter-plane era, setting the stage for far more technologically advanced efforts in the future. In the postwar age, many of the Soviet Union's most sophisticated and recognizable aircraft would bear the MiG prefix.

In addition to its own indigenous designs, the Soviet Union relied heavily on Lend-Lease aircraft as stop-gap measures during the war. One of the most important of the Lend-Lease aircraft was the American Bell P-63 Kingcobra, an improved version of the P-39 Airacobra. The P-63's prototype first flew exactly one year after the Japanese attack on Pearl Harbor, and orders were exported beginning the following year. Of the 3,300 produced, 2,421 went to the Soviet Union.

Minor Powers: Fighter and Attack Aircraft

Lacking the infrastructure to build their own aircraft, most small countries relied exclusively on imported aircraft to provide their fighters, which generally resulted in them obtaining fighters that were already becoming obsolete or that had been rejected for service in their country of origin. Those countries that did have sufficient capacity to produce fighters often lacked the technical expertise to develop their own designs and therefore entered into contracts that allowed them to manufacture design-built fighters. A few small nations, however, were able to manufacture and develop their aircraft. The most important of these were the Netherlands, the homeland of Anthony Fokker, who had designed some of the best German fighters in World War I; Australia, which had the advantage of being a member of the British Empire; Poland; Czechoslovakia; and Romania.

Having left Germany and returned to the Netherlands following the end of the First World War, Fokker introduced one of the most widely exported aircraft of the interwar period with the Fokker C V in 1924. The key to its success was that it could be fitted with any number of engine types. As was the case with his World War I–era aircraft, the CV featured steel tube construction, fabric covering, and wooden wings. It had a wingspan of 41 ft, a length of 31 ft 2 in, and a loaded weight of 4,079 lbs. Its most popular engine was the 336 hp Hispano-Suiza liquid-cooled inline, which provided a top speed of 140 mph, service ceiling of 18,045 ft, and range of 478 miles. Its two 7.92 mm synchronized machine guns provided excellent protection for its day, and it could also carry up to 441 lbs of bombs under its wings, making it both an effective fighter and light-bomber. More than 400 were produced in the Netherlands and many were still in service in the Dutch Air Force when Nazi Germany attacked it in May 1940.

Another popular Fokker fighter was the D XXI low-wing monoplane fighter. It was introduced in 1938, and its only modern feature was an enclosed canopy. It still used steel tube and fabric construction and wooden wings. More important, its undercarriage could not be retracted. Despite these deficiencies, the D XXI was easy to build and relatively inexpensive. It had a wingspan of 36 ft 1 in, a length of 26 ft 10 in, and a loaded weight of 4,519 lbs. Its 830 hp Bristol Mercury VIII radial engine gave it a top speed of 286 mph, service ceiling of 36,090 ft, and range of 590 miles. Even though it was underpowered and underarmed with four 7.92 mm machine guns, it nevertheless enjoyed brief success against unescorted Junkers Ju 52/3 transports on May

10, 1940. It was no match for the Messerschmitt BF-109, however. Approximately 150 were built in the Netherlands and Finland.

The Fokker G 1 was a far more successful aircraft than the D XXI and provided service as a fighter and light-bomber. Using a twin-engine figuration and twin-booms, it had a wingspan of 56 ft 3 in, a length of 37 ft 9 in, and a loaded weight of 10,582 lbs. Its two 830 hp Bristol Mercury VIII radial engines provided a maximum speed of 295 mph, service ceiling of 30,500 ft, and range of 870 miles. The G 1 was well defended with eight 7.92 mm machine guns in the nose and one 7.92 mm machine gun for the tailgunner. It could also carry up to 882 lbs of bombs. Like other Fokker aircraft, it relied upon steel tube, fabric, and wooden wing construction. The majority of the 23 G 1s in Dutch service on May 10, 1940, were destroyed on the ground.

Having relied upon imported aircraft for its air force, in 1931 the Polish National Aircraft Company (PZL) had introduced its first native fighter, a high, gull-winged fighter, which was followed in 1933 by the PZL P7. Further modifications resulted in the introduction of the outstanding PZL P 11 in 1935, which provided the Polish Air Force with the world's first all-metal fighter force. With a wingspan of 35 ft 2 in, a length of 24 ft 9 in, and a loaded weight of 3,968 lbs, it was ruggedly constructed, with stressed metal skin, and a rounded streamlined fuselage. Its 645 hp Bristol Mercury VIS radial engine provided a maximum speed of 242 mph, a service ceiling of 26,250 ft, and a range of 435 miles. Armed with two 7.92 mm machine guns, it was fast, highly maneuverable, and perhaps the world's best fighter at the time. It was unfortunate for Poland, however, that it was soon surpassed by low-wing monoplanes with retractable undercarriages. Although Polish pilots flying the PZL P 11 would shoot down 124 German aircraft while losing just 114 P 11s, the Poles had only produced 258 P 11s. Sheer force of number and fighters like the Messerschmitt BF-109 overwhelmed the P 11, and within two weeks it ceased to provide more than nuisance resistance.

Czechoslovakia had produced its first fighter in 1924, with the Avia BH 21 biplane, of which 120 were produced between 1924 and 1931. Although it was not as advanced as fighters produced by major powers, it gave the Czechs valuable technical experience, which would lead to the Avia B 534 in 1934. The B 534's steel-spar, fabric-covered construction, enclosed canopy, and 850 hp Hispano-Suizo 12Ydrs liquid-cooled engine provided the Czechoslovakian Air Force with one of the fastest, most maneuverable biplane fighters ever produced. It had a top speed of 245 mph, ceiling of 34,875 ft, and range of 360 miles. In addition, it was armed with four 7.62 mm machine guns mounted on the fuselage. At the Zurich International Flying Meet in 1937, it was surpassed only by the Messerschmitt BF-109 monoplane. Had the British and French not succumbed to Hitler's threats at Munich, the Avia B 534 would have been capable of providing credible resistance to the Luftwaffe. Instead, the 446 that had been constructed ended up in service with the Luftwaffe as trainers or with the Nazi-allied Slovak Air Force.

Desperate for fighters in World War II, the Australian government turned to the Commonwealth Aircraft Corporation to help fill the need. In 1943 it introduced the CA 12 Boomerang, which proved to be a rugged, agile aircraft, particularly useful in strafing operations. Similar to the Wirraway, Australia's first indigenous warplane, the Boomerang featured a low-wing, monoplane design, retractable undercarriage, and enclosed cockpit. It had a wingspan of 36 ft 3 in, length of 25 ft 6 in, and loaded weight of 7,600, and its 1,200 hp Pratt & Whitney R-1830 Twin Wasp radial engine provided a 296 mph top speed, 29,000 ft service ceiling, and 930-mile range. It was armed with four .303 caliber machine guns and two 20 mm cannon. A total of 250 were built by war's end.

Having produced licensed-built Polish fighters for the Romanian Air Force, Industria Aernautica Romania introduced its own fighter, the IAR 80, in 1939. A low-wing cantilever monoplane, it was quite remarkable in its performance and compared favorably with those being produced by major powers. It had a wingspan of 34 ft 6 in, a length of 29 ft 5 in, and a loaded weight of 5,489 lbs. Powered by a 1,025 hp IAR K 14–1000 radial, it had a maximum speed of 342 mph, a service ceiling of 34,450 ft, and a range of 454 miles. Most were armed with four 7.92 mm and two 13.2 mm machine guns in the wings, though later versions, the IAR 80C and IAR 81, replaced the 13.2 mm machine guns with 20 mm cannon. A total of 461 were produced between 1939 and 1943, with most seeing service on the Russian Front.

CHAPTER FOUR

Bomber Aircraft

As was the case with fighters, bomber design and use underwent dramatic changes over the course of World War II. The results certainly vindicated many claims of prewar air power theorists because strategic bombing of Germany undeniably contributed to Allied victory. Moreover, heavy bombers delivered the atomic weapons that directly led to Japan's immediate capitulation. Nevertheless, air power theorists dramatically overestimated the role bombers would play in this conflict; they were neither the difference-makers nor insignificant, but somewhere between. The nations that entered World War II overly reliant on merely one type of bomber (the German fixation on dive-bombers) ultimately regretted their inability to deploy different airframes for different missions. The United States and Great Britain boasted the most versatile bomber fleets, and ultimately demonstrated the utility of long-range heavy bombers even if they were not the amazing weapon of the theorists' dreams. Indeed, the Cold War that followed this world war featured a race to develop the best strategic bombers to deliver the newest, and most frightening, atomic and nuclear weapons. By failing to develop an indigenous long-range bomber during World War II, the Soviet Union would later begin the Cold War at a distinct disadvantage.

American Bombers

In contrast to the USAAC's fighter inventory, there were actually a number of capable American bombers in combat units at the onset of the Second World War. This is thanks in no small part to the influence of men like General William "Billy" Mitchell, and other proponents of strategic bombing. The focused efforts of the American aviation industry would ultimately produce some of the more memorable aircraft of the era in preparation for the time when the American bomber corps would be recognized as the world's most technologically advanced. Indeed, it would be an American bomber, the B-29 *Enola Gay*, that brought the first—and along with its cousin *Bockscar*, still the only— use of atomic technology in war. This was an extensive process, however, that long predates August 1945.

Even before the end of the First World War, the U.S. Army began investigating the utility of multiengine bomber designs. For example, as early as 1917 the Glenn L. Martin Company was solicited to develop a twin-engine bomber. It produced the prototype MB-1 in August 1918, but continued tinkering with the design. The following year, modifications to the initial design produced the MB-2, which entered service in 1920 as the U.S. Army Air Corps's first heavy bomber. It featured a wingspan of 74 ft, length of 42 ft 8 in, and height of 14 ft 8 in, the biplane bomber carried a crew of four, a 3,000 lb bomb load, and was armed with four .30 caliber defensive machine guns. The MB-2 possessed a maximum speed of 100 mph and operating ceiling of 8,500 ft, made capable by its dual 420 hp Liberty 12 vee-type engines. The bomber had a maximum range of approximately 560 miles. The MB-2 was less significant for its combat record—in fact it had none of which to speak—than it was for its role in advancing American tactical doctrines. On July 21, 1921, then-Brigadier General Billy Mitchell led a flight of six MB-2s in a bombing run on the prize dreadnought *Ostfriesland*. Their success in sinking the massive ship helped propel both the navy and army to see the promise of bombers in military strategies, although Mitchell's own impetuousness in pushing for an independent air service would eventually cost him his rank and make him a pariah within the military command.

The success of the MB-2 led the military to secure more multiengine bomber designs in the coming years. The Keystone Aircraft Company offered a design in 1925 that after a series of revisions would become the B-3A light bomber (itself introduced in 1930). The B-3A was a sturdy and safe, if obsolete in design, biplane with wingspan of 74 ft 9 in, length of 48 ft 10 in, and height of 17 ft 2 in. Powered by two 575 hp Pratt & Whitney Hornet radial engines, the aircraft could achieve a top speed of 121 mph, and possessed a service ceiling of 14,100 ft and maximum range of 855 miles. Its defensive armament consisted of three Browning machine guns; offensively, the B-3A could carry a

2,500 lb maximum bomb load. Although a few copies were still in service at the outbreak of World War II, none saw combat action. There were approximately 200 copies of this model, and it was the mainstay of the American bomber fleet until the arrival of the Martin B-10.

On its introduction in 1932, the B-10 was immediately the class of the USAAC's bomber inventory, and it is widely considered the Air Corps's first truly modern design of the class. The monoplane spanned 70 ft 6 in, length of 44 ft 9 in, and height of 15 ft 5 in. Powered by twin 775 hp Wright Cyclone R-1820 engines, the B-10 possessed an astonishing top speed in excess of 210 mph, greater than all but the most advanced fighters of the time. Along with a service ceiling of 24,400 ft and maximum operational range of more than 1,200 miles, the B-10 was a mightily impressive aircraft. In addition to a bomb load of 2,200 lbs carried in an internal bay, the B-10 featured a rotating gun turret for one of its three .30 caliber machine guns. In addition to a domestic production run of 152 copies, the model was popular as an export, with 190 copies serving with various foreign air forces. It was as important for its design innovations as it was for its role in furthering American bomber doctrines; in this regard, its place in American aviation history is not unlike that of the MB-2. Building on the operational principles demonstrated by Mitchell and his MB-2s, Colonel Henry "Hap" Arnold piloted the lead of a group of ten B-10s on a roughly 8,000 mile round-trip flight from Washington, D.C., to Fairbanks, Alaska. Mitchell proved bombers capable of sinking "unsinkable" ships, and Arnold had now showed them to be capable of undertaking long-range strategic bombing runs.

The most numerically important bomber by far in the American arsenal during the interwar years was the Douglas B-18 Bolo, one of the models that replaced the B-10 as the USAAC bomber group's standard-bearer. (The other model to in part replace the B-10 was the Northrop A-17 Nomad, which was discussed in Chapter 3.) A development of its popular and successful civilian DC-2 model, the Douglas B-18 won a 1934 open design competition, thanks in no small part to its cost-effectiveness as compared with its more expensive, although better performing, competitors from Boeing and Martin. In total, approximately 350 copies of the B-18 were purchased by the army beginning in 1936. The B-18 had a crew of six. The all-metal monoplane spanned 89 ft 6 in, with length of 57 ft 10 in, and height of 15 ft 2 in. Thanks to its power plant, twin 1,000 hp Wright R-1820-53 engines, the Bolo could achieve a top speed of 215 mph, service ceiling of nearly 24,000 ft, and range of 1,180 miles. The model was deemed obsolete after suffering heavy losses on the ground during the

Japanese attack on Pearl Harbor; however, approximately 40 B-18s were among the first group of aircraft redeployed as the Antilles Air Task Force, which was tasked with finding and destroying the German U-boats inflicting severe damage on American shipping in the Caribbean.

In September 1934, the Boeing Aircraft Company began a design process that would eventually produce one of the most famous American bombers of all time with the B-17 Flying Fortress. A massive, four-engine model flown by a 12-man crew, the heavy bomber was successfully pitched to the U.S. Congress as a coastal defense aircraft rather than the precision bomber it was truly designed to be. The USAAC ordered its first B-17s in 1935, but the aircraft was not ordered in quantity until the introduction of the F model. Beginning in May 1942, 3,405 B-17Fs were procured, with an additional 8,680 of the definitive G model from May 1943 through the end of the war. There was a total of more than 12,700 of all types produced for the USAAC. The G model spanned 103 ft 10 in, with length of 74 ft 4 in, and height of 19 ft 1 in. The airframe was frequently loaded far past its 65,500 lbs maximum recommended take-off weight, which resulted in substantially reduced range and maneuverability. The aircraft possessed an impressive maximum range of approximately 3,400 miles with standard loading, with a top speed in excess of 285 mph and service ceiling of 35,600 ft. To achieve these characteristics, the aircraft was powered by four 1,200 hp Wright Cyclone R-1820 radial engines. For defense the plane carried up to thirteen .50 caliber machine gun installations, including an innovative Bendix rotating ball turret on the plane's belly. Its offensive armament, the aircraft's chief raison d'être, featured a maximum 6,000 lb bomb load and a precision-accuracy Norden bombsight (whose precision in combat conditions generally left something to be desired). The B-17 was well-built and capable of sustaining almost unbelievable amounts of damage while remaining airborne. With its mindful use of such safety technologies as self-sealing fuel and oil tanks, the workmanlike B-17 proved invaluable for the USAAF throughout World War II.

Although a number of B-17s participated in the first American response in the Pacific after Pearl Harbor, their initial use was primarily over Europe. Despite its engineers' anticipations, the B-17 proved inefficient as a precision bomber, and the overloaded—and thus sluggishly handling—aircraft suffered heavy losses in raids against Ploesti (July 1943), Schweinfurt and Regensburg (August 1943), and Schweinfurt (October 1943). As a direct result, the USAAC largely abandoned precision bombing as a tactical doctrine for the remainder of the war, instead employing the B-17s and B-24 Liberators as carpet-bombers. The B-17 faced a similar doctrinal shift in the Pacific Theater, especially as demonstrated in the devastating fire-bombing of Tokyo (March 9–10, 1945) in which between 83,000 and 100,000 Japanese, mostly civilians, were killed.

Although it was perhaps a disappointment with regard to precision bombing, the B-17 did pave the way for other four-engine bomber models; from the Flying Fortress's earliest tests the USAAC recognized the strategic and tactical possibilities of heavy bombers, rather than employing only twin-engine medium bombers. In this vein, the Air Corps in 1939 solicited designs on a long-range heavy bomber, using the B-17 as a baseline for performance, range, and payload. Consolidated's B-24 Liberator model proved the best entry, and its reputation for excellence is borne out in its production numbers. With approximately 19,256 copies produced, the B-24 outnumbers any other American combat aircraft model of the war era. The introduction of several technological advancements enabled the B-24 to carry a greater payload, faster and farther, than did the B-17. The Liberator used a high-aspect ratio wing designed by David R. Davis, a far more efficient and aerodynamic element than the B-17's. It is also notable for its use of a tricycle landing gear, and its especially distinctive twin rudders. Powered by four 1,200 hp Pratt & Whitney R-1830 radials, these features allowed the B-24 to achieve remarkable performance benchmarks, such as a 303 mph maximum speed and 3,700 mile range, all while carrying up to 8,000 lbs of bombs.

Despite this, the model was generally viewed with great skepticism when it arrived at units for the first time. Pilots unaware of its superb in-flight capabilities regarded it as an ugly duckling, the "crate the B-17 came in." Although there are significantly fewer stories of Liberators than of Flying Fortresses sustaining incredible amounts of damage while still returning crews safely to base, the B-24 was in fact marginally safer for her 10-man crew than her more aesthetically pleasing predecessor; casualty rates for B-17 crews over the course of the war slightly outpaced those for B-24 crews. Spanning 110 ft, with length of 66 ft 4 in, and height of 17 ft 11 in, the model was defended by up to ten .50 caliber machine guns. It still proved to be susceptible to the more advanced German fighters as well as to heavy flak; roughly 20 percent of the B-24s tasked to the raid on Ploesti (August 1943) were lost to enemy fire. Despite isolated instances of such heavy losses, the B-24 Liberator served with aplomb in all theaters. Its bomb-load was especially suited to carpet-bombing missions over Europe, whereas its superlative range, which could be extended an additional 1,000 miles with the use of external drop tanks, made it ideal for long-range bombing runs over the Pacific and for the anti-submarine campaign in the Atlantic.

The B-25 "Mitchell" proved that despite the success of the B-17 (and future success of the B-24), the USAAC remained committed to the tactical usefulness of the twin-engine, medium bomber concept. Solicited in 1938 as a replacement for the outmoded medium bombers then in the Army's inventory, the North American Aircraft Company's distinctive twin-rudder model eventually became one of the most famous of all the American bombers. First flown in January 1939, the prototype possessed a wingspan of 67 ft 7 in, length of 54 ft 1 in, and height of 15 ft 9 in. Powered by twin 1,700 hp Wright R-2600 radials, the model achieved a top speed of 284 mph, range of approximately 1,500 miles, and service ceiling of 27,000 ft. In addition to her six-man crew, the B-25 carried as many as twelve .50 caliber machine guns mounted throughout the fuselage, and a maximum 4,000 lb bomb load in internal bays. With impressive performance and a reputation for ease-of-maintenance, the B-25 became a popular Lend-Lease aircraft in the early days of the Second World War. Its most famous use, however, came at the hands of the intrepid Colonel James Doolittle. In April 1942, a flight of 16 B-25s were led off the decks of the aircraft carrier *Hornet* by Colonel Doolittle himself in a daring one-way raid on Tokyo. Although the actual damage inflicted on the Japanese Home Islands was rather negligible, the "Doolittle Raid" proved to be a dramatic turning-point in terms of American morale in the Pacific Theater. It seems only appropriate that Doolittle's tactically innovative long-range bombing raid launched off the deck of an aircraft carrier featured bombers named after the first great American airpower pioneer, Brigadier General Billy Mitchell.

A far less successful model, at least initially, was the Martin B-26. The Glenn L. Martin Company pitched such a convincing case to the USAAC that this model was ordered into production despite the absence of a flying prototype. This proved rather dangerous for the pilots first tasked to the aircraft. Because they had little understanding of the plane's capabilities and in-flight characteristics, a number of crewmembers perished in training accidents, especially common on landing. Thus, the model's early, and decidedly unofficial, nickname was "Widowmaker." After a design modification increased the aircraft's wingspan for better stability on landing approach, the model's British-given moniker of Marauder stuck. Following this redesign, the B-26 spanned 71 feet, with length of 58 ft 6 in, and height of 20 ft 3 in. Carrying a crew of seven, the Marauder carried up to twelve .50

caliber machine guns and a maximum bomb load of 4,000 lbs. Some versions were fitted with torpedo racks, which made this model unique among American bombers. Its dual 2,000 hp Pratt & Whitney R-2800 radials afforded a maximum speed of 285 mph, with range of 1,100 miles and service ceiling of 19,800 ft. Once crews became more knowledgeable about the aircraft's inflight temperament, the B-26 became an impressively safe aircraft; in fact, despite its rather dubious beginnings, the model maintained a combat loss rate of less than 0.5 percent throughout the war. The Marauder, which also saw service at the hands of many foreign nations, served quite capably along with the B-25 Mitchell as the USAAC's primary medium bombers of the war. A total of 5,266 copies were produced through the end of the war.

The Boeing B-29 Superfortress is a model of which the names of two particular planes are more recognizable than the model itself, because the B-29s *Enola Gay* and *Bockscar* were used to drop atomic weapons on Hiroshima and Nagasaki in August 1945. Although this particular use was not the purpose for the B-29's creation, the model was the only aircraft in the American inventory with a bomb bay large enough to accommodate the atomic weapons. This notwithstanding, the B-29 was the most technologically advanced bomber of the Second World War, featuring such innovations as pressurized cabins for its ten crewmembers. Along with its four 2,200 hp Wright Cyclone R-3350 radial engines (themselves the site of another innovation; namely, the use of dual superchargers on each engine), the model was able to fly at heights up to 33,600 ft, at speeds in excess of 355 mph, and ranges of up to 3,250 miles. Its wingspan was 141 ft 3 in, with length of 99 ft, and height of 29 ft 7 in. The model featured twelve .50 caliber machine guns (a normal outfitting) and an unheard-of 20,000 lb maximum bomb load. Although the USAAF eagerly awaited its combat-readiness for this reason, a frustratingly long two-year development period followed the B-29's first test flight in September 1942. By the time it became operational, the aircraft's range and the pressing need for a long-range heavy bomber in the Pacific Theater directed it there only. Beginning in late 1944, B-29s raided Japanese cities from bases in China. When the United States secured the Mariana Islands in October, B-29s had yet another base for raids on the Home Islands. As discovered in Europe with the B-17s, high-altitude precision bombing was simply not as effective as low-level carpet-bombing. Thus, General Curtis E. LeMay, future head of the Strategic Air Command, redirected B-29s for use as night-time, low-level carpet bombers. They performed this duty with devastating and ruthless effectiveness, especially when loaded with incendiary bombs. By war's end, a total of

3,960 B-29s of all types were produced, with most remaining in service well into the 1950s.

As proudly noted by its manufacturers, the Douglas A/B-26 Invader bears the distinction of being the only American bomber to fly missions in World War II, Korea, and Vietnam. The A/B-26, which was first flown on July 10, 1942, was intended as a replacement for the North American B-25 Mitchell. Instead of dedicated use as a midlevel medium bomber, the A/B-26 served primarily in the "attack" role as a ground-support aircraft upon its combat entry in 1944. For this it was fitted with fourteen 5-inch rockets and eight .50 caliber machine guns. When it was used as a medium bomber, the Invader carried up to 5,000 lbs of bombs. It spanned 70 ft, with length of 50 ft, and height of 18 ft 6 in. Twin 2,000 hp Pratt & Whitney R-2800 radial engines carried a three-man crew at speeds of up to 355 mph; the aircraft also featured a service ceiling of 22,100 ft, and range of 1,400 miles. The USAAF was quite impressed with its performance capabilities and intrigued with its potential as a dual-use attack/bomber, so it quickly ordered more than 2,500 of the aircraft. There were approximately 2,450 delivered by the end of the war. Due in part to their primary use as close-air-support aircraft, the model suffered fewer combat losses than any other bomber in the USAAF inventory during World War II.

The Consolidated B-32 Dominator was on the other end of the spectrum, both in terms of service time and service record. The B-32 was excessively complex, and was the presumed successor to the B-24 based on a faulty concept (USAAC calls for an oversized, "hemispheric" defense bomber). Consolidated began work on the concept aircraft in 1939, but a prototype of the 11,500 lb (normal loading) aircraft did not successfully take to the skies until September 1942. The model spanned 135 ft, with length of 83 ft 1 in, and height of 32 ft 9 in. Four 2,300 hp Wright Cyclone R-3350 radial engines were needed to power the massive aircraft at approximately 360 mph (maximum speed), at heights up to 35,000 ft, and distances up to 800 miles. Its contingent of twelve .50 caliber machine guns were mounted in five powered turrets, and the eight-man crew was carried in a pressurized cabin; however, these innovations were removed as they proved continually problematic to the design crew. Instead, the weight saved by removing these systems afforded a 20,000 lb maximum bomb load. More than two years after its test flight, the B-32 was delivered to combat units beginning in December 1944, and restricted to low-level combat (due to the lack of a pressurized cabin system). Although generally performing without note in the Pacific, the last combat "kill" of the war does belong to a B-32, when on August 18, 1945, models on a reconnaissance mission over Tokyo downed two Japanese fighters. This was a far cry from the combat record envisioned by USAAF planners, who until December 1943 harbored hopes that the B-32 would join B-24 Liberators in precision-bombing Germany into surrender. Approximately 115 copies of the underachieving bomber were produced.

British Bombers

Although Great Britain had been slow to introduce bombers during the First World War, the German Gotha attacks had a definite impact upon the British that would make strategic bombing the core doctrine upon which the RAF was based throughout the interwar years. As a result, the British would be one of the world's leading producers of bombers during the interwar years and World War II.

Intended for use against Berlin, the Vickers FB 27 Vimy came too late for service in World War I, with only three reaching France prior to the Armistice. A total of 221 were produced during the 1920s, providing the RAF with the heavy bomber that Trenchard insisted was vital for British success in any future war. The Vimy had a wingspan of 68 ft, a length of 43 ft 6 in, and a loaded weight of 12,500 lbs, used a standard three-bay biplane configuration, had a biplane tail, and was wooden framed and canvas covered. It was powered by two 207 hp Hispano-Suiza water-cooled engines, had a maximum speed of 103 mph, a service ceiling of 12,000 ft, and a range of 900 miles. It was defended by two ring-mounted .303 caliber machine guns, one in the nose and one behind the pilot. In July 1919 a specially modified Vimy crossed the Atlantic, flying from Newfoundland to Ireland. It was gradually replaced by the similar Vimy Virginia, which remained in British service until the mid-1930s.

Designed with the RAF's strategic bombing mission in mind, the Handley Page Heyford was the last RAF biplane bomber. It was introduced in 1933 as a replacement for the Vickers Virginia, and had a wingspan of 75 ft, length of 58 ft, and loaded weight of 16,900 lbs. Its two 550 hp Rolls-Royce Kestrel liquid-cooled engines provided a maximum speed of 142 mph, service ceiling of 21,000 ft, and range of 920 miles. It was defended by three .303 caliber machine guns and could carry 3,500 lbs of bombs. Although supplanted by monoplane bombers that began to appear in 1937, the Heyford was a marked improvement to the Vickers Virginia it replaced. A total of 124 were produced.

Introduced in 1937, the Armstrong-Whitworth Whitley was the primary bomber in Bomber Command's arsenal at the start of the Second

World War. Featuring a midwing monoplane design, slab-sides, twin rudders, and retractable undercarriage, the Whitley marked a transition between the RAF's earlier bombers and the more modern Wellingtons and Hampdens that were beginning to replace it. It had a wingspan of 84 ft, length of 69 ft 3 in, and loaded weight of 33,500 lbs. Its two 1,145 hp Rolls-Royce Merlin X liquid-cooled engines produced a top speed of 222 mph and gave it a range of 1,650 miles. Armed with just two .303 caliber machine guns, the Whitley could carry a 7,000 lb bomb load. It participated in Bomber Command's August 25, 1940, retaliatory strike on Berlin, which caused Hitler to change the focus of the Luftwaffe's attack during the Battle of Britain. It was gradually replaced by more advanced bombers, but the Whitley remained in service until 1945 for patrol and training duties.

Introduced in 1938, the Vickers Wellington incorporated the geodetic construction techniques used on the single-engine Vickers Wellesley. With a wingspan of 86 ft 2 in, a length of 64 ft 7 in, and a loaded weight of 34,000 lbs, it was light, yet rugged. Powered by two 1,500 hp Bristol Hercules XI radial engines, the Wellington had a maximum speed of 255 mph, a service ceiling of 19,000 ft, and a range of 1,540 miles. It was defended by eight .303 caliber machine guns in nose and tail turrets and could carry 4,500 lbs of bombs. The heavy losses it suffered in a raid on Wilhelmshaven on December 18, 1939, led Bomber Command to switch to night bombing, and the Wellington carried the brunt of its bombing attacks well into 1942. After larger four-engine bombers became available, the Wellington was used increasingly by Coastal Command for antisubmarine duties, accounting for at least 26 U-boat kills. A total of 11,462 were built, making it the most produced British multiengine aircraft.

While the twin-engine Handley Page Hampden is not as famous as its larger four-engine cousins, it provided outstanding service as a medium bomber during the first two years of the war. It had a wingspan of 69 ft 2 in, a length of 53 ft 7 in, and a loaded weight of 18,756 lbs. Its two 1,000 hp Bristol Pegasus radial engines produced a top speed of 254 mph and provided a service ceiling of 19,000 ft and range of 1,885 miles. It was defended by six .303 caliber machine guns in nose and dorsal turrets and could deliver up to 4,000 lbs of bombs or torpedoes. Its chief weakness was its low armor, which relegated it to nighttime bombing or coastal patrol duties.

Based on 1938 specifications, the Short Stirling became Bomber Command's first strategic bomber when it entered service in early 1941. With a wingspan of 99 ft 1 in, a length of 87 ft 3 in, and a loaded weight of 70,000 lbs, it was large for its time and could carry a 14,000 lb bomb load, although no single bombs larger than 2,000 lbs. Its shoulder-mounted wings required a massive retractable undercarriage. Powered by four 1,650 hp Bristol Hercules XVI radial engines, it had a maximum speed of 270 mph, a service ceiling of 17,000 ft, and a range of 2,010 miles. Surpassed in performance capabilities by the Avro Lancaster and Handley-Page Halifax, it nevertheless remained an integral part of Bomber Command's night campaign over Germany. In 1944 it was put to more effective use as a glider tug during the Normandy Invasion. A total of 2,373 were constructed.

Although the Avro Lancaster became the backbone of Bomber Command's four-engine heavy bomber force, it originated in 1940 as the twin-engine Avro Manchester, of which 200 were built. Underpowered and unreliable, the Manchester was redesigned with a longer wingspan to accommodate four 1,460 hp Rolls-Royce Merlin XX liquid-cooled engines that produced a top speed of 287 mph and range of 600 miles. Renamed the Lancaster in 1942, it had a wingspan of 102 ft, length of 69 ft 6 in, and loaded weight of 68,000 lbs. Armed with eight .303 caliber machine guns in nose, dorsal, and tail turrets, it carried a 14,000 lb bomb load and could be modified to carry the 22,000 lb "Grand Slam" bomb, the largest used in the war. In its night-bombing role, Lancasters would drop more than 600,000 tons of bombs over German-held territory during the course of the war. A force of 31 Lancasters was dispatched on November 12, 1944, to Norway, where they sank the German battleship *Tirpitz*. A total of 7,377 Lancasters were built.

The Handley Page Halifax, like the Lancaster, was modified from a two-engine design that expanded to four engines because of the need for greater power. It had a wingspan of 104 ft 2 in, length of 71 ft 7 in, and loaded weight of 68,000 lbs. Its four 1,800 hp Bristol Hercules radial engines provided a maximum speed of 312 mph, service ceiling of 24,000 ft, and range of 1,260 miles. It was defended by three powered turrets in nose, dorsal, and tail positions, each of which had three .303 caliber machine guns. The Halifax could carry up to 13,000 lbs of bombs and was also used to tow the General Aircraft Hamilcar transport glider. A total of 6,176 were built for service in Bomber Command and Coastal Command.

Even though its medium and heavy bombers were designed to fulfill the strategic bombing role that Trenchard had emphasized, the British had not neglected light bombers that were designed for army support roles. In addition, the RAF would develop a number of land-based torpedo bombers to support Coastal Command's task of defending Great Britain from a seaborne attack. Both types would play an important role during the Second World War.

The Hawker Hart was designed as a replacement for World War I–era light bombers, and it entered service in 1930. With a wingspan of 37 ft 3 in, length of 29 ft 4 in, and loaded weight of 4,554 lbs, the Hart featured a streamlined design that improved performance over its predecessors. Its 525 hp Rolls-Royce Kestrel IB liquid-cooled engine provided a top speed of 184 mph, a service ceiling of 21,300 ft, and a range of 470 miles. It was defended by two .303 caliber machine guns and could carry a 500 lb bomb load. Several variants were introduced, including the Hawker Osprey naval version. There were approximately 1,000 of all types produced.

Featuring a more modern, all-metal, low-wing monoplane design, the Bristol Blenheim entered service as a light bomber in 1937. It had a wingspan of 56 ft 4 in, length of 42 ft 7 in, and loaded weight of 13,500 lbs. The Blenheim's two 920 hp Bristol Mercury XV radial engines provided a top speed of 266 mph, service ceiling of 22,000 ft, and range of 1,460 miles. It was defended by just three .303 caliber machine guns and carried a bomb load of 1,300 lbs. After it proved to be inadequate as a light bomber because of its low armament and slow speed, the Blenheim was converted for use as a night-fighter and remained in that role until 1944.

The Fairey Battle was introduced at the same time as the Bristol Blenheim, and was a vast improvement to Hawker Hart biplanes it replaced, but it proved to be even more ineffective than the Blenheim in World War II. The Battle had a wingspan of 54 ft, length of 42 ft 4 in, and loaded weight of 10,792 lbs. Its 1,073 hp Rolls-Royce Merlin I liquid-cooled engine gave it a top speed of 257 mph, service ceiling of 25,000 ft, and range of 1,000 miles. It was defended by just two .303 caliber machine guns and could carry just 1,000 lbs of bombs. After the German invasion of France in May 1940, the Luftwaffe had a field day against the Battle. On May 14, for example, 32 out of 63 Battles were shot down over Sedan. The Battle was withdrawn from light bombing service afterward and relegated to training service. Total production surpassed 1,000 prior to World War II.

The Vickers Vildebeest prototype, based on 1925 specifications that sought a more effective land-based torpedo bomber, was first introduced in 1928. It finally entered service with Coastal Command in 1933 after numerous modifications. The Vildebeest used a biplane configuration, metal framework, and fabric covering, and had a wingspan of 49 ft, a length of 37 ft 8 in, and a loaded weight of 8,500 lbs. Its 825 hp Bristol Perseus radial engine provided a maximum speed of 156 mph, a service ceiling of 17,000 ft, and a range of 630 miles. It was armed with one .303 caliber machine gun in the nose and rear cockpit and could carry one 18 in torpedo or 1,000 lbs of bombs. Delays with the Bristol Beaufort left the Vildebeest in service until 1942, well beyond its capabilities as the Japanese would demonstrate with devastating results in 1941.

The Bristol Beaufort was introduced in 1940 to replace the Vildebeest and served as Coastal Command's primary torpedo-bomber during World War II. The Beaufort had a midwing monoplane design, a wingspan of 57 ft 10 in, length of 44 ft 3 in, and loaded weight of 21,228 lbs. Its two 1,130 hp Bristol Taurus radial engines provided a top speed of 265 mph, service ceiling of 16,500 ft, and range of 1,600 miles. The Beaufort was protected by six .303 caliber machine guns and could deliver 2,000 lbs of bombs or torpedoes. A total of 1,429 were built in England. An additional 700 were built in Australia for service in the Pacific Theater.

Difficult to classify in any one category because of its great versatility, the two-seat de Havilland DH 98 Mosquito, dubbed the "Wooden Wonder" because of its all-wooden construction, was introduced in 1941 and utilized as a light bomber, high-speed reconnaissance plane, fighter, and night-fighter. It had a wingspan of 54 ft 2 in, length of 41 ft 6 in, and loaded weight of 25,550 lbs. Its two 1,710 hp Rolls-Royce Merlin 76 liquid-cooled engines produced an amazing 425 mph top speed and provided a service ceiling of 36,000 ft and range of 3,500 miles. The Mosquito was protected by four .303 caliber machine guns and four 20 mm cannon and it could deliver up to 4,000 lbs of bombs. Its ability to outrun German fighters and its extended range enabled the Mosquito to serve as a pathfinder for night bombing. Speeding ahead of slower bombers, the Mosquito would drop its incendiary bombs on the target to help the planes that followed it find the target.

French Bombers

In contrast to the British, the French had not been impressed with their attempts at strategic bombing during the First World War—in part because they had not made much of an effort—and consequently entered the 1920s without an air power doctrine based upon the bomber. Indeed, the French never developed a coherent air power doctrine, although it came close when Pierre Cot served two stints as minister of air during the 1930s. As a result, throughout the 1920s France continued to produce bombers that had been designed in World

War I, the most important of which was the Breguet 14, a light bomber that was introduced in 1917 and remained in service until 1932. The only bomber of note it did introduce during the 1920s was the Breuget 19, which entered service in 1924, stayed in production through the 1920s and 1930s, and was still in front-line service in 1939, a further indication of France's opinion on bombers and their role.

The Breguet 19, which was intended as a replacement for the Breguet 14, was built entirely of metal and featured a more stream-lined, circular fuselage. It had a wingspan of 48 ft 8 in, a length of 31 ft 2 in, and a loaded weight of 4,850 lbs. One of the reasons for its longevity was the ease with which more powerful engines could be adapted to it. With the 450 hp Lorraine water-cooled engine, it had a top speed of 137 mph, service ceiling of 22,970 ft, and range of 497 miles. It was armed with two 7.7 mm machine guns and could carry up to 1,543 lbs of bombs. More than 1,000 were produced for the Armée de l'Air for use as light bombers and reconnaissance craft. A number were also exported to Yugoslavia. CASA produced 177 licensed-models in Spain that served both Popular Front and Nationalists Forces during the Spanish Civil War.

The Amiot 143, which was based on 1928 specifications for an all-metal bomber capable of day or night service, did not begin production until 1934. It featured a high-wing cantilever design and fixed under-carriage, making the Amiot 143 an ugly aircraft, and one that was quickly obsolete when compared with the low-wing, retractable under-carriage bombers other powers soon began introducing. It had a wingspan of 80 ft 4 in, length of 59 ft, and weighed 21,385 lbs when fully loaded. Its two 870 hp Gnome-Rhone Mistral Major radial engines produced a maximum speed of 193 mph and it could carry approximately 1,750 lbs of bombs. A total of 138 entered service in the Armée de l'Air. Used to drop propaganda leaflets over Germany at the start of the war, it proved to be extremely vulnerable to German fighters during the Battle of France because it was defended by just four 7.5 mm machine guns and because of its slow speed and minimal armor. As a result, it was relegated primarily to service as a night-bomber. By 1942 the Vichy government scrapped the few that remained.

The Liore de Olivier LeO 20 was introduced in 1928 as a replacement for aging World War I–era bombers. It served as Armée de l'Air's primary medium bomber and was intended for nighttime service. It had a wingspan of 73 ft, length of 45 ft 3 in, and loaded weight of 12,037 lbs. Powered by two 420 hp Gnome-Rhone 9 Ady radial engines, it had a top speed of just 123 mph, a service ceiling of 18,900 ft, and a range of 621 miles. The LeO 20 was defended by five 7.7 mm machine guns and carried a bomb load of 2,205 lbs. A total of 320 entered French service, but unfortunately French designers struggled to develop a replacement, leaving the LeO 20 remaining in service until 1939, well beyond its usefulness.

The Farman F 221 entered service in 1935 and was based on 1929 specifications for a replacement for the aging LeO 20s. Although it provided the Armée de l'Air with its first all-metal heavy bomber, its high-wing, heavily strutted monoplane design, fixed undercarriage, and boxlike, angular fuselage made it an ugly aircraft. The F 222, an improved version that featured retractable landing gear, was introduced in 1938, but it was already obsolete by contemporary standards. The F 222 had a wingspan of 118 ft 1 in, length of 70 ft 8 in, and loaded weight of 39,242 lbs. Its four 860 hp Gnome-Rhone GR1Kbrs radial engines were mounted in tandem for a tractor pusher configuration that provided a top speed of 199 mph, service ceiling of 26,250 ft, and range of 1,240 miles. The F222 was defended by three 7.5 mm machine guns, and was designed to carry a 9,240 lb bomb load, but would spend the first part of the war dropping propaganda leaflets. After the Germans launched their invasion of France, it was relegated to nighttime bombing duties and participated in a raid on Berlin in June before France surrendered. A total of 45 were produced.

Although originally intended to be a twin-engine fighter, the Breguet 691 provided the Armée de l'Air one of its best light bombers of World War II. The Breguet 691 had a wingspan of 50 ft 5 in, length of 31 ft, and loaded weight of 10,803. Its all-metal construction and high-wing monoplane design, combined with its two 700 hp Gnome-Rhone 14M-6/7 radial engines, made it a rugged, yet fast aircraft. It was capable of a top speed of 304 mph and had a range of 840 miles. Four 7.7 mm machine guns and one .20 mm cannon provided defense, and it could carry a bomb load of 880 lbs. It provided excellent service after the May 1940 German invasion, but with only around 350 being produced there were not enough to make a difference.

The Potez 63 is difficult to classify because it was intended as a multipurpose aircraft that could provide bombing, fighting, and reconnaissance roles. It had a wingspan of 52 ft 6 in and a length of 35 ft 10 in. Its two 700 hp Gnome-Rhone 14M radial engines were underpowered, providing a maximum speed of just 276 mph, a service ceiling of 27,890 ft, and a range of 932 miles. It was armed with just five 7.5 mm and could deliver just 1,323 lbs of bombs. Unlike the De Havilland DH 98 Mosquito, which also performed several roles and did so well, the Potez 63 failed in all three roles because it was too slow, too undergunned, and too cumbersome.

The LeO 451 was introduced in 1939 and produced in good numbers (450 were available in May 1940). It was by far the best French bomber of the Second World War. Built entirely of metal, the LeO 451 was streamlined and elegant. It had a wingspan of 73 ft 9 in, length of 56 ft 4 in, and loaded weight of 25,133 lbs. Although its designers had intended it to use 1,600 hp engines, shortages forced the French to use two 1,140 hp Gnome-Rhone 14N 48/49 radial engines, making it underpowered with a top speed of 308 mph, service ceiling of 29,350 ft, and range of 1,429 miles. Although it could carry up to 3,307 lbs of bombs, it was seriously underarmed with just two 7.5 mm machine guns and one 20 mm cannon. As a result, it proved to be vulnerable to German fighters.

German Bombers

Coming into World War II, the Luftwaffe articulated a threefold mission. The first component, air superiority, was the function of its fighters. The second, close air support, was achieved by fighter/bombers and attack aircraft. The third, battlefield interdiction by attacking the enemy's combat strength and supply lines, was the primary purpose of its bombers. Even though the Battle of Britain indicated that the German air forces understood the power of strategic bombing, their inability to achieve air superiority there greatly limited the strategic importance of those bombing runs. This seemed to mesh with the lessons the Germans believed they had learned while assisting the fascist forces during the Spanish Civil War. Luftwaffe technologies and tactics were put to the test in combat there, and the results were a strong commitment to close air support rather than strategic bombing. Combined with the lack of a perceived need for a long-range heavy bomber, Luftwaffe commanders never fully appreciated—and thus never fully achieved—the great potential of bombers in modern warfare.

One of the earliest medium bombers developed for eventual use in the Luftwaffe was the Junkers Ju 86. In an indication of the ability of Germany to subvert the limitations of the Treaty of Versailles, a number of aircraft were designed as "civilian transports" with the knowledge that slight modifications would make the model suitable as a medium bomber. Such was the case with the Ju 86, which first appeared in November 1934. With a wingspan of 73 ft 10 in, length of 58 ft 7 in, and height of 16 ft 7 in, the military model accommodated a crew of four. It was powered by two 600 hp Junkers Jumo vertically opposed six cylinder diesel engines, capable of producing a maximum speed of 186 mph, service ceiling of 19,360 ft, and a range of 932 miles. There were approximately 470 of all types produced, with late models powered by 1,000 hp engines capable of reaching 38,000 ft and 260 mph in maximum speed. Most models featured three 7.92 mm machine guns, and an internal bomb load of up to 2,205 lbs. Although important for the lessons learned from its combat over Spain, the Ju 86 was obsolete by the onset of World War II.

The Heinkel He 111 was far more successful during the war. It initially competed against the Ju 86 in competitive service trials. Like the Ju 86, the He 111 was billed as a civilian airliner until Hitler's resurrection of the Luftwaffe in 1936. The aircraft carried a crew of four, spanned 74 ft 14 in, with length of 53 ft 10 in, and height of 13 ft 2 in. In excess of 7,300 of all types were produced, including 6,200 of the definitive H model. The He 111-H was powered by twin 1,350 hp Junkers Jumo 211F-2 inverted vee-type engines, which afforded the aircraft a top speed of 252 mph, service ceiling of 27,900 ft, and 1,750 mile maximum range. It was armed with a 20 mm cannon in the nose, along with four to six machine guns of varying caliber. This primary medium bomber of the Luftwaffe could carry up to 5,500 lbs of bombs using internal bay and external hardpoints. It served on all fronts with varying degrees of success, and production of the model continued through October 1944 despite the plane's obvious obsolescence. Although heavily involved in the Battle of Britain, the aircraft suffered numerous casualties at the hands of more advanced British fighters and in the absence of a serviceable long-range German escort fighter.

A dedicated dive-bomber, the Junkers Ju 87 "Stuka" was one of the Luftwaffe's best-performing, and one of the war's most memorable, aircraft. More than 5,700 of all types were produced following the model's first successful flight in November 1936. The inverted gull wings spanned 45 ft 3 in, and the fuselage was 36 ft 5 in long, with height of 12 ft 9 in. The B model featured a single 1,100 hp Junkers Jumo 211 inverted V-12 engine, which afforded the aircraft a top speed of 242 mph, service ceiling of 26,250 ft, and loaded range of 373 miles. The Ju 87 was armed with three 7.92 mm machine guns, and could carry up to 1,510 lbs of bombs on external hardpoints. After stunning successes in Spain, the Ju 87 "Stuka" made dive-bombers an integral part of the German offensive; however, the model remained in front-line service long after its technological era had passed. By the latter phases of the war, the "Stuka" could safely operate only in German-controlled skies. Later models were rededicated as tank-killers, and thus armed with two 37 mm cannons under the wings. The Ju 87-Gs were rather successful in this role, but they proved increasingly vulnerable to Allied fighters and losses mounted.

The Junkers Ju 88 was a veritable workhorse for the Luftwaffe, serving in such varied roles as medium bomber, attack aircraft, night-fighter, and reconnaissance platform. The Ju 88, generally regarded as one of the most reliable and best-performing German aircraft of the war, answered a call for a high-speed medium bomber and dive-bomber. Although later models featured 1,700–1,810 hp BMW 14 cylinder radials or 1,730–2,125 hp Junkers Jumo V-12s, the most numerous model was the Ju 88-A (7,000 of the 14,980 produced), which featured the 1,200 hp Junkers Jumo inverted V-12 engines. This produced a maximum speed of 292 mph, along with a service ceiling of 26,900 ft, and maximum extended range of 1,700 miles. With a wingspan of 65 ft 7 in, length of 48 ft 9 in, and height of 15 ft 8 in, the bomber was capable of carrying a bomb load in excess of 4,000 lbs. Its three-man crew was defended by up to seven machine guns of various calibers. Some models were fitted with a 75 mm antitank cannon for close air support, whereas night-fighters featured radar sets. In this configuration, the Ju 88 is credited with more "kills" of Allied bombers than all other German night-fighters combined. Despite Allied aviation advances, production of the capable Ju 88 continued until the Junkers factories were overrun in early 1945.

The Dornier Do 17 offered a similarly versatile platform for the Luftwaffe, especially upon the introduction of the Do 217, essentially a redesigned version of the Do 17. The Do 17 was offered to Lufthansa as a fast mail carrier and civilian transport, but was rejected for lack of adequate cabin volume. With a wingspan of 59 ft, length of 52 ft 10 in, and height of 14 ft 11 in, the aircraft presented a long and slender profile and was thus dubbed by its aircrews the "Flying Pencil." A maximum speed of 255 mph, service ceiling of 26,900 ft, and normal range of 205 miles (extendable to 930 miles with use of auxiliary fuel tanks) were afforded by twin 1,000 hp BMW-Bramo Fafnir power plant. The four-man crew commanded defensive armament consisting of seven or eight 7.9 mm machine guns, and an offensive bomb load of up to 2,205 lbs. There were approximately 1,200 of all types produced, including approximately 370 in service at the beginning of the war.

By December 1942, however, the Do 17 had been removed from front-line service and instead relegated to use as a rear-echelon transport. It was replaced on the front lines by the Do 217, which was first produced in 1938 and first entered combat in 1940. Although it retained visual similarities to its predecessor (wingspan of 62 ft 4 in, length of 59 ft 9 in, and height of 16 ft 4 in), the Do 217 featured so many new elements it essentially represents an entirely new bomber. The aircraft's power plant was conspicuously different, now featuring twin 1,850 hp BMW 14 cylinder radials that allowed the Do 217 a top speed of 320 mph, with a service ceiling of 24,600 ft and a range of approximately 1,400 miles. There were approximately 1,730 of all types produced, with most featuring a 15 mm cannon, two 13 mm machine guns, and up to five 7.9 mm machine guns, in addition to an 8,800 lb bomb load. Although the dive-bombing gear was stripped from the model to increase speed, decrease weight, and make it more suitable as a true medium bomber, the Do 217 remained extraordinarily versatile, seeing service as a night-fighter, reconnaissance, and transport aircraft.

The Junkers Ju 188 was the final medium bomber entering Luftwaffe service during the war. It first flew in 1940. The Ju 188 was to the Ju 88 what the Do 217 was to the Do 17; outwardly similar but larger, faster, and more powerful. The Ju 188 spanned 72 ft 2 in, with length of 49 ft, and height of 14 ft 7 in, and it accommodated a crew of five. In addition to its larger size, it is visually distinguishable from its predecessor by the addition of a large glass nose and a larger, squared vertical tail. The model was powered by two 1,776 hp Junkers Jumo inverted V-12 engines, which produced a maximum speed of 325 mph. With an operational ceiling of 20,500 ft and maximum range of 1,550 miles, the medium bomber carried a payload in excess of 6,600 lbs. In terms of defense it carried a 20 mm cannon in the nose, two 13 mm and two 7.9 mm machine guns. Although produced in relatively small numbers (roughly 1,036 of all types), the model served with workmanlike efficiency on both fronts and in various capacities, including night-fighting and reconnaissance.

The most innovative German bomber was undoubtedly the Arado Ar 234 Blitz (Lightning), which lays claim to being the world's first operational jet-powered bomber. A single-seat reconnaissance/bomber aircraft, the model's prototype first flew on June 8, 1944 and was delivered to combat units just three months later. There were only 274 ultimately produced. The Ar 234 spanned 46 ft 4 in, with length of 41 ft 6 in, and height of 14 ft 1 in. It was powered by twin Junkers Jumo 004B turbojets that produced 1,980 lbs of thrust, and afforded the aircraft a maximum speed in excess of 460 mph. As during flight, the Ar 234 landed at high speeds, so designers fitted it with a deployable drag chute to slow the plane on wheels-down. Its service ceiling was 32,800 ft, and its maximum range exceeded 1,000 miles. The model also featured twin 20 mm rear-firing cannons and a maximum 3,300 lb bomb load on external hardpoints. Due to its long development period, the

Ar 234 saw little combat service. It did participate in the Battle of the Bulge and ill-fated bombing runs on the bridge at Remagen (March 7–17, 1945).

The Ar 234 and Ju 188 (-S and T models) each served in some capacity as the impetus for the late-arriving German experimentation with high-altitude and jet-powered heavy bombers. Various experimental programs yielded little more than frustration, and even the most successful of these efforts generated negligible returns. The Junkers Ju 388, for instance, was an expedited development primarily from the Ju 188 that possessed a 44,000 ft service ceiling. Production delays and the shortage of strategic materials limited production of the model to 103, of which most were reconnaissance, not bomber, aircraft. Other companies similarly attempted to join Arado in the jet-powered bomber arena, but with little-to-no success. The Junkers Ju 287, with its distinctive forward-swept wings, did actually fly during the war, but it was not involved in any recorded combat. In the end, these last gasps of German technological innovation were seized by the Allies as spoils of war.

Italian Bombers

Although Italy had been among the first countries to produce large bombers prior to the First World War, when Gianni Caproni introduced the Ca 1 trimotor, and produced a number of derivatives, including the Caproni Ca 5, it was slow to introduce new bomber types during the 1920s. Indeed, the Caproni Ca 5 remained in front-line service until 1928. Two factors help account for this. First, although Douhet was the leading proponent of the bomber as a strategic weapon and even a terror weapon, he had so viciously attacked his superiors within the army that it had the effect of turning them against his ideas, in effect killing both the messenger and the message. Second, based upon the failures of the army in World War I, Italian commanders were far more interested in having an air force that provided close support for its troops, a view that was shared by top commanders in the Regia Aeronautica.

After several failed attempts to introduce a replacement for the Ca 5, the Caproni Ca 101 began entering service in the late 1920s. The Ca 101 used a biplane configuration, had a wingspan of 64 ft 6 in, a length of 45 ft 3 in, and a loaded weight of 10,968 lbs. Its three 240 hp Alfa Romeo D2 radial engines provided a top speed of 103 mph, a service ceiling of 20,000 ft, and a range of 621 miles. The Ca 101 was armed with three 7.7 mm machine guns and carried a 1,102 lb bomb load. As more powerful engines, at least by Italian standards, became available, the Ca 101 developed into the Ca 111 and the Ca 133. There were several hundred produced and they were used in the Ethiopian campaign as bombers and transports.

The Fiat Br 20 Cignona, which used a long-wing design with retractable undercarriage, metal framework, and a combination of metal stressed skin throughout, except for its fabric-covered aft fuselage, marked a transition in Italian bombers. It had a wingspan of 70 ft 9 in, a length of 52 ft 9 in, and a loaded weight of 22,046 lbs. Its two 1,000 hp Fiat A.80 radial engines produced a maximum speed of 264 mph and provided a 22,145 ft service ceiling with a 1,710 mile range. The Br 20 was defended by four 7.7 mm machine guns and capable of carrying up to 3,527 lbs of bombs. The plane was introduced in 1936 and provided excellent service in the Spanish Civil War, but it would find the going much tougher when it was confronted by RAF fighters in World War II. Although a few participated in the Battle of Britain, they were confined primarily to the Mediterranean Theatre. Of the 602 constructed, only a few remained in service in 1943.

The Savoia-Marchetti SM 81 Pipistrello (Bat) was introduced in 1935 and was one of the best bombers in the world. It also served as a transport for up to 18 troops. Mussolini adopted one that he flew himself, recognizing the propaganda effect this had. Using a metal framework and fabric covering, the SM 81 had a wingspan of 78 ft 8 in, length of 58 ft 4 in, and loaded weight of 23,040 lbs. It was powered by three 700 hp Piaggio P.X radial engines, which provided a top speed of 211 mph, a service ceiling of 26,240 ft, and a range of 1,336 miles. It was armed with up to six 7.7 machine guns and had a maximum bomb load of 2,205 lbs. The plane was used to perform multiple roles in the Spanish Civil War, and it served in the same fashion throughout World War II. As a bomber, it was employed from Ethiopia to strike British targets in eastern Africa. Although it was relegated to night bombing in North Africa, it proved to be vital in airlifting troops and supplies to supply Rommel's forces. A total of 534 were built by 1944.

When the Savoia-Marchetti SM 79 Sparviero (Sparrow) entered the Regia Aeronautica in 1936, it quickly emerged as one of the best all around warplanes that Italy produced, serving as a medium bomber, torpedo-bomber, reconnaissance aircraft, and transport. It combined steel tube, wood, and fabric construction, and had a wingspan of 69 ft 6 in, a length of 51 ft 10 in, and a loaded weight of 23,104 lbs. Its low wing design and retractable undercarriage greatly improved its performance over earlier Italian aircraft. The SM 79 was powered by three 780 hp Alfa-Romeo 126 RC34 engines, and had a maximum speed of 267 mph, a service ceiling of 21,325 ft, and a range of 1,180 miles. Although defended with just three 12.7 mm machine guns, it could carry 2,755 lbs of bombs or two 17.7 in torpedoes. It earned a reputation during the Spanish Civil War as a fast, rugged aircraft that maneuvered well for its size. During World War II it created havoc with Allied shipping in the Mediterranean. After Italy surrendered in September 1943, SM 79s fought on both sides and sometimes against one another. There were approximately 1370 of all types produced.

The Caproni Ca 310 was introduced in 1938 and gave the Regia Aeronautica one of its most versatile aircraft series, providing service as a light bomber, torpedo-bomber, and long-range reconnaissance plane. The Ca 310 series combined wood, metal, and fabric construction, had a wingspan of 53 ft 2 in, length of 40 ft, and loaded weight of 10,252 lbs. Its two 470 hp Piaggio P.VII radial engines made it somewhat underpowered with a top speed of 227, service ceiling of 22,956 ft, and range of 1,025 miles. It was also weakly defended by just two 7.7 mm machine guns, but it could deliver up to 1,764 lbs of bombs. A total of 2,400 were built and several were exported to Norway, Hungary, Spain, and Yugoslavia prior to Italy entering the war.

The Cant Z 1007 Alcione (Kingfisher) was surpassed in importance only by the Savoia-Marchetti SM 79 Sparviero. It entered production in 1939 as a land-based version of the Cant Z 506 floatplane. It had a wingspan of 81 ft 4 in, length of 60 ft, and loaded weight of 30,029 lbs. Its three 1,000 hp Piaggio P.XI radial engines provided a top speed of 280 mph, service ceiling of 24,600 ft, and range of 1,370 miles, and they enabled it to carry a 4,410 lb bomb load. The plane was also capable of being modified to carry two 1,000 lb torpedoes, so it proved to be useful in antishipping duties. Defended by just four 7.7 mm or 12.7 mm machine guns and using wooden construction, the Alcione proved to be vulnerable to enemy fighters. Nevertheless, they served throughout the Mediterranean Theater and saw brief service in Russia.

As Italy's only four-engine heavy bomber, the Piaggio P 108B proved to be highly effective, but it was not produced in sufficient numbers to make a difference. It had a wingspan of 104 ft 11 in, a length of 73 ft 1 in, and a loaded weight of 65,885 lbs. Unlike most other Italian aircraft, it was well-armed, having a total of eight 12.7 mm machine guns, four of which were mounted in remote-controlled barbettes over the engines. Its four 1,500 hp Piaggio P.XII RC.35 radial engines provided a maximum speed of 267 mph, a service ceiling of 27,890 ft, and a range of 2,187 miles. It was capable of carrying a 7,716 lb bomb load.

A total of 182 were built, 12 of which were modified troop transports that were later seized by the Luftwaffe.

Japanese Bombers

In order to wage an effective war from their relatively isolated position, the island nation of Japan, perhaps more than most other powers, had to develop a highly effective first-strike–capable air force. One significant wing of this force would necessarily be a fleet of bombers to carry the offensive across the sea. It is easy to trace the rise and fall of the entire Japanese war machine through its bombers: a group rising virtually unnoticed to a place of self-sufficiency and even superiority in comparison to the Western powers, but one whose early successes were as quick and stunning as its dramatic fall from dominance. In the end, the innovative spirit that helped launch the Japanese war machine across the Pacific turned its energies toward the creation of dedicated suicide aircraft, a symbolically powerful statement of their status in the conflict.

In its push to modernize and make its air fleet self-sufficient, the Japanese military solicited a vast number of designs of various types. Many of these would propel the air fleet toward, and eventually past, equality with the Western air forces, but many, especially in the early days of the modernization program, met with little success. The Kawasaki Ki-32 embodied both of these characterizations. It was designed by Isamu Imashi and Shiro Ota in response to a call by the Japanese Army Air Force (JAAF) for a new, Japanese-built light bomber. Their model, which first flew in March 1932, was a midwing cantilever monoplane featuring a fixed spatted undercarriage and an internal bomb bay. In most respects it was unremarkable. Difficult maintenance plagued the model, dubbed "Mary" by the Allies, from its inception and throughout its 854-copy production program. Despite rampant mechanical difficulties, the Ki-32 did achieve more than acceptable performance stats, including a maximum speed of 263 mph and a range of 1,200 miles. Although it was in service through 1942, it never achieved notable combat success and incorporated no real innovative design elements. Nevertheless, the Ki-32 outperformed the Fairey Battle, its British contemporary, and it was a portent of things to come from the Japanese design bureaus.

The Mitsubishi Ki-21 signaled Japanese equivalency with the other air forces of the world, at least symbolically; however, the Ki-21 ironically was obsolete nearly as soon as it was built. This seeming contradiction indicates just how rapidly Japanese aviation technology advanced in the interwar years. In February 1936, the army solicited designs for a new heavy bomber that could carry a bomb load of between 1,650 and 2,200 lbs. The Mitsubishi entry, designed by Nakata and Ozawa, beat out prototypes from Nakajima and Kawasaki in competitive trials in 1937 and early 1938. By the spring of 1938, the army had ordered quantity production of the plane the Allies would soon come to call "Sally." The Ki-21 spanned 73 ft 9 in, length of 52 ft 6 in, 14 ft 3 in height, and had 749 sq feet of wing area. It was powered by dual 850 hp Army Type 97 14 cylinder radial engines that were air cooled, the first integration of this technology with Japanese bombers. The Ki-21 carried a crew of five (with accommodations for two additional gunners), and could achieve a top speed of 268 mph with a range of between 932 and 1,680 miles. Its offensive armaments consisted of up to 2,200 lbs of bombs. It carried at least five Type 89 machine guns positioned all around the body of the aircraft for defense. Ki-21s served as the primary Japanese offensive bomber throughout the remainder of the decade, but both its defensive armament and performance capabilities proved insufficient in the face of such technologically superior Allied aircraft as the British Hurricane. As a result, most were eventually modified for use as transports between the Home Islands, Manchuria, and China, or relegated to second-line status as invasion-support aircraft. Its ease in flying and maintenance helped keep the roughly 2,064 Ki-21s in service far beyond their days as the most technologically advanced Japanese bombers.

The Tachikawa Ki-36 entered production shortly after the Ki-21. It was designed as a two-seat cooperation aircraft. The training version was dubbed the Ki-55, a solo flight of which was the last major step before earning one's wings. (See Chapter 5 for additional design information regarding the Ki-36/-55.) The smallish Ki-55 (span: 38 ft 8 in; length: 26 ft 3 in; height: 11 ft 11 in; wing area: 215 sq feet) proved quite adept at close combat support operations, despite lacking impressive performance capabilities (217 mph top speed) and defensive armament (a single 7.7 mm Type 89 machine gun). This was mostly due to its scant runway requirements (it could lift off in roughly 770 feet and land in only slightly more). It could thus be launched from makeshift runways close to the front lines, and when loaded with ten 27.5 lb or fifteen 33 lb bombs, was useful for close-in combat support as well as various reconnaissance purposes. Of the 1,334 produced, those that remained by 1943 were largely tasked to suicide missions.

The aforementioned bombers saw a majority of their front-line action in and over China. Although most Japanese aircraft proved vastly superior to their opponents there, the JAAF was quite impressed by the Soviet Tupolev SB-2 flown by the Chinese in the early stages of the Sino-Japanese conflict. The JAAF therefore solicited a design from Kawasaki in December 1937 for a plane that could approximate the capabilities of the SB-2. It was to have a maximum speed of nearly 300 mph, a climb rate of more than 16,000 ft in 10 minutes, an 880 lb bomb load, and was to be cold-weather compliant. Designer Takeo Doi's response was the Ki-48, which incorporated many elements of the Ki-45 fighter. The midwing cantilever design afforded the use of an internal bomb bay, but the 661–882 lb bomb load proved woefully inadequate shortly after its adoption as a JAAF light bomber in late 1939. The Ki-48-I spanned 57 ft 4 in, with a length of 41 ft 4 in, height of 12 ft 5 in, and wing area of 430.5 sq feet. It was powered by dual 950 hp Army Type 99 radials, and the first model could achieve a top speed just less than 300 mph, could climb to 16,405 ft in nine minutes, and it possessed a range of between 1,200 and 1,500 miles. By early 1942, however, the JAAF realized that the Ki-48-I was ill-equipped for front-line service. A revision program gave the Ki-48-IIs dual 1,150 hp Army Type I radials, which increased maximum speed, range, and climb rate, while still allowing the bomb load effectively to be doubled. The 1,408 Ki-48-IIs produced also featured dive brakes and other minor modifications aimed at increasing their combat usefulness. Nonetheless, by the time the JAAF reacted to the Ki-48's inadequacies, the aircraft's time had passed. For a majority of its service time, the "Lily" was effective only under the cover of darkness or when unchallenged in the air. It was too slow and too lightly armed (offensively and defensively) to prove much of a threat except under the most ideal of circumstances. As a result many were later modified as flying bombs (Type 99 Special Attack Plane).

The JAAF, believing it had satisfied the need for an effective new light bomber, turned its attention to soliciting designs for a new heavy bomber to replace Mitsubishi's Ki-21 in early 1938. The JAAF wanted a bomber that could operate effectively beyond the range of fighter escorts, using speed and heavy armament as its own defense. The rigorous specifications called for a 2,000-plus pound bomb load that could be carried at more than 300 mph across 1,800 miles. The plane was also to feature self-sealing fuel tanks for safety, and an array of defensive armaments (multiple flexible 7.7 mm machine guns, including one mounted in a tail turret, and a 20 mm flexible cannon mounted in a dorsal turret). Nakajima appointed senior engineers Nishimura,

Itokawa, and Koyama as the design team. Their prototype first flew in August 1939, and was adopted for production by the JAAF in March 1941. After first seeing combat in China, the Ki-49 Donryu (translated as Storm Dragon, Dragon Eater, or Dragon Swallower; called "Helen" by the Allies) also participated in action all across the Pacific Theatre. There were approximately 819 Ki-49s built, with one major revision to install improved engines on the frame. The aircraft spanned roughly 67 ft, with a length of 55 ft 2 in, height of 13 ft 11 in, and a wing area of 743 sq feet. It carried a crew of eight, a bomb load of between 1,653 and 2,205 lbs, and featured no fewer than five 12.7 mm Type 1 machine guns and a 20 mm Ho-1 cannon mounted at different points around the frame. With the better engines (rated at 1,450 hp), the Ki-48 could achieve a top speed in excess of 300 mph, with a climb rate of 16,405 ft in 13 minutes and 40 seconds. Although faster and more heavily armed and armored than virtually any of their fellow Japanese bombers, Ki-48s suffered heavy losses in the face of increasingly superior Allied opposition.

Planning for an invasion that would never occur, the JAAF in 1941 called for a tactical bomber for use against the Soviet Union. Mitsubishi received the specifications, calling for a bomber with a maximum speed of 342 mph, a 435 mile combat radius with a 1,100 lb bomb load, and an operating altitude range between 13,125 and 22,965 ft. Mitsubishi designer Ozawa went for efficiency in design, production, and flight after considering the situation in which the empire found itself. The result, the Ki-67, carried a crew of between six and eight in a plane that spanned 73 ft 9 in, with a length of 61 ft 4 in, height of 25 ft 3 in, and wing area of 708.8 sq ft. Two Army Type 4 18 cylinder air-cooled radials powered the Ki-67 Hiryu (Flying Dragon), which could achieve a top speed of more than 330 mph and a range between 1,740 and 2,360 miles. Offensive armament consisted of a bomb load of between 1,102 and 1,764 lbs. For defensive, most models carried four or five flexible 12.7 mm Type 1 machine guns and a flexible 20 mm Ho-5 cannon mounted in a dorsal turret. In addition, all combustibles (fuel, engine oil) were enclosed in self-sealing tanks, and rather heavily armored. Ozawa's first prototype flew on December 27, 1942, even as design modifications were underway to fit the Ki-67 as a torpedo bomber. Indeed, it was in this latter model that the "Peggy" (as the Allies dubbed it) first saw combat, off Formosa in October 1944. Standard models later appeared over Formosa, as well as in combat operations in China and the Marianas. This was by far the best bomber in the entire Japanese inventory, although it appeared too late in the war to stem the tide then turning against Japan.

The Imperial Japanese Navy (IJN) engaged in a similar program to first modernize, and then make self-sufficient, their bomber fleet. A prime example of the fusion of self-sufficiency and native innovation with foreign designs or ideas comes in the development of the Mitsubishi G3M, a plane the Allies came to call "Nell." Admiral Isoroku Yamamoto determined that the IJN needed a long-range medium bomber to supplement its growing carrier-based attack arm. The design team of Sueo Honjo, Tomio Kubo, and Nobuhiko Kusabake "borrowed" elements common to Junkers aircraft (prominently, twin fins and rudders) in creating the all-metal K-9, which first flew in April 1934 at the hands of Yoshitaka Kajima. The plane's superlative range and handling characteristics led the IJN to issue a formal, noncompetitive call to Mitsubishi for an attack bomber capable of delivering a 1,700 lb bomb load over a great range. The resulting Ka-15 featured a wider fuselage, larger tail surface, and various other structural modifications aimed at improving the frame's strength and aerodynamics. Production continued after a test flight revealed the need for further upgrades. Twenty-one different prototypes followed, with modifications ranging from unglazed to glazed noses, various power plants, and increased dihedral in the wings. It finally entered production in June 1936 as the G3M, but just 34 of this initial type were produced. A major modification (i.e., G3M2 Model 21) in 1937 replaced the dual Mitsubishi Kinsei 3 radial engines with more powerful Kinsei 41s or 42s. This provided the 343 copies of this type approximately 20 mph more speed, a substantially increased climb rate (to 9,845 ft in 1 minute 30 seconds less than the G3M1s), and increased service ceiling and range. Beginning in 1939 yet another engine modification further improved performance: There were 238 G3M3s produced under this set-up. The vast majority of the 1,048 total G3Ms produced were of these latter two types. The aircraft spanned just more than 82 ft, was 53 ft 11 in long, 12 ft 1 in high, with a wing area of roughly 807 sq feet. It could carry between five and seven crewmembers and a single 1,764 lb torpedo or a total of 1,764 lbs of bombs on external fixtures over a range of 2,700 (G3M2) to 3,800 (G3M3) miles. The most powerful G3Ms could achieve a top speed in excess of 250 mph, could climb to 9,845 ft in under 5 minutes 30 seconds, and possessed a service ceiling of more than 33,000 ft. The later models featured improved defensive armament, including up to four flexible 7.7 mm Type 92 machine guns and a flexible Type 99 Model 1 20 mm cannon mounted in a dorsal turret.

On August 14, 1937, Yamamoto's brainchild made history. A flight of G3Ms launched a 1,250-mile, transoceanic bombing raid from Formosa to Hangchow and Kwangteh on the Chinese mainland, the first ever assault of its kind. The following day, another flight of G3Ms repeated the feat. This experience undoubtedly greatly shaped the future war plans of the IJN. Indeed, when the Japanese war machine first directed its energies toward seizing control of the Pacific, G3Ms played an important role. They participated in actions against Wake Island, the Philippines, the Marianas, and other sites. GM3s perhaps most famously participated with great effect in the sinking of the HMS *Repulse* and the HMS *Prince of Wales* near Malaysia on December 10, 1941; however, once the Allies rebounded and their production facilities began churning out modern aircraft of their own, the G3M rather quickly became obsolete. After these initial successes, G3Ms were limited to the range of their fighter escorts, and even then suffered increasingly heavy losses at the hands of technologically superior Allied interceptors. As a result, many were relegated to second-line status or converted to use as transports (Type 96 Transport, "Tina").

In a recurring theme for all of Japan's aircraft types, almost as soon as one model began achieving combat success Japanese leadership called for an even better type to replace it. This was the case with the G3M. In late 1938 and early 1939 Mitsubishi was tasked with besting their already wildly successful G3M design. Kiro Honjo headed the program, and in September 1939 produced the first prototype of the G4M ("Betty"). It made its first flight on October 23, 1939, with Katsuzo Shima at the controls. It was initially too successful a design (its range far exceeded that of any available escorts). In mid-1940, however, the model was finally adopted for quantity production, and more than 2,440 copies would roll off the lines between September 1939 and August 1945. It was a large bomber, spanning 82 ft, with a length of 65 ft 7 in, height of 19 ft 8 in, and wing area of nearly 841 sq feet. It carried a crew of between seven and 10. The modified copies powered by two Mitsubishi MK3T-B Kasei 25b engines could achieve a max speed of 292 mph, climb nearly 23,000 ft in just more than 20 minutes, with a range of nearly 2,700 (standard) miles. Knowing the aircraft was rangier than any of its potential escorts, it was designed to be heavily armed. In addition to its 2,205 lb bomb load, the most heavily defended G4M featured 7.7 mm machine guns in the nose and multiple 20 mm Type 99 Model 1 cannons mounted in dorsal, beam, and tail turrets. The model lacked much armor plating, however, sacrificing it for speed and range, and its fuel tanks failed to incorporate self-sealing technology. When directly hit it was prone to spectacular midair explosions; as a result, Allied personnel gave the "Betty" a far more descriptive nickname: the "Flying Lighter."

Its first combat experiences came over Chungking in early 1941, and G4Ms were soon participating in virtually every Japanese air campaign throughout the rest of the war. It became the most widely-produced and widely used bomber in the Japanese inventory, and is particularly noted for assaults on Clark Field (Philippines) on December 8, 1941, and contributed a few days later to the sinking of the HMS *Repulse* and HMS *Prince of Wales* off the coast of Malaya. G4M raids during the fighting on Guadalcanal were less successful because its vulnerabilities were more widely known by that time. On April 18, 1943, a flight of G4Ms carrying Admiral Yamamoto and his staff was downed near Bougainville. Despite increasingly heavy combat losses, G4Ms continued to participate in Japanese military operations quite literally until the end of the war, when a G4M transport plane carried the Japanese delegation to the surrender talks.

In 1938 the IJN solicited designs for an attack bomber with even greater range than the Mitsubishi G4M. As such, Nakajima turned to the Japan Air Lines Company (Nippon Koku K.K.), which had obtained the four-engine variant of the Douglas DC-4. Nakajima's designers essentially copied the American-designed plane, albeit with a slightly modified fuselage, glazed nose, ventral bomb bay, twin fins and rudders, and Japanese-built engines. The first prototype of the G5N Shinzan ("Mountain Recess") was completed in late 1940 and first flew on April 10, 1941. "Liz," as the Allies called it, was a massive plane, weighing more than 44,000 lbs unloaded and up to 70,700 lbs with a maximum load. The G5N carried a crew of seven to 10 and could haul a maximum of 8,818 lbs of bombs. It was defended by dual 20 mm cannons and four 7.7 mm machine guns mounted throughout the fuselage. It spanned 138 ft 3 in, was 101 ft 9 in long, with height of 19 ft 8 in, and wing area of just over 2,172 sq feet. Four G5N1s were powered by four Nakajima NK7A Mamoru 11 14-cylinder air-cooled radial engines, whereas the two G5N2s produced featured four Mitsubishi Kasei 12 14-cylinder air-cooled radials. The massive aircraft had a top speed of 261 mph and range of over 2,600 miles. It is notable for its size because it is the first such mammoth to be produced by the Japanese; unfortunately, this is also the reason for the project's abandonment. After producing only six G5Ns, the IJN shifted their resources elsewhere. The Japanese firms simply had no experience designing, manufacturing, and maintaining an aircraft of this size. The few that survived testing saw limited service as transports during the war.

In 1940 the IJN issued specifications for a fast bomber capable of low-altitude, torpedo-, or dive-bombing missions. Yokosuka designers Tadano Mitsuzi and Masao Yamana created the P1Y Ginga ("Milky Way"), which suffered from excruciating production delays and would not enter the field until the war was virtually lost; nevertheless, when it did appear the P1Y was welcomed as a reliable and respectable combat aircraft. It first flew a few months after the completion of its prototype in August 1943, but it did not see combat action until the spring of 1945. It carried a crew of three and featured twin Nakajima NK9B Homare 11 18-cylinder air-cooled radials; the P1Y sacrificed armor and armament for speed. It generally featured only two 20 mm cannons for defense, and could carry approximately 2,200 lbs of bombs. It also possessed a cruising speed of 230 mph and a top speed in excess of 340 mph. It also had an impressive climb rate of 9,845 ft in 4 minutes 15 seconds, and possessed a range of 1,190 to 3,330 miles. The model spanned 65 ft 7 in, had a 49 ft 2 in length, a height of 14 ft 1 in, and a wing area of 592 sq feet. Nearly 1,100 of this type, called "Frances" by the Allies, were built between 1943 and 1945. Despite the potential of this aircraft, it appeared too late in the war to make much of an impact.

The Kyushu Q1W Tokai ("Eastern Sea") is notable for being the IJN's first dedicated antisubmarine warfare (ASW) aircraft. It was the design of Kyushu engineer Nojiri, whose prototype rolled off the assembly lines in September 1943. There were 153 ultimately produced, although most did not see service in ASW, but rather as transports and escorts; however, the Q1W was badly suited for both roles. Code named "Lorna" by the Allies, the Q1W carried a crew of three or four and was armed with between one and three guns (a 7.7 mm machine gun and 20 mm cannons) and could carry two 551 lb bombs or depth charges on external points. It spanned 52 ft 6 in, with a length of 39 ft 8 in, height of 13 ft 6 in, and wing area of 411 sq feet. The aircraft's top speed was 200 mph, and it cruised near 150 mph with a range of approximately 830 miles.

One additional type merits note in this section if only because it symbolizes the rather unique mindset employed by the Japanese fighting forces. As the war turned increasingly against Japan, more and more obsolete aircraft were refitted as suicide aircraft (most were simply stripped of any materials not vital for flight, and the remaining space filled with explosives). Some aircraft were modified with rockets, which could be fired to increase the speed at which the kamikaze aircraft struck its target. It was in this spirit that Ensign Mitsui Ohta envisaged a suicide aircraft that was little more than a piloted missile. Indeed, in 1944 the IJN began modifying Type 93 torpedoes for use as suicide submarines ("Kaiten" submarines). Yokosuka's Masao Yamana, Tadano Mitsugi, and Rokuro Hattori developed the MXY7 Ohka ("Cherry Blossom") along similar lines. It was designed to be ferried in the bomb bay of a modified G4M, just as the Kaiten were launched from "mother" submarines, and was essentially a wooden bomb powered by three solid-propellant rockets with a rudimentary steering system. It was planned for use in the kamikaze spirit as a weapon of last resort, and was designed out of easy-to-obtain materials, was mass-producible by unskilled labor, and required very little skill and no special training to pilot. More than 750 of these were produced from September 1944 through March 1945. It spanned just 16 ft 9 in, 19 ft 11 in long, with a height less than 3 ft 10 in, and wing area of roughly 64.5 sq feet. When firing its rockets in unison, the MXY7 could achieve a maximum speed of more than 400 mph, and could reach a terminal velocity in excess of 575 mph in steep dive. It could carry its 2,646 lb warhead more than 23 miles after launch from the belly of a G4M. The first combat deployment of MXY7s came on March 21, 1945, but the flight of G4Ms was intercepted by Allied fighters. Their first combat success came about a few days later when four ships, including the American battleship *West Virginia*, were damaged by MXY7 suicide bombers on April 1. In the end, however, these represented the last aviation innovation of a dying empire.

Soviet Bombers

Following the Bolshevik Revolution, virtually the entire Soviet air force had to be restored from the ground up. What had been a respectable air force at the end of Russia's involvement in the Great War was utterly destroyed by the end of the Russian Civil War. Throughout the interwar period, however, Soviet air strength grew by leaps and bounds. There were fewer than 2,500 aircraft in 1917, and perhaps less than 400 serviceable planes by 1923. As the New Economic Policy and first two Five Year Plans took effect, however, production surpassed pre-Revolution levels. A growing percentage of these aircraft were dedicated bombers.

On December 22, 1930, the prototype for Andrei Nikolaevich Tupolev bureau's historic ANT-6/TB-3 bomber flew for the first time at the hands of pilot M.M. Gromov. This model set new standards for heavy bomber forces, and its position at the forefront of four-engine cantilever bombers makes the project, guided by lead-designer V.M. Petlyakov, truly remarkable. The success of the TB-3 would help revolutionize tactics regarding the strategic use of bomber forces. The prototype owed its design to its twin-engine predecessor, the TB-1. Tupolev's late-1920s project produced a medium bomber that served on the Soviet Union's frontlines into the mid-1930s. The TB-1's combat record is unclear, but it is widely regarded as a sound and reliable aircraft. It was used in early experiments with such postproduction improvements as firing rockets to decrease take-off distances, although it is perhaps otherwise undistinguished. Production of the TB-1 gradually died out as the TB-3 was adopted; production on the latter, much larger aircraft began in late 1931 and early 1932. Although the TB-1 had been powered by dual 680-hp BMW VI engines, most of the 818 TB-3s produced featured four of the slightly more powerful 730 hp M-17 12 cylinder vee-type water-cooled engines (themselves upgraded license copies of the BMW VIz engine), but beyond this similarity, comparisons between the TB-1 and TB-3 generally cease. The TB-3 dwarfed most of its contemporary aircraft, spanning 129 ft 7 in, with length just more than 80 ft, height of perhaps 20 ft, and wing area in excess of 247.5 sq feet. It was also much heavier than its peers, weighing more than 24,000 lbs empty and nearly 38,000 lbs at maximum loading. This contributed to understandably sluggish in-air performance, including a top speed of just 122 mph and range of approximately 840 miles. Its true performance, however, came in its payload capacity. In addition to the placement of up to ten 7.62 mm ShKAS machine guns at various points around the fuselage, the TB-3's defining trait was its 4,400-plus lb bomb load. The aircraft's size and defensive requirements necessitated a crew of eight.

TB-3s saw combat action against Japanese forces in late 1938 over China, and later against Finland in the opening thrusts of the Second World War. Even by its combat baptism in 1938, however, Soviet leaders realized that the TB-3 simply lacked the speed and maneuverability required to protect it from modern fighter attacks. The model was thus shifted to use as a paratroop carrier and general transport plane. In the former role, it could carry 30–35 paratroops, as well as loads of equipment or even smaller vehicles attached to special external hardpoints. The TB-3 was also used as the "mother" aircraft in a number of V.S. Vakhmistrov's Zveno experiments (launching "parasite" fighter aircraft from a parent vehicle) in the 1930s. As the German army advanced into the Soviet Union in 1941, however, the outmoded TB-3 and all its fellow Soviet aircraft saw increased service in various roles in an attempt to stave off the German advance. For the TB-3, this meant a brief, and relatively unsuccessful, return to service as a frontline heavy bomber, as well as increasing use as a desperation night-bomber—a role to which it was not well adapted. As a transport, however, the TB-3 (more commonly referred to in this vein as the ANT-6) earned well-deserved praise for its role in maintaining supply lines to the Soviet defenders during the epic Battle of Leningrad.

Konstantin Alekseevich Kalinin took things a step further in his design of the K-7, a project no fewer than eight years in the making. Kalinin claimed he first envisioned the creation of a massive flying wing around 1925, yet the aircraft did not complete its maiden flight until August 11, 1935, with M.M. Gromov piloting and Kalinin assisting. After failed experiments with wooden construction, Kalinin decided to employ an all-metal design of the nearly 174 ft wide wing. The aircraft was also 91 ft 10 in long, with a staggering wing area of nearly 1,490 sq feet. Booms extended to the twin tails and rudders, and the aircraft was powered by seven Soviet-built 750-hp AM-34 engines. The power plant provided 145 mph in top speed, an impressive figure considering the plane's girth (well more than 83,000 lbs maximum loading). The K-7 also featured a quite distinctive landing gear system (four large wheels, two each in covered housings set fairly wide apart underneath the giant elliptical wing). The graceful-looking aircraft required no fewer than 12 crewmembers, and it could be fitted to carry more than 19,000 lbs of cargo in internal bays. The promise of such an aircraft was immense (some saw its potential for a 150-plus passenger transport, whereas others envisioned it as a massive heavy bomber, guarded by up to 12 machine gun fixtures). On November 21, however, the prototype unfortunately crashed during testing, killing its entire 20-man crew. Kalinin continued to pitch the necessity of such an aircraft to the military authorities, but found himself increasingly out of favor and was eventually executed in a 1938 Communist purge.

A far more reasonable, and successful, design was proffered by Tupolev in the mid-1930s as the eventual successor to the TB-3. Direction of the project was eventually given over Vladimir Mikhailovich Petlyakov, whose ANT-42 prototype completed its first flight under M.M Gromov's guidance on December 27, 1936. Despite the lack of a suitable engine at the time, reviews for the ANT-42, eventually renamed the Pe.8, were promising after some initial problems with the power plant; it seemed capable of fulfilling the VVS's demand for a high-speed and high-altitude frontline bomber; development of a production-quality model proved to be quite frustrating. The model continued to be plagued by insufficient power from available engines. One early solution rigged a fifth engine in the fuselage to power a rudimentary fuel-injection system for the four main, wing-mounted engines. The aircraft's progress was no doubt hindered by the incarceration of its chief designer, and the first production model was not delivered to combat forces until Petlyakov was "rehabilitated" and released from the gulag (and entrusted with his own design firm) in 1940. Production Pe.8s were powered by four 1,350 hp AM-35A engines, although supply shortages led to the use of Shvetsov M-82 air-cooled radials. These were more powerful, but they required slight modification of the mounting design and proved to be somewhat less-reliable engines. The Pe.8 could attain a top speed of 265 mph, and it possessed a service ceiling of 27,560 ft and impressive range approaching 3,000 miles. The latter made the Pe.8 increasingly useful as a transport, and it indeed served this purpose well (in 1942 it ferried Foreign Minister Vyacheslav Molotov from Moscow to Washington, D.C.). As a combat aircraft, the Pe.8 was well designed even though circumstances quickly rendered it ill-suited to the war the Soviets were fighting. Its defensive armament consisted of twin 7.62 mm ShVAK machine guns in a nose turret, as well as 20 mm ShVAK cannons mounted dorsally and in the tail section of the aircraft. On offensive, the Pe.8 was well served by its range, speed, service ceiling, and 8,800 lb bomb load. The aircraft spanned 128 ft 3 in, with length of 77 ft 5 in, height of 20 ft 4 in, and wing area of approximately 2,030 sq feet. It carried a standard complement of nine crewmembers. It was the most effective strategic bomber in the Soviet inventory at the onset of the Second World War. Although it led Soviet strikes into the heart of Berlin on August 10, 1941, Operation Barbarossa forced the Soviet strategy toward a defensive war (strategic, long-range bombing became far less important than close air support). Pe.8s were adapted to this role, and they served admirably, but they were never given much of a trial run as the long-reaching arm of the VVS. Many observers indicate that had it been used as intended the Pe.8 would have outclassed most, if not all, of her Western competitors. Production figures are difficult to ascertain. Most non-Soviet sources estimate fewer than 90 Pe.8s were turned out before the production facilities fell to German forces, although Soviet claims far exceed that figure.

Although the Soviet aviation leadership spent some of their earliest efforts focusing on massive heavy bombers, measures were also taken to modernize their more standard-type bomber fleet. Tupolev's talents assisted this goal as well. In stark contrast to the plodding TB-3, the Tupolev SB-2 (ANT-40) was designed to be a fast-moving, quick-strike bomber. The design team, led by A.A. Arhangelsky, adapted twin-engine fighter technology into a bomber-sized airframe, creating a midwing monoplane that would become arguably the world's most advanced bomber of its time. The design progressed quickly after the stringent 1933 specifications (including and especially a maximum speed of 205 mph) were issued by the VVS. The first prototype flew on October 7, 1933, and the aircraft went into production and was delivered to units in 1936 after a series of revisions to the power plant. Production-series SB-2s featured dual 860 hp M-100 engines (i.e., license-built copies of the Hispano-Suiza 12Y), affording a top speed in excess of 240 mph. Authorities were quite impressed with the latter, as well as with its climb rate of 16,400 ft in 8.5 minutes. Later revisions, designated the SB-2bis, featured the more powerful 960 hp M-103 engines, increasing the maximum speed by 40 mph. The SB-2 spanned 66 ft 8 in, with height of 14 ft 4 in, and wing area of approximately 168.4 sq feet. It possessed four 7.62 mm ShKAS machine guns, two forward- and two aft-firing, and could carry a single 1,100 lb or six 221 lb bombs internally. The SB-2 was manned by a crew of three. A total of 6,656 were produced, and SB-2s comprised the bulk of the Soviet bomber fleet during the first phases of World War II, despite being relatively outdated by that point. During action in the Spanish Civil War, as well as over China and later Finland, the SB-2 proved to be an admirable foe that was generally able to outmaneuver and in most ways outclass even its fighter-plane enemies. Once the Messerschmitt Me BF-109 burst onto the scene, however, the SB-2 had more than met its match. The Me BF-109's superior speed and agility allowed it to take advantage of the SB-2's weaknesses (nonsealing fuel tanks, which increasingly showed a proclivity for spectacular explosion when hit by enemy fire).

Like Petlyakov, Pavel Sukhoi probably owed his start in aircraft design to Tupolev. Sukhoi's first solo design originated from his time under Tupolev's tutelage. The ANT-51 monoplane eventually became the Su-2, a low-wing, single-engine attack bomber intended for reconnaissance and tactical ground-support missions. In preparation for competitive trials, Sukhoi's prototype completed its first test-flight on August 25, 1937. By the time of the trials, in late 1940, the Su-2 featured a more powerful engine and retractable landing gear. Its performance was sufficient to merit a production contract. After producing several copies with the 950 hp Shvetsov M-88 radial engine, Soviet leadership called for a switch to the more powerful M-82, rated at 1,400 hp. This produced a maximum speed in excess of 300 mph and afforded a service ceiling of 29,500 ft. The Su-2 spanned 46 ft 1 in, with a length of 34 ft 3 in, and wing area of 312.16 sq feet. It carried a two-man crew and was rather heavily armored for its time. Combined with its speed and armament of as many as five 7.62 mm ShKAS machine guns, and up to 882 lbs in bomb load, the Su-2 was considered to be a very safe and reliable medium bomber. When it was fitted with RS-82 or RS-130 rockets on underwing mounts, it was considered to be a capable close air support aircraft. Although it did serve admirably in this latter role, the Su-2 was neither up to the task, nor was it produced in enough quantity to stem the tide of the German invasion. The German Me BF-109 proved to be quite superior to almost anything the Soviet designers had envisioned because it and other German aircraft showed the Soviet armor and defensive armament designs to be lacking. As the war progressed, the Su-2 regressed further from the front lines. Production figures are sketchy, at best, although it seems certain that no more than 500 copies of the Su-2 were ever produced. Sukhoi would produce a successor, the Su-6, designed specifically for close air support, but this model was overshadowed by Sergei Vladimorovic Ilyushin's "tank-buster," the famed Il-2 (discussed in detail in Chapter 3).

Even though the Il-2 (along with its upgraded model, the Il-10) was certainly his most famous contribution to the VVS, it was not Sergei Ilyushin's only successful design. In 1935 an Ilyushin prototype long-range bomber took its first flight, with a great deal of its body actually taken from the Polikarpov I-16 fighter. Revisions to the entire fuselage followed in 1936, and the DB-3 entered production and soon thereafter became the Soviet VVS's premier long-range bomber. There were approximately 1,528 DB-3s entering service before the start of the Second World War. Experimentation with the design continued, and in 1942 the implementation of M-88 engines led to the production of the Il-4. An estimated 5,200 copies of this aircraft were produced for the VVS before the German surrender, and perhaps as many as 6,800 when combining the production figures for all models in this series. Although the DB-3 had proved vulnerable to enemy fire during the Winter War phase of combat, the Il-4's improved power plant afforded an increase in armor without substantial reduction in top speed, and various structural modifications actually improved the aircraft's in-flight handling and the ease of in-the-field maintenance. Ilyushin's design also proved to be quite adaptable, serving admirably in its intended role of long-range bomber, but easily tasked to reconnaissance and naval operations as well. In addition to antishipping duties, it was in fact a naval tasking of Il-4's that spearheaded the first Soviet bombing raids on Berlin. A three-person crew manned the bomber, which was powered by twin 1,100 hp M-88B air-cooled radial engines. The aircraft could achieve a top speed of more than 265 mph, possessed a service ceiling approaching 32,000 ft and a range of more than 2,300 miles. The Il-4 was armed with a single 12.7 mm UBT and twin 7.62 mm ShKAS machine guns, and carried up to a 5,500 lb bomb load (when using both internal bays and external hardpoints). It spanned 70 ft 4 in, with length of 48 ft 7 in, height of 13 ft 5 in, and wing area of approximately 718 sq feet.

Alexander Sergeevich Yakovlev's Yak-2 and Yak-4 were both byproducts of a late 1930s movement in most design bureaus worldwide to develop high-speed, multipurpose aircraft. By 1938, Yakovlev had a wealth of expertise in developing smaller, faster aircraft, and far less experience working on dedicated bombers; however, the new fascination with speed as a chief defensive weapon made for a logical transitioning of Yakovlev's prior work into this new field. His first prototype, designated BB-22, flew in February 1939 and immediately generated substantial interest (its first tests managed to exceed 345 mph in top speed). During later flight tests by the VVS, the crew of Shevarev, Tretyakov, and Holopov managed to push the aircraft past 355 mph, which was an extraordinary feat for a bomber design. Even more tantalizing to the VVS, the BB-22's test crew promised a top speed in excess of 370 mph if the power plant could be made more efficient. These claims were made even more surprising because the BB-22, redesignated the Yak-2 upon its entry into quantity production, was powered by the same M-103 engines as the Tupolev SB-2bis, yet managed substantially improved top-end performance characteristics. This is due largely to Yakovlev's design, which sacrificed many other qualities for speed. The aircraft lacked any armor plating, and was far less armed than most that would follow; additionally, in seeking to use as many weight-reducing components as possible, the graceful-looking sweep of the aircraft belied a number of structural weaknesses that were only uncovered with the testing of production models. The Yak-2 program did not pass its VVS testing until November 1940, and then at the expense of its trademark speed. Maximum speed of the Yak-2 barely exceeded 325 mph, fully 50 mph less than initially desired; the aircraft was so unstable in flight that it was recommended that it be used only for unarmed reconnaissance because carrying even a small bomb load could pose large risks to the crew. Needless to say, this was unacceptable.

A radical overhaul of the design resulted in the Yak-4, which was powered by a pair of the 1,050 hp M-105 vee-type engines. This increased maximum speed to nearly 340 mph, while also allowing for the addition of at least a thin plate of armor around the crew. The Yak-4's service ceiling was also improved, to 31,170 ft. Its range remained stunted, although it was slightly improved at 745 miles. It spanned 45 ft 11 in, with length of 30 ft 7 in, and wing area of 319.7 sq feet. It carried two 7.62 mm ShKAS machine guns and up to 1,765 lbs in bombs. These aircraft were quickly produced and delivered, but complaints about instability in flight and unreliability in service dogged them throughout their brief tenure in the Soviet air forces. Although

Yakovlev claimed that more than 600 were produced, independent estimates claim roughly one third of that figure were actually delivered to combat units, where most of them were destroyed on the ground or in the air during the opening stages of Operation Barbarossa. Most important about this project, however, is probably that it gave impetus to the notion that speed could be as important an offensive and defensive weapon as guns and bombs. For that reason, the Yak-2/Yak-4, though itself reasonably considered a failed project, nevertheless occupies an important place in the history of Soviet design and tactics.

One example of the new tactical use of speed is seen in the use of the Petlyakov Pe.2. Designed while Petlyakov was still incarcerated in a gulag, the Pe.2 was initially intended as an escort fighter to be paired with Tupolev's ANT-42 high-altitude heavy bomber; however, shortly after being adopted for production, the VVS ordered it retasked for use as a tactical dive-bomber, evidence of the change in air-power doctrine. What had been a rather technologically advanced aircraft (i.e., featuring a pressurized cabin and comparatively modern electronics systems) was stripped of most of its innovative features, with the notable exception of its fighter-class speed. Despite this shift in its intended use, the aircraft's promise and performance won Petlyakov his release. The dive-bomber version of the Pe.2 completed its first flight tests on December 15, 1940, and entered production immediately thereafter. By the summer of 1941, deliveries had already been made to combat units. The three-man aircraft featured a twin fin and rudder assembly, and was powered by two 1,300 hp Klimov M-105 12 cylinder liquid-cooled engines. This gave the Pe.2 a top speed in excess of 360 mph, and service ceiling of 28,800 ft. It spanned approximately 56 ft 2 in, with length of 41 ft 6 in, height of 11 ft 5 in, and wing area of 435.9 sq feet. For defensive purposes, the Pe.2 featured four 7.62 mm ShKAS machine guns, two mounted in the nose and two in a rear-firing mount. Its offensive armament consisted of approximately 1,500 lbs of bombs, although the latest models could carry up to three and perhaps four times that payload. Pe.2s participated to great effect in battles from Stalingrad to Kursk, and along the Soviet counteroffensive all the way into Berlin. More than 11,425 copies of the Pe.2 were produced, making it the most numerous twin-engined, and likely the most accurate (of any configuration), bomber in the Soviet arsenal. Even though it was not as vital to the ultimate Soviet victory along the Eastern Front as the Il-2, the Petlyakov Pe.2 was a closer second-place than any other component of the Soviet air fleet.

Like Petlyakov, Tupolev also produced a spectacularly successful bomber design while incarcerated in the gulag for allegedly hindering the Soviet war effort, for espionage, or for both. Tupolev's prototype, initially dubbed the ANT-58, completed its maiden flight in late January 1941, followed four months later by the first flight of the upgraded ANT-59 prototype. After 12 more months of such experimentation, primarily with different power plants, the ANT-61 (later redesignated the Tu-2) entered production. Combat unit deliveries were made beginning in late 1942. The Tu-2 spanned 61 ft 10 in, with length of 45 ft 3 in, height of 14 ft 10 in, and wing area of approximately 525.3 sq feet. It carried a crew of four, two wing-mounted 20 mm ShVAK cannons, a complement of between three and five machine guns (7.62 mm ShKAS, 12.7 mm UBT machine guns, or both, depending on the model), and up to 6,600 lbs of bombs in an internal bay. The most numerous revision carried the designation Tu-2S, distinguished by power plant. This model featured two 1,850 hp Shvetsov Ash-82FN radials, providing a top speed in excess of 340 mph, and climb rate of 16,400 ft in 9 minutes and 30 seconds. The Tu-2 possessed a range of approximately 1,200–1,300 miles. Despite interruptions in production (caused by the war as well as by Stalin's whimsy), Tu-2s proved to be one of the more important Soviet aircraft in the battlefield in the middle and latter stages of the war in Europe, helping lead the assault on German forces at Stalingrad and thereafter. The model earned high marks from flight and ground crews alike: Where the Yak-2/Yak-4 had provided speed with little armor or armament, the Tu-2 provided all three, as well as range and payload capacity, in a tough and reliable package that made it ideally suited to frontline duties. There were approximately 1,040 Tu-2s produced during World War II, but production continued even after the war because of its versatility and venerability; ultimately, it is estimated that at least 2,525 copies of what NATO later called the "Bat" saw service into the 1960s as part of various Soviet-bloc air forces, and as part of the North Korean air force.

Minor Powers: Bombers

Entering service in 1933, the Letov S 328 was intended for both light bomber and reconnaissance use for the Czechoslovakian Air Force. With a wingspan of 44 ft 11 in, length of 33 ft 11 in, and loaded weight of 5,820 lbs, it was ruggedly constructed with a metal framework and fabric covering. Powered by a 635 hp Bristol Pegasus radial engine, the Letov S 328 had a top speed of 174 mph, service ceiling of 23,620 ft, and range of 435 miles. It was protected by four 7.92 mm machine guns and could carry up to 1,102 lbs of bombs. A total of 445 had been built prior to the Nazi takeover of Czechoslovakia. Recognizing their value, the Luftwaffe adopted it for use in the Polish Campaign. Based on its excellent performance, the Germans kept the Letov S 328 in production although most were then transferred to its allies.

The Commonwealth CA 1 Wirraway (Challenge) provided Australia with its first indigenous warplane. Based on the North American BT-9 trainer, the Wirraway was modified to serve as a light bomber, torpedo bomber, trainer, and reconnaissance aircraft. It used a combination of metal skin and fabric covering and had a wingspan of 43 ft, length of 27 ft 10 in, and loaded weight of 6,595 lbs. The Wirraway's 600 hp Pratt & Whitney CAC R-1340 Wasp radial engine provided a 220 mph top speed, 23,000 ft service ceiling, and 720 mile range. It was armed with two .303 caliber machine guns in the nose and one in the rear cockpit and could carry up to 500 lbs of bombs. A total of 755 were produced, and it remained in service as a trainer until 1958.

Having developed its first successful native fighter, the PZL P 1, in 1931, the Polish government initiated a program to develop a light bomber of its own making. After going through several prototypes, it finally introduced the PZL P 23 Karas in front-line units in 1937. With a wingspan of 45 ft 9 in, a length of 31 ft 9 in, and a loaded weight of 7,771 lbs, the Karas featured a low-wing design with a fixed, spatted undercarriage and sandwiched stressed-metal/balsa skin. Its 680 hp Bristol Pegasus VIII radial engine provided a maximum speed of 199 mph, a service ceiling of 23,950 ft, and a range of 783 miles. Although it could carry up to 1,543 lbs of bombs, it was defended by just three 7.7 mm machine guns, which made it extremely vulnerable to German fighters during the Polish campaign. Of the 253 built, 54 were exported to Bulgaria. The remainder formed 12 light bombing and reconnaissance squadrons. Contrary to popular belief, most of these were not destroyed on the ground. In fact, it inflicted a lot of damage on German panzer forces during the first couple of weeks of the Polish campaign, although most had been destroyed by German fighters and ground fire by the time Poland fell. A few pilots managed to escape to neutral Romania. The Romanian Air Force later flew them in the Russian Campaign.

On the eve of World War II, PZL introduced the all-metal P 37 Los, which was one of the best medium bombers in the world. It featured a low-wing design with a retractable undercarriage and twin rudders. The P 37 had a wingspan of 58 ft 8 in, a length of 42 ft 4 in, and a loaded weight of 19,577 lbs. Powered by two 925 hp Bristol Pegasus radial engines, it had a maximum speed of 273 mph, a service ceiling of 19,685 ft, and a range of 1,616 miles. More important, it could carry up to 5,688 lbs of bombs, which was more than half its empty weight. Sleek and aerodynamic, it handled well, even though it was under-armed with just three 7.7 mm machine guns. The Polish High Command, unfortunately, considered bombers a waste of money and purchased only 50 of the 153 built (the others were sold to Bulgaria, Turkey, Romania, and Yugoslavia). Although it inflicted a lot of damage on German forces, its numbers were too small to make a difference. Approximately 40 pilots escaped in their P 37s to neutral Romania, where their machines were later seized by the Romanian Air Force and used in Russia by the Romanian Air Force.

CHAPTER FIVE

Reconnaissance and Auxiliary Aircraft

WITHOUT A DOUBT, THE UNSUNG workhorses of the air forces of World War II were reconnaissance and other "auxiliary" airframes. As aircraft and their instruments became ever more complex, nations required increasingly sophisticated trainer aircraft and training regimens before their pilots could effectively fly combat missions. Being a truly "world" war, the conflict required great mobility of its participants. Moving troops, equipment, and supplies quickly and efficiently presented a unique challenge that the boom in civil air travel of the interwar years actually predicted—and for which it unwittingly prepared some nations. The most unsung component of the air war perhaps remained the original military use of aircraft—reconnaissance; however, even this demanded, and incorporated, radical innovations and improvements throughout the war. Advances in these types provided the backbone for the development and deployment of the modern air forces of the world.

American Reconnaissance and Auxiliary Aircraft

Trainers

Recognizing the newfound importance of air power in military doctrines, the U.S. Army Air Corps (USAAC) and the U.S. Navy agreed on a three-part training program after World War I: primary, basic, and advanced. Specific aircraft were thus needed to satisfy each stage of pilot development. This facilitated quantity production of a number of training aircraft in the period before and during World War II.

It was in this vein that one of the most venerable, yet unsung, aircraft in American military aviation history was produced. In 1925 the USAAC purchased 221 copies of the Consolidated PT-1 "Trusty" tandem biplane trainer. The transaction is notable as both the first aircraft purchase by the military following the Great War, and also as being the largest single production order of its time. Replacing the Curtiss JN-4 "Jenny" was no easy task, but the Trusty proved more than apt, serving as the army's primary training aircraft for more than a decade. It did so with an impeccable service record, which along with its steel tube framing earned the model its moniker. The Trusty spanned 34 ft 5 in, with length of 27 ft 9 in, and height of 9 ft 10 in. It was powered by a single 180 hp Wright E engine, which produced a top speed of 90 mph. The aircraft possessed a service ceiling of approximately 14,000 ft, and a maximum range of 350 miles. Beginning in 1928, Curtiss introduced the PT-3, matching a stronger engine with the PT-1's airframe. In all, approximately 469 copies of the model were produced, serving as a trainer in both the USAAC and the National Guard through 1936.

Perhaps even more popular a model was the Stearman Kaydet series, which was first introduced in 1936 as the PT-13. A tandem biplane of mixed construction, the aircraft possessed a wingspan of 32 ft 2 in, length of 24 ft 10 in, and height of 9 ft 8 in. Powered by a single 220 hp Lycoming R-680, the PT-13 could achieve a top speed of 125 mph, with a range of 450 miles and operational ceiling of approximately 13,000 ft. When the aircraft was given a 220 hp Continental R-670 radial, it became the PT-17; however, it was redesignated the N2S when ordered by the Navy. The PT-18 was powered by a 225 hp Jacobs R-755 engine. The model became the PT-27 with an enclosed canopy. In total, more than 10,000 copies of this training aircraft were produced, many of which were exported to other nations for use. The U.S. military employed more than 8,200 PT-13s, -17s, and –18s from 1935 through the end of the war.

Just as the Kaydet was rising to prominence, the Army Air Corps was holding open competitions for new basic trainers; in 1935, the North American BT-9 monoplane won a production contract for 42 copies. Spanning 42 ft, with length of 27 ft 7 in, and height of 13 ft 7 in, the aircraft was powered by a 400 hp Wright R-975 engine. Its two-man crew, in an enclosed glass cockpit, could achieve a top speed of approximately 170 mph. The model also featured a range of 750 miles, and service ceiling of nearly 20,000 ft. The model, and its next-generation successor, the BT-14, served prominently until 1940. The USAAC procured 250 "Yales" for use in training, but in hindsight the model is even more significant as the technological forebear of the superlative AT-6 Texan advanced trainer. It was also on this production run of aircraft that guns were added (as on the BT-9A and subsequent models) for further pilot/gunner training. Several BT-9Cs served in the Navy as NJ-1s.

By the mid 1930s the U.S. military recognized the need for a new generation of dedicated, high-performance trainers. Responding to a 1935 solicitation for an all-metal, monoplane trainer, famed Russian aircraft designer Alexander P. De Seversky offered his world record–holding SEV-3 (the world's fastest naval aircraft in 1933) as the BT-8. For training purposes, however, the model was purposefully limited to a relatively small power plant. Its 400 hp Pratt & Whitney R-985 Wasp Junior engine afforded a top speed in excess of 175 mph, a 15,000 ft service ceiling, and a maximum range of approximately 740 miles—reasonable but unimpressive performance characteristics. The Seversky BT-8 spanned 36 ft, with length of 24 ft 4 in, and height of 8 ft 10 in, which is not remarkable for its performance or production numbers. Only 30 or so were delivered to the army. The model, however, symbolically represented the advance of American military aviation technology and industry. It was not a modified biplane or surplus World War I–era fighter; rather, it was a high-performance, low-wing monoplane trainer built specifically for this purpose.

The Fairchild PT-19 appeared on the scene as the United States began mobilizing for war in 1940; indeed, the PT-19 served as the primary trainer for the majority of Allied World War II pilots. The PT-19 Cornell was introduced in 1939 as the replacement for the almost-too-easy-to-fly PT-17. It was ultimately produced for the USAAC in quantities exceeding 7,740. The plane was also exported, so the total production run amounted to an estimated 8,400 copies. The PT-19 spanned 36 ft, with length of 27 ft 8 in, and height of 7 ft 7 in. It was initially powered by a 200 hp Ranger L-440 engine, which produced 122 mph in maximum speed, as well as 400 miles in range and a service ceiling of 16,000 ft. Later models, designated PT-23, featured surplus Continental R-670 power plants.

The Vultee BT-13—or SNV (U.S. Navy)—Valiant, of which more than 12,000 were produced for the U.S. military through the end of the Second World War, also entered service in 1940. When Vultee entered the prototype for their BT-13 into a competitive trial, the Army Air Corps responded by immediately ordering 300 copies of the aircraft for use as a basic trainer. It was constructed entirely of metal, and it had a glass canopy to enclose its two-man cockpit. The Valiant spanned 42 feet, with length of 28 ft 10 in, and height of 11 ft 6 in. The 450 hp Pratt & Whitney R-985 Wasp Junior radial engine gave it a top speed of 180 mph, range of 725 miles, and operational ceiling of 21,000 ft.

For advanced training, the United States relied heavily on the North American AT-6 Texan, perhaps the most famous—and almost certainly the most important—American trainer of the era. American biplane trainers could not keep pace as fighter-plane technology improved throughout the 1930s. The USAAC soon realized the need for a higher-performing advanced monoplane suitable for training the pilots of their new, more advanced fighter-planes. In 1937 North American introduced an upgraded version of its popular BT-9. The army ordered more than 180 of the AT-6, and the navy procured several designated SNJ. Great Britain also ordered a number, which they dubbed the Harvard. Almost 15,000 copies were produced for the United States alone, and approximately 100,000 pilots received their wings after checking out in the AT-6. The model had a wingspan of 42 ft, length of 29 ft, and height of 11 ft 9 in. The Texan was powered by a 600 hp Pratt & Whitney R-1340 radial engine and possessed a top speed of 210 mph, with a service ceiling in excess of 24,000 ft, and maximum range of 625 miles. A number of these venerable planes remained in military service into the 1950s as spotting aircraft. Some of the 40 nations to which the aircraft was exported flew the aircraft in active duty into the 1990s.

In addition to training pilots for flying fighters, the army and navy needed to train pilots on multiengine aircraft. With a mind toward conserving strategic materials in the face of looming war, the USAAC tapped the Beech Aircraft Company in 1940 to fill this need with an all-wood—neoprene-lined fuel tanks included—multiengine trainer, the AT-10 Wichita. With a wingspan of 44 ft, length of 34 ft 4 in, and height of 10 ft 4 in, the aircraft was powered by twin 295 hp Lycoming R-680 radials. It could achieve a top speed of approximately 200 mph, ceiling of 19,700 ft, and range of 770 miles. The Wichita likely trained more American multiengine pilots than any other single trainer. More than 2,200 copies of the model were ultimately produced.

Beginning in 1941, the widely successful Cessna T-50 was adapted into military use as the UC-78 light transport and AT-8 trainer; the latter model was redeployed as the AT-17 with a less powerful engine more suitable for training purposes. An estimated 4,600 of all types were ultimately produced through the end of the decade. The aircraft spanned 41 ft 11 in, with length of 32 ft 9 in, and height of 9 ft 11 in.

It was powered by dual 245 hp Jacobs R-775 radials, producing a top speed just shy of 200 mph, along with a service ceiling of 15,000 ft and range of 750 miles.

Other notable American trainers of the World War II era include the Curtiss AT-9 Jeep, the Seversky AT-12, the North American P-64, and the Fairchild AT-21 Gunner. The Curtiss AT-9 was originally intended as a transitional trainer for pilots of multiengine aircraft, and approximately 800 were ordered for this purpose; however, bomber design advances made the trainer virtually obsolete almost immediately on its introduction into active service. The Seversky AT-12 preceded the AT-6 Texan in service as an advanced fighter-plane trainer, although it was initially exported as a fighter/bomber. The North American P-64 was similarly initially exported, but Japanese threats in the Pacific led to its recall by the United States, where it served briefly as a trainer and later as a liaison aircraft. The Fairchild AT-21 Gunner was aptly named because it was the sole American aircraft designed specifically for training machine gunners for service on bomber crews.

Transports and Gliders

By the end of World War I, the USAAC recognized the necessity of equipping itself with cargo and transport aircraft; however, a majority of the early designs in this category were foreign aircraft. The Douglas C-1 was one of the first successful indigenous designs in the American inventory. First introduced in 1925, the C-1 helped establish Douglas as one of the chief American cargo and transport designers even through the Cold War era. The C-1 biplane prototype spanned 56 ft 7 in, with length of 35 ft 4 in and height of 14 ft, and was powered by a 420 hp Liberty engine; this produced a top speed of 121 mph, and a service ceiling of 15,900 ft. It could carry six passengers or equivalent weight in cargo more than 750 miles. The C-1 was essentially a modified O-2 observation biplane, but it was nevertheless the USAAC's first dedicated "C" (Cargo) type aircraft. There were approximately 26 copies of this transport produced through the end of the decade.

Douglas's next major entry into the class was the C-39/R2D. The USAAC placed an order for the C-39 in 1939, the components for which were mostly the civilian transport DC-3. The model was designated R2D when purchased by the navy. There were ultimately 39 copies produced, many of which were pressed into emergency service during the first days of World War II. The model spanned 85 ft, with length of 61 ft 6 in, and height of 19 ft 7 in. It was powered by two 975 hp Wright R-1820 radials, providing 202 mph in maximum speed, 20,600 ft in operational ceiling, and 900 miles in maximum range. Although relatively outmoded, it did serve admirably as a stand-in until the development of the C-47 Skytrain.

The famous Douglas Skytrain first appeared in service in 1940, and, in a testament to the venerability of its design and manufacturing, remained in active service in one capacity or another well into the 1970s. Whereas the C-39 was a menagerie of parts from DC-3s, B-19s, and other aircraft, the C-47 was a military version of a complete DC-3. Well more than 10,000 copies of the aircraft saw service in the United States military (designated R4D in the navy). The aircraft's wingspan was 95 ft, its length was 64 ft 2 in, and its height was 16 ft 11 in. The C-47 featured two 1,200 hp Pratt & Whitney Twin Wasp R-1830 radials, generating a top speed of 229 mph. Along with a service ceiling of 23,200 ft, range in excess of 1,500 miles, and cargo of 28 passengers (along with three to six crewmembers) or more than 9,900 lbs, the C-47 was ideally suited to being the USAAC's transport workhorse well into the post–World War II era. During the Second World War, the model ran supplies into Asia and dropped more than 20,000 paratroopers on D-Day. In Vietnam, AC-47 gunships provided devastating close air support with their 20 mm cannons. Other models included rescue aircraft, trainers, and electronic warfare planes, making the C-47 one of the most versatile, and most famous, cargo planes in American aviation history.

Two years after the C-47's first appearance in the USAAC, the C-54/RD5 became Douglas's next great transport plane. Although first produced in 1938, a lack of domestic demand led to its export overseas. The model was recalled upon the buildup of threats from Japan, and the USAAC expressed newfound interest in it. There were approximately 1,200 eventually produced, many of which served as V.I.P. carriers due to the aircraft's superlative range, safety, and roominess. The C-54 "Skymaster" spanned 117 ft 6 in, with length of 93 ft 10 in, and height of 27 ft 6 in. Powered by four 1,290 hp Pratt & Whitney R-2000 radials, it could accommodate more than 32,000 lbs (or 50 passengers) over a distance of 3,900 miles. It also possessed a top speed of 265 mph, and service ceiling of 22,000 ft. The Skymaster was a very modern cargo plane, featuring all-metal construction and pressurized cabins. It remained in active military service through 1976, and formed the backbone of the famous Berlin Airlift of 1948.

Douglas was not the only successful transport manufacturer in the United States, only the most prolific. In 1940 Curtiss put its C-46/ R5C transport forward for consideration, and it was adopted in modest numbers by the army and navy (i.e., approximately 3,340 were produced through 1945). It spanned 108 ft, with length of 76 ft 4 in, and height of 21 ft 9 in. The model was powered by twin 2,000 hp Pratt & Whitney Double Wasp R-2800 radials. It could achieve a top speed in excess of 250 mph, and possessed a service ceiling of approximately 27,000 ft. The model served efficiently in all World War II theaters, especially in the China-Burma-India Theater. It could carry 40 troops, or a cargo load of more than 12,000 lbs over a 1,500 mile range.

Another notable aircraft of this type was the Waco CG-4 Haig/Hadrian. The CG-4 was the only glider produced in quantity within the United States during the Second World War, with total production by several companies totaling 12,400. Haigs (called Hadrians by the British), which were especially prevalent in the CBI Theater, were also used in great numbers during the Allied invasions of Sicily (1943) and the Normandy (D-Day, 1944) and Dutch coasts (Operation Market Garden, 1944). A single C-47 "mother" aircraft could haul as many as three Haigs into the air. The CG-4 spanned 83 ft 8 in, with length of 48 ft 3 in, and height of 12 ft 7 in. It was piloted by a two-member crew. It could accommodate a troop contingent of 15, or could even be loaded with a jeep or 75-mm howitzer artillery gun.

Reconnaissance and Liaison Aircraft

From their first military uses, aircraft have served as reconnaissance and liaison vehicles. The USAAC and U.S. Navy continued to procure aircraft to meet these needs even as the role of military aviation was rapidly changing in the 1920s, 1930s, and even into the 1940s. Indeed, almost immediately after World War I, the army placed an order for a light liaison aircraft. Alfred Verville's M-1 Messenger design won an open competition, and the Sperry Aircraft Corporation won a competitive bid to build it. With a 20 ft wingspan, length of 17 ft 9 in, height of 6 ft 9 in, and weighing just 623 lbs (empty), the M-1 still stands as the smallest military aircraft in U.S. aviation history. Its power plant was a 60 hp Lawrence J-4 three-cylinder radial engine, which produced just 96 mph in top speed. The aircraft possessed a maximum range of approximately 500 miles. There were approximately 42 copies of the tiny M-1 produced, although they were withdrawn from active duty shortly after Elmer Sperry, owner of the aircraft's production plant, died upon crashing his own M-1 into the English Channel. Nevertheless, the model proved an important transitional step for the USAAC.

The USAAC in 1924 awarded a production contract to Douglas for its O-2 model to replace the M-1 as a liaison aircraft, as well as the aging De Havilland DH-4 photo-reconnaissance aircraft of World War I. The observation ("O") biplane, which was first flown in 1924, spanned 40 ft, with length of 30 ft, and height of 10 ft 5 in. Most of the 649 of all models produced featured the 525 hp Pratt & Whitney Hornet R-1690 radial, affording 149 mph in top speed, a service ceiling in excess of 20,000 ft, and a range of approximately 300 miles. The aircraft was overhauled and reproduced in 1930 as the O-25, and again a couple of years later as the O-38. It could be armed with two .30 caliber machine guns and up to 400 lbs of bombs. The plane accommodated a two-man crew. The O-2 was out of front-line duty by the outbreak of war.

Although defeated by the Douglas O-2 in competitive trials in 1924, the Thomas-Morse observation biplane was redesigned as a slightly smaller, all-metal version of the Douglas O-2. The USAAC eventually purchased more than 170 copies of Thomas-Morse's O-19 in this configuration. The aircraft possessed a wingspan of 39 ft 9 in, length of 28 ft 4 in, and height of 10 ft 6 in. The 450 hp Pratt & Whitney R-1340 radial engine powered the aircraft to 137 mph in maximum speed. It also featured a service ceiling of 20,500 ft and a range of 450 miles. Armed with two .30 caliber machine guns, the O-19 carried a crew of two, and served in active duty through 1938 in a variety of roles (including that of personal transport for the secretary of war).

Douglas would make both of these aircraft obsolete upon the introduction of its O-31, which was a high-wing monoplane featuring a crew of two in an enclosed cockpit. The O-31, which first appeared in 1930, was redesigned with a parasol-mounted wing (O-43), and later with wing struts and aft-of-center canopy (O-46); all told, more than 100 models were produced through 1941. The aircraft had a wingspan of 45 ft 9 in, length of 34 ft 6 in, and height of 10 ft 8 in, and it featured a 725 hp Pratt & Whitney Wasp Junior R-1535 radial. The model was armed with two .30 caliber machine guns, and could reach a top speed of 200 mph, with an operational ceiling of 24,000 ft, and range of approximately 435 miles.

The O-31, however modern it was in 1930, was dramatically outclassed in 1935 by the North American O-47, an all-metal, midwing monoplane spanning 46 ft 5 in, with length of 33 ft 7 in, and height of 12 ft 2 in. The O-47 had such innovations as retractable landing gear, and it was, technologically, the world's most advanced observation aircraft of its time. The 0-47 carried a crew of three, including a photographer stationed in a belly pod. Its 975 hp Wright R-1820 radial provided an impressive 220 mph of maximum speed, as well as a service ceiling in excess of 32,000 ft, and a maximum range of approximately 400 mph. Although relatively outmoded by the time of World War II, the model did serve in front-line observation duties through 1942, with approximately 220 copies procured by the USAAC during that time.

Curtiss's O-52 Owl was the USAAC's final observation-series ("O") aircraft. First flying in 1940, the Owl featured fine performance characteristics, including a top speed of 220 mph, ceiling of 21,000 ft, and range of 700 miles. The army ordered more than 200 copies, but the outbreak of war soon after determined it to be underpowered and ill-suited for combat, despite being armed with three .30 caliber machine guns. The Owl spanned 40 ft 9 in, had a length of 26 ft 4 in, a height of 9 ft 3 in, and was powered by a 600 hp Pratt & Whitney R-1340 radial. It accommodated a crew of two. Most saw service during the war as trainers.

The O-52 was replaced tactically with bombers for long-range reconnaissance and such models as the Stinson O-49/L-1, the first in the army's new "L" series of short-range reconnaissance and liaison aircraft. The Stinson originated as an "O"-type observation aircraft, but was redesignated in 1942 upon the adoption of these new tactical guidelines for aerial reconnaissance. The O-49/L-1 Vigilant was first flown in 1940. It transitioned the USAAC from the dedicated reconnaissance class of the interwar era to the multipurpose reconnaissance/ bombers and smaller liaison aircraft of the World War II era. The Vigilant had a wingspan of 50 ft 11 in, length of 34 ft 3 in, height of 10 ft 2 in, and was powered by a 295 hp Lycoming R-680 radial. It proved adept at short takeoff and landing, a feature that made it extremely attractive to the USAAC as a close-support reconnaissance vehicle; however, the Air Corps was beginning to recognize that such aircraft as the Vigilant would not survive modern combat due to such lackluster performance characteristics as a mere 122 mph top speed, ceiling of 12,800 ft, and range of 280 miles. There were approximately 325 copies of the model built for the army, and many saw service with foreign nations via the Lend-Lease program.

The USAAC turned to the Grasshopper series of aircraft for quantity of shorter range tactical reconnaissance: Piper's O-59/L-4 was the most numerous of this series, with more than 5,400 produced. In addition, Stinson's L-5 model featured more than 3,200 produced; Taylorcraft's L-2 numbered 1,900, and Aeronca's, almost 1,500. The Piper variant spanned 34 ft 3 in, with length of 22 ft 4 in, and height of 6 ft 8 in. The tiny aircraft weighed less than 700 lbs (empty) and was powered by a mere 65 hp (the Continental engine afforded a top speed of approximately 87 mph). The Grasshopper featured a range of 250 miles, and a ceiling of 9,500 ft, and was thus designed for multipurpose liaison and rear-echelon duty. The Grasshopper was also notable in that it was of a mixed construction, an important war-time feature for saving strategic materials for the larger fighters and bombers. Still, the model was ruggedly built, and it served admirably in a variety of roles throughout the war.

British Auxiliary Aircraft

Given the RAF's budgetary restrictions throughout most of the inter-war years, it tended to rely upon decommissioned fighters and bombers to provide auxiliary roles as reconnaissance aircraft or trainers, although a few (the de Havilland DH 60 Gypsy Moth trainer) were designed specifically for these roles. In addition, just as surplus bombers had been purchased and converted to provide commercial passenger service, the RAF could achieve the same thing with its bombers and did so, using many to carry troops and supplies to various hot spots within the Empire as indicated in the first chapter.

Trainers

The last biplane trainer to be designed for the RAF, the de Havilland DH 82 Tiger Moth, was introduced in 1932 after modifications to the earlier DH 60T Gypsy Moth. With a wingspan of 29 ft 4 in, length of 23 ft 11 in, and loaded weight of 1,825 lbs, the fabric-covered Tiger Moth was light and compact, and it was one of the most acrobatic biplane trainers ever produced. More important, it was easy to handle and forgiving, which made it well-suited for novices. It served as one of the primary trainers for Allied pilots who flew in World War II. The Tiger Moth was powered by a 120 hp DH Gypsy liquid-cooled engine and had a 109 mph top speed, 13,600 ft service ceiling, and 300 mile range.

In addition to the 8,796 trainers produced in Great Britain and the dominions, 420 radio-operated, wooden-constructed versions, known as "Queen Bee Drones," were manufactured to serve as anti-aircraft gunnery targets.

The twin-engine Avro Anson was designed in 1935 and entered service the following year as an armed coastal patrol aircraft. It used a combination of steel-tube, wood, and fabric construction and was the RAF's first monoplane as well as the first with a retractable undercarriage. The

Anson had a wingspan of 56 ft 6 in, length of 42 ft 3 in, and loaded weight of 9,900 lbs. Powered by two 420 hp Cheetah XV radial engines, it had a top speed of 188 mph and range of 700 miles. At the outbreak of the war, the Anson outfitted 12 Coastal Command squadrons. Even though it continued in that role until 1941, it made its primary contribution to the British war effort as an air crew trainer, training navigators, radio operators, and air gun operators. One variant, the Mk.X, was used for transporting freight or up to eight passengers. A total of 10,996 were produced until 1952, and it remained in service until 1968.

The twin-engine De Havilland Dominie was introduced originally as a passenger liner (the DH 89 Dragon Rapide), and it served primarily as a radio and navigator trainer and as a communications aircraft. With the outbreak of the war, civilian versions were pressed into military service in an effort to supply the British Expeditionary Force in France. A total of 730 of all varieties were constructed.

The Airspeed Oxford, which was introduced in 1937, was a military version of the twin-engine Envoy small passenger craft. Dubbed the "Ox-box" by British airmen, the Oxford provided the RAF with its first twin-engine trainer. With a 53 ft 4 in wingspan, 34 ft 6 in length, and loaded weight of 8,000 lbs, the Oxford's two 370 hp Armstrong-Siddley Cheetah radial engines could reach a top speed of 188 mph. Even though the plane was easy to handle in flight, landing it proved to be difficult, but this was precisely what pilots needed in training. It also came equipped with a single-gun turret to train gunners and sophisticated systems to train radio operators, navigators, and bombardiers. There were approximately 8,750 built by war's end and it remained in RAF service until 1954.

The Miles Master provided a performance nearly meeting that of early versions of the Hurricane and Spitfire. It also provided the RAF with its most widely used advanced trainer during World War II. It had a wooden frame and plywood cover, and a wingspan of 39 ft, length of 35 ft 7 in, and loaded weight of 5,573 lbs. The Master was powered by an 870 hp Bristol Mercury XX radial, and had a top speed of 242 mph, a service ceiling of 25,100 ft, and a range of 393 miles. It was armed with a single .303 caliber machine gun for gunning practice. A total of 3,227 entered service between 1939 and the end of the war.

Transports and Gliders

Although the twin-engine Bristol Bombay was designed as a troop transport carrier in 1931, the Great Depression delayed its production until early 1939. It had a wingspan of 95 ft 9 in, a length of 69 ft 3 in, and loaded weight of 20,000 lbs, and its two 1010 hp Bristol Pegaus XXII radial engines gave it a maximum speed of 192 mph, a service ceiling of 25,000 ft, and a range of 880 miles. Although only 51 were produced, the Bristol Bombay, which was capable of carrying up to 24 troops or a payload of 7,200 lbs, saw significant action during the first half of the war, ferrying troops and supplies across the English Channel in 1940, evacuating British forces from Crete in 1941, and dropping paratroopers behind enemy lines in North Africa.

The Armstrong Whitworth Albemarle, which was originally intended as a bomber, was instead converted to transport service. It had a wingspan of 77 ft, a length of 59 ft 11 in, and a loaded weight of 36,500 lbs. The Albemarle was powered by two 1560 hp Bristol Hercules XI radials that produced a maximum speed of 265 mph, a service ceiling of 18,000 ft, and a range of 1,300 miles. A total of 310 were used as special operations transports (dropping paratroopers behind enemy lines). An additional 247 served as the standard tug for the Airspeed Horsa assault glider, seeing action in invasion of Sicily in 1943 and the D-Day landings in June 1944. At least 10 were shipped to the Soviet Union.

The success of German glider-borne troops in May 1940, particularly the seizure of the Belgian fortress of Eban Emael, convinced the British to develop similar capabilities. Great Britain produced two primary transport gliders during the war: the Airspeed Horsa and the General Aircraft Hamilcar. The high-wing, monoplane Horsa was constructed of wood and covered with heavy canvas with a wingspan of 88 ft and length of 67 ft. It came in two varieties: the Mk.1, which was configured for carrying up to 25 troops, and the Mk.2, which could carry up to 7,000 lbs of freight and featured a hinged nose section for easier loading and unloading. The Horsa was towed by a twin-engine bomber and it jettisoned its undercarriage after taking off and relied upon compressed air to extend underwing dive brakes, which allowed it to land on its retractable skid in relatively small areas. First used on a large scale, it carried airborne troops during the Normandy Landing and Rhine River crossing. There were approximately 3,800 of the Horsa gliders constructed. The Hamilcar was the largest Allied glider of the war with a wingspan of 110 ft, length of 68 ft, and loaded weight of 36,000 ft. It was capable of carrying a payload of 17,500 lbs. It first saw action in the D-Day landings and proved immensely significant because it could provide heavy equipment (the British Tetrarch Mk.IV tank) to airborne troops operating behind enemy lines. A total of 390 were produced.

Reconnaissance and Liaison Aircraft

Although the British used a number of multipurpose aircraft, such as the de Havilland DH 98 Mosquito, for reconnaissance duties, the Westland Wapiti was one of the few designed primarily for reconnaissance purposes, although it also had light bombing capabilities that made it ideally suited for use in policing the empire. Using wings and tail units from de Havilland DH 9a surplus aircraft as a cost-saving measure, the Wapiti had wingspan of 46 ft 5 in, a length of 32 ft 6 in, and a loaded weight of 5,400 lbs. Its 460 hp Bristol Jupiter VI radial engine provided a maximum speed of 140 mph, a service ceiling of 20,600 ft, and a range of 360 miles. Because it was intended for use throughout the empire, the Wapiti used an all metal framework to stand up to the wear and tear it would encounter. It could be modified to operate with skis in Arctic environments, with twin floats in coastal areas, or with additional fuel tanks for desert patrols. More than 1,000 were built, and 500 entered RAF service between 1927 and 1939.

The Westland Lysander, which entered service in 1938, was based on 1934 specifications for an aircraft with STOL (short takeoff and landing) characteristics to provide reconnaissance and liaison service. With a wingspan of 50 ft, a length of 30 ft 6 in, and loaded weight of 6,318 lbs, it featured a high-wing monoplane configuration, spatted wheels, and slotted flaps that allowed it to take off and land at just 65 mph. Its 870 hp Bristol Mercury XX radial engine provided a top speed of 212 miles, a service ceiling of 21,500 ft, and a range of 600 miles. Armed with three .303 caliber machine guns, it was called upon to provide strafing attacks during the height of the German invasion of France, resulting in 112 being lost fulfilling a role for which they were not intended. They proved most useful in dropping special agents into Nazi-occupied Europe. A total of 1,593 were built.

French Reconnaissance and Auxiliary Aircraft

Like Great Britain, France relied heavily upon many of its World War I aircraft and decommissioned fighters to provide auxiliary roles throughout the 1920s and 1930 as a cost-saving measure. In addition, budgetary pressures led the French to develop a number of multipurpose fighter, bomber, reconnaissance (B.C.R.) types during the 1930s (these are discussed in other chapters). The most important factor for the lack of specialized auxiliary aircraft, however, was that the French military was designed to fight a defensive war, as evidenced by its construction of the massive Maginot Line. Content to wait for the German Army to come to it, the French Army did not have the same offensive-mindedness with which it had entered the First World War. As a result, the French did not develop transports or gliders as did Germany. To an extent, its lack of these types of auxiliary aircraft was a casualty of World War I.

The Breguet 19 was introduced in 1924 as a replacement for its World War I predecessors. The plane was also a principal light bomber, was one of the best two-seat reconnaissance biplanes of the interwar years, and remained in service until 1939. Although it was fabric-covered, its all metal structure made it a rugged aircraft and its semi-circular fuselage gave it a more streamlined appearance and improved performance. With a wingspan of 48 ft 8 in, length of 31 ft 2 in, loaded weight of 4,850 lbs, and 450 hp Lorraine water-cooled engine, the Breguet 19 could reach a top speed of 137 mph and had a range of 497 miles. In its reconnaissance version, the Breguet 19 retained the two 7.7 mm machine guns, but it was fitted with extra tanks to extend its range. As a result, it would set numerous long-distance records, including an incredible 1929 nonstop flight from Paris to Manchuria. The Breguet 19 was also ideally suited for service on long patrols in French possessions in North and West Africa and dominions in the Middle East.

The Bloch MB 174 entered service on the eve of World War II and was the first major aircraft designed specifically to provide reconnaissance for the Armée de l'Air. With a wingspan of 58 ft 8 in, length of 40 ft 2 in, loaded weight of 15,784 lbs, and two 1,110 hp Gnome-Rhone 14N-48/49 radial engines, the MB 174 had a range of 1,025 miles, which made it ideal for reconnaissance. It was well-defended with seven 7.5 mm machine guns and could also carry up to 882 lbs of bombs. More important, it had a top speed of 329 mph, which enabled it to escape Luftwaffe fighters. There were approximately 80 built before France fell to the Germans, who continued production of them for use as trainers. The French resumed production after the war, reconfiguring them as torpedo bombers.

German Reconnaissance and Auxiliary Aircraft

Trainers

There was no formal, official German training program because the Luftwaffe was banned under the terms of the Treaty of Versailles.

However, the 1920s and 1930s witnessed the popularization of private flying clubs, as interest in flying became a world-wide phenomenon. Germany was no exception, and it was in these ostensibly civilian clubs that future Luftwaffe pilots first learned to fly. By 1935, Hitler was openly flaunting the treaty, and restarted the air force. From that time on, the underground training program was made officially sanctioned.

The Arado Flugzeugwerke GmbH produced a series of training aircraft throughout the interwar years. The Ar 66, first flown in 1932, proved to one of the most symbolically important trainers in their series. Although it initially equipped private flight schools, it was soon part of the primary training program for the reborn Luftwaffe. The model spanned 32 ft 9 in, with a length of 26 ft 6 in and a height of 10 ft. It was powered by a 240 hp Argus As 10C engine, which produced a top speed of 130 mph, range of 445 miles, and service ceiling of 17,000 ft. Although total production figures are difficult to ascertain, more than 6,000 copies were definitely produced, with the model serving as one of the last biplane trainers in the German inventory. Several thousand were refitted for use as stop-gap night-fighters against the Soviet Union on the Eastern Front.

Along with the Ar 66 the Gotha Go 145 was the last great German biplane trainer. More than 9,960 copies were produced in Germany, with an additional 1,000 or so being produced in Spain and elsewhere. Spanning 29 ft 6 in, with length of 28 ft 6 in, and height of 9 ft 6 in, the Go 145 was, like the Ar 66, powered by the Argus As 10C eight-cylinder vee-type engine. The model possessed a top speed of 130 mph and was first delivered to training programs in 1935, where it continued to serve throughout the war. As the Eastern Front stagnated into stalemate, a number of Go 145s were used as raiders and light bombers.

Another Arado, the Ar 96, served as the Luftwaffe's primary monoplane trainer from its first flight in 1938. Of entirely metal construction, the Ar 96 spanned 36 ft 1 in, with a length of 27 ft 1 in, and height of 8 ft 6 in. It was initially powered by a 240 hp Argus As 10C engine, but later models featured the more powerful As 410A 12 cylinder engine. The aircraft possessed a top speed of approximately 205 mph, an operational ceiling of 23,000 ft, and range of 615 miles. With more than 11,546 copies produced, the Ar 96 was a vital cog in the Luftwaffe training program. The Ar 96 was highly successful in this task, and it served through the end of the decade in foreign air forces.

The Messerschmitt BF-108 Taifun served as a trainer for pilots, but the lessons learned from its production proved equally instructive for the designers of the great monoplane fighter, the BF-109. The 108 trainer spanned 24 ft 10 in, with length of 27 ft 3 in, and height of 7 ft 6 in. Powered by the As 10C, the model featured a top speed of 196 mph, 870 mile range, and 16,400 ft service ceiling. Along with the Ar 96, it formed the basis of advanced training for Luftwaffe pilots. During the war, it also mimicked the other trainers, which were all employed in auxiliary use as necessary (liaison, harassment bombing, or night-fighting duties).

Focke-Wulf's Fw 58 Weihe was an important transitional aircraft. Although primarily a multiengine trainer, it also served in a variety of transport, light bombing, and other utility roles. The Fw 58 was first flown in 1935 and was a small civilian airliner. By 1937, the Luftwaffe adopted it into military service. A low-wing monoplane, the Fw 58 spanned 68 ft 11 in, with length of 45 ft 11 in, and height of 13 ft 10 in. The aircraft was powered by twin Argus As 10C engines, and possessed a top speed of 174 mph, with range of approximately 500 miles and service ceiling of 18,000 ft. Armed with up to three 7.92 mm machine guns, the aircraft was manned by a crew of two, but could carry six passengers or similar cargo. Some models were fitted with bomb racks on underwing hardpoints. It is estimated that no fewer than 2,000 copies of the versatile Fw 58 were produced.

Transports and Gliders

As with most German manufacturers, the Junkers Flugzeug und Motorenwerke AG produced civilian aircraft that were readily adaptable into military use. The Ju 52, first flown on October 13, 1930, was first marketed as a civilian airliner. Shortly after its introduction, however, the German air force adopted it into service as their chief transport aircraft; in this role, the venerable Ju 52 shone. There were approximately 4,835 copies of the model produced, and some remained in service in foreign air forces into the 1980s. The Ju 52 featured a wingspan of 95 ft 11 in, with length of 62 ft, and height of 14 ft 9 in. The aircraft was powered by three 830 hp BMW 132A nine cylinder air-cooled radials, and it possessed a maximum speed of 190 mph, service ceiling of 18,000 ft, and range of more than 800 miles. In addition to a crew of three, it could accommodate up to 17 passengers or equivalent cargo. Most models were lightly armed, with a single 13 mm and twin 7.92 mm machine guns. As a light bomber, the Ju 52 could carry a maximum bomb load of 1,102 lbs. The Ju 52 was a versatile and reliable aircraft that was affectionately known by her crews as "Auntie Junkers" or, perhaps more appropriately, "Iron Annie."

The Luftwaffe generally lacked the impetus for designing long-range heavy transports, similar to their want of a long-range heavy bomber. The lack of both ultimately would greatly hinder the flexibility of Germany's war plans; however, the Luftwaffe did make great use of gliders as transport aircraft to help partially fill this void. The design company DFS had long been a producer of high-performance gliders, and in 1937 they offered the 230, a transport and assault glider designed by Hans Jacobs. Total production reached 1,022 copies of the DFS 230, which spanned 68 ft 6 in, with length of 36 ft 11 in, and height of just less than 9 ft. The glider was generally hauled into flight by a Junkers Ju 52 and could accommodate a pilot and up to nine passengers. It was armed with three 7.9 mm machine guns. The DFS 230 has a colorful World War II service record, being the aircraft of choice for the raid on the Belgian fort, Eban-Emael (May 10, 1940), as well as the German invasion of Crete (May 1941). The model most famously allowed impetuous Waffen SS Colonel Otto Skorzeny to raid Gran Sasso in the Italian Alps on September 12, 1943, rescuing Benito Mussolini from his captivity.

The Gotha Go 242 performed more traditional transport duties. It first flew in 1941, and more than 1,520 copies of the glider were produced through the end of the war. With a distinctive twin boom and tail assembly, the Go 242 was 51 ft 10 in long, with height of 14 ft 4 in, and wingspan of 80 ft 4 in. It could be armed with four 7.92 mm machine guns, and it accommodated 23 passengers in addition to a two-man crew. It could be towed airborne by a Heinkel He 111, or, less commonly, a Messerschmitt BF-110. There were approximately 130 models fitted with two 700 hp Gnome-Rhone 14 cylinder radials that were redesignated the Go 244. Most Go 242s and 244s saw service along the Eastern Front, although a few were used in the Mediterranean and North African Theaters.

The Messerschmitt 321 was quite distinctive compared with any other glider. Aptly named the Gigant ("Giant"), the glider possessed a wingspan of 180 ft 5 in, length of 92 ft 4 in, and height of 33 ft 4 in, as well as a maximum takeoff weight in excess of 75,000 lbs. It could carry a fully loaded 120-man company of troops, or up to 22,000 lbs of cargo. The aircraft was so large and heavy that it took three BF-110s, usually with the assistance of rocket-boosters, to tow the Me 321 into the air; in fact, 10 He 111s were fitted with a fifth engine specifically for the purposes of serving as the tug for Me 321s. There were approximately 200 Me 321s fitted with six 1,140 hp Gnome-Rhone 14 cylinder radials, scoured from captured French equipment, and designated as Me 323 transports. These massive aircraft possessed a pedestrian maximum speed of approximately 150 mph, service ceiling of 13,000 ft, and range of 680 miles. The Luftwaffe even experimented with a gunship version, which featured as many as eleven 20 mm cannons and four 13 mm machine guns. The aircraft was ultimately too slow and insufficiently armored to be of much service in any area where the Luftwaffe did not possess air superiority.

Reconnaissance and Liaison Aircraft

Although there were a number of reconnaissance types produced in interwar Germany, one of the earliest ordered into quantity production by the still-underground Luftwaffe was the Heinkel He 45. The –A model was a trainer, whereas types –B and –C were used as reconnaissance and light bomber aircraft. The models entered service in late 1932. The He 45 spanned 37 ft 8 in, with length of 34 ft 9 in, and height of 11 ft 10 in. It was powered by a single 750 hp BMW VI 12 cylinder vee-type engine, which afforded a top speed of 180 mph, service ceiling of 18,000 ft, and range of 746 miles. More than 500 copies of the He 45 were produced, although most all were out of front-line service by the outbreak of World War II.

Heinkel's He 46 was designed as a reconnaissance and light attack cooperation aircraft. First flying in 1931, it entered the Luftwaffe in 1936, with more than 480 eventually produced by various manufacturers. Powered by a 650 hp Bramo 322B SAM nine cylinder radial engine, it possessed a top speed of 160 mph, with range of approximately 620 miles and service ceiling of 19,700 ft. It spanned 45 ft 11 in, with length of 31 ft 2 in, and height of 12 ft. Like its predecessor, the He 45, the He 46 accommodated a two-man crew. It was armed with a single 7.92 mm machine gun, and could also be outfitted with up to twenty 22-lb bombs. After seeing some combat service as reconnaissance and close air support aircraft in Spain, the model was retired in favor of the Henschel Hs 126.

The Hs 126 proved to be a worthy successor to the He 46, and served with great effectiveness as the Luftwaffe's primary tactical reconnaissance aircraft well into the war. Following its first flight in August 1936, the Luftwaffe ordered production and received its first Hs 126s approximately 10 months later. The model featured the 900 hp Bramo Fafnir 323A nine cylinder radial engine and could achieve a top speed in excess of 220 mph, as well as a ceiling of 27,000 ft, and range of 360 miles. The Hs 126 spanned 47 ft 5 in, with length of 35 ft 8 in, and height of 12 ft 3 in. It also featured two 7.92 mm machine guns for defense, and could carry an offensive armament of up to 110 lbs; alternatively, it could be fitted with an external fuel tank to extend its range. There were approximately 800 copies of the two-seat reconnaissance aircraft built.

The Fieseler Fi 156 Storch was far more famous, and important, to the Luftwaffe. When the Luftwaffe organized an open design competition calling for a short takeoff and landing (STOL) capable reconnaissance aircraft, Feiseler's ungainly Storch beat out models from such design firms as Messerschmitt and Focke-Wulf. In the sincerest form of flattery, the Fi 156 was copied by several foreign nations, including Japan and Russia. For the Luftwaffe alone, more than 2,549 were produced, forming the backbone of Germany's liaison and multipurpose reconnaissance air corps from its first delivery in May 1937 through the end of the war. The model spanned 46 ft 9 in, with length of 32 ft 5 in, and height of 9 ft 10 in. It was powered by a single Argus As 10C engine, whose 240 hp generated a maximum speed of 109 mph. The Fi 156 also featured a service ceiling of approximately 15,000 ft, and a range of approximately 375 miles. Its performance characteristics belie its ruggedness, however, because the Fi 156's durability and STOL capabilities made it an invaluable part of the German military infrastructure throughout the entire war and in every theater.

The Focke-Wulf Fw 189 Uhu (Owl) was another important reconnaissance aircraft in the Luftwaffe inventory. The Fw 189, with twin booms, was 39 ft 5 in long, with height of 10 ft 2 in, and wingspan of 60 ft 5 in. Powered by twin 465 hp Argus As 410A 12 cylinder engines, the model possessed a maximum speed of 217 mph, service ceiling of 24,000 ft, and range of 415 miles. It was typically armed with up to five 7.92 mm machine guns and external hardpoints for up to 440 lbs of bombs. Beginning with its first delivery in late 1940, approximately 864 copies of the three-seat Fw 189s were produced for the Luftwaffe. It earned high marks from its crews and its opponents alike, and proved to be a highly reliable and effective reconnaissance aircraft.

The Focke-Wulf 200 Condor was equally important, especially in its unique (for the Luftwaffe) role as a maritime reconnaissance bomber. The Condor was initially designed in 1937 as a civilian transport plane, and it proved readily adaptable to long flights over water thanks to its maximum range of 2,750 miles. The model spanned 107 ft 7 in, with length of 77 ft 1 in, and height of 20 ft 8 in. The Fw 200 was powered by four 1,610 hp BMW 323 nine cylinder radials, and it possessed a maximum speed of 224 mph with a service ceiling of 19,000 ft. A crew of eight operated the aircraft, which was armed with five 13 mm machine guns and a 20 mm cannon. It also carried more than 4,600 lbs of bombs. Several of the 278 total copies produced were equipped with a Fug 200 Hohentwiel radar set, which greatly enhanced their capabilities as shipping interdictor. In this role, Fw 200s claimed more than 365,000 tons of Allied shipping through early 1941, when Allied fighters made the skies too dangerous for the rather fragile Condor. Because it was designed with civilian uses in mind, the airframe was simply not durable enough for extended combat duty, although it was rather successful in limited use. Through the end of the war, the Fw 200 continually served as one of the few dedicated long-range transport options in the German inventory.

Italian Auxiliary Aircraft

The same sort of budgetary pressures that limited the development of specially designed auxiliary aircraft in France applied to Italy as well. In many respects, however, Italy is more similar to Great Britain because it would use its bombers and fighters for multiple purposes. The Fiat CR 20, for example, was also produced in two-seat reconnaissance versions, and almost every Italian bomber also saw service as transport aircraft both before being decommissioned as bombers and afterwards. Nevertheless, the Regia Aeronautica did possess a few transports that were designed specifically for that purpose.

Although Italy relied upon a number of aircraft for transport duties (the Caproni CA 309–316, the Piaggio P 108, and the Savoia-Marchetti SM 81 Pipistrello), the Savoia-Marchetti SM 75 and the Savoia-Marchetti SM 82 Canguru were exceptions. With a wingspan of 97 ft 5 in, a length of 70 ft, and a loaded weight of 28,700 lbs, the SM75 had originally been designed for passenger service for Ala Littoria in 1937. Powered by three Alfa Romeo AR 126 RC34 radial engines, it had a top speed of 225 mph, a service ceiling of 20,500 ft, and a range of 1,070 miles. The SM 75 was requisitioned for military service when Italy entered the war in June 1940. It could carry up to 30 troops and saw action throughout the Mediterranean until the end of the war with a total of 98 being constructed. The three-engine SM 82 proved to be one of the best heavy transports available to the Axis. With a wingspan of 97 ft 4 in, a length of 75 ft 1 in, and a maximum weight of 44,092, the SM 82 was powered by three 950 hp Alfa Romeo 128 RC 21 radial engines, which provided a top speed of 230 mph, a service ceiling of 19,685 ft, and a range of 1,864 miles. The plane was capable of carrying up to 40 fully equipped troops or almost 9,000 lbs of freight, and it proved to be invaluable in keeping Rommel's Afrika Korps supplied

in North Africa, prolonging the fighting in that theater. Of the approximately 400 SM 82s that were constructed between 1941 and 1943,
at least 50 entered service with the Luftwaffe in the Baltic on the Eastern Front. Those that survived the war continued in service with the
Italian Air Force into the 1950s.

Japanese Reconnaissance and Auxiliary Aircraft

Trainers

The Japanese armed forces surely learned from their experiences in
World War I the value of air power in modern combat operations. In
the interwar years, the modernization program, which had severed
Japan's former dependence on foreign designs, airframes, and engines
by the mid-1930s, impelled the production of various training, reconnaissance, and other auxiliary types. Although many of the early
designs were modeled after or inspired by foreign aircraft, like several
of Japan's fighters and bombers, this arm of their air forces was effectively built up from scratch.

As their air forces grew in number and self-sufficiency, the Japanese military began encouraging the development of both Japanese-
designed and Japanese-built fighters, bombers, and reconnaissance
planes and of other auxiliary aircraft as well. One of the first generated
from this effort was the Mitsubishi K3M, a single-engine crew trainer.
The navy asked Mitsubishi, which in turn commissioned British engineer Herbert Smith, to construct a training aircraft. Smith began the
project in 1928, but soon abandoned it. Joji Hattori revived the design
the following year. In May 1930, Hattori's prototype undertook its
maiden flight under the hand of Mitsubishi test pilot Nakawa.
Although performance proved satisfactory, the navy sought several
modifications, particularly to the power plant, before ordering the
model in volume. There were approximately 624 K3Ms produced, the
bulk of which were of the K3M3 revision, powered by a 300 hp Nakajima Kotobuki 2 KAI 2 nine cylinder air-cooled radial engine. It was a
full-service trainer, housing a pilot, gunner, instructor, and two
observers, and it was armed with a rear-firing, flexible 7.7 mm machine
gun and up to four 66-lb bombs. The K3M was constructed out of a
combination of wood and metal, and it spanned 51 ft 9 in, with a
length of 31 ft 3 in, wing area of 371 sq feet, and a height of 12 ft 6 in.
The K3M, which was eventually replaced by Kyushu's K11W (1943),

proved a capable trainer, but it is most noteworthy for its place at the lead of the line of Japanese-designed, Japanese-built auxiliary aircraft.

The Yokosuka K5Y, code-named "Willow" by the Allies, was far more important for its role in the Japanese air forces' training regimen. In 1932, the navy issued a series of specifications calling for an updated intermediate ground-based trainer. Yokosuka's prototype, which first flew in December 1933, was of sesquiplane design with a fixed under-carriage, powered by a 300 hp Hitachi Amakaze 11 nine cylinder air-cooled radial engine. The aircraft, 36 ft in span, 26 ft 4 in in length, 10 ft 5 in in height, and wing area of 289 sq feet, achieved relatively modest performance characteristics (a 132 mph maximum speed and a climb rate of 9,845 in 13 minutes 30 seconds). Of course, perfor-mance was less important for training purposes than reliability and ease-of-handling, and based on production numbers one can safely assume that the K5Y performed well at both tasks. The K5Y entered production almost immediately after its maiden flight, and it remained in production and service throughout the war. There were ultimately 5,770 of this type produced, making it by far the most-produced trainer in the Japanese fleet.

In the JAAF's training program, successful completion of a solo flight in a Tachikawa Ki-55 trainer was the last step toward getting one's pilot's wings. A noncombat twin to the Ki-36 close air support craft, the Ki-55 was of identical dimensions and could achieve virtu-ally identical speed, even though it was slightly heavier (2,848 lbs empty compared with the Ki-36's empty weight of 2,749 lbs) and had a more sluggish climb rate (30 seconds longer to 9,845 ft). Toward the end of the war, some of the 1,389 Ki-55's built for the army saw serv-ice as kamikaze craft, packed with either a 551 lb or 1,102 lb bomb.

Transports

As the Pacific war loomed in August 1939, the army solicited designs on a heavy transport plane. Mitsubishi had developed a commercial transport aircraft earlier that year, a design based largely on one of their military types (the Ki-21, "Sally"). The army requested an air-craft capable of hauling 11 passengers and 600–700 lbs of freight more than 800–1,800 miles. With a crew of four, the plane was not to exceed a maximum loaded weight of 17,417 lbs. Mitsubishi took their Ki-21, redesigned the fuselage and lowered the placement of the wings, and in July 1940 produced the first prototype of the Ki-57, which the Allies would come to call "Topsy." It first flew in August of that year, and was immediately placed into production. With a span of 74 ft 1 in, length of 52 ft 9 in, wing area of 754 sq feet, and height of 15 ft 8 in, the Ki-57 would quickly become the army's standard large transport. Most of the 507 Ki-57s produced were of the –II modification, differing only in power plant (dual 1,050 hp Army Type 100 fourteen-cylinder air-cooled radial engines) from the –I type (dual 850 hp Army Type 97 engines). The Ki-57 proved quite durable and could operate at fairly long ranges (900–1,800 miles), so both the army and navy came to use the plane as a troop transport. On February 14, 1942, Ki-57s comprised part of the fleet that dropped 360 Japanese paratroopers over Palembang. Ki-57s similarly dropped more than 400 paratroopers over Leyte Island on December 6, 1944, in an ill-fated Japanese assault on Allied positions there. The JAAF and IJN ultimately relied on converted bombers for the bulk of their transport duties.

Reconnaissance and Liaison Aircraft

One of the most important of the early Japanese reconnaissance types was the Kawasaki Army Type 88 reconnaissance and light bomber. It was the genesis of a series of army specifications calling for a Japanese-built reconnaissance aircraft to replace the French Salmson 2-A.2, which was at that time the chief reconnaissance plane in the Japanese air fleet. The army issued the design call in early 1926, soliciting entries from Ishikawajima, Kawasaki, Mitsubishi, and Nakajima. None of the companies had experience in a project of this magnitude, so each retained German engineers for assistance. Kawasaki turned to Richard Vogt, who with the assistance of Hisashi Tojo produced a design to meet the rigorous specifications (a speed in excess of 120 mph, a range to exceed 600 miles, equipped with one fixed, forward-firing machine gun and one flexible, dorsal-mounted 7.7 twin machine gun, a large aerial camera and radio). Vogt's prototype, finished in February 1927, exceeded these expectations. In competition against the other prototypes, Kawasaki's outclassed them all. The company won a ¥ 200,000 prize, and the army adopted the model for production in February 1928.

The Type 88 was the first Japanese plane to employ an entirely metal airframe, and it was this sturdiness and workmanlike reliability, combined with the Type 88's performance, that led the army to return time and again to Kawasaki as its chief supplier throughout the Second World War. The Type 88 was designed as a single-engine biplane, housing a two-man crew in an open cockpit. It employed a 450–600 hp BMW VI 12 cylinder water-cooled engine, built by Kawasaki through a licensing agreement with the German company. Its dimensions were 49 ft 3 in (span), 42 ft (length), 11 ft 2 in (height), with a wing area of 516 sq feet. The aircraft weighed roughly 3,900 lbs empty, and 6,200 lbs when loaded. After some minor modifications to the BWM VI engine, the Type 88-2 achieved a top speed of 137 mph, could climb to 9,800 ft in 16 minutes, and possessed a service ceiling of more than 20,000 ft. The army was also quite impressed with its 6 hour endurance rating. It performed admirably in Japanese combat throughout the 1930s and remained in service into the war in various capacities. There were approximately 710 reconnaissance types built, as well as more than 400 that were modified for use as light bombers. These modifications included "W"-shaped struts added to the wing and removable bomb racks under the wings. The Type 88, intended as a stopgap measure while the army solicited new bomber designs, was slow-moving and lightly-armed, but its reliability made it a rather popular aircraft.

Even though the Type 88 gave Kawasaki the inside track to most of the army's orders in the coming decades, three Mitsubishi designs helped further modernize the Imperial Japanese Army's reconnaissance wing. The first of these, the Ki-15, answered specifications calling for another two-seat reconnaissance plane with roughly double the top speed of the Type 88, to be achieved by cutting its loaded weight roughly in half, which would allow for a 1 hour endurance at a 250 mi combat radius. Mitsubishi tasked a three-man design team to meet these requirements: Kumihiko Kono, Tomio Kubo, Shokichi Mizumo. Their prototype, which first flew in May 1936, was a low-wing cantilever monoplane with fixed spatted undercarriage, and it more than fulfilled expectations when put through its trials by the army a year later. Mitsubishi sold the second prototype to a Japanese newspaper. The paper hired Masaaki Iinuma and Kenji Tsukagoshi to record a world record flight to Great Britain in honor of the coronation of George VI. The plane was eerily dubbed *Kamikaze* (Divine Wind); it completed its 9,542 mile flight in 95 hours. The aircraft proved equally adept in combat, and its performance in the Sino-Japanese conflict highlighted the strategic importance of reconnaissance aircraft to both the army and the navy. Based on its successes in China, the navy solicited a version (called the C5M), which later contributed to the sinking of the HMS *Repulse* and HMS *Prince of Wales* at the outset of the Pacific War, although it was soon thereafter found to be too slow and too lightly armored to serve a significant role in the conflict. There were four main variants of the design, mostly distinguished by engine. Each housed a two-man crew in an enclosed cockpit, armed with a flexible rear-firing 7.7 mm machine gun (Type 89 for the army models; Type 92 for the navy models). Each spanned 39 ft 4 in, with a length from 27 ft 10 in (Ki-15-I) to 28 ft 6 in (Ki-15-II, C5M1, C5M2), a height of 10 ft 11 in (Ki-15 I and II) or 11 ft 4 in (C5M 1 and 2), and a wing area of 219 sq feet. The Ki-15s transitioned from a 550 hp Army Type 94 nine cylinder air-cooled radial engine, providing a top speed of 298 mph, to a 900 hp Army Type 99 Model 1 fourteen cylinder air-cooled radial engine, increasing top speed to 317 mph. For the C5Ms, the 875 hp Mitsubishi Zuisei 12 fourteen cylinder air-cooled radial (291 mph) was replaced by the 950 hp Nakajima Sakae 12, driving a three-blade instead of a two-blade propeller, thus increasing top speed by slightly 10 mph. More than 430 Ki-15s were produced for the army, and 50 C5Ms for the navy. They came to be dubbed "Babs" by the Allies.

The army solicited Mitsubishi for another design in February 1938 that was brought about largely by the urgings of a prominent Japanese pilot, Captain Yuzo Fujita. Combat operations led Fujita to call for a quick, agile, and heavily armored aircraft for close air support. The specifications called for a max speed of 260 mph at 6,560 ft, a bomb load of twelve 33 lb or four 110 lb bombs, with two forward-firing and one flexible rear-firing machine guns. The prototype of the Mitsubishi Ki-51 was completed in June 1939. It accommodated two crewmembers in tandem enclosed cockpits, and was powered by a 900 hp Army Type 99 Model 2 fourteen cylinder air-cooled radial engine. The plane achieved admirable speeds of up to 263 mph, climb rates (16,000 ft in just under 10 minutes), and range (660 mi), with a span of 39 ft 8 in, length of 30 ft 2 in, height of 8 ft 11 in, and wing area of 258 sq feet. In combat, the Ki-51 (coded "Sonia" by the Allies) proved well-designed, and 2,385 copies of the venerable aircraft were built for the army.

Mitsubishi's third major contribution to the JAAF was the Ki-46. Japan's geography necessitated long-range and high-speed reconnaissance aircraft, and the aircraft known to the Allies as "Dinah" was solicited to fill this need. A team of Fujita, Tanaka, and Ando fulfilled rather rigorous army specifications with a graceful design. The Ki-46 was small-bodied with an abnormally large fuel tank, spanning 48 ft 3 in, with a length of 36 ft 1 in, height of 12 ft 9 in, and wing area of 344 sq feet. These, in tandem with twin engines of 900–1,250 hp, allowed for a maximum speed of 540–630 mph, and a maximum operating altitude of 35,000–36,000 ft. The Ki-46, however, performed with far less grace than its looks indicated. First flown in November 1939, Ki-46's performance tended to overstress its frame. Despite many revisions, the model tended to lack agility, and its speed and climb rates often overstressed the frame, resulting in engine problems and balky landing gear. Their first combat service came in July 1941 in Manchuria and China, where any such mechanical issues were masked as the model vastly overmatched its outmoded Chinese opposition. The Ki-46, however, proved vulnerable when the Allies introduced such new interceptors as Spitfires and P-38s into combat. Nonetheless, it was a quite serviceable reconnaissance aircraft, of which the army ordered 1,742 copies.

In an odd instance of noncooperation, Japan continually refused to license the Ki-46 to its German allies; however, the Japanese felt free to "borrow" design innovations from the Fieseler Fi 156 Storch and incorporate them into Kokusai's Ki-76. Although Kozo Masuhara's design commenced roughly 10 months prior to Japan obtaining a copy of the Storch, he did in fact model his aircraft on what he knew of the German plane. Masuhara used a different set of flaps (of Fowler type instead of slotted) and a different engine (a 280 hp Hitachi Ha-42 nine cylinder air-cooled radial) to produce an easy-to-fly and easy-to-maintain aircraft that proved superior in virtually every way to its muse. It housed a pilot and observer, who operated a flexible rear-firing 7.7 mm Type 89 machine gun, in a tandem-enclosed cockpit. For antisubmarine patrol, the Ki-76 also carried two 132-lb depth charges, although it was primarily used for artillery-spotting duties. It achieved a top speed of 111 mph, a range of 466 miles, with a service ceiling of 18,400 ft. First flown in May 1941, the Ki-76 was known to the Allies as "Stella," and it saw widespread, although little noted, use in reconnaissance and command liaison roles throughout the Pacific.

Soviet Reconnaissance and Auxiliary Aircraft

Trainers

The Soviet air forces became as self-sufficient as possible, as quickly as possible. Hitler's devastating successes during the first phase of Operation Barbarossa forced the Soviets into a more reliant position than they would have liked. Many of the VVS's World War II transport and reconnaissance aircraft were license-built copies or imports through the Lend-Lease program. This is only a consequence of the war, however, and not an indication of the capabilities of Soviet design bureaus. Many Soviet designs in this auxiliary class had the potential to surpass their Western counterpart aircraft if the Soviet Union had the industrial resources to fuel continued improvements to the initial designs. Once the war was over, however, the VVS was in prime position to ascend to dominance in the coming years.

One obvious key to building the Soviet air fleet to a place of prominence even before the war was training a large squadron of pilots. Mirroring the rise of the VVS was the rise of the Polikarpov U-2 (redesignated Po-2 following Polikarpov's death in 1944), a simple biplane trainer of which a reported 30,000 were eventually produced. Under the supervision of Nikolai Nikolayevich Polikarpov's design bureau, plans for the trainer proceeded slowly at first. Initial designs attempted to be overly efficient, resulting in a sluggish flying machine essentially unusable for its designated function. The Polikarpov team retrenched subsequent to these 1927 experiments and soon produced a simpler and more effective aircraft. The U-2 was first flown on January 7, 1928, by test pilot M. M. Gromov, and it proved to be an ideal trainer that was maneuverable, but extraordinarily stable and easy to fly. Ordered into production thereafter, the Soviet Union produced approximately 1,000 U-2s per year between 1928 and 1941. Powered by a 100 hp Shvetsov M-11 five cylinder air-cooled radial engine, the U-2 could achieve a top speed of 97 mph, and had a service ceiling of 13,125 ft. It housed a pilot and instructor in tandem open cockpits, and spanned 37 ft 5 in, with length of 26 ft 10 in, height of 10 ft 2 in, and wing area of 358.86 sq feet.

The U-2 saw a greatly expanded service role after Hitler's invasion in 1941. Many built prior to the war were converted for use as close air support aircraft, adding underwing racks for bombs and rails for RS 82 rockets to the standard 7.7 mm ShKAS machine gun mounted on the rear cockpit. Several were employed as nighttime light bombers or artillery-spotting reconnaissance vehicles, whereas others were reportedly fitted with loudspeakers and used to broadcast propaganda. A relatively small number, approximately 860, were converted for use as flying ambulances. Well more than 9,000 saw extensive use as transports for Soviet VIPs. Production of the U-2 and its variants continued in many different forms into 1953, mostly carried on in such Soviet Bloc countries as Poland. It is widely considered to be the single most-produced aircraft in history.

Another noteworthy trainer from this era is the Yakovlev UT-1, a cantilever monoplane designed to ready pilots for the I-16, MiG-1, and LaGG-3. The UT-1 was the product of Aleksandr Sergeyevich Yakovlev's fertile mind, and the winning entrant in a design competition that called for an aerobatic monoplane trainer. Prototypes flew in

1931 and the following years, as Yakovlev experimented with different power plants before settling on the Shvetsov M-11 engine, a 100 hp, five cylinder air-cooled radial. This is the configuration that won the aircraft the competitive trials, although most production-class aircraft featured the upgraded 150 hp Shvetsov M-11 E. There were approximately 1,241 UT-1s built from 1937 through 1942. More production capacity was being devoted to the two-seat version by this time; approximately 7,243 UT-2s were produced by 1945. With the more powerful M-11 E engine, the UT-2 could achieve a top speed in excess of 140 mph, and it possessed a service ceiling of 11,485 ft. The model spanned 33 ft 5 in, with length of 22 ft 11 in, height of 8 ft 1 in, and wing area of 184.28 sq feet. Standard armament featured wing-mounted 7.62 mm ShKAS machine guns, along with a set of four RS-82 rocket rails underneath. During the worst of the German invasion, virtually all available aircraft were used in combat, and these trainers were no exception. Although it was never designed to be a primary fighter or tactical support aircraft, it did prove to be an acceptable combat aircraft thanks to its remarkable design. Over its lifetime, the UT-1 set eight separate world records for various performance characteristics, a testament to A. S. Yakovlev's talents.

Transports

Although not memorable for its performance characteristics, the venerable Lisunov Li-2 transport, a license-built copy of the American Douglas DC-3, is notable for its ruggedness, durability, and reliability. It is estimated that more than 2,500 Li-2s were produced, and perhaps as many as 5,000 were built or obtained by the Soviet Union throughout the war. These differed from their American counterparts primarily in the power plant. For the license-built versions, the Soviets employed 1,000 hp Shvetsov M-62 nine cylinder air-cooled radials.

The Soviet air force was not nearly as dependent on Lend-Lease aircraft for their transport arm as they were in other types (their sea-plane fleet, relied rather heavily on the famous PBY Catalina). In 1929, designer A. N. Tupolev's prototype ANT-9 completed its first flight. It made its public debut on May 1 of that year, an appropriate coming-out considering this was specifically requisitioned as a Soviet-built civilian airliner that was equal or superior to any foreign airliner. The ANT-9 can thus be seen as a key step toward Soviet self-sufficiency in this industry. Indeed, it accomplished its goal, becoming as much a propaganda tool as a civilian airliner. It initially carried a crew of two and could accommodate nine passengers, and was powered by a set of three 300 hp Wright Whirlwind radials. The ANT-9 spanned just more than 78 ft, with length of 54 ft 7 in, and wing area of 275.59 sq feet. Although ANT-9s did perform several goodwill tours of Europe, it is perhaps more notable for its role in the development of the much larger ANT-14. This aircraft was quite remarkable, accommodating 36 passengers and a five-man crew, and was essentially an enlargement of the ANT-9. The ANT-14 spanned 132 ft 1 in, with length of 86 ft 11 in, height of 17 ft 8 in, and wing area of 787.4 sq feet. It was powered by five 480 hp Gnome-Rhone Jupiter engines. It could achieve a top speed approaching 150 mph, and had a range of approximately 745 miles. Following its first test-flight on August 14, 1931, by M. M. Gromov, the ANT-14 immediately became a propaganda symbol of the potential of Soviet air power because it was immediately one of the largest aircraft of its time. Total production numbers are unknown, but the extremely limited quantity of aircraft carried an estimated 40,000 passengers on more than 1,000 flights in a 10-year span, and one even served as a traveling movie theater during the early days of the Second World War.

Alexander Yakovlev is more renowned for his design bureau's fighters and bombers, but as the Soviet Union began to feel the pressures of the war with Germany, Yakovlev lent his efforts to a utilitarian project (the production of a transport plane out of nonvital materials). Instead of metal airframes, as had been standard on Soviet aircraft for some time, Yakovlev experimented with a primarily wooden frame in designing the Yak-6 light transport. The first prototype was put into the air in mid-1942, with production of some 1,000 copies beginning shortly thereafter. Spanning 45 ft 1 in, with length of 33 ft 1 in, and wing area of 318.62 sq feet, the Yak-6 accommodated a crew of two and up to six passengers or comparable weight in freight. It was powered by twin 140 hp Shvetsov M-11 nine cylinder air-cooled radials, which contributed to a maximum speed exceeding 140 mph and service ceiling of 11,090 ft. Armed with a 7.62 mm ShKAS machine gun, and with external hardpoints for up to 1,100 lbs of bombs or, for close-air-support missions, 10 RS-82 rockets, the Yak-6 was a capable support or night bombing aircraft, although its limited armor and even more limited range made it far better suited for transport and ambulance services.

Reconnaissance and Liaison Aircraft

The various reconnaissance aircraft designed in the period following the Russian Civil War were more central to the Soviet war effort. (A number of these types are discussed in the next chapter on naval air-craft, including floatplanes and flying boats.) Polikarpov's successes with the U-2 trainer led him to extend his design efforts into this area. Drawings and experimentations originating in 1925 finally gave way to flight in 1928. By 1931 the Polikarpov R.5 biplane entered production as a two-seat light bomber and reconnaissance aircraft. Most featured the 680 hp M-17B engine, which rated a top speed exceeding 140 mph, service ceiling of 19,488 ft, and range in excess of 600 miles. The R.5 spanned 50 ft 10 in, with length of 34 ft 7 in, and wing area of 540.37 sq feet. Housing a two-man crew in open cockpits, it possessed a single 7.62 mm PV-1 machine gun mounted in the fuselage, along with a ring-mounted set of 7.62 mm DA machine guns over the rear cockpit and an 882 lb bomb load capacity. Although an accurate count is impossible, an estimated 5,000–7,000 R.5s were produced from 1931 through the end of the war. Throughout the conflict, the R.5 continued to serve as a venerable reconnaissance, liaison, and light bombing aircraft. Indeed, the R.5 saw a great deal of combat time before Hitler's invasion with extensive service over China in the Sino-Japanese conflicts, and combat with Republican forces in the Spanish Civil War before the Soviets launched their Winter War offensive against Finland in 1939.

CHAPTER SIX

Naval Aircraft

WORLD WAR II MARRIED TWO of the great innovations in military theory: sea power and air power. Where the theories of an Alfred Thayer Mahan met the thesis of a Billy Mitchell, naval air power was born. Although venerable float-planes remained important for transporting people and goods to remote locations, their utility as offensive weapons was severely limited from the very beginning of the war. With the advent of carrier-launched fighters and attack aircraft, however, the nature of war and power changed dramatically. A nation's battleships alone would never again determine its offensive capabilities; rather, its aircraft carriers would "project" power far beyond the reach of any deck gun. This era indeed witnessed the birth and demonstrated the effectiveness of a wholly new means of power projection, one no modern nation can be without and still claim influence in world affairs. As a result, naval airpower was almost the exclusive purview of the great powers as indicated in this chapter.

American Naval Aircraft

Fighters and Attack Aircraft

The navy's official history accurately documents the 1920s as a period of tremendous growth and technological advance. No area of aviation better bears this out than the development for the U.S. Navy of dedicated carrier-launched fighter aircraft. The first in this line was the Curtiss TS-1, a small biplane that weighed just 1,239 lbs (empty). It spanned 25 ft, with length of 22 ft, and height of 8 ft, making it a good match for the navy's new line of aircraft carriers. Powered by an air-cooled 200 hp Lawrence J-1 radial engine (itself a design innovation for a naval aircraft), the model could achieve a top speed of 130 mph, along with an operational ceiling of 14,400 ft, and range of approximately 465 miles. On offensive the single-seat fighter featured two .30 caliber machine guns. The plane was originally designed by the Naval Aircraft Factory, but the Curtiss-Wright Corporation secured the production contracts for all 43 TS1s produced beginning in 1923.

By the end of the decade, the Boeing F2B and F3B replaced the TS1 as the navy's primary fighter planes. The F2B was first introduced in 1928, and it proved highly maneuverable; indeed, it was the platform of choice for the navy's Three Seahawks aerobatics team. Only 35 copies of the model were produced, however; roughly twice as many F3Bs were built for the navy. The F3B was the more memorable of the two models, and featured a wingspan of 33 ft, length of 24 ft 10 in, and height of 9 ft 2 in. The F3B was powered by a 425 hp Pratt & Whitney Wasp R-1340 radial, and it retained the hallmark agility and speed (158 mph) of the F2B, and featured an improved service ceiling (22,500 ft) and range (340 miles) over its predecessor (21,500 ft and 317 miles, respectively). In addition to its two .30 caliber machine guns, the aircraft could carry up to 125 lbs of bombs. Although it was initially developed as a floatplane fighter, the U.S. Navy requested that Boeing redesign it for use with fixed landing gear. By the time Boeing completed the requested modifications, two Grumman designs would bring the biplane age to its apex. For this reason, even though it performed well and was relatively easy to maintain, the F3B was rather quickly outmoded.

Grumman's FF, dubbed "FiFi" by her admiring crews, was first adopted into service in 1933. The model was an odd mix of forward-thinking and traditional elements: Even though it was the first U.S. Navy fighter to employ retractable landing gear, it was a two-seat biplane. Nevertheless, the FF was a well-designed and maneuverable aircraft, featuring a top speed of approximately 244 mph, with service ceiling of 21,000 ft, and range of 932 miles. It spanned 34 ft 6 in, with length of 24 ft 6 in, and height of 11 ft 1 in, and was powered by a 700 hp Wright Cyclone R-1820 radial. The FF served reliably through the end of the decade, with approximately 120 copies purchased by the navy.

The Grumman F2F and F3F, both stubby, single-seat biplanes, would be the last biplane fighters active in the U.S. Navy arsenal. Although impressive in performance, these Grumman aircraft would be relatively quickly outmoded because the age of the monoplane fast approached. Still, when first introduced in 1934, the F2F was greeted with much anticipation for its performance characteristics, including a service ceiling of 27,000 ft, range of 985 miles, and maximum speed of 230 mph thanks to a 700 hp Pratt & Whitney R-1535 engine. The F2F was 28 ft in span, with length of just 21 ft 5 in, and height of 10 ft 6 in. It carried two .30 caliber machine guns and up to 332 lbs of bombs. An initial run of 55 was followed by a series of design modifications, leading to the total production of roughly 164 copies of the F3F. This model spanned 32 ft, with length of 23 ft 2 in, and height of 9 ft 4 in, and was powered by a 950 hp Wright R-1820 engine. This produced roughly similar performance characteristics as the F2F, including a maximum speed of 264 mph, operational ceiling of 33,200 ft, and range of 980 miles. The F3F was armed similarly to its predecessor, but was ultimately replaced by the navy's first monoplane fighter, the Brewster F2A Buffalo.

An all-metal fighter, the Brewster F2A owed much of its appearance to the Grumman line. It was just 26 ft 4 in long, with height of 12 ft 1 in, and wingspan of 35 ft. A production order of 54 copies followed the Buffalo's first successful test flight in January 1938, and ultimately 509 were produced with a number serving in foreign air forces. A 1,100 hp Wright Cyclone R-1620 engine produced a top speed of approximately 300 mph, service ceiling of 30,500 ft, and range of 950 miles. Although it represented a great leap forward for U.S. Navy fighter designs, the Buffalo proved hopelessly outclassed by the far superior Japanese opponents in the opening phases of the Pacific War.

By that point Grumman's F4F Wildcat was the primary carrier-based fighter of the U.S. Navy. Although it was initially defeated in competitive trials by the F2A, the Wildcat ultimately outclassed the Buffalo with the addition of a larger power plant. With a 1,200 hp Wright Cyclone R-1830 engine, the model possessed a top speed of 318 mph, service ceiling of 35,000 ft, and range of 900 miles. The model spanned 38 ft, with length of 28 ft 9 in, and height of 11 ft 11 in. It was heavily armed for the fighters of its time, featuring up to six .50 caliber machine guns. The F4F could also be fitted with up to 500 lbs of bombs. With the introduction of folding wings, an invaluable trait for a carrier-based aircraft, the F4F-4 saw the greatest production quantity (1,169) of all models (7,815 in total). Although the Mitsubishi A6M Zero was a superior fighter, the F4F Wildcat proved a capable foe. On the introduction of a covering maneuver known as the Thatch Weave, F4F pilots (flying in two-plane groups) downed approximately seven enemies for every Wildcat lost in combat. Indeed, ground-based F4Fs from Wake Island scored the first American aerial victories of the war, including sinking the Japanese destroyer *Kisaragi* on December 8, 1941.

The F6F Hellcat was Grumman's next great contribution to the U.S. Navy's fighter arm, first appearing in 1943 and widely credited with turning the tide of the air war in the Pacific. The Hellcat spanned 42 ft 10 in, with length of 33 ft 7 in, and height of 13 ft 1 in, and was powered by a 2,000 hp Pratt & Whitney Double Wasp R-2800. Constructed specifically to counter the Japanese Zero fighter, the F6F proved superior in virtually every category. Its maximum speed was in excess of 375 mph, and it possessed a service ceiling of 37,500 ft with a maximum range of 1,000 miles. The aircraft was armed with two or three .50 caliber machine guns, and could be fitted with up to a 2,000 lb bomb load. On its introduction into service, the Hellcat garnered a well-deserved reputation for its combat abilities. In an F6F, David McCampbell became the navy's most decorated ace, with 34 confirmed "kills." During the famed "Marianas Turkey Shoot" of June 1944, during which American naval aircraft, primarily Hellcats, downed more than 300 Japanese aircraft, McCampbell scored seven confirmed kills. He and fellow Hellcat pilot Roy Rushing splashed 15 Japanese aircraft in a single sortie during the Battle of Leyte Gulf (October 1944). Even at the hands of less prolific combat pilots, the F6F was a superb aircraft, accumulating approximately 19 "kills" for every Hellcat lost in combat. A testament to its effectiveness, records indicate that at peak production Grumman's plants could produce a new F6F roughly every 60 seconds, for a total wartime production run of more than 12,270 aircraft. Many of these remained in active service into the Korean Conflict.

The final great U.S. Navy fighter of the World War II era was the Vought F4U Corsair. The plane was distinctively shaped, with an inverted gull wing. It was also heavily armed with either six .50 caliber machine guns or four 20 mm cannons. In its adapted role as a close air support or air-to-ground bomber, the Corsair could carry a 2,000 lb bomb load. The F4U first appeared in late 1942 after an often frustrating four-year development period, during which it failed repeatedly to be qualified for carrier use. Instead, a majority of its flights were from ground bases. (Note: The model is retained in this chapter because it was used solely by the U.S. Navy and U.S. Marine Corps in the Pacific.) Indeed, one of the most famous flying squadrons of the war, the "Black Sheep" of the Marine Fighting Squadron 214 (September 1943 through January 1944), produced nine aces, including the U.S. Marine Corps's most decorated flying ace, famed Major Gregory "Pappy" Boyington. In all combat, it produced a kill-to-loss ratio of roughly 11:1, making it one of the winningest of all American fighter planes. More than 12,570 of all types were built by several manufacturers, and many F4Us continued in active service through 1952, making it one of the longest-serving models in the navy's inventory. The Corsair spanned 40 ft 11 in, with length of 33 ft 8 in, and height of 14 ft 9 in, and was powered by a 2,850 Pratt & Whitney Double Wasp R-2800 radial engine. This produced a top speed of 462 mph, making it one of the fastest propeller-driven aircraft of any service. It also featured a service ceiling of 44,000 ft, and maximum range in excess of 1,000 miles.

The development of naval attack aircraft, or torpedo bombers, followed a similar course. Among the first of these was the Douglas DT, a civilian aircraft modified for sea use via the attachment of a set of pontoon floats. A two-seat open cockpit biplane, the DT served as a groundbreaking torpedo-bomber for the U.S. Navy from 1921 through the end of the decade. Two U.S. Army DTs circumnavigated the globe in 1924, and the navy was similarly impressed with their performance. A 400 hp Liberty liquid-cooled engine provided a top speed of approximately 100 mph, service ceiling of 7,800 ft, and range of approximately 300 miles. With a wingspan of 50 ft, length of 34 ft 2 in, and height of 13 ft 7 in, the DT could be armed with a single 1,835 lb torpedo. A total of 86 copies of the DT were procured by the U.S. military.

The Martin T3M, a biplane torpedo bomber spanning 53 ft, with length of 35 ft 7 in, and height of 14 ft 9 in, entered service in 1926. There were approximately 125 copies of the T3M produced, featuring a Wright T3B liquid-cooled engine. Although this provided relatively good performance, including a maximum speed of 108 mph, navy air corps leaders solicited a similar design from Martin that would make use of the easier-to-maintain air-cooled radial engines then being produced. The result was the T4M, featuring a 525 hp Pratt & Whitney R-1690, which had a top speed of 114 mph, service ceiling of 10,150 ft, and range of 363 miles. The model was armed with a .30 caliber machine gun and a single 1,800 lb torpedo. More than 100 additional T4Ms were produced for the navy, each featuring a three-man crew and either wheeled landing gear or floats. Few carrier-based aircraft were larger than the T3M/T4M.

The Douglas T2D/P2D biplane torpedo bomber entered service in 1927. Although used primarily as a seaplane, the T2D was officially the first multiengine, carrier-based aircraft in the U.S. Navy inventory. Because the latter was its initial design impetus, the T2D featured folding wings. It spanned 57 ft, with length of 44 ft, and height of 14 ft 7 in, and was powered by twin 525 hp Wright Cyclone R-1820 radials. This power plant afforded a top speed of 125 mph, with a service ceiling of 13,830 ft, and range in excess of 400 miles. Armed with two .30 caliber machine guns and a single 1,618 lb torpedo, the aircraft accommodated a crew of four.

By 1936, however, the Douglas TBD Devastator was the class of the U.S. naval attack aircraft corps. It was a low-wing monoplane of entirely metal construction that accommodated a crew of three. With an 850 hp Pratt & Whitney R-1830 radial, producing a top speed of 205 mph, ceiling of 19,700 ft, and range of 415 miles, the Devastator was among the most advanced aircraft of its class in the late 1930s. Indeed, it was still among the front-line aircraft in the U.S. Navy upon the outbreak of war, although by that time foreign fighter aircraft far overmatched the now outmoded TBDs. The 130 TBDs built for the navy represented a tremendous technological advancement for torpedo bombers. The three-man crew was housed in an aircraft that spanned 50 ft, was 35 ft in length, and 15 ft 1 in high. It featured .30 caliber and .50 caliber machine guns, and could carry a 1,000 lb bomb or torpedo load. In Pacific Theater combat, where U.S. fighters could protect it from Japanese aircraft, Devastators performed admirably until staggeringly high losses in the Battle of Midway (June 4, 1942) forced them into immediate and complete retirement.

The TBF/TBM Avenger, a Grumman product widely considered to be one of the keys to the American victory in the Pacific, took the place of the Devastator. There were approximately 9,839 copies of this gold-standard for World War II–era carrier-based torpedo bombers built, several of which served as the navy's primary carrier-borne antisubmarine/attack aircraft well into the 1950s. After an ominous introduction, which saw five of six TBFs lost to Japanese fighters at Midway, American and British RAF Avengers went on to sink thousands of tons of Japanese shipping, two of the IJN's largest battleships (*Muashi* and *Yamato*), nearly 100 enemy aircraft, as well as roughly 45 German U-boats in the Atlantic. Their 2,000 lb torpedo was a devastating payload, and the model proved well-armed defensively with three .50 caliber and one .30 caliber machine guns. The Avenger was powered by a 1,700 hp Wright Cyclone R-2600 radial, and it possessed a top speed of 278 mph, service ceiling of 23,400 ft, and range of up to 1,215 miles that could be extended to roughly 2,500 miles with external fuel tanks. It spanned 54 ft 2 in, with length of 40 ft, and height of 16 ft 5 in, and it accommodated a three-man crew. The TBF/TBM served with several nations and totaled 9,842 copies. It is of note that future U.S. President George H.W. Bush earned a Distinguished Flying Cross for his World War II piloting of a TBF Avenger.

Bombers

Throughout the interwar years, the U.S. Navy continually experimented with the maritime uses of bombers. This is especially seen in the navy's determined efforts to procure an effective carrier-based dive-bomber. The Martin BM, which first appeared in 1932, represented a highly successful first foray into this niche for the U.S. Navy, which had never before issued specifications for a dedicated dive-bomber. With a wingspan of 41 ft, length of 28 ft 9 in, and height of 12 ft 4 in, the BM was powered by a 625 hp Pratt & Whitney R-1690 radial producing 146 mph in top speed. The model possessed a service ceiling of 16,500 ft, and range of 413 miles with a 1,000 lb bomb load. It accommodated a two-man crew, and served through the end of the decade. Just 33 were produced, but the BM's lasting legacy is its status as the aircraft that proved the strategic importance and possibilities of dive bombing to the navy.

This provided new life for the Vought F3U two-seat biplane fighter, which was converted to dive-bombing duties as the SBU. The Navy began adopting approximately 120 into service in 1935 through 1940. Many were still in service on the eve of World War II because of their impressive performance capabilities. A 700 hp Pratt & Whitney R-1535 radial produced a top speed in excess of 205 mph. Along with the Curtiss SBC Helldiver, the SBU was among the last biplane dive-bombers in naval service. The Helldiver featured a more powerful Wright Cyclone R-1820 engine and a top speed of approximately 235 mph. It also carried double the bomb load of the SBU (1,000 lbs to the SBU's 500 lbs). There were approximately 250 SBC Helldivers built for the navy, and they served well into World War II despite being outclassed by almost all fighters in the various services.

Vought produced the next great dive-bomber, a carrier-friendly monoplane featuring retractable wheels and folding wings. The SB2U Vindicator entered service in 1938, two years after its prototype's first flight, and more than 7,200 copies were produced through 1942. The SB2U was of mixed construction and carried a two-man crew. It spanned 42 ft, with a length of 34 ft and a height of 10 ft 3 in. Its 825 hp Pratt & Whitney Twin Wasp Junior R-1535 radial engine afforded it a top speed of 243 mph, service ceiling in excess of 23,500 ft, and range of 1,100 miles. It was armed with two .50 caliber machine guns and also carried a 1,000 lb bomb load. Despite their readily apparent obsolescence, Vindicators participated in numerous actions in the Pacific Theater during the opening stages of World War II.

The Douglas SBD Dauntless, which first entered naval service in 1940 was far more adept in combat. A development produced out of the defunct Northrop BT-1 and BT-2 models, the SBD became one of the most important U.S. Navy aircraft of the war despite poor handling and performance characteristics that left it derisively referred to as a flying "Barge." Its in-combat performance, however, gave the SBD a somewhat more positive nickname, "Slow, But Deadly." One of the innovations born out of the five-year development-to-production period was the use of perforated flaps, which greatly improved the accuracy of dive-bombing by slowing the aircraft on its descent. It was well-armed for this task, with up to 1,200 lbs of bombs and four machine guns (two each of .50 and .30 caliber). The Dauntless spanned 41 ft 6 in, with length of 33 ft, and height of 12 ft 11 in. It was manned by a crew of two. The plane was powered by a 1,200 hp Wright Cyclone R-1820 engine, and it could attain a top speed of 252 mph, possessed an operational ceiling of 24,300 ft, and a range of approximately 450 miles. These characteristics led to the sinking of more than 300,000 tons of Japanese shipping; only the British Fairey Swordfish was responsible for more Axis tonnage during the war. This followed an inauspicious beginning when several Dauntlesses ran headlong into the attacking Japanese force over Pearl Harbor on December 7, 1941. Thereafter, Dauntlesses proved to be among the safest American aircraft of the war, sporting a microscopic loss rate of less than 0.02 percent of the 5,936 aircraft produced. This is especially impressive considering the six Japanese aircraft carriers lost to SBDs through late 1944.

It would take a truly remarkable aircraft to supplant the SBD Dauntless as the class of the American dive-bomber corps, and the Curtiss SB2C proved to be up to the enormous task despite decidedly negative reviews from pilots and crews alike. The plane was also developed for the USAAC as the A-25 Shrike. It was highly successful as a dive-bomber in spite of its difficulty to fly and maneuver. Helldivers were employed in strikes throughout the Pacific Theater, where their sturdy build absorbed much damage and their 2,000 lb bomb load inflicted even more damage. The SB2C spanned 49 ft 9 in, with length of 36 ft 8 in, and height of 13 ft 2 in, and it was powered by a 1,900 hp Wright Cyclone R-2600 radial engine. This power plant afforded a generous top speed approaching 300 mph. Together with an operational ceiling of more than 29,000 ft, and a range in excess of 1,100 miles, the Helldiver was good fit for the nature of combat in the Pacific. It was defended by two 20 mm cannons and two .30 caliber machine guns. The plane continued in service through the end of the decade, and more than 7,000 were delivered to the navy beginning in 1943.

In addition to carrier-based dive-bombers, the U.S. Navy developed a number of ground-based patrol bombers. In this field, Lockheed proved especially influential. Their PBO Hudson first flew in late 1938 as a modified version of the civilian Model 14 Super Electra. Within a year, more than 250 Hudsons served the Royal Air Force (RAF) as patrol bombers. The U.S. Navy placed an order two years later, in late 1941, and total production of the model eventually reached 2,822. Hudsons were used primarily for coastal patrol and antisubmarine warfare, and they scored numerous "kills" of German U-boats in the Atlantic in service through 1944. The model spanned 65 ft 6 in, with length of 44 ft 4 in, and height of 11 ft 10 in. The 1,200 hp Pratt & Whitney R-1830 power plant afforded a top speed of 246 mph, service ceiling of 24,500 ft, and a range of 1,960 miles, making it well-suited to long over-water patrols. It was armed with seven .303 caliber machine guns and could carry a bomb load of 1,600 lbs.

A series of design modifications to the Hudson created the PV-1 Ventura. It was slightly larger than its predecessor, spanning 65 ft 6 in, with length of 51 ft 5 in, and height of 13 ft 2 in, and could carry a greater payload (3,000 lbs). The Ventura featured an improved power plant, the 2,000 hp Pratt & Whitney Double Wasp R-2800 radial, providing a top speed of 300 mph, ceiling of 26,300 ft, and range of 900 miles. In addition to its bomb load, the PV-1 was armed with four .50 caliber and two .30 caliber machine guns. The plane was primarily used in the Pacific Theater by the U.S. Navy, which procured 1,600 copies; however, the USAAC purchased approximately 200, which it dubbed the B-34. Although it was more heavily armed, it possessed a shorter range than the Hudson. In response to this, Lockheed produced the PV-2 Harpoon. The same basic design as the Hudson and Ventura, the Harpoon was larger, with greater payload, and range closer to that of the original model. It spanned 74 ft 11 in, with length of 52 ft, and height of 11 ft 11 in, and it was powered by a 2,000 hp Pratt & Whitney R-2800 radial. This generated a top speed of 282 mph, ceiling of 23,900 ft, and range of 1,800 miles. The Harpoon was armed with up to seven .50 caliber machine guns, and could carry a payload of up to 6,000 lbs. Because of its late arrival, it saw limited service in the Pacific war, but served for several years after the war as part of the Naval Air Reserve.

A final U.S. Navy patrol bomber of the World War II era that bears mentioning is the Consolidated PB4Y. A maritime version of the B-24 Liberator, the PB4Y Privateer spanned 100 ft, with length of 74 ft 7 in, and height of 30 ft 1 in. It was powered by four 1,350 hp Pratt & Whitney Twin Wasp R-1830 radials. It possessed a top speed of 237 mph, operational ceiling of 20,700 ft, and had a superlative range of 2,800 miles. The PB4Y prototype first flew in 1943, with combat units being supplied them beginning in mid-1944. The last of the 739 Privateers delivered to the U.S. Navy came in September 1945. Despite a limited combat record, the PB4Y garnered positive reviews for its payload and range capabilities. Armed with up to twelve .50 caliber machine guns, it could deliver 12,800 lbs of bombs on target. It was a U.S. Navy Privateer that dropped radar-guided bombs on Japanese ships on April 23, 1945, a combat first for the revolutionary technology. PB4Ys continued to serve with the navy's air corps well into the 1950s as reconnaissance and patrol bombers.

Reconnaissance and Auxiliary Aircraft

Although there were a number of trainers used by the U.S. Navy during the interwar and World War II years, most of which were models shared with the USAAC, there are four dedicated naval models meriting special notice. Although Boeing's NB was among the first of the post–World War I generation of sea-plane trainers, it was Consolidated's NY that was produced in noteworthy numbers. A two-seat biplane, the NY became the navy's standard trainer for approximately a decade following its introduction in 1926. In many ways it is the navy's cousin of the Army's PT-1 Trusty. Like the NB, the NY could be outfitted with floats for sea-plane training. It spanned 40 ft, with length of 27 ft 10 in, and height of 9 ft 11 in, and it was powered by a 220 hp Wright R-790 radial engine. This produced a top speed of approximately 98 mph, service ceiling of 15,200 ft, and range of approximately 300 miles. More than 300 copies of the easy-to-fly machine were produced for the navy, where it served admirably, if unspectacularly, until being replaced in part by the Naval Aircraft Factory's N3N.

Despite its nickname, the "Yellow Peril," the N3N was a safe and worthy trainer that served from 1935 through the end of World War II; indeed, a vast majority of World War II navy pilots spent time in one of these aircraft with the distinctive yellow paint. The N3N spanned 34 ft, with length of 25 ft 6 in, and height of 10 ft 10 in. It was powered by a 235 hp Wright R-760 radial, with a top speed of 125 mph, operational ceiling of 15,200 ft, and range of 470 miles. The N3N was a biplane that, like the NY, was capable of being fitted with sea-plane floats, and it served with the U.S. Navy through 1961, even though by that time it was relegated to instructional duties at the U.S. Naval Academy. As a primary trainer, however, the model excelled, with a total of 996 being built.

The Curtiss SNC Falcon was an intermediate trainer and among the first monoplane trainers designed specifically for the U.S. Navy. The model spanned 35 ft, with length of 26 ft 6 in, and height of 7 ft 6 in. It was powered by a 420 hp Wright Whirlwind R-975 radial, and was capable of more than 200 mph in top speed, a service ceiling approaching 22,000 ft, and range of 515 miles. More than 300 copies of the SNC were built for the navy, despite their structural inadequacy for carrier-landing training. It remained in service as an intermediate instrument trainer, extending its service life through 1944.

The Timm N2T Tutor, a monoplane built from bonded plywood to save on the use of strategic materials, was equally important. More than 260 copies of this unique aircraft were constructed for the navy, where they served in a niche as a mass-produced, cheap, and easy-to-fly formation trainer. It spanned 36 ft, with length of 24 ft 10 in, and height of 10 ft 8 in, and was powered by a 220 hp Continental R-670 radial. This produced a top speed of just 144 mph, service ceiling of 16,000 ft, and range of approximately 400 miles. The Tutor stood as an example of the navy's wartime ingenuity, and it served only through the end of 1944.

There are also a number of naval reconnaissance, transport, and liaison aircraft of the interwar and World War II era that demand attention. The first postwar addition to this important, but often overlooked class, was the Loening OL. The model, originally based on Grover Cleveland Loening's civilian "Air Yacht," featured Loening's original "unitary hull" design—with main pontoon float built directly into the aircraft's hull—as well as manually retractable wheeled landing gear, and other modern features. The "unitary hull" gave it a unique appearance that led to the nickname "Flying Shoehorn." It spanned 45 ft, with length of 34 ft 9 in, and height of 12 ft 9 in, with a 450 hp Pratt & Whitney R-1340 power plant. The OL could achieve a top speed of 122 mph, and it possessed a ceiling of 14,300 ft, and range of 625 miles. The OL was impressively rugged, and it explored the Arctic in 1925, demonstrating the possibilities of sea-based reconnaissance aircraft.

Vought began a successful run of auxiliary naval aircraft in 1923 with the introduction of its UO. The UO was a two-seat, catapult-launched biplane scout, which served for approximately a decade after its introduction. The biplane spanned 34 ft 3 in, with length of 24 ft 5 in, and height of 8 ft 9 in, and was powered by a 200 hp Wright J-3 radial engine. It possessed a top speed of 125 mph, ceiling of 18,800 ft, and maximum range of 398 miles. As a float-plane fighter, the model could be fitted with two .30 caliber machine guns; in this format, it outfitted several battleships in the Pacific Fleet in the late 1920s; however, Vought rather quickly offered an improved observation plane, the O2U. The O2U Corsair accommodated a crew of two in a biplane spanning 34 ft 6 in, with length of 24 ft 5 in, and height of 10 ft 1 in. The model notably featured the 450 hp Pratt & Whitney R-1340 Wasp radial, the first aircraft so fitted with the venerable power plant. It generated a top speed of 150 mph, operational ceiling of 18,700 ft, and range of more than 600 miles. The O2U could be fitted with wheeled landing gear or floats for use at sea, and was armed with three .30 caliber machine guns. Several models saw combat in Latin America in the late 1920s, and many of the 289 produced continued in active duty into the 1930s.

By the turn of the decade, Vought produced the quintessential biplane scout of the era, the O3U Corsair. It spanned 36 ft, with length of 27 ft 5 in, and height of 11 ft 4 in, and it was powered by a 600 hp Pratt & Whitney R-1690 radial. The O3U boasted a top speed in excess of 165 mph, ceiling of 18,600 ft, and range of 680 miles. Of the navy's initial order of 87, every copy was immediately tasked to a warship, where its adaptability into a float-plane proved highly useful. For the Marine Corps, several copies were procured and designated SU (Scout, Utility). More than 140 of the approximately 300 copies of the O3U/SU remained in active service through the Japanese attacks in the Pacific in December 1941.

Vought's run of successful sea-plane scouts was briefly interrupted by the introduction of Curtiss's SOC Seagull. A biplane of 36 ft wingspan, with length of 26 ft 6 in, and height of 14 ft 9 in, the Seagull was the navy's replacement for the O2U-series of observation and reconnaissance sea-planes. The model featured removable floats for ground use, foldable wings for being carried aboard ship, and a two-man crew in a tandem, enclosed cockpit. Its 600 hp Pratt & Whitney Wasp R-1340 radial engine produced a top speed of 165 mph, service ceiling of 14,900 ft, and range of 675 miles. Just 262 copies of the Seagull were produced, but virtually every one of them served aboard a U.S. Navy cruiser or battleship and offered reliable aerial scouting from their introduction in 1935 and throughout the war. They were briefly retired in favor of the ostensibly upgraded SO3C Seamew, but the Seagull returned to active duty on cruisers as the navy realized that the Seamew was ill-suited to the rigors of combat. Although nearly

800 SO3C Seamews were produced, the navy was quite dissatisfied with their performance and ruggedness, and relied instead on the older Seagull and the new Vought OS2U Kingfisher.

This last of the great Vought sea-plane observation aircraft served on the frontlines with U.S. Navy battleships from its introduction in 1940 through the end of the war. The Kingfisher in 1940 became the navy's first monoplane reconnaissance float-plane successfully cata-pulted into flight, and from then on became the standard and most reliable such aircraft in the U.S. Navy arsenal. Vought developed the design from their O3U biplane, and produced a monoplane spanning 35 ft 11 in, with length of 33 ft 10 in, and height of 15 ft 1 in. The frame was matched with a 450 hp Pratt & Whitney R-985 Wasp Jun-ior power plant, which afforded a maximum speed of 165 mph, with service ceiling of 13,000 ft, and range in excess of 805 miles. Armed with two .30 caliber machine guns and up to 325 lbs of bombs, the Kingfisher was not intended for use in aerial combat, but rather excelled as a reconnaissance and air–sea rescue platform. More than 1,300 copies of the highly successful Kingfisher were produced for the U.S. Navy as well as various other national forces.

The final aircraft of this type was the Curtiss SC Seahawk, spanning 41 ft, with length of 36 ft, and height of 12 ft 9 in. Its 1,350 hp Wright Cyclone R-1820 radial engine produced an impressive top speed of 313 mph, service ceiling of 28,600 ft, and range of 625 miles. The all-metal monoplane accommodated a single pilot, and was armed with two .50 caliber machine guns and hardpoints for up to a 650 lb bomb load. Its performance characteristics made it the class of the navy's World War II scout planes, but it arrived in late 1944 and saw little combat. In fact, just 576 copies of the aircraft were produced for the navy before the end of the war, at which point the outstanding contracts were canceled. Nev-ertheless, the capable Seahawk continued in naval service through the end of the decade as a land- or warship-based scout.

Flying Boats

A special naval class of patrol bombers, reconnaissance, and transport aircraft are flying boats. Although the technology was not new in the 1920s, that era would prove to be one of rapid modernization of the class. The Naval Aircraft Factory began this process with its PN-series of flying boats, which appeared in U.S. Navy service from 1922 through the end of the decade. Each iteration tested a new design ele-ment or feature, and many were produced by such rival aircraft firms as Martin, Keystone, and Douglas. The ultimate flying boat of this generation came in the Hall PH, a biplane spanning 72 ft 10 in, with length of 51 ft, and height of 19 ft 10 in. It was powered by two 750 hp Wright Cyclone R-1820 radials, and possessed a top speed of 160 mph, service ceiling of 21,300 ft, and range in excess of 1,900 miles. The U.S. Coast Guard found the model, which accommodated a crew of five and had the space for more than a dozen passengers, ideal for water-rescue purposes, whereas the navy was drawn to its ruggedness and ranginess. Production was modest, yet several copies remained in service well into World War II.

The Douglas OA-4/RD entered naval service in 1931 and continued to perform transport and observation functions throughout the Second World War. An amphibian flying boat, the OA-4/RD Dolphin in part replaced the Loening OA/OLs, discussed later, and in part carved out a new niche all its own. It could carry up to eight passengers in addition to its two-man crew more than 720 miles. The Dolphin spanned 60 ft, with length of 45 ft 1 in, and height of 14 ft. It featured two 450 hp Pratt & Whitney Wasp R-1340 radials producing a top speed in excess of 150 mph and service ceiling of 17,000 ft. Copies of the model served in every U.S. military branch, including the Coast Guard, which was the first service branch to order production copies.

Beginning in 1934, Consolidated had a long and successful career producing flying boats. The P2Y Ranger, the first monoplane flying boat in the navy inventory, owned several distance and endurance records during its heyday, and it continued to serve into the opening stages of World War I. It is perhaps more memorable as the muse for Japan's successful flying boat, the Kawanishi H6K Mavis, and as the foundation for Consolidated's famous PBY Catalina. The Catalina was introduced beginning in 1936, and served through 1957, with production figures totaling well more than 4,000. In addition to use in the U.S. Navy, Catalinas served as primary flying boats for several Allied nations, including Great Britain and the Soviet Union. The Catalina was less useful as a patrol bomber, but it was the ideal platform for transoceanic transport, reconnaissance, and air–sea rescue, and it performed these duties with admirable efficiency, making it undoubtedly the most famous and most widely used flying boat in aviation history. The PBY spanned 104 ft, with length of 63 ft 11 in, and height of 18 ft 10 in. The Catalina was powered by two 1,200 hp Pratt & Whitney Twin Wasp R-1830 radials, and it could achieve a top speed of 196 mph, with an operational ceiling of 18,200 ft and range in excess of 3,100 miles. The PBY was lightly armed, with a single .30 caliber and twin .50 caliber machine guns, but it could be outfitted with 4,000 lbs of bombs: however, this space was more often used for cargo or passengers.

The Grumman JF/J2F Duck similarly offered ruggedness and versatility in one efficient, if ungainly, package. It spanned 39 ft, with length of 34 ft, and height of 13 ft 11 in. The Duck was powered by a single 900 hp Wright Cyclone R-1820 radial. This produced a top speed of 190 mph, service ceiling of 25,000 ft, and range of 750 miles. The model, an amphibian biplane, was upgraded with twin .30 caliber machine guns and hardpoints for two 325-lb depth charges for use as antisubmarine platforms. It performed these duties with equal aplomb as it did general reconnaissance and scouting, as well as air-sea rescue, transport and liaison duties. There were approximately 645 copies of the model produced, with active service spanning from 1936 through 1948.

The Grumman JRF Goose was another amphibious cargo plane, purportedly better performing than the Duck, although never as popular or as widely used (JRFs were produced in roughly half as many copies as the JF/J2F Duck). The Goose possessed a wingspan of 49 ft, with length of 38 ft 6 in, and height of 16 ft 2 in. Its power plant consisted of twin 450 hp Pratt & Whitney R-985 radials, producing a top speed in excess of 200 mph, ceiling of 21,300 ft, and operational range of approximately 640 miles. It was unarmed, save for hardpoints for two 125 lb bombs or depth charges. As such, it was kept largely out of harm's way, but it did perform valuable rear-echelon transport, reconnaissance, and air-sea rescue duties, in addition to antisubmarine patrols.

In 1940, Consolidated offered a heavy-duty flying boat in the PB2Y Coronado. A large aircraft, it spanned 115 ft, with length of 79 ft 3 in, and height of 27 ft 6 in, and weighed more than 40,000 lbs empty. Four 1,200 hp Pratt & Whitney R-1830 radials were required to lift it airborne, and this power plant afforded a top speed of 210 mph, ceiling of 20,000 ft, and range of approximately 1,500 miles. Although rather slow and plodding, the Coronado's selling point was its amphibious capabilities (thanks to retractable wingtip floats and wheeled landing gear that retracted into the fuselage) and its large payload or cargo capacity. It could carry a total of 12,000 lbs of bombs in an internal bay and on external hardpoints, or, alternatively, a similar weight in cargo (more than 40 combat-ready soldiers, or, in some models, approximately 25 medical litters). A total of 210 were produced for the U.S. Navy through the end of the war.

Two Martin products also outfitted the U.S. Navy's flying boat corps during the World War II era. Martin's PBM Mariner was originally slated to replace the Consolidated PBY Catalina, but it never fully did so. The Mariner spanned 118 ft, with length of 79 ft 10 in, and height of 27 ft 6 in. It was powered by two 1,900 hp Wright Cyclone R-2600 radials that provided a top speed in excess of 210 mph. Its most distinguishing characteristic was a twin rudder with marked dihedral tilt. The PBM featured a service ceiling of 19,800 ft and a range of 2,240 miles. Armed with eight .50 caliber machine guns, the Mariner could carry 8,000 lbs of bombs or depth charges, making it an able antisubmarine and patrol aircraft. The Mariner was manned by a crew of nine and could carry up to 20 passengers. It was produced through the end of the decade, and 1,366 copies ultimately reached the U.S. Navy. Although the Mariner was never as popular as its Consolidated predecessor, it was equally as sea- and airworthy as the Catalina, and in many ways a superior flying boat.

Martin's final World War II–era flying boat was the massive JRM Mars, which first entered service in 1943. It possessed a wingspan of 200 ft, length of 117 ft 3 in, and height of 38 ft 5 in, and it weighed more than 75,000 lbs empty, making it the largest flying boat to enter active service. Four 2,200 hp Wright Duplex Cyclone R-3350 engines produced a top speed of more than 220 mph, and an operational ceiling of 14,600 ft. It accommodated a crew of 11, and up to 132 additional passengers or well more than 20,000 lbs of cargo, which it could carry more than 4,950 miles. Because of its lateness in arriving, the JRM saw little action during World War II, but some of the seven copies of the enormous flying boat transport did remain active in the U.S. service through the mid-1950s.

British Naval Aircraft

In many respects the Royal Navy suffered from the establishment of the RAF as an independent branch of service. With the RAF's focus on strategic bombing, the Fleet Air Arm, which was not given back to the Royal Navy until right before World War II, was not a huge priority. As a result, the Royal Navy did not have as advanced naval aircraft as did the U.S. Navy or the Japanese Imperial Navy, which were free to develop their own aircraft. Nevertheless, the British were far better off than all of the other powers.

Fighters and Attack Aircraft

The Fairey Flycatcher, introduced in 1923, was the Fleet Air Arm's first postwar carrier-based fighter, a role that it played exclusively until

1934. Its wood and metal constructed fuselage had a unique bent look because it titled upward aft of the cockpit and both wings were equipped with extended flaps to provide greater lift for takeoff and reduced speed for landing. Its hydraulic brakes, a new development, made it ideally suited for carrier service. The Flycatcher had a wingspan of 29 ft, length of 22 ft 10 in, and loaded weight of 3,028 lbs. Its 410 hp Armstrong-Siddeley Jaguar IV radial engine provided a maximum speed of 134 mph, a service ceiling of 19,000 ft, and a range of 263 miles. The Flycatcher was armed with two .303 caliber machine guns and carried up to 80 lbs of bombs.

The Blackburn Skua, which was intended as a replacement for the Hawker Osprey and Hawker Nimrod, provided the Royal Navy with its first carrier-based monoplane when it entered service in 1938. It had a wingspan of 46 ft 2 in, length of 35 ft 7 in, and loaded weight of 8,228. Its 890 hp Bristol Perseus XII radial engine unfortunately proved to be underpowered, giving it a top speed of 225 mph and a range of 760 miles. The Skua was armed with just five .303 caliber machine guns and proved to be too underarmed to be an effective fighter. As a result, the Fleet Air Arm ended up using it primarily as a dive-bomber, a role in which it proved to be more effective, as demonstrated by the sinking of the heavy cruiser *Konigsberg* off the coast of Norway on April 10, 1940. A total of 192 were built before it was replaced by the Fairey Fulmar and Hawker Sea Hurricane.

Although the Skua had proven to be a disappointment as a carrier-based fighter, the Fairey Fulmar entered service in 1940 and provided the Fleet Air Arm with a two-seat fighter that was superior to the land-based fighters that the Regia Aeronautica sent to support its bombers in their attacks on Malta. The Fulmar had a wingspan of 46 ft 4 in, a length of 40 ft 2 in, and a loaded weight of 10,200. Its 1,080 hp Rolls-Royce Merlin VIII liquid-cooled engines provided a top speed of 272 mph, service ceiling of 27,200 ft, and range of 780 miles. The Fulmar was armed with eight .303 caliber machine guns in its wings, could also be fitted with a .303 caliber machine gun in the rear cockpit, and carried two 250 lb bombs under its wings. A total of 600 were produced before the Fulmar was gradually phased out of service as naval versions of the Hurricane and Spitfire became available in 1943.

The Fairey Firefly was introduced in 1943 as a replacement for the Fulmar, and it provided the Royal Navy with the best two-seat fighter of the war. The Firefly used a low-wing monoplane design with folding wings and was well-suited for service on carriers. Although its wingspan of 44 ft 6 in, length of 37 ft 7 in, and loaded weight of 14,020 lbs made it larger and heavier than many of its contemporaries, it was nevertheless a surprisingly nimble aircraft. The Firefly was powered by a 1,730 hp Rolls-Royce Griffon IIIB liquid-cooled engine and had a top speed of 316 mph, a service ceiling of 28,000 ft, and a range of 1300 miles. It was armed with four 20 mm cannons and could carry up to 2,000 lbs of bombs. It remained in service until 1956, and a total of 1,638 were built.

Bombers

The Blackburn Shark entered service in 1934 and provided the RAF's Fleet Air Arm with a torpedo bomber that could operate off carriers or as a floatplane. Its biplane configuration was unique in that both wings were equipped with flaps. Although the wings were metal-framed and fabric-covered, the fuselage was constructed entirely of metal. The Shark had a wingspan of 46 ft, length of 35 ft 3 in, and loaded weight of 8,050 lbs and was fairly maneuverable. Its 800 hp Bristol Pegasus radial engine provided a top speed of 150 mph and range of 625 miles. The Shark was armed with two .303 caliber machine guns and delivered a 1,150 lb torpedo. The Shark was replaced by the Fairey Swordfish for carrier service in 1938 and was relegated to training and target-towing duties. A total of 238 were produced.

Although its biplane configuration made it look obsolete compared with monoplane torpedo-bombers employed during the Second World War, the Fairey Swordfish, which had been introduced in 1936, accounted for more sunk Axis ships than any other British aircraft. Its most stunning success came on November 10, 1940, when 20 Swordfish launched from the HMS *Illustrious* sank the battleship *Duilio* and damaged the battleships *Cavour* and *Littorio* at Taranto. The Swordfish had a wingspan of 45 ft 6 in, length of 35 ft 8 in, and loaded weight of 7,510 lbs. Its 750 hp Bristol Pegasus radial engine provided a top speed of 138 mph, service ceiling of 10,700 ft, and range of 1,030 miles. It was armed with two .303 caliber machine guns and carried a 1,610 lb torpedo or 1500 lb mine. A total of 2,391 had been produced by the time the Swordfish was retired in 1945.

Seeking a monoplane torpedo-bomber to replace the Fairey Swordfish biplane, the Royal Navy issued specifications in 1937 that ultimately resulted in the introduction of the Fairey Barracuda in 1943. With a wingspan of 49 ft 2 in, length of 39 ft 9 in, and loaded weight of 14,250 lbs, the Barracuda featured a distinctive look with its shoulder-mounted wings and raised tail. Despite its weight, the Barracuda's 1,640 hp Rolls-Royce Merlin 32 liquid-cooled engine provided a top speed of 240 mph, service ceiling of 16,600 ft, and range of 1,150 miles. It was armed with two .303 caliber machine guns and carried a 2,610 lb torpedo or up to 2,000 lbs of bombs, mines, or depth charges. Barracudas were used on several attacks against the German battleship *Tirpitz* in 1944 in Norwegian waters, and they conducted numerous raids on Japanese shipping in the Pacific theater. A total of 2,602 were built and the last Barracuda was taken out of service in 1953.

Reconnaissance and Auxiliary Aircraft

The Fairey IIIF was introduced in 1928 and served until 1940. It became the most numerous aircraft used by the Fleet Air Arm during the interwar years, primarily providing reconnaissance and liaison service. It could be fitted with floats for service from capital ships or landing gear for service from carriers. The Fairey III had a wingspan of 45 ft 9 in, length of 35 ft 6 in, and loaded weight of 6,300 lbs. Its 570 hp Napier Lion XIA liquid-cooled engine gave it a maximum speed of 130 mph, a service ceiling of 20,000 ft, and a range of 400 miles. It was defended by two .303 machine guns and could also carry up to 550 lbs of bombs. A total of 622 were built.

Flying Boats

After the First World War, the British would introduce a series of flying boats based on the design of its highly successful Felixstowe F5. One of the first was the Supermarine Southampton, of which 78 were manufactured for the RAF, beginning in the mid-1920s, and the Scapa, which entered service in 1933. The last in the series, all of which featured a biplane configuration, was the Supermarine Stranraer, which entered service in 1938. It had a wingspan of 85 ft, length of 54 ft 10 in, and loaded weight of 19,000 lbs, and it featured twin rudders and a fully enclosed cockpit. The Stranraer was powered by two 875 hp Bristol Pegasus X radial engines and had a top speed of 165 mph, a service ceiling of 18,500 ft, and a range of 1,000 miles. It came equipped with three .303 machine guns and could carry up to 1,000 lbs. Although 24 were delivered in 1935, the RAF recognized that a larger flying boat capable of carrying more bombs and having a longer range was needed. Nevertheless, the Stranraer remained in RAF service into 1942. The Royal Canadian Air Force purchased 47, which were used until 1954.

The four-engine Short Sunderland was a maritime patrol and anti-submarine flying boat introduced to replace the Stranraer in 1938. It was powered by four 1,200 hp Pratt & Whitney R-1830 Twin Wasp radial engines that provided a top speed of 213 mph, a service ceiling of 17,900 ft, and a maximum range of 2,690 miles. The aircraft used a monoplane configuration and had a wingspan of 112 ft 9 in, a length of 85 ft 3 in, and a loaded weight of 65,000 lbs. It was nicknamed the "Flying Porcupine" because it came equipped with eight .303 caliber machine guns, which made the Sunderland more than capable of defending itself, and with a 2,000 lb bomb load it proved deadly to German shipping and U-boats. In addition to its reconnaissance and antisubmarine roles, it was also used for transport and air–sea rescue operations. It played an important role in successfully evacuating forces from Norway, Greece, and Crete. A total of 749 were constructed and it remained in service with the RAF until 1959.

The single-engine Supermarine Walrus was first introduced in 1935 by Australia, where it was known as the Seagull V and intended as a maritime patrol and antisubmarine aircraft. It entered British service in 1936 as an amphibious biplane used for search and air–sea rescue operations. It used a biplane configuration, and had a wingspan of 45 ft, a length of 37 ft 3 in, and a loaded weight of 7,200 lbs. The Walrus was powered by a 755 hp Bristol Pegasus radial engine, had a top speed of 135 mph, a service ceiling of 18,500 ft, and a range of 600 miles. It was capable of operating in rough seas and successfully rescued as many as 5,000 downed pilots around Britain and another 2,500 in the Mediterranean. A total of 771 were constructed.

French Naval Aircraft

Throughout the interwar years French naval aviation lagged behind the other great powers. This was in part because France considered Germany to be the greatest threat to its security. Because Germany had been deprived of its navy at the end of the First World War, the French did not have the same concerns that had prompted it to develop naval aircraft prior to and during World War I. Another major factor in France's failure to develop naval air power is that its naval commanders still placed a heavy emphasis upon battleships and did not develop modern aircraft carriers. Nevertheless, the French did develop flying boats and float planes for naval reconnaissance during the interwar years.

During the 1920s, France introduced two primary flying boats for reconnaissance service. The three-person CAMS 37, which was based at naval air stations and also catapulted from capital ships, entered production in 1926. It used a biplane configuration and had a wingspan of 47 ft 7 in, a length of 37 ft 6 in, and a loaded weight of 6,614 lbs. Its 450 hp Lorraine 12Ed engine provided a top speed of 115 mph, a service ceiling of 11,480 ft, and a range of 748 miles. It was armed with four 7.7 mm machine guns in the bow and dorsal position and could carry up to 660 lbs of bombs under its lower wings. A total of 80 were manufactured, with the bulk of them serving with the French Navy and with a few exported to Portugal. They were gradually phased out of service during the 1930s, but a few were still in use upon the outbreak of the Second World War. The larger CAMS 55, designed for a five-man crew, had a wingspan of 66 ft 11 in, a length of 49 ft 4 in, and a loaded weight of 15,212 lbs. It was powered by two 500 hp Bristol Jupiter engines in a tandem, tractor-pusher configuration, and had a maximum speed of 121 mph, a service ceiling of 11,155 ft, and a range of 1,165 miles. It had the same armament as the CAMS 37, but carried only two 165 lb bombs under the lower wing. A total of 112 were built and equipped 15 escadrilles at French naval air stations.

The Loire 130 monoplane flying boat, which was developed in the mid-1930s, had replaced most flying boat and seaborne reconnaissance floatplanes in French service by the start of World War II. It had a wingspan of 52 ft 6 in, a length of 37 ft, and loaded weight of 7,716, and its heavy struts made it one of the ugliest flying boats of its era. The Loire 130 was powered by a 720 hp Hispano-Suiza 12Xirs. It had a maximum speed of 139 mph and carried a crew of four or five. It was armed with two 7.5 mm machine guns and carried two 165 lb bombs under its wings. There were approximately 125 built between 1937 and 1942.

After Great Britain signed a treaty with Germany that allowed the Germans to develop capital ships, the French would introduce the Latécoère Laté 298 torpedo-reconnaissance floatplane and the Loire-Nieuport LN 401 dive bomber on the eve of World War II to deal with the possibility of a German naval attack. The all-metal Laté 298, which entered service in February 1939, had a wingspan of 50 ft 10 in, a length of 41 ft 2 in, and loaded weight of 10,582 lbs. It used a low-wing monoplane, twin float configuration. The plane was powered by an 880 hp Hispano-Suiza 12Ycrs liquid-cooled engine, and it had a maximum speed of 180 mph, a service ceiling of 16,732 ft, and a range of 621 miles. The Laté 298 was armed with two 7.5 mm machine guns in its wings and one 7.5 mm machine gun in its rear cockpit, and it could deploy one 1,477 lb torpedo, 1,102 lb of bombs, or depth charges. There were approximately 110 built.

The LN 401 dive bomber, which was introduced in 1938, had a wingspan of 46 ft, a length of 32 ft, and a loaded weight of 6,223 lbs. It was powered by a 690 hp Hispano-Suiza 12XCrs liquid-cooled engine, and had a maximum speed of 236 mph and range of 745 miles. The plane was armed with two 7.5 mm machine guns, and carried a bomb load of just 496 lbs. Although intended for service with the navy, it was used in an effort to disrupt German armored divisions during the Battle of France. A total of 68 were built.

German Naval Aircraft

Both deprived of its capital ships and forbidden to have an air force at the end of the First World War, Germany did not begin naval air power until late in the interwar period, although it did rely upon small floatplanes for coastal patrols before the resurrection of the Luftwaffe and Germany Navy in the 1930s. When it did begin its military buildup Germany placed a far higher priority on meeting the needs of the Luftwaffe and its army rather than the navy. Nevertheless, the Germans did develop a few naval air assets that would serve it well during World War II.

The single engine, two-seat Arado Ar 196, introduced in August 1939, proved to be one of the most versatile reconnaissance seaplanes in the German Navy's arsenal. It used a low-wing monoplane configuration, had a wingspan of 40 ft 10 in, a length of 36 ft 1 in, and a loaded weight of 8,226 lbs. The Ar 196 was powered by a 900 hp BMW 132K radial engine that provided a maximum speed of 193 mph, a service ceiling of 22,965 ft, and a range of 670 miles. It was well-defended with two 20 mm cannon in its wings, one 7.9 mm machine gun in the upper cowling, and one or two 7.9 mm machine guns in the rear cockpit; additionally, it could also carry two 110 lb bombs under its wings. The aircraft was designed as a catapult-launched aircraft and was carried on board Germany's major capital ships to provide reconnaissance at sea. It also conducted coastal and maritime patrol, antisubmarine hunting, and convoy escort operations in the North Sea, the English Channel, and the Bay of Biscay while operating out of coastal bases. A total of 546 were produced.

Germany also relied upon three primary flying boats for reconnaissance and auxiliary purposes during World War II. The three-engine, six-seat Blohm und Voss Bv 138 was originally designed for passenger service by Hamburger Flugzeugbau. There were 279 constructed, and it entered military service in late 1940. The Bv 138 had a wingspan of 88 ft 4 in, a length of 65 ft 11 in, and a loaded weight of 34,100 lbs. It was powered by three 880 hp Junkers Jumo 205D diesel engines that provided a top speed of 170 mph, a service ceiling of 18,700 ft, and a maximum range of 2,500 miles. The Bv 138 was capable of remaining aloft for up to 18 hours and was well-suited for conducting long-range patrols in the North Atlantic, where it reported on the positions of Allied convoys to German U-Boats. It was armed with two 20 mm cannon, one 13 mm machine gun, and carried up to six 110 lb bombs or four 331 lb depth charges.

The twin-engine, four- or five-seat Dornier Do 18 was designed prior to the war as a trans-Atlantic mail carrier. There were 152 constructed, and it was quickly adopted for military use when Germany began its rearmament program. It had a wingspan of 77 ft 9 in, a length of 63 ft 7 in, and a loaded weight of 23,000 lbs. The Do 18 was powered by two 700 hp Junker Jumo 205D diesel engines, which provided a top speed of 166 mph, a service ceiling of 17,200 ft, and a range of 2,175 miles. The Do 18 was used primarily in the Baltic and North Sea for maritime patrol and air–sea rescue operations. It saved the lives of numerous grateful pilots shot down over the English Channel during the Battle of Britain.

The Dornier Do 24, introduced in 1937, had a wingspan of 59 ft, a length of 52 ft 9 in, and a loaded weight of 16,887 lbs. The Do 24 was powered by two 865 hp BMW 132N radial engines and was faster than the Do 18, with a maximum speed of 214 mph, a service ceiling of 22,965 ft, and a range of 845 miles. A total of 294 were constructed for maritime patrol and air–sea rescue operations as well as transport and troop evacuation.

Italian Naval Aircraft

Although Italy had developed a number of floatplanes and flying boats during the First World War, several factors limited its development of specifically designed naval aircraft during the interwar years. From a budgetary standpoint, it saved money to maintain a number of World War I flying boats well into the 1920s. In addition, many of the fighters that Italy produced, including the Fiat CR 20, were adapted for naval service by converting them into floatplanes that could operate from naval bases or be catapulted from capital ships. Italy's geography also allowed land-based aircraft to provide many of its naval needs, which were restricted to the Mediterranean, particularly as aircraft gained more extended range. Nevertheless, Italy did develop a few aircraft that were specifically designed for use by its navy.

The single-engine, four- to five-seat Cant Z 501 Gabbiano, introduced in 1934, served as Italy's only flying boat during World War II. It had a wingspan of 73 ft 10 in, length of 46 ft 10 in, and loaded weight of 15,510 lbs. It was powered by a 900 hp Isotta-Franchini liquid-cooled engine, had a top speed of 171 mph, service ceiling of 22,965 ft, and normal range of 1,490 miles. The wooden-constructed Gabbiano was intended as an armed reconnaissance/maritime patrol aircraft, and it had set numerous long-distance records in the mid-1930s, including a 3,080 mile flight from Monfalcone to Somalia in 1935. With Italy's entry into World War II, however, the plane quickly proved to be extremely vulnerable to enemy fire, relegating it primarily to coastal patrol service. By the time Italy surrendered in September 1943, only 40 remained out of the 445 that had been produced.

The Cant Z 506B Airone was an all-wood trimotor floatplane that gave Italy one of the most versatile aircraft in its arsenal. It had a wingspan of 81 ft 4 in, length of 60 ft 2 in, and loaded weight of 30,029 lbs. Its three 1,000 hp Piaggio P.XI radial engines produced a maximum speed of 280 mph, provided a service ceiling of 24,600 ft, and a range of 1,370 miles. The aircraft entered service in 1937 and was used toward the end of the Spanish Civil War. It was originally intended for transport services, but would be used for reconnaissance, convoy escort, rescue service, and torpedo-bombing duties. Total production reached 563.

The twin-engine Fiat RS 14, introduced in 1941, was originally designed as a coastal reconnaissance floatplane, but its performance soon proved to be far better than that of the Cant Z 506, allowing it to be used as a torpedo-bomber. With a wingspan of 64 ft 1 in, a length of 46 ft 3 in, and loaded weight of 17,637 lbs, the RS 14 was powered by two 840 hp Fiat A 74 RC38 radial engines, which provided a top speed of 254 mph, a service ceiling of 16,400 ft, and a maximum range of 1,553 miles. It was armed with one 12.7 mm machine gun in the dorsal turret, two 7.7 mm machine guns in its beam hatches, and carried up to 880 lbs of bombs or two 353 lb depth charges. A total of 187 were produced, providing convoy escort, maritime reconnaissance, and air–sea rescue service in the Adriatic and Mediterranean. After Italy's surrender to the Allies in 1943, it had the distinction of serving on both sides for the remainder of the war.

Japanese Naval Aircraft

Fighters and Attack Aircraft

The Imperial Japanese Navy (IJN) followed a similar but independent path to that of the JAAF toward self-sufficiency and modern military aviation. Beginning their move away from license-built copies of foreign designs, the IJN solicited designs for a carrier-based fighter as early as February 1934. Specifications called for a top speed of 217 mph, with a climb rate of 16,405 ft in 6 minutes 30 seconds, and an aircraft small enough (less than 36 ft in span and 26 ft in length) so as to fit on the standard Japanese carrier. Mitsubishi's Jiro Horikoshi designed a cantilevered monoplane, which first flew in February 1935 and entered into production shortly thereafter. It became the first monoplane in the IJN inventory on its service delivery in 1937. Of the 1,094 produced through 1944, the majority featured the following specifications: single crewmember in an open cockpit, with span of 36 ft 1 in, length of 25 ft 3 in, height of 10 ft 6 in, and wing area of 191.5 sq feet (later models varied slightly in these regards). The first production-class model was built around the Nakajima Kotobuki 2 KAI 1 nine cylinder air-cooled radial engine, with later models featuring upgraded power plants that provided for a top speed between 252 mph (A5M1) and 270 mph (A5M4). Almost all copies housed twin 7.7 mm Type 89 machine guns, although some experimented with a single 20 mm Hispano cannon (A5M3a). The A5M, or "Claude" as the Allies came to call it, proved to be quite robust and fulfilled every expectation of the IJN. Its superior agility, a hallmark of Japanese military aviation designs, and its impressive capability to absorb damage and still return to base helped immediately catapult the A5M to the forefront of the navy's arsenal. It delivered air superiority over China in the Second Sino-Japanese Conflict, and even though it was not in front-line use it nevertheless saw a good deal of action at the outset of the war in the Pacific.

Jiro Horikoshi, however, would become famous from another design. The IJN began planning for the A5M's replacement beginning in 1937, so it returned to Horikoshi for a new design. This model was to be faster, more maneuverable, and with greater endurance and armament than the A5M, and Mitsubishi would deliver. From its first flight on April 1, 1939, at the hands of Katsuzo Shima, the A6M Reisen, more popularly known as the "Zero," impressed all observers. Like its predecessor, the A6M was a single-seat, low-wing monoplane carrier-based fighter of cantilever design; however, unlike its predecessor this model featured an enclosed cockpit and retractable undercarriage. It was similar in dimension to the A5M, spanning 36 ft 1 in, with length of 29 ft 9 in, height of 11 ft 6 in, and wing area of approximately 231 sq feet. The first few A6Ms were delivered in July 1940 for combat trials, and proved so wildly successful that the IJN immediately ordered quantity production. By the end of the war, more than 10,440 A6Ms were manufactured. The A6M underwent numerous revisions throughout its lifetime, mostly as new engines became available for use in the same, or very slightly modified, airframes. The first production models featured the Nakajima NK1C Sakae 12, a 940 hp radial engine, whereas later revisions replaced this power plant with the Nakajima NK1F Sakae 21, Nakajima NK1F Sakae 31, and finally the Mitsubishi MK8P Kinsei 62 engines. Top-end performance increased accordingly, from what was even then an impressive 331 mph maximum speed to one in excess of 350 mph; similarly, climb rates improved from 19,685 ft in 7 minutes 27 seconds down to 6 minutes 50 seconds. Most models featured dual 7.7 mm Type 97 machine guns mounted in the upper fuselage, along with a 20 mm Type 99 cannon mounted on each wing. Some later models upgraded the fuselage-mounted machine guns to 13.2 mm Type 3s, and a very few models were modified for use as night-fighters, featuring obliquely mounted 20 mm Type 99 cannon for this purpose. The model could also carry two 132 lb bombs, whereas a few late models even featured air-to-air rockets.

Such experimentation was as common a theme for the IJN as it was for the JAAF because the burdens of the war placed severe restrictions on new designs and production of new models. Thus, the A6M, like many other Japanese aircraft, remained the service's featured model long after its technological peak. Nevertheless, the A6M entered the Western consciousness in a stunning manner, doubtless contributing to its well-earned reputation as the finest—and certainly the most famous—aircraft ever produced by the Japanese. Approximately 400 Zeros were on IJN carriers in early December 1941, having already proven their unquestioned superiority to every other aircraft being flown over China in 1940 and early 1941. When the Japanese Navy launched its surprise attack on Allied stations across the Pacific, A6Ms helped spearhead the charge. After securing some strategically key islands to use as launch sites, land-based Zeros provided air superiority and combat support for Japanese invasion forces all across the Pacific. Precisely the type of "imperial overreach" that Japan soon encountered was perhaps the only thing that could derail the stunning success of the A6M-led IJN air fleet. Production of aircraft, parts, and pilots could not keep pace with the war, and even though the A6M was still the unchallenged ruler of the Pacific skies in early May 1942, the course of the war and the role of the Zero would shift dramatically. After the battles of Coral Sea (May 7–8, 1942) and Midway (June 3–4, 1942), the Japanese lost the offensive, and the Zeros were now a defensive weapon. This changing role was one to which the aircraft was simply ill-suited. Encounters with increasingly capable Allied fighters forced the Japanese to improve the plane's performance, but even so the A6M (code-named "Zeke" by the Allies) never again dominated as it had at the outset of the Pacific War. The Zero's story of stunning initial success and gradual recession from dominance, as its role shifted from offense to defense in nature, parallels that of the entire empire. Thus, the A6M "Zero" remains, for many different reasons, the virtual flag of the entire Japanese war machine.

In the latter part of 1940, as their war plans took shape, the IJN began looking for planes suitable for providing air supremacy in remote regions of the Pacific in places where the ground forces had not yet secured a foothold. Kawanishi thus began to design a floatplane for this task, but the IJN became so infatuated with the A6M that it directed Nakajima to adapt its design and build a seaplane version of the famed "Zero." The A6M2-N project was under the direction of Nakajima designers Tajima and Niitake, who created an intriguing design by installing a fuel tank inside the oversized main float. Otherwise, its dimensions mirrored the carrier-borne A6M (span of 39 ft 4 in, length of 33 ft 1 in, height of 14 ft 1 in, and wing area of 241.5 sq feet). It carried a single pilot in an enclosed cockpit and was armed with twin 7.7 mm Type 97 machine guns mounted on the fuselage and a 20 mm Type 99 cannon on each wing. The "Rufe," as it was known to the Allies, could also carry two 132 lb bombs on external fixtures. It was powered by the Nakajima NK1C Sakae 12 fourteen cylinder air-cooled radial engine. After flight tests showed it to be surprisingly fast and agile, with a top speed in excess of 270 mph and climb rate of 16,405 ft in 6 minutes 43 seconds, the A6M2-N was ordered into production in late 1941. Through mid-1943, approximately 237 copies were delivered to combat units, where the model proved mostly ineffective despite the encouraging early tests. The IJN was so disappointed with its performance under fire that the A6M2-N was rather quickly relegated to service as a trainer for the Kawanishi N1K1 floatplane.

As evidenced by the development of the A6M2-N, the IJN was unique among the major World War II powers in soliciting designs for sea-based air-superiority fighters. It was this notion (that Japan would be fighting an offensive war across the Pacific and would need air cover

for island-hopping ground troops) that led to the design of the Kawanishi N1K1 Kyofu ("Mighty Wind"). By the time this aircraft, which was
almost without question the most impressive seaplane fighter ever produced, entered production the IJN's war strategy was forced into a radical shift. The navy no longer needed a front-line seaplane for an
offensive role and was looking instead for a fighter capable of stem-
ming the Allied tide in the Pacific (an aircraft capable of holding its
own against the technologically advanced Allied Hellcats and Corsairs). The ground-based version of the Kyofu was redesignated the
N1K1-J Shiden ("Violet Lightning"), coded "George" by the Allied
intelligence services, and entered production in 1943. The N1K1
spanned 39 ft 4 in, with length of 29 ft 2 in, height of 13 ft 4 in, and
wing area of approximately 253 sq feet. It was powered by the
extremely powerful Nakajima NK9B Homare 11 eighteen cylinder air-
cooled radial. This enabled it to achieve a top speed of more than 360
mph, which along with a climb rate of 19,685 ft in less than 8 minutes
helped give the N1K1 a good reputation among its Allied opponents.
The model was armed with dual 7.7 mm Type 97 machine guns on the
body and a 20 mm Type 99 Model 2 cannon on each wing. Although
quite capable in combat, and in some respects superior to most Allied
fighters it faced, the 1,435 Shidens delivered through 1945 faced the
same production delays and pilot shortages as plagued many other
technologically advanced Japanese models produced late in the war.

Bombers

One of the first significant steps toward Japanese self-sufficiency in
naval bomber aircraft came in February 1928 when the IJN issued
specifications calling for a carrier attack aircraft; the IJN, it seems,
realized very early on that a carrier-based bombing fleet might be a
very powerful weapon in modern warfare. Aichi, Kawanishi, Nakajima,
and Mitsubishi would all submit designs. Mitsubishi itself solicited
designs from three sources: a team led by Herbert Smith, the Handley
Page Company, and Blackburn. Blackburn's design, featuring a 600 hp
Hispano-Suiza engine, won the competition. The Mitsubishi team of
Hajime Matsuhara, Arikawa, Yui, and Fukui traveled to Great Britain
to observe the chief engineer of the Blackburn design, G.E. Petty, at
work. The first B2M prototype was delivered to Japan in February
1930. The IJN adopted it for production two years later, in March
1932. About 205 were built between 1930 and 1935. The B2M frame,
which housed a crew of three, was of a mixed steel, aluminum, and

fabric construction. It spanned 49 ft 11 in, with a length of 33 ft 8 in, height of 12 ft 2 in, and wing area of 592 sq feet. This single-engine biplane achieved a top speed of 132 mph, and had a climb rate of 9,840 ft in approximately 18 minutes. Its defensive armament consisted of a fixed forward-firing and a dorsal-mounted flexible 7.7 mm machine gun. Its offensive armament consisted of a single torpedo (Type 91 or Type 94) or a single 1,763-lb bomb. Although the B2M represented an important step forward in Japan's modernization program, the aircraft proved difficult to maintain and lacked any superlative performance capabilities of which to speak. Although some saw combat action in the Shanghai Incident (the brief Japanese invasion from January 28 to March 3, 1932, leading directly to the demilitarization of Shanghai and indirectly to the outbreak of the Second Sino-Japanese War five years later), B2Ms were woefully obsolescent by the outbreak of the Pacific War.

The IJN's claimant to the title of world's most effective and modern carrier-borne attack bomber would be the Nakajima B5N. The IJN issued specs for a modern torpedo bomber even though the G3M ground-based attack bomber was still in its initial design phases. They sought a plane with foldable wings, a slight length, and short runway requirements, which were all necessary components for a carrier-borne aircraft. Nakajima's first prototype took to the air in January 1937 and the INJ was impressed, but it feared that the design's many innovations (e.g., hydraulically powered folding wings) would make the aircraft far too difficult to maintain in a combat theater. Nakajima dumbed-down their ambitious design to satisfy the IJN's request for ease of maintenance by, among other things, removing the hydraulic system on the folding wing apparatus. In competitive trial, the Nakajima design still beat out its peers, and the B5N (code-named "Kate" by the Allies) was ordered into production in November 1937. The model underwent one major revision during its production run (replacement of the Nakajima Hikari 3 nine cylinder air-cooled radial engine with the Nakajima NK1B Sakae 11 fourteen cylinder power plant). There were a total 1,149 produced. The B5N carried a crew of three, 50 ft 11 in, and had a length of 33 ft 9 in, height of 12 ft 1 in, and wing area of approximately 405 sq feet. The B5N2 model (with the more powerful engine) could achieve a top speed of 235 mph, climb to 9,845 ft in less than eight minutes, and had a range of between 600 and 1,200 (standard) miles. Defensive armament was scarce (a single rear-firing 7.7 mm Type 92 machine gun). Offensive armament consisted of a single 1,764-lb torpedo, or an external bomb load of a similar weight. The B5N immediately became Japan's premier front-line carrier attack bomber. After impressive performance during the Sino-Japanese conflict, the B5N went on to score some of the most memorable attacks in the Pacific War. On December 7, 1941, 144 Nakajima B5Ns led Admiral Yamamoto's surprise attack on the American fleet at Pearl Harbor. Within the next year, B5Ns also participated in the sinking of four different U.S. carriers, the *Yorktown*, *Lexington*, *Wasp*, and *Hornet*. Several B5Ns were refitted as ASW aircraft when their effectiveness as a primary torpedo bomber was severely reduced by the introduction of advanced Allied fighters into the Pacific Theater.

Even though B5Ns led the assault on Pearl Harbor, the first bombs dropped on Oahu that day were carried by Aichi D3As. The D3A resulted from a navy specification calling for a replacement to the Aichi D1A2 carrier-borne dive-bomber. Aichi, Nakajima, and Mitsubishi competed for the contract, with Tokuhishiro Goake's Aichi design winning the IJN's favor. Goake incorporated visual elements of the Heinkel He 70, particularly the wing structure, into his airframe, which was to be the final Japanese carrier aircraft to feature a fixed spatted undercarriage. The prototype flew in December 1937, and was adopted into production two years later as the Navy Type 99 Carrier Bomber Model 11. More than 143 participated in the campaign against the U.S. installations in Hawaii (these were some of the 470 D3A1s produced between 1939 and August 1942, when the model's power plant was replaced). There were approximately 815 D3A2s produced from late 1942 through June 1944. The plane was powered by a single Kinsei 43, 44, or 54 fourteen cylinder air-cooled radial. The aircraft, with a crew of two, was armed with dual forward-firing and flexible rear-firing 7.7 mm Type 97 machine guns. It could carry a 551 lb bomb under the frame along with a 132 lb bomb under each wing. The D3A spanned 47 ft 1 in, and was 33 ft 5 in length, 12 ft 7 in high, with a wing area of approximately 376 sq feet. The D3A2 could achieve a top speed of more than 265 mph, with a climb rate of 9,845 ft in less than 6 minutes, and it possessed a range of 840 (standard) miles. A total of 1,495 D3As were produced. In addition to action over Hawaii, many delivered ruthlessly effective and devastatingly accurate strikes on the HMS *Cornwall*, the HMS *Dorsetshire*, and the HMS *Hermes*, which were attacked off the coast of Ceylon on April 5–9, 1942.

In early 1938 the IJN secured licensing rights to the Heinkel He 118V4; subsequently, a few months later, Yokosuka was commissioned to design a smaller and more agile version of the same plane. Masao Yamana designed a midwing monoplane of all-metal construction that was smaller and lighter, yet with a far superior fuel capacity, than its muse. Yamana's prototype was completed in November 1940, with its first flight occurring in December. It was determined during extensive testing that the D4Y Suisei ("Comet") was ill-suited for its intended role as a dive-bomber because it was more powerful and more agile than its frame could handle, and high-speed diving runs tended to cause stress fractures along the plane's wings. Aichi built a number of D4Ys modified for reconnaissance use, whereas Yokosuka continued to tweak its design. The IJN adopted the model as a dive-bomber in March 1943. More than 2,000 D4Ys were produced, in four major revisions by adapting more powerful engines into the aircraft from 1942 through August 1945. The plane, called "Judy" by the Allies, had a wing area of 254 sq feet, span of 37 ft 9 in, length of 33 ft 6 in, and height of slightly more than 12 ft. Its top speed ranged from 343 to 360 mph depending on its power plant, and it featured a climb rate of 9,845 ft in approximately 5 minutes or less, along with a service ceiling of between 32,000 and 35,000 ft. Its range was between 900 (normal) and 2,400 miles (maximum range), also depending on its power plant and weapon load. The D4Y was designed to carry a crew of two, between 683 and 1,234 lbs in bombs, and two 7.7 mm Type 97 machine guns mounted on the fuselage. Some D4Ys were modified for use as night-fighters, and these featured an oblique-firing 20 mm Type 99 Model 2 cannon. The plane ultimately lacked sufficient armament or speed to be a truly effective medium bomber; indeed, D4Ys were some of the models hardest hit during the infamous Marianas "Turkey Shoot" on June 19, 1944.

Reconnaissance and Auxiliary Aircraft

The IJN forced self-sufficiency in the aircraft industry by soliciting only Japanese designs for their air fleet, even in reconnaissance and auxiliary models. In 1933, for instance, Nakajima answered a navy specification calling for a two-seat reconnaissance floatplane by producing the E8N. The single-engine, all metal floatplane, with a span of 36 ft, length of 29 ft 11 in, height of 12 ft 7 in, and wing area of 285 sq feet, carried a pilot and observer in open cockpits. It was armed with fixed forward-firing and flexible rear-firing 7.7 machine guns, and could be fitted with two 66-lb external bombs. Nakajima's prototype first flew in March 1934, and it immediately became the IJN's most modern reconnaissance aircraft when it was adopted by them. It achieved a top speed of 186 mph, could climb to 9,845 ft in 6 minutes 30 seconds, and had an operational range of 558 miles. The navy obtained 755 E8Ns between 1934 and 1940. "Dave," as Allies called the E8N, remained in service during the war even though it was by that time rather obsolete.

The navy began planning for the E8N's retirement, however, almost immediately as it was put into service. The navy issued a call for designs specifically to replace the E8N in 1934. Mitsubishi's Joji Hattori produced the winning design, a single-engine observation floatplane dubbed the F1M that would become the only reconnaissance seaplane adopted by the navy for mass production. The first prototype flew in June 1936, although the plane was not adopted until a major revision replaced the 820 hp Nakajima Hikari 1 engine with the 875 hp Mitsubishi Zuisei 13 fourteen cylinder air-cooled radial and reduced the interplane struts, thereby making the plane both faster and more aerodynamic. Two 7.7 mm Type 97 machine guns were fixed and forward-firing, with one rear-firing and flexible. The standard external load included two 132 lb bombs. The F1M, which was code-named "Pete" by the Allied forces, proved to be adept at reconnaissance, air-to-air combat, dive-bombing, escort, and patrol duties, thanks in no small part to its armament and its performance capabilities (particularly a maximum speed of 230 mph and a climb rate of 16,405 ft in 9 minutes 30 seconds). Four F1M1 prototypes were produced before the revisions, of which 1,114 were ultimately manufactured.

The navy issued a call to Kawanishi in 1934 for a long-range, four-engine, flying-boat of monoplane design. Kawanishi assigned Yoshio Hashiguchi and Shizuo Kikahura to this task, one made easier by the incorporation of technological innovations drawn from visits to the Short Brothers aircraft manufacturing plants in Great Britain. Their design featured a parasol wing mounted above the fuselage by inverted-V shaped struts, and was powered by four Nakajima Hikari 2 nine cylinder air-cooled radial engines. The H6K was first flown by Katsuji Kondo on July 14, 1936, and it impressed the navy enough to be adopted into the air fleet. The aircraft underwent several modifications, and its large size enabled use for reconnaissance, bombing, and transport. Its span was 131 ft 2 in, with a length of 84 ft, height of 20 ft 6 in, and 1,829 sq feet of wing area. Although it generally carried a crew of nine, it could be easily modified to carry 10–18 passengers along with an eight-man crew. It was a heavily armed aircraft for its time, and early models housed no fewer than three 7.7 mm Type 92 machine guns in various positions around the fuselage; however, later models rearranged these guns and added a Type 99 Model 1 cannon in the tail. The plane could also carry two 1,764 lb torpedoes or up to a 2,205 lb bomb load, while still surpassing 200 mph in maximum speed. This is even more impressive considering its 50,000 lb maximum weight, which was approximately double its empty weight. Although only 215 H6Ks were produced, the "Mavis" (Allied codename) served the Japanese navy quite admirably from January 1938 and throughout the war in its intended role as a long-range reconnaissance aircraft and, increasingly, as a transport. H6Ks, however, also participated in bombing raids against Rabaul and the Dutch East Indies. The bulk of those produced were of the –4 designation, which had an upgraded power plant (four 1,070 hp Mitsubishi Kinsei 46 fourteen cylinder air-cooled radials) and increased fuel capacity over its predecessors, for a maximum range of nearly 3,800 miles and a reported 24-hour patrol capability. The final version (H6K5) had a superlative maximum range of more than 4,200 miles, but only 36 of this type were produced.

In September 1937 the navy issued a set of specifications calling for a three-seat reconnaissance floatplane. Aichi's Kishiro Matsuo debuted a single-engine monoplane design in December 1940 that beat out competition from Nakajima and Kawanishi. The result was that 1,418 E13As were ultimately produced for the navy between 1938 and 1945. The plane the Allies called "Jake" made its combat debut in late 1941, and garnered rave reviews for its performance on antishipping patrols in the Pacific, for which its 15-hour endurance rating made it ideally suited. E13As were also used to bomb the Canton-Hankow railway, and for reconnaissance purposes during the Hawaiian campaign. The E13A was driven by a 1,080 hp Mitsubishi Kinsei 43 engine, and it spanned 47 ft 7 in, with a length of 37 ft, height of 24 ft 3 in, and wing area of 387 sq feet. It could climb to 9,845 ft in just more than 6 minutes, and it achieved a maximum speed of 233 mph. It was initially armed with a flexible rear-firing 7.7 mm Type 92 machine gun; however, later production aircraft were modified by their field service crews to also house a flexible downward-firing 20 mm Type 99 Model 1 cannon that was used to devastating effect against shipping convoys. The E13A could carry a single 551 lb bomb or four 132 lb bombs or depth charges for use in antisubmarine patrol or as a light bomber. Like many of its generation of aircraft, the E13A's final combat tasking came as a kamikaze suicide craft during the war's closing days.

The IJN commissioned Kawanishi for another large, four-engine seaplane in 1938 that would outperform its British and American cousins, the Short Sunderland and the Sikorsky XPBS-1, as well as its Japanese predecessor, the H6K "Mavis." The latter was indeed a tall order because the H6K proved to be one of the most capable of the

Japanese aircraft of the Second World War. Still, the Kawanishi design team was able to meet these lofty expectations, and the H8K entered production in late 1941, just a few months after its maiden flight in January of that year. Its fuselage was longer (at 92 ft 3 in) and taller (at 30 ft) than the H6K, but it had shorter (124 ft 8 in) and smaller wings (1,722 sq feet). It also had a quite innovative fuel system. In order to meet the stringent range requirements, eight tanks were fitted to the wings, along with six, larger, main tanks in the fuselage. These eight made partial use of self-sealing technology, and had a transfer system allowing fuel from damaged tanks to be drained into bilges, and then recycled into the other tanks. Although it was officially coded "Emily," most Allied servicemen dubbed the H8K the "Flying Porcupine" because it was easily the most heavily armed flying boat in the entire conflict. Its defensive armament, consisting of five 20 mm Type 99 Model 1 cannon arranged all around the aircraft, along with two manually operated 7.7 mm Type 92 machine guns that could be used from a number of different turrets, along with its surprising speed for a plane of its size (270–282 mph maximum speed, 40,000 lb empty and 71,650 lb maximum loaded weight) made the H8K a quite adept reconnaissance and patrol craft. Its offensive armament (two 1,764 lb torpedoes, or eight 551 lb bombs, or 16 132 lb bombs or depth charges fitted on underwing racks) made it easily adaptable to light bombing, antishipping, and antisubmarine duties. Later models were fitted with Mark VI Model 1 radar sets for these purposes. The H8K normally carried a crew of ten and could easily be modified to carry a nine-man crew, and either 29 passengers or 64 troops (model designated H8K2-L). Of the 167 produced, the vast majority were of the H8K2 variant, distinguished chiefly by the use of Mitsubishi MK4Q Kasei 14 cylinder, 1,680 hp engines as the power plant. It represented, without a doubt, the apex of flying-boat design and technology, and despite its relatively small production numbers it served the IJN with distinction in front-line units from its introduction in August 1941 and throughout the remainder of the war.

Following the pattern shown by the H6K and H8K, the IJN liked to plan in advance for the phasing-out of models only shortly after they had become operational. Almost as soon as the E13A was ordered for production, the navy began looking for an even better design. In October 1940, Aichi-based designers Kishiro Matsuo and Yasushiro Ozawa began work on a project that became more urgent upon the issuance of a navy specification in January 1941 that essentially formulated around the new Aichi design. The prototype was not completed until May 1942, and by this time the exigencies of war forced rather innovative accommodations. In this case, the E16A Zuiun ("Auspicious Cloud") used a comparatively limited amount of metal in its construction, using instead reinforced wood for the wingtips and tailplane, and covering the control surfaces with fabric. Matsuo and Ozawa also used perforated dive brakes on this single-engine twin-float reconnaissance aircraft. It carried a crew of two, armed with two wing-mounted 20 mm Type 99 Model 2 cannon and a flexible rear-firing 13 mm Type 2 machine gun, and up to a 551 lb external bomb load. The E16A (code-named "Paul) was powered by a Mitsubishi MK8D Kinsei 54 fourteen cylinder air-cooled radial, rated at 1,200 hp; the plane could achieve a top speed of 273 mph, had a service ceiling of 32,810 ft, and a maximum range of 1,504 miles. Of the 256 acquired by the navy, the most concentrated combat use of the type came in kamikaze attacks around Okinawa in the final stages of the war.

The final naval reconnaissance type to appear under the Rising Sun flag during the war was Nakajima's C6N Saiun ("Painted Cloud"). The IJN realized their fleet lacked a long-range carrier-borne reconnaissance aircraft almost as soon as the Pacific War had begun. Such a design was solicited from Nakajima in early 1942. The plane was to be a three-seat, carrier-borne model capable of achieving a top speed in excess of 400 mph, a 19,685 ft climb in less than 8 minutes, and a range of from 1,700 to more than 3,000 miles. Yasuo Fukuda and Yoshizo Yamamoto were entrusted with the task, and they decided to take advantage of the new Nakajima Homare turbocharged, 1,980 hp power-plant, essentially building the C6N's fuselage around the engine. They also employed a system combining Fowler and split flaps, an element characteristic of what was perhaps an overly innovative design. It failed to meet its specifications when first flight tested, on May 15, 1943, due largely to problems with the new and relatively untested engine; however, necessity took precedence over preference, and the IJN ordered the C6N into production despite these concerns. The first of the 463 C6Ns were delivered in the summer of 1944, and even though it was far from perfect the plane proved to be superior to Japan's existing carrier-based reconnaissance options.

"Myrt" saw combat over the Marianas, and proved especially useful in shadowing the U.S. Pacific Fleet thanks to its impressive speed (379 mph at 20,000 ft) and range (3,299 mi). It was lightly armed with a single 7.7 mm flexible rear-firing Type 2 machine gun in the rear cockpit, but necessity again forced the design into a task for which it was ill-suited because the C6N was retasked as a night-fighter used to defend the Home Islands against Allied bombing raids shortly after it made its combat debut. For this task, late production models added dual fuselage-mounted, oblique-firing 7.92 mm Type 99 cannon and removed the third crewmember. Although its speed and impressive performance at high altitudes (with a service ceiling of more than 35,000 ft) made it a capable night-fighter, the C6N was never intended for this purpose and ultimately represented simply one of an ever-increasing number of stop-gap measures undertaken by the rapidly retreating Japanese war machine. On August 15, 1945, Lt. Cmdr. T.H. Reidy of the U.S. Navy shot down a C6N over Tokyo with his F4U Corsair, recording the final confirmed "kill" of the Pacific air war.

Soviet Naval Aircraft

Due to the internal upheaval caused by the revolution and the nature of the war once the German Army invaded along the Eastern Front, the Soviet Union dedicated few aircraft to maritime service. Those produced were floatplanes or flying boats that were tasked primarily to reconnaissance and auxiliary functions.

In 1932 Georgii Mikhailovich Beriev, drawing upon his experiences as an assistant to French design master Paul-Aimé Richard, put a prototype of the MBR-2 short-range reconnaissance floatplane into the air. The MBR-2 featured a cantilever design with a single 680-hp M-17B engine mounted above the wing. This allowed for a top speed of 152 mph, service ceiling of 14,435 ft, and climb rate of 3,280 ft in approximately 5 minutes. The MBR-2 had a span of 62 ft 4 in, length of 44 ft 3 in, height of 15 ft 9 in, and wing area of just more than 592 sq ft. It featured ring-mounted 7.62 mm ShKAS machine guns mounted in the front and at the midsection of the fuselage, and external points for 1,100 lbs of bombs or depth charges. The plane entered into production in 1934, and approximately 1,300 were ultimately produced of a variety of modified versions. The MBR-2 was both versatile and venerable, and it served in all Soviet theaters and was well-regarded by both its ground and air crews. Different MBR-2s featured floats, wheels, and even skis as landing gear, thereby exemplifying its adaptability. The aircraft could be rather easily modified for use as a light transport, carrying up to six passengers. It was also the aircraft of choice for Paulina Osipenka, who flew a civilian model to numerous records for female pilots. There were approximately 1,500 copies of a revised model, the MP-2bis, featuring the more powerful 860 hp AM-34NB engine; however, despite the improvements in speed, range, and maneuverability, the model remained ill-equipped for combat in the face of concerted German attacks, and was best suited for reconnaissance and rescue missions.

In November 1934 the Soviet military command issued orders for a single float biplane, but orders were given for catapult launching systems to be installed on Soviet aircraft carriers the following year. Beriev thus designed a biplane suitable for use as a catapult-launched aircraft. On September 4, 1934, his KOR-1 design prototype successfully completed its maiden flight. Carrying a crew of two in open cockpits, the KOR-1 spanned just more than 36 ft, with length of 28 ft 5 in, and wing area of 96.12 sq feet. Although initial flight reviews were disappointing (the aircraft was far less maneuverable than desired) the KOR-1 was nevertheless adopted for production as a catapult-launched reconnaissance plane. It was powered by a single 635 hp M-25 nine cylinder air-cooled engine, it could top 149 mph in speed, and it possessed a service ceiling of 22,965 ft. It also featured one of the most lethargic turn rates of any Soviet aircraft of the era. This, combined with its light armament (two 7.62 mm machine guns and points for two 220-lb bombs), meant the KOR-1 was suited for little other than reconnaissance and artillery spotting duties. It performed these duties well into the 1940s, although by 1942 it was no longer the featured catapult aircraft.

Igor Chetverikov was far less prolific than either Beriev or Polikarpov in designing aircraft for the Soviet Union. His most noteworthy contribution was probably the MDR-6, a monoplane flying boat powered by a twin set of engines mounted above the wing. Chetverikov had unsuccessfully experimented with several flying boat designs (the single-engine ARK-3/ARK-4, which was abandoned after a pair of its prototypes broke up during flight testing). Chetverikov returned to the design a few years later, hoping to produce a vehicle with acceptable flight characteristics, but one suitably capable of handling the rough seas in which Soviet naval planes would unavoidably operate. Military authorities ran the MDR-6 prototype through its paces in December 1937, finding it to be a worthy addition to the air fleet. It was ordered into production in 1938, and only a relatively small number—approximately 50—were produced before the advancing German army overran its production facilities in 1941. Although Chetverikov doggedly continued mockups and revisions for improved models of the MDR-6, none of these variants ever saw full-scale production; it simply was not a model worth much of the Soviet Union's increasingly strained productive capacity, and the introduction of several PBY Catalinas into Soviet service under the Lend-Lease program further reduced demand for the

MDR-6. For several years, however, Chetverikov's design did fill a need in the Soviet air arm by providing a three-seat, long-range, reconnaissance seaplane. The basic MDR-6 spanned 63 ft 7 in, with length of 51 ft 7 in, height of 14 ft 1 in, and wing area of approximately 563 sq feet. Dual 1,100 hp Klimov M-63 nine cylinder air-cooled radials powered the MDR-6 to a top speed of 224 mph and climb rate of 16,405 ft in 12 minutes. It also featured a service ceiling of 29,530 ft, and range in excess of 1,640 miles. The MDR-6 was lightly armed because it was intended for reconnoitering, not for combat, and it featured a 7.62 mm ShKAS machine gun in the bow, and a dorsally mounted 12.7 mm UBT machine gun; additionally, it could carry a bomb load of up to 2,200 lbs. Chetverikov's variations on the MDR-6 experimented with different hull designs, different gun configurations and placements, and multiple power plants, but none was ever adopted for production and its designer finally shelved the model in 1946.

The Beriev KOR-2 possesses a story similar to that of the Chetverikov MDR-6. Both were produced in relatively small numbers before their production plants were seized by the advancing Germans, and both saw their usefulness greatly reduced by the introduction of Lend-Lease Catalinas. Nevertheless, the KOR-2 was a step in the determined Soviet attempts to reach self-sufficiency, parity, and superiority to Western air forces. The KOR-1 was ordered into production out of necessity, but Beriev decided to develop a concurrent project to afford greater latitude in the design process. The KOR-2 (later renamed the Be-4) was essentially an improved model of the KOR-1. In this design Beriev created what would have been a quite graceful-looking seaplane were it not for the mounting of an oversized engine atop the single wing. This was a feature that spoiled any aesthetically pleasing aspects of the aircraft. Designed for the same purposes as the KOR-1 (i.e., short-range, sea-launched reconnaissance), the KOR-2 greatly improved upon the performance of its predecessor. The plane was powered by the Shvetsov M-62 nine cylinder air-cooled radial, and it possessed a maximum speed of 223 mph, range approaching 600 miles, service ceiling of 26,575 ft, and featured a climb rate of 16,404 ft in 12 minutes, as well as a vastly improved turn rate over the KOR-1. The KOR-2 spanned 39 ft 4 in, with length of 34 ft 5 in, height of 13 ft 2 in, and wing area of 274.5 sq feet, and it carried a two-man crew in enclosed cockpits. It was armed with a 7.62 mm ShKAS machine gun over the rear cockpit, and had underwing racks for 661 lbs of bombs or depth charges. An accurate count of the production totals of the KOR-2 is virtually impossible because of the shifting of facilities forced on the Soviets by German advances.

The PBY Catalina was likely the most numerous seaplane reconnaissance aircraft in the Soviet air force during World War II. Impressed with a Catalina's performance during a search-and-rescue mission in 1937, the Soviet government contracted with PBY to build licensed copies of the aircraft. Although only 27 GSTs (the Soviet designation for native-produced Catalinas) were produced, the Soviet military procured approximately 190 others through the Lend-Lease program. As was the case with other nations that flew the Catalina, its durability and reliability allowed its participation in virtually all the Soviet theaters.

AIRCRAFT BY COUNTRY

Czechoslovakia
Avia B 534

France
Amiot AM.143
Bloch MB.174
Breguet 19
Dewoitine D.510
Nieuport-Delage NiD.29
Potez 63 Series

Germany
Arado Ar 196
Dornier Do 24
Dornier Do 217
Fieseler Fi 156 Storch
Focke-Wulf Fw 190
Focke-Wulf Fw 200 Condor
Heinkel He 111
Junkers Ju 52/3m
Junkers Ju 87
Junkers Ju 88
Messerschmitt Me BF-109
Messerschmitt Me BF-110
Messerschmitt Me 262

Great Britain
Airspeed Horsa
Avro Lancaster
Bristol Beaufighter

Bristol Bulldog
De Havilland DH.82 Tiger Moth
De Havilland DH.98 Mosquito
Fairey Flycatcher
Fairey Swordfish
Handley-Page Halifax
Hawker Hurricane
Supermarine Spitfire

Italy

Cant Z.501 Gabbiano
Caproni Ca.310
Fiat CR.32 Chirri
Fiat G.50 Freccia
Macchi MC.202 Folgore
Savoia-Marchetti S.M.79 Sparviero
Savoia-Marchetti S.M.81

Japan

Kawanishi N1K1
Kawasaki Ki-61
Kawasaki Type 88
Mitsubishi A6M
Mitsubishi G4M
Mitsubishi Ki-21
Nakajimi B5N
Nakajima Ki-43
Kakajima Ki-84

Poland

PZL P.11

Soviet Union

Ilyushin Il-2
Lavochkin La-7
Lavochkin LaGG-3
Petlyakov Pe.2
Polikarpov I-15
Polikarpov I-16
Polikarpov U-2
Tupolev SB-2
Tupolev TB-3

Tupolev Tu-2
Yakovlev Yak-1
Yakovlev Yak-9

United States

Boeing B-17 Flying Fortress
Boeing B-29 Superfortress
Boeing F4B/P-12
Boeing P-26 Peashooter
Brewster F2A Buffalo
Consolidated B-24 Liberator
Consolidated PBY Catalina
Consolidated PT-1/PT-3 Trusty
Curtiss P-40 Warhawk
Douglas C-47 Skytrain and Dakota
Grumman F2F
Grumman F6F Hellcat
Grumman TBF/TBM Avenger
Lockheed P-38 Lightning
Martin B-10
North American AT-6 Texan/Harvard
North American B-25 Mitchell
North American P-51 Mustang
Republic P-47 Thunderbolt
Vought F4U-1 Corsair

AIRSPEED HORSA
(Courtesy Art-Tech)

COUNTRY OF ORIGIN: Great Britain

MANUFACTURER: Airspeed, Ltd. (Subcontractors: Austin Motor Co., and Harris Lebus and Associates)

TYPE: Glider Transport

CREW: 1

DIMENSIONS: Wingspan 88 ft 0 in.; Length 67 ft 0 in; Height 19 ft 6 in

LOADED WEIGHT: 15,250 lbs

POWER PLANT: none

PERFORMANCE: 150 mph maximum towing speed; 100 mph gliding speed

ARMAMENT: none

TOTAL PRODUCTION: 3,799

SERVICE DATES: 1942–1945

SUMMARY: Designed as a high-wing monoplane of wooden construction, the Horsa came in two types: the Mk.I troop carrier, which could accommodate up to 25 men, and the Mk.II freight carrier, which featured a hinged nose section to make it eas-

ier to load and unload supplies. Its ease of construction allowed approximately 70 percent of those produced to be manufactured by Harris Lebus and Associates, a furniture manufacturer. Towed by such large bombers as the Armstrong Whitworth Albemarle or Handle Page Halifax, it jettisoned its tricycle landing gear after takeoff and landed on a retractable nose wheel and skid. It came equipped with flaps and air brakes, which allowed it to slow down for relatively short landings. The Horsa entered service in 1942 and played a crucial role in the Allied invasions of Sicily and Normandy, as well as in the crossing of the Rhine.

AMIOT AM.143

COUNTRY OF ORIGIN: France

MANUFACTURER: Société d'Emboutissage et de Constructions Mécaniques

TYPE: Medium Bomber

CREW: 5

DIMENSIONS: Wingspan 80 ft 6 in; Length 59 ft 11 in; Height 18 ft 8 in

LOADED WEIGHT: 21,385 lbs

POWER PLANT: 2 x 900 hp Gnome-Rhône 14K Mistral Major radial engines

PERFORMANCE: 193 mph maximum speed; 25,920 ft (7,900 m) service ceiling; 746 mile normal range, 1,240 mile maximum range

ARMAMENT: 3,960 lb maximum bomb load; 4 x 7.5 mm machine guns

TOTAL PRODUCTION: 144

SERVICE DATES: 1935–1942

SUMMARY: Based on 1928 design specifications for a day and night bomber, the Amiot Am.143 did not enter service until 1935. Although it was an all-metal monoplane, it still used a fixed undercarriage and featured an angular, slab-sided fuselage, making it an ugly aircraft with poor aerodynamic characteristics. It was already obsolete by the time war broke out in 1939, but it still supplied six bomber groups in the Armée de l'Air. Its slow speed relegated it primarily to night bombing. After Germany launched its invasion of France, the French desperately pressed the Amiot Am.143 into daytime service, but lost 13 of 14 aircraft in a single sortie. Following France's surrender to Nazi Germany, a few Amiot Am.143s were relegated to transport duties for the Vichy regime.

ARADO AR 196
(Courtesy Art-Tech)

COUNTRY OF ORIGIN: Germany
MANUFACTURER: Arado Flugzeugwerke GmbH
TYPE: Reconnaissance Seaplane
CREW: 2
DIMENSIONS: Wingspan 40 ft 10 in; Length 36 ft 1 in; Height 14 ft 1 in
LOADED WEIGHT: 8,223 lbs
POWER PLANT: 1 x 900 hp BMW radial
PERFORMANCE: 193 mph maximum speed; 22,965 ft (7,000 m) service ceiling; 670 mile range
ARMAMENT: 2 x 20 mm cannon; 1–3 x 7.9 mm machine guns; 220 lb maximum bomb load
TOTAL PRODUCTION: 546 of all types
SERVICE DATES: 1939–1945

SUMMARY: Considered one of the most versatile of its type, the Ar 196 replaced the He 60 as the standard catapult-launched aircraft on the Kriegsmarine's capital ships beginning in August 1939. The Ar 196 was also flown in some numbers by Bulgaria, Finland, and Romania, and was used for reconnaissance, coastal patrol, antisubmarine, light-bombing, and convoy escort duties.

AVIA B 534
(Courtesy Art-Tech)

COUNTRY OF ORIGIN: Czechoslovakia
MANUFACTURER: Avia Akciova Spolecnost Pro Prumysl Letecky
TYPE: Fighter
CREW: 1
DIMENSIONS: Wingspan 30 ft 10 in; Length 26 ft 7 in; Height 10 ft 2 in
LOADED WEIGHT: 4,376 lbs
POWER PLANT: 1 x 860 hp Avia Hispano-Suiza 12 Ydrs liquid-cooled V-12 engine
PERFORMANCE: 245 mph maximum speed; 36,089 ft (11,000 m) ceiling; 373 mile range
ARMAMENT: 4 x 7.92 mm machine guns
TOTAL PRODUCTION: Approximately 500
SERVICE DATES: 1934–1944

SUMMARY: Designed by Frantisek Novotny as an improvement to the earlier Avia B 34, the B 534 was one of the fastest and best maneuverable biplane fighters produced between the wars. It combined metal framing and fabric covering construction, featured ailerons on both wings, and sported a sliding canopy to enclose the cockpit. Although its performance was slightly eclipsed by Nazi Germany's Messerschmitt BF-109 monoplane, the B 534 would have offered capable resistance had the British and French not capitulated to Hitler at the Munich Conference. After Czechoslovakia was absorbed by Nazi Germany in March 1939, the B 534 was used as a trainer and tug by the Luftwaffe and saw service as a fighter in the Slovakia and Bulgarian air forces.

AVRO LANCASTER
(Courtesy Art-Tech)

COUNTRY OF ORIGIN: Great Britain

MANUFACTURER: A. V. Roe & Co. Ltd. and numerous subcontractors

TYPE: Heavy Bomber

CREW: 7–8

DIMENSIONS: Wingspan 102 ft 0 in; Length 68 ft 10 in; Height 20 ft 4 in

LOADED WEIGHT: 68,000 lbs (normal); 72,000 lbs (maximum)

POWER PLANT: 4 x 1,280 hp or 1,620 hp Rolls-Royce Merlin 20, 22, or 24 liquid-cooled V-12 engines

PERFORMANCE: 287 mph maximum speed; 24,500 ft (7,465 m) service ceiling; 1,040 mile range

ARMAMENT: Normal bomb load of 14,000 lbs; 8 x .303 caliber machine guns in powered turrets

TOTAL PRODUCTION: 7,377 of all models

SERVICE DATES: 1942–1954

SUMMARY: A replacement for the under-powered Avro Manchester, the Avro Lancaster entered service in March 1942 and quickly became the centerpiece of RAF Bomber Command, flying approximately 156,000 sorties and dropping more than 600,000 tons of bombs during the war. It featured an all-metal construction monoplane design with twin rudders, which allowed for a powered machine gun turret to be placed in the tail for added protection. Lancasters gained notoriety for sinking the German battleship *Tirpitz* and for raids against German dams, gaining the nickname the "Dam Buster." A modified version of the Lancaster was designed to carry the the 22,000 lb Grand Slam bomb, which was designed to penetrate into the ground before exploding in order to destroy underground structures. Lancasters remained in service with RAF Coastal Command until 1954.

BLOCH MB.174/175
(Courtesy Art-Tech)

COUNTRY OF ORIGIN: France
MANUFACTURER: Avions Marcel Bloch
TYPE: Reconnaissance and Light Bomber
CREW: 3
DIMENSIONS: Wingspan 58 ft 9.5 in; Length 40 ft 1.5 in; Height 11 ft 8 in
LOADED WEIGHT: 15,748 lbs
POWER PLANT: 2 x 1140 hp Gnome-Rhône 14N 48/49 radial engines
PERFORMANCE: 335 mph maximum speed; 36,089 ft (11,000 m) service ceiling; 1,025 mile range
ARMAMENT: 7 x 7.5 mm machine guns and up to 1,102 lbs of bombs
TOTAL PRODUCTION: 227 of all types
SERVICE DATES: 1939–1953
SUMMARY: Introduced in 1939, the Bloch MB.174 proved to be an outstanding reconnaissance aircraft that was fast enough to escape from German fighters. Production unfortunately began so late that not enough were available to make a significant difference. Nevertheless, it was an advanced aircraft of all metal construction and low-wing monoplane design that included fully retractable wheels, an enclosed cockpit, and twin rudders. The MB.175 was a light bombing version. With France's defeat, several MB.174s and MB.175s were destroyed by their pilots to prevent their use by the Germans. A few managed to fly to North Africa, where they served with Free French Forces. Production continued during the German occupation and served the Luftwaffe as trainers. The French Navy ordered 80 after the war to serve as torpedo bombers, a role in which they served until 1953.

BOEING B-17 FLYING FORTRESS
(Courtesy Art-Tech)

COUNTRY OF ORIGIN: United States
MANUFACTURER: Boeing Aircraft Company
TYPE: Medium/Heavy Bomber
CREW: 10
DIMENSIONS: Wingspan 103 ft 9 in; Length 74 ft 9 in; Height 19 ft 1 in
LOADED WEIGHT: 65,500 lbs
POWER PLANT: 3 x 1,200 hp Wright R-1820–97 radials
PERFORMANCE: 302 mph maximum speed; 35,600 ft (10,850 m) service ceiling; 1,800 mile maximum range
ARMAMENT: 10–13 x .50 caliber machine guns; 9,600 lb maximum bomb load
TOTAL PRODUCTION: 12,731 of all types
SERVICE DATES: 1937–1945
SUMMARY: Developed to replace the Martin B-10, the B-17's prototype crashed during testing and was initially disqualified from competitive service trials. The Army Air Force was so intrigued by the design, however, that a small number were ordered for further evaluation. Once accepted into service, B-17 production peaked at 330 per month between 1943 and July 1945. The Flying Fortress became the stalwart of the U.S. air offensive in Europe, easy to fly and capable of sustaining plenty of damage; a typical long-range bomb load of 4,000 lbs increased the aircraft's range while also aiding its inflight stability. The most capable model was the –G version, which entered production in mid-1943 and eventually accounted for nearly 8,700 of the total produced.

BOEING B-29 SUPERFORTRESS
(Courtesy Art-Tech)

COUNTRY OF ORIGIN: United States
MANUFACTURER: Boeing Aircraft Company
TYPE: Heavy Bomber
CREW: 10–14
DIMENSIONS: Wingspan 141 ft 3 in; Length 99 ft; Height 27 ft 9 in
LOADED WEIGHT: 138,000 lbs
POWER PLANT: 4 x 2,200 hp Wright Cyclone R-3350 radials
PERFORMANCE: 344 mph maximum speed; 31,850 ft (9,700 m) service ceiling; 3,250 mile maximum range
ARMAMENT: 10–12 x .50 caliber machine guns; 20,000 lb maximum bomb load
TOTAL PRODUCTION: 3,960 of all types
SERVICE DATES: 1944–1954
SUMMARY: The B-29 was the most technologically advanced bomber in the American arsenal, featuring a tricycle undercarriage, pressurized cabin, remotely controlled defensive guns, a high payload, and extended range capability. Its initial deployment was to the China-India-Burma Theater, and it remained tasked solely to the Pacific region during the war. The B-29's superior range and size made it the choice as carrier for the atomic weapons developed by the Manhattan Project. On August 6, 1945, the B-29 "Enola Gay" dropped the atomic weapon, dubbed "Little Boy," on Hiroshima; three days later, the weapon dubbed "Fat Man" was dropped on Nagasaki by the B-29 "Bockscar." In late August 1945, Soviet forces downed a B-29, which was reverse-engineered and reproduced as the Tupolev Tu-4.

BOEING F4B/P-12
(Courtesy Art-Tech)

COUNTRY OF ORIGIN: United States
MANUFACTURER: Boeing Aircraft Company
TYPE: Fighter
CREW: 1
DIMENSIONS: Wingspan 30 ft; Length 20 ft; Height 9 ft 3 in
LOADED WEIGHT: 2,750 lbs
POWER PLANT: 1 x 550 hp Pratt & Whitney R-1340 radial
PERFORMANCE: 189 mph maximum speed; 27,000 ft (8,230 m) service ceiling; 520 mile range
ARMAMENT: 2 x .30 caliber machine guns; 232 lb maximum bomb load
TOTAL PRODUCTION: 562
SERVICE DATES: 1929–1937

SUMMARY: The Boeing F4B was arguably the most capable biplane fighter in the American inventory during the interwar years; indeed, it was built in greater numbers than any other American military aircraft prior to World War II. First adopted by the navy, which purchased 170 copies, the Army Air Force also liked the design and secured more than 360 F4Bs. The army quickly phased the fighter out after 1934, however, because it proved too slow to engage the B-10 bomber and was thus considered obsolete.

BOEING P-26 PEASHOOTER
(Courtesy Art-Tech)

COUNTRY OF ORIGIN: United States
MANUFACTURER: Boeing Aircraft Company
TYPE: Fighter
CREW: 1
DIMENSIONS: Wingspan 27 ft 11 in; Length 23 ft 9 in; Height 10 ft
LOADED WEIGHT: 3,075 lbs
POWER PLANT: 1 x 600 hp Pratt & Whitney Wasp radial
PERFORMANCE: 235 mph maximum speed; 28,000 ft (8,500 m) service ceiling; 635 mile range
ARMAMENT: 1 x .30 caliber machine gun; 1 x .50 caliber machine gun; 200 lb maximum bomb load
TOTAL PRODUCTION: 113
SERVICE DATES: 1934–1939

SUMMARY: The P-26 was the first monoplane fighter produced by American manufacturing; it is also notable as the first all-metal fighter produced. Pilots, somewhat suspicious of the new design elements, derisively dubbed the aircraft the "Peashooter." Nevertheless, it was a fast and maneuverable aircraft for its time. As such, it served as the Army Air Force's front-line fighter plane until the arrival of such fighters as the Seversky P-35 and Curtiss P-36. Although out of front-line service by the time of the Japanese attack on Pearl Harbor, six P-26s were destroyed on the ground at Wheeler Field. It should be best remembered as a transitional aircraft, helping to bring the American aircraft industry into the modern technological age.

BREGUET 19
(Courtesy Art-Tech)

COUNTRY OF ORIGIN: France

MANUFACTURER: Société des Avions Louis Breguet

TYPE: Reconnaissance and Light Bomber

CREW: 2

DIMENSIONS: Wingspan 48 ft 8 in; Length 31 ft 2 in; Height 10 ft 11 in

LOADED WEIGHT: 4,850 lbs

POWER PLANT: 1 x 500 hp Hispano Suiza 12HB V-12

PERFORMANCE: 143 mph maximum speed; 21,982 ft (6,700 m) ceiling; 497 mile range

ARMAMENT: 3–4 x 7.5 mm Darne or 7.7 mm Vickers machine guns; up to 1,543 lbs of bombs

TOTAL PRODUCTION: Approximately 3,200 including licensed built versions

SERVICE DATES: 1924–1939

SUMMARY: The Breguet 19, introduced in 1924, proved to be one of the most successful aircraft of the early interwar years with more than 1,000 entering French service and approximately twice that number entering service with other countries. It was consequently one of the most widely produced aircraft of the interwar period. It combined all-metal framing with fabric covering. The Breguet 19 set many long-distance records in international competitions during the 1920s and was used militarily by the French to suppress uprisings in North Africa. It also served on both sides during the Spanish Civil War.

BREWSTER F2A BUFFALO
(Courtesy Art-Tech)

COUNTRY OF ORIGIN: United States

MANUFACTURER: Brewster Aeronautical Corporation

TYPE: Fighter

CREW: 1

DIMENSIONS: Wingspan 35 ft; Length 26 ft 4 in; Height 12 ft 1 in

LOADED WEIGHT: 7,055 lbs

POWER PLANT: 1 x 1,100 hp Wright Cyclone R-1820 radial

PERFORMANCE: 300 mph maximum speed; 30,500 ft (9,300 m) service ceiling; 950 mile range

ARMAMENT: 4 x .50 caliber machine guns

TOTAL PRODUCTION: 509

SERVICE DATES: 1939–1942

SUMMARY: The F2A, dubbed "Buffalo" by the British, was the U.S. Navy's first all-metal monoplane fighter. Although considered technologically advanced upon its service delivery in 1939, it was obsolete by 1942.

Of the first batch of production aircraft, only 11 were delivered to the navy. The remainder were shipped to Finland, where they were employed along the Soviet front. The model saw greater success in this region than it did in the Pacific because they were no match for the clearly superior A6M "Zero" fighter.

BRISTOL BEAUFIGHTER
(Courtesy Art-Tech)

COUNTRY OF ORIGIN: Great Britain

MANUFACTURER: Bristol Aeroplane Co. Ltd.

TYPE: Fighter, Night-Fighter, Torpedo-Bomber

CREW: 2

DIMENSIONS: Wingspan 57 ft 10 in; Length 41 ft 4 in; Height 15 ft 10 in

LOADED WEIGHT: 21,600 lbs

POWER PLANT: 2 x 1,670 hp Bristol Hercules VI or XVI radial engines

PERFORMANCE: 333 mph maximum speed; 26,500 ft (8,077 m) ceiling; 1,540 mile range

ARMAMENT: 4 x 20 mm cannon; 6 x .303 caliber machine guns; up to 1,000 lbs of bombs or a 1,650 lb or 2,127 lb torpedo.

TOTAL PRODUCTION: 5,584

SERVICE DATES: 1940–1957

SUMMARY: The Bristol Beaufighter, adapted from the earlier Bristol Beaufort by lead designer Leslie Frise, was intended to provide the RAF with a long-range night fighter that was to be directed to its targets by the A/I radar system. After they entered service in October 1940 they proved highly effective against German bombers attempting to strike Britain at night. Beaufighters also served throughout the North African and Mediterranean Theaters. The British and Australians also adapted them to deliver torpedoes against enemy shipping.

BRISTOL BULLDOG
(Courtesy Art-Tech)

COUNTRY OF ORIGIN: Great Britain
MANUFACTURER: Bristol Aeroplane Co. Ltd.
TYPE: Fighter
CREW: 1
DIMENSIONS: Wingspan 33 ft 11 in; Length 25 ft 2 in; Height 9 ft 10 in
LOADED WEIGHT: 3,530 lbs
POWER PLANT: 1 x 490 hp Bristol Jupiter VIIF radial engine
PERFORMANCE: 174 mph maximum speed; 27,000 ft (8,230 m) ceiling; 350 mile range
ARMAMENT: 2 x .303 caliber synchronized Vickers machine guns; 80 lbs of bombs
TOTAL PRODUCTION: 449
SERVICE DATES: 1929–1937
SUMMARY: Introduced in 1929 as a replacement for the Gloster Gamecock and Armstrong-Whitworth Siskins IIIA, the Bristol Bulldog would comprise approximately 70 percent of the RAF's fighter strength in the early 1930s. It marked a transitional aircraft between the immediate post–World War I era fighters and those that would enter service on the eve of World War II. Although its frame used all metal construction, it was fabric covered except for the area around the engine. It also still used wire bracing. Approximately one third of the number produced were exported to other countries, including Finland, which relied upon them heavily during the Russo-Finnish War.

CANT Z.501 GABBIANO

(Courtesy Art-Tech)

COUNTRY OF ORIGIN: Italy

MANUFACTURER: Cantieri Riuniti dell'Adriatico

TYPE: Patrol-Bomber Flying Boat

CREW: 4–5

DIMENSIONS: Wingspan 73 ft 10 in; Length 46 ft 11 in; Height 14 ft 6 in

LOADED WEIGHT: 13,117 lbs (normal); 15,542 lbs (maximum)

POWER PLANT: 1 x 900 hp Isotta-Fraschini Asso XI R2 C15 V-12 engine

PERFORMANCE: 171 mph maximum speed; 22,966 ft (7,000 m) ceiling; 1,490 mile range

ARMAMENT: 3 x 7.7 mm machine guns; 1,404 lb bomb load

TOTAL PRODUCTION: 445

SERVICE DATES: 1936–1950

SUMMARY: The Cant Z.501 Gabbiano, designed by Filippo Zappata, set numerous speed and distance records for a flying boat after its introduction in 1934. It entered service with the Regia Aeronautica and was used as a bomber in support of Nationalist forces during the Spanish Civil War. Although produced in relatively large numbers, its wood and fabric construction made it ill equipped for service in the Second World War, resulting in heavy losses.

CAPRONI CA.310

(*Courtesy Art-Tech*)

COUNTRY OF ORIGIN: Italy

MANUFACTURER: Società di Aviazione Ing. Caproni

TYPE: Light Bomber, Torpedo-Bomber, and Reconnaissance

CREW: 3

DIMENSIONS: Wingspan 53 ft 2 in; Length 40 ft 0.5 in; Height 11 ft 7 in

LOADED WEIGHT: 12,450 lbs

POWER PLANT: 2 x 470 hp Piaggio P.VII C 16 radial engines

PERFORMANCE: 227 mph maximum speed; 22,956 ft (7,000 m) ceiling; 1,025 mile range

ARMAMENT: 3 x 7.7 mm machine guns; 1,764 lb maximum bomb load

TOTAL PRODUCTION: 2,400 of all types (Ca.309–316)

SERVICE DATES: 1938–1945

SUMMARY: The Caproni Ca.310 was derived from an earlier civil transport model and was part of the most widely produced series of Italian military aircraft made during the war. The Ca.310 featured all-metal construction and retractable landing gear. Even though it was somewhat underpowered, it was easy to fly and generally well-received by Italian aircrews. It saw extensive service in the Mediterranean and North Africa Theaters.

CONSOLIDATED B-24 LIBERATOR
(Courtesy Art-Tech)

COUNTRY OF ORIGIN: United States
MANUFACTURER: Consolidated Aircraft Corporation
TYPE: Medium/Heavy Bomber
CREW: 8–10
DIMENSIONS: Wingspan 110 ft; Length 66 ft 4 in; Height 17 ft 11 in
LOADED WEIGHT: 64,000 lbs
POWER PLANT: 4 x 1,200 hp Pratt & Whitney Twin Wasp radials
PERFORMANCE: 303 mph maximum speed; 32,000 ft (9,750 m) service ceiling; 2,850 mile range
ARMAMENT: 10 x .50 caliber machine guns; 8,000 lb maximum bomb load
TOTAL PRODUCTION: 18,482 of all types
SERVICE DATES: 1940–1950

SUMMARY: The B-24 in all its versions was produced in greater quantity than any other American combat aircraft of the war. In addition to its primary role as bomber, variants of the B-24 were also used as transport, tanker, reconnaissance, and maritime patrol aircraft. Orders from Great Britain and France immediately followed the prototype's first successful test flight in December 1939; however, by the time of production France had fallen and those aircraft were instead rerouted to Great Britain. The USAAC adopted the B-24 into service ranks in early 1941, with production greatly increased after Pearl Harbor. The –D version was the most numerous production model, at 2,738 copies. Despite being able to absorb less damage than the B-17, B-24s are estimated to have dropped more than 600,000 tons of bombs in all theaters during the war.

CONSOLIDATED PBY CATALINA
(Courtesy Art-Tech)

COUNTRY OF ORIGIN: United States

MANUFACTURER: Consolidated Aircraft Corporation

TYPE: Reconnaissance Flying Boat

CREW: 7–9

DIMENSIONS: Wingspan 104 ft; Length 63 ft 10 in; Height 18 ft 10 in

LOADED WEIGHT: 34,000 lbs

POWER PLANT: 2 x 1,200 hp Pratt & Whitney Twin Wasp radials

PERFORMANCE: 196 mph maximum speed; 18,100 ft (5,500 m) service ceiling; 3,100 mile range

ARMAMENT: 5 x .30 or .50 caliber machine guns; 4,000 lb maximum bomb/depth charge load

TOTAL PRODUCTION: 3,290 of all types

SERVICE DATES: 1936–1957

SUMMARY: The Catalina was by far the most widely used flying boat of the war, seeing service in the hands of the United States, Australia, Brazil, Great Britain, Canada, Chile, the Netherlands, New Zealand, Norway, South Africa, and the Soviet Union. Indeed, the Soviets produced approximately 150 copies of the PBY Catalina, redesignated the GST. The PBY was stationed on all fronts, and it served in a variety of offensive and secondary roles, including antisubmarine warfare, air–sea rescue, mine-laying, bombing, and transport duties. Its versatility, reliability, and range made it one of the more venerable aircraft of the era.

CONSOLIDATED PT-1/PT-3 TRUSTY
(Courtesy Art-Tech)

COUNTRY OF ORIGIN: United States

MANUFACTURER: Consolidated Aircraft Corporation

TYPE: Trainer

CREW: 2

DIMENSIONS: Wingspan 34 ft 5 in; Length 27 ft 9 in; Height 9 ft 10 in

LOADED WEIGHT: 2,577 lbs

POWER PLANT: 1 x 180 hp Wright E vee-type

PERFORMANCE: 92 mph maximum speed; 14,000 ft (4,250 m) service ceiling; 350 mile range

ARMAMENT: None

TOTAL PRODUCTION: 469 of all types

SERVICE DATES: 1924–1936

SUMMARY: The PT-1 was the army's first post–World War I trainer, and the first ordered in quantity (221 ordered in 1921). The plane was extraordinarily easy to fly, and pilot-trainees soon dubbed it the "Trusty." The biplane had a steel tubing frame and fabric covering, and was strongly built and served admirably as the USAAC's primary trainer for 10 years. In 1928, the PT-3 incorporated a stronger engine into virtually the same airframe; this variant of the "Trusty" served as the primary trainer through 1936.

CURTISS P-40 WARHAWK
(Courtesy Art-Tech)

COUNTRY OF ORIGIN: United States

MANUFACTURER: Curtiss-Wright Corporation

TYPE: Fighter

CREW: 1

DIMENSIONS: Wingspan 37 ft 4 in; Length 33 ft 4 in; Height 12 ft 4 in

LOADED WEIGHT: 8,500 lbs

POWER PLANT: 1 x 1,300 hp Packard Merlin vee-type

PERFORMANCE: 320 mph maximum speed; 32,400 ft (9,875 m) service ceiling; 800 mile range

ARMAMENT: 6 x .50 caliber machine guns; 500 lb maximum bomb load

TOTAL PRODUCTION: 13,738 of all types

SERVICE DATES: 1939–1944

SUMMARY: The P-40, developed in an attempt to improve the performance characteristics of the P-36 Hawk model, improved on little other than this feature. Upon entering combat at the hands of the RAF, the P-40 was discovered to lack the altitude and speed capabilities of its German enemies. It is most notable for its use by the AVG "Flying Tigers" in China, where the American pilots capitalized on the Warhawk's fast diving speed and ability to absorb damage. The P-40 was used in a more conventional manner in the European theater, where it showed its obsolescence; however, it was far more successful when adapted to night-fighting duties over North Africa and Italy.

DE HAVILLAND DH.82 TIGER MOTH

(Courtesy Art-Tech)

COUNTRY OF ORIGIN: Great Britain

MANUFACTURER: De Havilland Aircraft Company

TYPE: Trainer

CREW: 2

DIMENSIONS: Wingspan 29 ft 4 in; Length 23 ft 11 in; Height 8 ft 9.5 in

LOADED WEIGHT: 1,825 lbs

POWER PLANT: 1 x 130 hp de Havilland Gipsy Major inline engine

PERFORMANCE: 109 mph maximum speed; 14,000 ft (4,267 m) service ceiling; 300 mile range

ARMAMENT: none

TOTAL PRODUCTION: 8,796

SERVICE DATES: 1932–1947

SUMMARY: The Tiger Moth, derived from the earlier De Havilland Moth series, entered service in 1932 as a basic trainer for the RAF and other Commonwealth nations until 1947. Its metal framework and fabric covering made it highly acrobatic. Later versions included one with a canvas cover for the rear cockpit so that a trainee could learn to fly by instruments, as well as a radio-operated drone that was used for gunnery practice.

DE HAVILLAND DH.98 MOSQUITO
(Courtesy Art-Tech)

COUNTRY OF ORIGIN: Great Britain

MANUFACTURER: De Havilland Aircraft Company

TYPE: Reconnaissance, Light Bomber, Fighter, and Night Fighter

CREW: 2

DIMENSIONS: Wingspan 54 ft 2 in; Length 41 ft 6 in; Height 15 ft 3 in

LOADED WEIGHT: 25,500 lbs

POWER PLANT: 2 x 1,710 hp Rolls-Royce Merlin 76/77 V-12 engines

PERFORMANCE: 425 mph maximum speed; 36,000 ft (10,973 m) ceiling; up to 3,500 miles

ARMAMENT: 4 x 20 mm cannons; 4 x .303 caliber machine guns; 4,000 lb maximum bomb load

TOTAL PRODUCTION: 7,781 of all types (including 1,245 produced in Australia and Canada)

SERVICE DATES: 1941–1955

SUMMARY: The De Havilland DH.98 Mosquito, introduced in 1941, proved to be one of the most versatile aircraft of the Second World War, serving in a variety of roles. The Mosquito, unique for its time because of its wooden construction, proved to be as fast and maneuverable as many single-engine fighters. Indeed, as a reconnaissance aircraft it could rely upon its speed to outrun pursuing German fighters.

DEWOITINE D.510
(Courtesy Art-Tech)

COUNTRY OF ORIGIN: France

MANUFACTURER: Constructions Aeronautiques Emile Dewoitine

TYPE: Fighter

CREW: 1

DIMENSIONS: Wingspan 39 ft 8 in; Length 26 ft 0 in; Height 8 ft 10 in

LOADED WEIGHT: 4,235 lbs

POWER PLANT: 1 x 860 hp Hispano-Suiza 12Ycrs V-12 engine

PERFORMANCE: 250 mph maximum speed; 34,448 ft (10,500 m) ceiling; 435 mile range

ARMAMENT: 1 x 20 mm cannon; 2 x 7.7 mm machine guns

TOTAL PRODUCTION: 121

SERVICE DATES: 1935–1940

SUMMARY: The Dewoitine D.510, introduced in 1935, marked a clear transition in fighter design away from biplanes and toward the low-wing monoplane fighters of the Second World War. Of all metal construction, it featured stressed metal sheeting, cantilever wings, and enclosed engine cowling, but it still utilized a fixed landing gear and open cockpit. Although it was soon surpassed by the Messerschmitt BF-109, the Dewoitine D.510 remained in service until 1940 because of production delays in the more advanced Dewoitine D.520.

DORNIER DO 24
(Courtesy Art-Tech)

COUNTRY OF ORIGIN: Germany

MANUFACTURER: Dornier Werke GmbH

TYPE: Reconnaissance Flying Boat, Air/Sea Rescue

CREW: 6

DIMENSIONS: Wingspan 88 ft 7 in; Length 72 ft 2 in; Height 18 ft 10 in

LOADED WEIGHT: 28,600 lbs

POWER PLANT: 3 x 760 hp Wright Cyclone radials

PERFORMANCE: 195 mph maximum speed; 17,390 ft (5,300 m) service ceiling; 2,048 mile range

ARMAMENT: 2 x 7.92 mm machine guns; 1 x 20 mm or 30 mm cannon; 1,320 lb maximum bomb load

TOTAL PRODUCTION: 214 of all types

SERVICE DATES: 1939–1945

SUMMARY: The Do 24 was originally designed for the Dutch government, and most of the original production line was destroyed by the Japanese in their attacks on the Dutch East Indies. The model saw its most extensive use within the Luftwaffe. The German air force used it for a variety of missions, including air–sea rescue, convoy escort, reconnaissance, transport, and troop movements.

DORNIER DO 217
(Courtesy Art-Tech)

COUNTRY OF ORIGIN: Germany
MANUFACTURER: Dornier Werke GmbH
TYPE: Medium/Heavy Bomber, Night Fighter
CREW: 3–4
DIMENSIONS: Wingspan 62 ft 4 in; Length 55 ft 9.25 in; Height 16 ft 3 in
LOADED WEIGHT: 36,917 lbs (maximum takeoff)
POWER PLANT: 2 x 1,750 hp Daimler Benz radials
PERFORMANCE: 348 mph maximum speed; 29,200 ft (8,900 m) service ceiling; 1,550 mile maximum range
ARMAMENT: 4 x 7.9 mm machine guns; 2 x 13 mm machine guns; 8,818 lb maximum bomb load
TOTAL PRODUCTION: 1,730 of all types
SERVICE DATES: 1937–1945

SUMMARY: The Do 217 was developed from the Do 17 series medium bomber. It was larger, heavier, better armed, and was able to carry a greater bomb load. The famed "Flying Pencil" was a workhorse for German forces throughout the war as a bomber. Proving its versatility, models (-J and –N versions) were also adapted for use as night fighters. In this configuration, four 20 mm MG 151 cannons would be mounted in the Schräge Musik ("Slanted Music" or "Jazz") upward-firing position. Beginning in 1942, the night-fighter version flew with 15 groups defending Germany over the Eastern Front, and in the Mediterranean.

DOUGLAS C-47 SKYTRAIN AND DAKOTA

(Courtesy Art-Tech)

COUNTRY OF ORIGIN: United States
MANUFACTURER: Douglas Aircraft Company, Inc.
TYPE: Transport
CREW: 2
DIMENSIONS: Wingspan 95 ft; Length 64 ft 5.5 in; Height 16 ft 11 in
LOADED WEIGHT: 29,300 lbs
POWER PLANT: 2 x 1,200 hp Pratt & Whitney Twin Wasp radials
PERFORMANCE: 229 mph maximum speed; 24,000 ft (7,315 m) service ceiling; 1,500 mile range
ARMAMENT: None
TOTAL PRODUCTION: 10,665 of all types
SERVICE DATES: 1940–1976

SUMMARY: The C-47 Dakota was considered by many aviation historians to be the most famous aircraft of its type in the world. It was derived from the Douglas DC-3 commercial airliner and could carry a load of 28 troops, or up to 10,000 lbs in cargo. American entry into the Pacific war in 1941 prompted the USAAC to call for quantity production of the model. Thanks to its durability, the C-47 served on every front of the war, with production peaking at 4,878 in 1944. It remained in service in some capacities into the Vietnam War (as a gunship). In addition to the United States, Dakotas served with Australia, Great Britain, Canada, Germany, India, Japan, and the Soviet Union.

FAIREY FLYCATCHER
(Courtesy Art-Tech)

COUNTRY OF ORIGIN: Great Britain
MANUFACTURER: The Fairey Aviation Co. Ltd.
TYPE: Fighter
CREW: 1
DIMENSIONS: Wingspan 29 ft 0 in; Length 22 ft 10 in; Height 10 ft 0 in
LOADED WEIGHT: 3,028 lbs
POWER PLANT: 1 x 410 hp Armstrong-Siddeley Jaguar IV radial engine
PERFORMANCE: 134 mph maximum speed; 19,000 ft (5,791 m) service ceiling; 263 mile range
ARMAMENT: 2 x .303 caliber machine guns; 80 lb maximum bomb load
TOTAL PRODUCTION: 192
SERVICE DATES: 1923–1934

SUMMARY: The Fairey Flycatcher, introduced in 1923, provided the Royal Navy's Fleet Air Arm with its first specifically designed carrier fighter. Although it was a rather ugly aircraft, its diving ability and maneuverability were superb. More important, the Flycatcher did not require a catapult in order to take off from carriers. Its use of flaps and hydraulic wheel brakes also made it easy to land onboard the carrier.

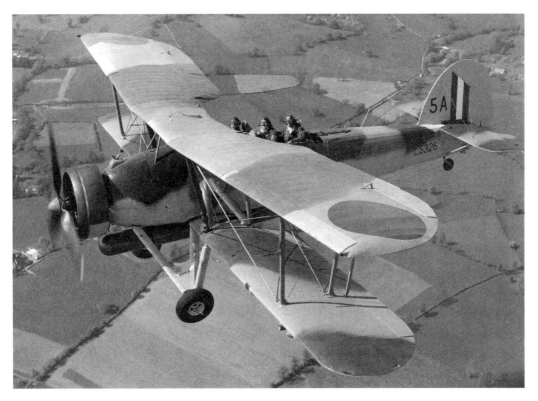

FAIREY SWORDFISH
(Courtesy Art-Tech)

COUNTRY OF ORIGIN: Great Britain

MANUFACTURER: The Fairey Aviation Co. Ltd.

TYPE: Torpedo-Bomber and Reconnaissance

CREW: 3

DIMENSIONS: Wingspan 45 ft 6 in; Length 35 ft 8 in; Height 12 ft 4 in

LOADED WEIGHT: 7,510 lbs

POWER PLANT: 1 x 750 hp Bristol Pegasus 30 radial engine

PERFORMANCE: 138 mph maximum speed; 10,700 ft (3,261 m) service ceiling; 1,030 mile range

ARMAMENT: 2 x .303 caliber machine guns; 1,680 lbs of bombs, torpedoes, rockets, or mines

TOTAL PRODUCTION: 2,391

SERVICE DATES: 1936–1945

SUMMARY: Although its appearance had more in common with aircraft of the First World War, the Fairey Swordfish accounted for more Axis tonnage than any other British aircraft of the Second World War. The Swordfish, introduced in 1936, featured an all-metal frame and fabric covered construction. Rugged and highly maneuverable, it excelled in taking off from aircraft carriers and accurately striking enemy ships with torpedoes. They remained in service throughout the war, operating in all naval theaters.

FIAT C.R.32 CHIRRI
(Courtesy Art-Tech)

COUNTRY OF ORIGIN: Italy

MANUFACTURER: Aeronautica d'Italia Fiat SA

TYPE: Fighter

CREW: 1

DIMENSIONS: Wingspan 31 ft 2 in; Length 24 ft 5.5 in; Height 8 ft 11 in

LOADED WEIGHT: 4,200 lbs

POWER PLANT: 1 x 600 hp Fiat A.30 RA V-12 engine

PERFORMANCE: 221 mph maximum speed; 25,755 ft (7,850 m) ceiling; 485 mile range

ARMAMENT: 2 x 12.7 mm machine guns; 2 x 7.7 mm machine guns; 220 lbs of bombs

TOTAL PRODUCTION: 1,272

SERVICE DATES: 1935–1941

SUMMARY: The Fiat C R.32 Chirri, designed by Celestino Rosatelli, combined metal framework and fabric covering to produce a rugged and highly acrobatic aircraft that quickly proved itself in the Spanish Civil War; unfortunately, the Italians would learn the wrong lesson from the conflict. Because the C R.32 outperformed the Soviet-built Polikarpov I-16 monoplane, the Italians continued production well into the Second World War. Indeed, Italy would introduce the C R.42 biplane in 1939, even as the other major air powers were turning to the low-wing cantilever monoplane.

FIAT G.50 FRECCIA
(Courtesy Art-Tech)

COUNTRY OF ORIGIN: Italy

MANUFACTURER: Aeronautica d'Italia Fiat SA

TYPE: Fighter

CREW: 1

DIMENSIONS: Wingspan 36 ft 1 in; Length 26 ft 4 in; Height 10 ft 9 in

LOADED WEIGHT: 5,290 lbs

POWER PLANT: 1 x 840 hp Fiat A.74 RC.38 radial engine

PERFORMANCE: 293 mph maximum speed; 32,480 ft (9,900 m) ceiling; 620 mile maximum range

ARMAMENT: 2 x 12.7 mm machine guns

TOTAL PRODUCTION: 777

SERVICE DATES: 1938–1943

SUMMARY: Designed by Giuseppe Gabrielli, the Fiat G.50 Freccia was introduced in 1938 as Italy's first all-metal monoplane fighter. It featured a cantilever low-wing design and closed canopy. Although it performed well in the closing stages of the Spanish Civil War, by 1940 it was too slow and underarmed compared with more contemporary monoplane fighters. Nevertheless, Italy would continue producing them even when the far superior Macchi M.C.200 Saetta and M.C.202 Folgore were available.

FIESELER Fi 156 STORCH
(Courtesy Art-Tech)

COUNTRY OF ORIGIN: Germany
MANUFACTURER: Fieseler Werke GmbH
TYPE: Transport and Reconnaissance
CREW: 1
DIMENSIONS: Wingspan 46 ft 9 in; Length 32 ft 5.75 in; Height 9 ft 10 in
LOADED WEIGHT: 2,910 lbs
POWER PLANT: 1 x 240 hp Argus vee-type
PERFORMANCE: 109 mph maximum speed; 17,060 ft (5,200 m) service ceiling; 236 mile range
ARMAMENT: 1 x 7.9 mm machine gun
TOTAL PRODUCTION: 2,834 of all types
SERVICE DATES: 1937–1945

SUMMARY: The Storch was a slow and ungainly aircraft, but it saw extensive use thanks to its remarkable short field take-off and landing capabilities. Used on every European, African, and Mediterranean battlefield, the Storch remained in service in many nations, even after the war. On its most famous mission, an Fi 156 flown by Walter Gerlach was the central component in Otto Skorzeny's daring rescue of Benito Mussolini from his Allied captivity.

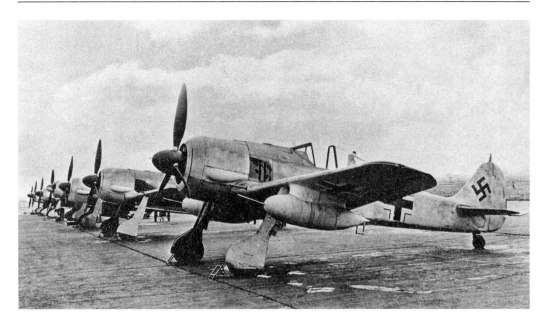

FOCKE-WULF Fw 190
(Courtesy Art-Tech)

COUNTRY OF ORIGIN: Germany
MANUFACTURER: Focke-Wulf Flugzeugbau AG
TYPE: Fighter-Bomber
CREW: 1
DIMENSIONS: Wingspan 34 ft 5.5 in; Length 29 ft; Height 13 ft
LOADED WEIGHT: 8,770 lbs
POWER PLANT: 1 x 1,700 hp BMW 801 D radial
PERFORMANCE: 382 mph maximum speed; 34,775 ft (10,600 m) service ceiling; 497 mile range
ARMAMENT: 2 x 7.9 mm machine guns; 4 x 20 mm cannon
TOTAL PRODUCTION: 20,051 of all types
SERVICE DATES: 1940–1945

SUMMARY: The Fw 190 was considered by many aviation historians as the best German fighter of the war. It shocked its Allied enemies over France in 1941; it was clearly superior to the performance of the Spitfire V, and its unexpected appearance helped the Luftwaffe establish air superiority. Nicknamed the "Butcher Bird," the Fw 190 served in various roles throughout the war, including night fighter, close air support, and long-range fighter/bomber. The –D version, the "Long-nose Dora," was delivered to combat units in August 1944, and was the finest fighter model in the Luftwaffe inventory.

FOCKE-WULF Fw 200 CONDOR
(Courtesy Art-Tech)

COUNTRY OF ORIGIN: Germany

MANUFACTURER: Focke-Wulf Flugzeugbau AG

TYPE: Reconnaissance Bomber and Transport

CREW: 6

DIMENSIONS: Wingspan 108 ft 3 in; Length 78 ft 3 in; Height 20 ft 8 in

LOADED WEIGHT: 50,045 lbs

POWER PLANT: 4 x 1,200 hp BMW Bramo-Fafnir 323R2 radials

PERFORMANCE: 240 mph maximum speed; 19,000 ft (5, 790 m) service ceiling; 2,759 mile range

ARMAMENT: 1 x 20 mm cannon; 4 x 12 mm machine guns; 1 x 7.9 mm machine gun; 3,307 lbs normal bomb load

TOTAL PRODUCTION: 276 of all types

SERVICE DATES: 1940–1945

SUMMARY: The Fw 200 Condor, described as the "scourge of the Atlantic" by Winston Churchill, was originally modified from a 26-passenger commercial airliner in January 1940. It entered combat service in July 1940, with production continuing through 1944. Assigned primarily to the North Atlantic, the Condor also served in Norway and during the ill-fated attempts to resupply the German Sixth Army at Stalingrad.

GRUMMAN F2F
(Courtesy Art-Tech)

COUNTRY OF ORIGIN: United States

MANUFACTURER: Grumman Aircraft Engineering Corporation

TYPE: Fighter

CREW: 1

DIMENSIONS: Wingspan 28 ft; Length 21 ft 5 in; Height 10 ft 6 in

LOADED WEIGHT: 3,539 lbs

POWER PLANT: 1 x 700 hp Pratt & Whitney R-1535 radial

PERFORMANCE: 231 mph maximum speed; 27,100 ft (8,260 m) service ceiling; 985 mile range

ARMAMENT: 2 x .30 caliber machine guns; 332 lb bomb load

TOTAL PRODUCTION: 55 of all types

SERVICE DATES: 1935–1940

SUMMARY: The F2F, designed as the replacement for the Grumman FF, had a metal fuselage with fabric-covered wings and retractable landing gear. The single-bay biplane had a very rotund silhouette, leading to its pilots dubbing it the "Flying Barrel." The F2F also incorporated a streamlined cowling and completely enclosed cockpit. It served on the USS *Lexington* and USS *Saratoga* prior to being withdrawn from front-line service in 1940.

GRUMMAN F6F HELLCAT
(Courtesy Art-Tech)

COUNTRY OF ORIGIN: United States

MANUFACTURER: Grumman Aircraft Engineering Corporation

TYPE: Fighter

CREW: 1

DIMENSIONS: Wingspan 42 ft 10 in; Length 33 ft 7 in; Height 13 ft 1 in

LOADED WEIGHT: 12,186 lbs

POWER PLANT: 1 x 2,000 hp Pratt & Whitney Double Wasp radial

PERFORMANCE: 380 mph maximum speed; 37,300 ft (11,370 m) service ceiling; 945 mile range

ARMAMENT: 6 x .50 caliber machine guns; 6 x 5 in. rockets or 2,000 lb bomb load

TOTAL PRODUCTION: 12,275 of all types

SERVICE DATES: 1943–1950

SUMMARY: From a rapid development phase (12 months) through an even more rapid deployment (i.e., more than 12,000 built in just 24 months), the F4F is considered one of the best, most rugged, and efficient naval fighters of the war. The Hellcat contributed greatly to the winning Allied effort in the Pacific; from its first appearance in the Theater in 1943 through the end of the war, Hellcat pilots claimed 5,156 enemy "kills." The model especially proved its worth during the "Marianas Turkey Shoot" portion of the Battle of the Philippine Sea in June 1944.

GRUMMAN TBF/TBM AVENGER
(Courtesy Art-Tech)

COUNTRY OF ORIGIN: United States

MANUFACTURER: Grumman Aircraft Engineering Corporation

TYPE: Torpedo Bomber

CREW: 3

DIMENSIONS: Wingspan 54 ft 2 in; Length 40 ft; Height 16 ft 5 in

LOADED WEIGHT: 15,905 lbs

POWER PLANT: 1 x 1,700 hp Wright R-2600 or 1,900 hp R-2600 Double Cyclone radial

PERFORMANCE: 271 mph maximum speed; 22,400 ft (6,825 m) service ceiling; 1,215 mile range

ARMAMENT: 2 x .30 caliber machine guns; 1–3 x .50 caliber machine gun; 8 x 60 lb rockets (late models); 1 x 22 in. torpedo or 1,600 lb bomb load internally; 2,000 total bomb load

TOTAL PRODUCTION: 9,836 of all types

SERVICE DATES: 1942–1954

SUMMARY: Grumman continued its production of superior naval aircraft with the introduction of the TBF/TBM Avenger in 1942. The model made its debut at Midway and participated in all major Pacific battles thereafter, in addition to seeing service in both the Mediterranean and Atlantic. Its versatility showed in its ability to adapt to ground-attack and antisubmarine roles.

HANDLEY-PAGE HALIFAX
(Courtesy Art-Tech)

COUNTRY OF ORIGIN: Great Britain

MANUFACTURER: Handley Page Ltd.

TYPE: Heavy Bomber, Reconnaissance, and Transport

CREW: 7

DIMENSIONS: Wingspan 104 ft 2 in; Length 71 ft 7 in; Height 20 ft 9 in

LOADED WEIGHT: 65,000 lbs

POWER PLANT: 4 x 1,800 hp Bristol Hercules 100 radial engines

PERFORMANCE: 309 mph maximum speed; 22,000 ft (6,706 m) ceiling; 1,260 mile range

ARMAMENT: 9 x .303 caliber machine guns in turret positions; 13,000 lb maximum bomb load

TOTAL PRODUCTION: 6,176 of all types

SERVICE DATES: 1941–1952

SUMMARY: The Handley Page Halifax, introduced in 1941, replaced the Short Stirling and provided Britain with its chief heavy bomber until the Avro Lancaster became available in 1942. As the Lancaster began to take on more of the load in the strategic bombing campaign against Germany, the Halifax was adapted for maritime patrol operations and transport duties. It also served as the primary tug for the General Aircraft Hamilcar and other Allied transport gliders.

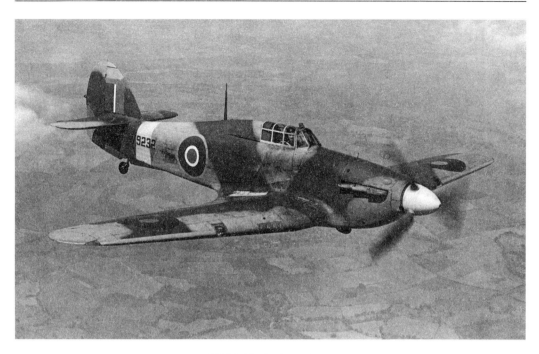

HAWKER HURRICANE
(Courtesy Art-Tech)

COUNTRY OF ORIGIN: Great Britain

MANUFACTURER: Hawker Aircraft Ltd.

TYPE: Fighter and Light Bomber

CREW: 1

DIMENSIONS: Wingspan 40 ft 0 in; Length 32 ft 3 in; Height 13 ft 3 in

LOADED WEIGHT: 8,100 lbs

POWER PLANT: 1 x 1,460 hp Rolls-Royce Merlin 20 V-12 engine

PERFORMANCE: 328 mph maximum speed; 36,000 ft (10,973 m) ceiling; 465 mile normal range, 935 mile range with drop tanks

ARMAMENT: 8–12 x .303 caliber machine guns or 4 x 20 mm cannon; 1,000 lb maximum bomb load

TOTAL PRODUCTION: 14,449 of all types

SERVICE DATES: 1938–1945

SUMMARY: The Hawker Huricane, designed by Sydney Camm, marked a tremendous technological leap forward by the British. Whereas the prototype had used metal tube framework and fabric covering, the production version was all-metal throughout. In addition, it featured a variable-pitch propeller, retractable landing gear, and eight wing-mounted machine guns. Subsequent variants would incorporate 20 mm cannons. Although the Messerschmitt BF-109 proved to be slightly superior during the Battle of France, the Hurricane was used highly effectively against German bombers during the ensuing Battle of Britain, accounting for more downed German aircraft than the more highly touted Supermarine Spitfire. Hurricanes would later be adapted for use as light bombers and ground attack aircraft.

HEINKEL HE 111

COUNTRY OF ORIGIN: Germany

MANUFACTURER: Heinkel Flugzeugwerke

TYPE: Medium Bomber

CREW: 4–6

DIMENSIONS: Wingspan 74 ft 1.75 in; Length 53 ft 9.5 in; Height 13 ft 1.5 in

LOADED WEIGHT: 30,865 lbs

POWER PLANT: 2 x 1,200 hp Junkers Jumo vee-types

PERFORMANCE: 252 mph maximum speed; 21,980 ft (6,700 m) service ceiling; 1,280 mile range

ARMAMENT: 1 x 20 mm cannon; up to 7 x 7.9 mm machine guns; 1 x 13 mm machine gun; 7,165 lb maximum bomb load

TOTAL PRODUCTION: Approximately 7,300 of all types

SERVICE DATES: 1936–1945

SUMMARY: The He 111, one of the earlier aircraft developed for the then-clandestine Luftwaffe, was originally a civilian model produced in 1935. The –B version entered Luftwaffe service in 1936. The He 111 saw extensive service in Spain during the Civil War, as well as over Poland, Scandinavia, the Low Countries, France, and the Battle of Britain. The most numerous model, the –H type, first flew in January 1938.

ILYUSHIN IL-2
(Courtesy Art-Tech)

COUNTRY OF ORIGIN: Soviet Union

MANUFACTURER: State Industries; Ilyushin, Central Design Bureau (TsKB)

TYPE: Anti-Tank, Light Bomber

CREW: 1–2

DIMENSIONS: Wingspan 47 ft 10.75 in; Length 38 ft 2.5 in; Height 13 ft. 8 in

LOADED WEIGHT: 14,021 lbs

POWER PLANT: 1 x 1,770 hp Mikulin AM-38F vee-type

PERFORMANCE: 255 mph maximum speed; 14,845 ft (4,525 m) service ceiling; 476 mile maximum range

ARMAMENT: 2 x 7.62 mm machine guns; 2 x 23 mm cannon; 8 x RS-82 rockets; 880 lb maximum bomb load

TOTAL PRODUCTION: 36,163 of all types

SERVICE DATES: 1941–1955

SUMMARY: The Il-2 "Shturmovik" was arguably the most famous, and important, Soviet aircraft of World War II, and it was certainly the most produced. It was the perfect aerial counter to the tank-led German offensive. Designed specifically as a tankbuster, the Il-2 featured thick armor plating around the crew quarters and was heavily armed. Despite its relatively pedestrian speed, it proved to be one of the safer aircraft in the war for its crew, and one of the most feared for its foes. The Soviet "Flying Tank" was, to those German tank crews, the "Black Death." The emergence of the Il-2 is widely credited for turning the tide of the battles of Stalingrad and Kursk on the Eastern Front, and in leading the Soviet counteroffensive. Derivative models (e.g., the Il-10) remained in service in Soviet Bloc countries into the 1950s.

JUNKERS JU 52/3M
(Courtesy Art-Tech)

COUNTRY OF ORIGIN: Germany

MANUFACTURER: Junkers Flugzeug- and Motorenwerke AG

TYPE: Transport and Bomber

CREW: 3–4

DIMENSIONS: Wingspan 95 ft 11.5 in; Length 62 ft; Height 18 ft 2 in

LOADED WEIGHT: 24,250 lbs

POWER PLANT: 3 x 830 hp BMW 123-A radials

PERFORMANCE: 171 mph maximum speed; 19,360 ft (5,900 m) service ceiling; 621 mile range

ARMAMENT: 2 x 7.9 mm machine guns; 1,102 lb bomb load

TOTAL PRODUCTION: Approximately 4,845 of all types

SERVICE DATES: 1935–1945

SUMMARY: The Ju52, known by her aircrews as "Auntie Junkers" or "Iron Annie," was the most significant German transports of the war. Serving on all fronts, the military version of what was initially a civilian airliner was a workhorse for the Luftwaffe, accommodating up to 18 troops. Although production officially ended in 1944, a Ju52 remained in service in Spain into the 1970s.

JUNKERS JU 87
(Courtesy Art-Tech)

COUNTRY OF ORIGIN: Germany

MANUFACTURER: Junkers Flugzeug- and Motorenwerke AG

TYPE: Dive-Bomber

CREW: 2

DIMENSIONS: Wingspan 45 ft 3.25 in; Length 36 ft 5 in; Height 13 ft 2 in

LOADED WEIGHT: 9,369 lbs

POWER PLANT: 1 x 1,100 hp Junkers Jumo 211 Da vee-type

PERFORMANCE: 238 mph maximum speed; 26,150 ft (7,970 m) service ceiling; 490 mile range

ARMAMENT: 3 x 7.9 mm machine guns; up to 1,542 lb bomb load

TOTAL PRODUCTION: 5,709 of all types

SERVICE DATES: 1936–1945

SUMMARY: Although technically applied to every German dive bomber, "Stuka" has been most commonly tied to the Junkers Ju 87. As a dive bomber, it was highly effective and extraordinarily accurate. It was proven to be susceptible to enemy fire by the time of the Battle of Britain; when assigned to regions where the Luftwaffe maintained a greater degree of air superiority, the Ju 87 continued to operate with great effectiveness. It is also notable for its role in the development of the aerial component of the Blitzkrieg tactic, cutting its combat teeth in Spain and Poland.

JUNKERS JU 88

(Courtesy Art-Tech)

COUNTRY OF ORIGIN: Germany

MANUFACTURER: Junkers Flugzeug- and Motorenwerke AG

TYPE: Medium and Dive-Bomber

CREW: 4

DIMENSIONS: Wingspan 59 ft 11 in; Length 47 ft 2 in; Height 15 ft 11 in

LOADED WEIGHT: 32,350 lbs (maximum takeoff)

POWER PLANT: 2 x 1,200 hp Junkers Jumo 211 B/G vee-types

PERFORMANCE: 292 mph maximum speed; 26,900 ft (8,200 m) service ceiling; 1,696 mile range

ARMAMENT: 3 x 7.9 mm machine guns; 2 x 13 mm machine guns or 4 x 7.92 mm machine guns; 4,409 lb maximum bomb load

TOTAL PRODUCTION: 14,980 of all types

SERVICE DATES: 1939–1945

SUMMARY: The most numerous and multi-faceted German bomber of the entire war, the Ju 88 offered the Luftwaffe reliable performance and great versatility. As a result, the aircraft served in several different modes: medium bomber, dive bomber, night fighter, intruder, long-range reconnaissance, antitank, and long-range heavy escort fighter. The venerable aircraft made its combat debut in late September 1939 against the British.

KAWANISHI N1K1
(Courtesy Art-Tech)

COUNTRY OF ORIGIN: Japan
MANUFACTURER: Kawanishi Kokuki K.K.
TYPE: Fighter
CREW: 1
DIMENSIONS: Wingspan 39 ft 4.44 in; Length 29 ft 1.78 in; Height 13 ft 3.84 in
LOADED WEIGHT: 8,598 lbs
POWER PLANT: 1 x 1,820 hp Nakajima KN9H Homare 23 radial
PERFORMANCE: 363 mph maximum speed; 41,010 ft (12,500 m) service ceiling; 1,581 mile maximum range
ARMAMENT: 2 x 7.7 mm machine guns; 2–4 x 20 mm cannon
TOTAL PRODUCTION: 1,435 of all types
SERVICE DATES: 1943–1945

SUMMARY: The N1K1 Kyofo ("Mighty Wind"), produced in both floatplane and ground-based fighter models, is generally regarded as the world's best seaplane fighter. The ground-based Shiden ("Violet Lightning") was the last major fighter type to enter the fray for the Japanese air forces. Although it was in some respects (i.e., maximum speed and maneuverability) a capable foe for the superior Allied fighters, it possessed the same weaknesses as virtually every other Japanese design (i.e., a lack of armor and armament, sacrificed for speed and agility). Perhaps more than any other issue, however, there were increasingly few pilots qualified and capable of flying the N1K1, severely limiting the impact of a promising fighter.

KAWASAKI KI-61
(Courtesy Art-Tech)

COUNTRY OF ORIGIN: Japan

MANUFACTURER: Kawasaki Kokuki Kogyo K.K.

TYPE: Fighter

CREW: 1

DIMENSIONS: Wingspan 39 ft 4.44 in; Length 28 ft 8.5 in; Height 12 ft 1.68 in

LOADED WEIGHT: 6,504 lbs

POWER PLANT: 1 x 1,100 hp Army Type 2 (Kawasaki Ha-40) vee-type

PERFORMANCE: 368 mph maximum speed; 37,730 ft (11,600 m) service ceiling; 684 mile maximum range

ARMAMENT: 4 x 12.7 mm machine guns

TOTAL PRODUCTION: 3,078 of all types

SERVICE DATES: 1943–1945

SUMMARY: The Ki-61, from a design partially adapted from the Messerschmitt BF-109, actually outperformed both the Messerschmitt and a Curtiss P-40E, as well as its Japanese competitors, in design trials. The Hien ("Swallow") proved similarly capable in the air, ably defending airspace against P-51 Mustangs thanks to a powerful engine that produced impressive speeds and maneuverability. The model proved one of the most difficult to maintain in the entire Japanese inventory, however, and never amassed the flying time totals envisioned for it. Its poor performance at higher altitudes was equally problematic; this would become a considerable drawback as the model became increasingly tasked to defend the Home Islands against high-flying B-29 raids.

KAWASAKI TYPE 88
(Courtesy Art-Tech)

COUNTRY OF ORIGIN: Japan
MANUFACTURER: Kawasaki
TYPE: Light Bomber
CREW: 2
DIMENSIONS: Wingspan 49 ft 2.75 in; Length 42 ft; Height 11 ft 2 in
LOADED WEIGHT: 6,834 lbs
POWER PLANT: 1 x 450–600 hp Kawasaki BMW VI vee-type
PERFORMANCE: 132 mph maximum speed; 18,044 ft (5,500 m) service ceiling; 6 hour endurance
ARMAMENT: 3 x 7.7 mm machine guns
TOTAL PRODUCTION: 407 of all types
SERVICE DATES: 1928

SUMMARY: The Type 88 was the principal reconnaissance and light-bomber aircraft in the Japanese inventory upon its introduction. It is also notable for being the first Japanese model to employ an entirely metal airframe. Kawasaki's success in this competitive trial established it as the Japanese Army Air Force's preferred supplier throughout World War II. The model itself was rather quickly outmoded, but it remained in service far beyond its technological age thanks to its reliability and ease-of-maintenance. It saw reconnaissance and light-bombing duties throughout the Sino-Japanese conflicts, and it served during World War II in various rear-echelon duties.

LAVOCHKIN LA-7
(Courtesy Art-Tech)

COUNTRY OF ORIGIN: Soviet Union

MANUFACTURER: State Industries; Lavochkin Design Bureau

TYPE: Fighter

CREW: 1

DIMENSIONS: Wingspan 31 ft 1.75 in; Length 28 ft 2.52 in; Height 8 ft 4 in

LOADED WEIGHT: 7,496 lbs

POWER PLANT: 1 x 1,850 hp Shvetsov M-82FN radial

PERFORMANCE: 423 mph maximum speed; 35,435 ft (10,800 m) service ceiling; 395 mile maximum range

ARMAMENT: 2–3 x 20 mm cannon; 440 lb maximum bomb load

TOTAL PRODUCTION: 5,753 of all types

SERVICE DATES: 1942–1945

SUMMARY: The La-7 was developed from the La-5 series as a dedicated high-altitude interceptor. Many of the Soviet Union's most famous aces of the war logged combat time in La-7s. Ivan Kozhedub, for instance, recorded approximately one third of his Soviet-record 62 kills, including one of a Messerschmitt Me-262 jet fighter, in an La-7. Highly maneuverable and with impressive top-end speed, the La-7 symbolized the apex of the prop-driven fighter age. It recorded perhaps as high as a 30:1 kill-to-loss ratio in World War II combat.

LAVOCHKIN LGG-3
(Courtesy Art-Tech)

COUNTRY OF ORIGIN: Soviet Union

MANUFACTURER: State Industries; Lavochkin-Gorbunov-Gudkov, Lavochkin Design Bureau

TYPE: Fighter

CREW: 1

DIMENSIONS: Wingspan 32 ft 2 in; Length 29 ft 1.75 in; Height 8 ft 10 in

LOADED WEIGHT: 7,275 lbs (maximum take-off)

POWER PLANT: 1 x 1,240 hp Klimov M-105PF vee-type

PERFORMANCE: 348 maximum speed; 29,527 ft (9,000 m) service ceiling; 404 mile maximum range

ARMAMENT: 1 x 20 mm cannon; 2 x 7.62 mm machine guns; 8 x RS-82 rockets or 440 lb maximum bomb load

TOTAL PRODUCTION: 6,258 of all types

SERVICE DATES: 1940–1945

SUMMARY: The LaGG-3, at more than 600 lbs lighter, with greater speed, agility, and armament than the LaGG-1 (which inspired the gallows-humor nickname: *Lakirovannii Garantirovannii Grob*, or, Varnished Guaranteed Coffin), was a dramatic step forward from its predecessor. It was slightly more reliable, and it performed better than the LaGG-1. Due to a mix of poor construction standards and inadequate pilot training, however, it proved equally as dangerous. Thus, it earned the dubious nickname of "mortician's mate" in some quarters. It is most notable for its technological advancements, including the use of the new Klimov M-105 engine; this engine served as the power plant for a trio of new fighters (i.e., the LaGG-3, Yak-1, and Yak-3), which, along with the MiG-1, collectively signaled Soviet parity with the fighter forces of the Western powers.

LOCKHEED P-38 LIGHTNING

(U.S. Air Force photo)

COUNTRY OF ORIGIN: United States

MANUFACTURER: Lockheed Aircraft Corporation

TYPE: Fighter-Bomber

CREW: 1

DIMENSIONS: Wingspan 52 ft; Length 37 ft 10 in; Height 9 ft 10 in

LOADED WEIGHT: 15,500 lbs

POWER PLANT: 2 x 1,425 hp Allison V-1710 vee-types

PERFORMANCE: 414 mph maximum speed; 43,800 ft (13,350 m) service ceiling; 1,950 mile maximum range

ARMAMENT: 1 x 20 mm cannon; 4 x 0.50 caliber machine guns; 4,000 lb maximum bomb load

TOTAL PRODUCTION: 10,036 of all types

SERVICE DATES: 1940–1949

SUMMARY: The P-38 was a radical design and a dramatic departure from the standard USAAF designs. It featured a unique twin-boom, twin-engine configuration, with a single pilot in a central pod, tricycle undercarriage, counterrotating props, and turbocharged engines. Its performance and its appearance led German crews to dub it the "Fork-Tailed Devil." After production models reached British hands, the American crews adopted the British moniker of "Lightning" to describe the aircraft. After undergoing several revisions, the –E version was considered the first truly combat-capable model, with the –F model claiming the first American "kill" of a German aircraft in combat in August 1942. The most numerous, and most capable, was the –J model, of which 2,970 were produced. An additional 1,400 were reconfigured after the war as the F-4 and F-5, and tasked to photo reconnaissance.

MACCHI MC 202 FOLGORE
(Courtesy Art-Tech)

COUNTRY OF ORIGIN: Italy
MANUFACTURER: Aeronautica Macchi S.p.A.
TYPE: Fighter
CREW: 1
DIMENSIONS: Wingspan 34 ft 8.5 in; Length 29 ft 0.5 in; Height 9 ft 11.5 in
LOADED WEIGHT: 6,766 lbs
POWER PLANT: 1 x 1175 hp Daimler-Benz DB 601A V-12 engine
PERFORMANCE: 372 mph maximum speed; 11,500 m (37,730 ft) ceiling; 475 mile range
ARMAMENT: 2 x 7.7 mm machine guns; 2 x 12.7 mm machine guns (some with 20 mm cannon)
TOTAL PRODUCTION: Approximately 1,200
SERVICE DATES: 1941–1945

SUMMARY: The Macchi MC 202 Folgore was generally considered to be the best overall Italian fighter of the Second World War. It was designed by Dr. Mario Castoldi as an improvement to the MC 202 Saetta. Improved streamlining, particularly with its enclosed engine cowling and propeller design, along with a higher-performing engine imported from Germany, increased performance from the Saetta by approximately 20 percent. The MC 202 outperformed the Hawker Hurricane and Curtiss P-40 Tomahawk in the Mediterranean Theater and Russian fighters on the Eastern Front. It came too late, however, to make a significant difference, in part because Italy foolishly continued production of the poorer performing Fiat G.50.

MARTIN B-10
(Courtesy Art-Tech)

COUNTRY OF ORIGIN: United States

MANUFACTURER: Glenn L. Martin Company

TYPE: Bomber

CREW: 4

DIMENSIONS: 70 ft 6 in; Length 44 ft 9 in; Height 15 ft 5 in

LOADED WEIGHT: 16,400 lbs

POWER PLANT: 2 x 775 hp Wright R-1820 Cyclone radials

PERFORMANCE: 213 mph maximum speed; 24,400 ft (7,435 m) service ceiling; 1,240 mile range

ARMAMENT: 3 x .30 caliber machine guns; 2,260 lb bomb load

TOTAL PRODUCTION: 152 of all types

SERVICE DATES: 1933–1940

SUMMARY: The first modern bomber in the American air force, the B-10 first flew in 1932 and proved faster than the American fighters currently in the inventory. The all-metal, midwing monoplane also featured retractable landing gear, an enclosed cockpit, variable pitch propellers, an internal bomb bay, and even a powered nose turret. The model was in great demand overseas, and eventually more than 190 copies were exported to Argentina, China, Siam, and the Dutch East Indies. The Dutch B-10s were still in service when World War II began.

MESSERSCHMITT ME BF-109
(Courtesy Art-Tech)

COUNTRY OF ORIGIN: Germany

MANUFACTURER: Messerschmitt AG

TYPE: Fighter

CREW: 1

DIMENSIONS: Wingspan 32 ft 6.5 in; Length 29 ft 7.5 in; Height 8 ft 2.5 in

LOADED WEIGHT: 6,834 lbs

POWER PLANT: 1 x 1,475 hp Daimler-Benz DB 605A vee-type

PERFORMANCE: 386 mph maximum speed; 37,890 ft (11,550 m) service ceiling; 350 mile normal range

ARMAMENT: 1 x 20 mm cannon; 2 x 7.9 mm machine guns

TOTAL PRODUCTION: Approximately 35,000 of all types

SERVICE DATES: 1937–1945

SUMMARY: The most important German fighter of the war, the Messerschmitt BF-109, served on all fronts. With the exception of the British Spitfire, the BF-109 was the superior fighter in Europe between 1938 and 1940. Although the –F version, comprising perhaps two thirds of the Luftwaffe's entire fighter contingent in 1941, was considered the pinnacle of the aircraft's development (2,200 produced), the –G version was the most numerous. The –G model made its debut in 1942 and an estimated 23,500 were produced. The failure to develop replacement fighters led to the continued production of the BF-109 long after it was outclassed by new Allied fighters. Despite this, the Luftwaffe's leading ace, Eric Hartmann, scored all of his 451 victories in a BF-109. The Spanish continued production until 1956; similarly, the model served in both Czech and Israeli air forces following the war.

MESSERSCHMITT ME BF-110
(Courtesy Art-Tech)

COUNTRY OF ORIGIN: Germany

MANUFACTURER: Messerschmitt AG

TYPE: Fighter-Bomber, Night Fighter

CREW: 2–3

DIMENSIONS: Wingspan 53 ft 4.75 in; Length 39 ft 8.5 in; Height 11 ft 6 in

LOADED WEIGHT: 15,300 lbs

POWER PLANT: 2 x 1,100 hp Daimler-Benz DB 601 A vee-type

PERFORMANCE: 349 mph maximum speed; 32,000 ft (9,750 m) service ceiling; 565 mile range

ARMAMENT: 4–5 x 7.9 mm machine gun; 2 x 20 mm cannon; 1,102 lb maximum bomb load

TOTAL PRODUCTION: 6,050 of all types

SERVICE DATES: 1939–1945

SUMMARY: Although first solicited in 1935, the BF-110 did not enter combat service until 1939, first over Poland, then later over Norway, the Low Countries, and France. Its performance against British fighters during the Battle of Britain showed that despite its promise, the fighter was not comparable to the more modern, single-engine fighters. Because it was a fast and relatively stable and reliable aircraft, however, the BF-110 continued to serve in a variety of roles for the Luftwaffe. It seemed to find a niche as a night fighter beginning in 1942, accounting for up to 60 percent of all of Germany's night air defenses.

MESSERSCHMITT ME 262
(Courtesy Art-Tech)

COUNTRY OF ORIGIN: Germany
MANUFACTURER: Messerschmitt AG
TYPE: Fighter-Bomber, Night Fighter
CREW: 1–2
DIMENSIONS: Wingspan 40 ft 11.5 in; Length 34 ft 9.5 in; Height 12 ft 7 in
LOADED WEIGHT: 14,101 lbs
POWER PLANT: 2 x 1,980 lbs thrust Junkers Jumo 004B turbojets
PERFORMANCE: 540 mph maximum speed; 37,565 ft (1,450 m) service ceiling; 652 mile maximum range
ARMAMENT: 4 x 30 mm cannon; 1,102 lb maximum bomb load
TOTAL PRODUCTION: 1,433 of all types
SERVICE DATES: 1944–1945

SUMMARY: With the introduction of the Me 262 into combat, Germany became the first power to field an operational jet-powered fighter/bomber. Although the first test flights had been taken in 1941, full production of the model did not begin until 1944; Hitler's insistence on adapting the Me 262 to a bomber delayed the aircraft's deployment to the detriment of the Luftwaffe. Of the roughly 1,400 built, only 200 reached combat squadrons. Nevertheless, the Me 262 inflicted a great deal of damage in a short period of time, downing more than 100 Allied aircraft before the end of the war. Nicknamed the "Swallow," the Me 262 might well have reestablished German air superiority over Europe if sufficient numbers, pilots, and fuel had been available.

MITSUBISHI A6M
(Courtesy Art-Tech)

COUNTRY OF ORIGIN: Japan

MANUFACTURER: Mitsubishi Jukogyo K.K., Nakajima Hikoki K.K.

TYPE: Fighter

CREW: 1

DIMENSIONS: Wingspan 39 ft 4.44 in; Length 29 ft 8.68 in; Height 10 ft

LOADED WEIGHT: 5,313 lbs

POWER PLANT: 1 x 940 hp Nakajima NK1C Sakae 12 radial

PERFORMANCE: 331 mph maximum speed; 32,810 ft (10,000 m) service ceiling; 1,930 mile maximum range

ARMAMENT: 2 x 7.7 mm machine guns; 2 x 20 mm cannon

TOTAL PRODUCTION: 10,449 of all types

SERVICE DATES: 1940–1945

SUMMARY: The "Zero" fighter was Japan's most successful, and most recognizable, fighter of the World War II era. It made use of relatively new design elements (e.g., canopied cockpit and retractable landing gear). The A6M provided for Japanese air superiority across the Pacific in the early stages of the war. It only became obsolete when Allied designs (e.g., the Grumman F4F) were finally able to marry improved performance with heavier armor and armament, thus negating the Japanese doctrine of sacrificing such elements for speed and maneuverability. In combat against these technologically superior foes at Midway, the Coral Sea, and the Philippine Sea, Zeros sustained heavy losses.

MITSUBISHI G4M
(Courtesy Art-Tech)

COUNTRY OF ORIGIN: Japan
MANUFACTURER: Mitsubishi Jukogyo K.K.
TYPE: Medium Bomber, Torpedo Bomber
CREW: 7
DIMENSIONS: Wingspan 82 ft; Length 65 ft 7.40 in; Height 19 ft 8.21 in
LOADED WEIGHT: 20,944 lbs
POWER PLANT: 2 x 1,530 hp Mitsubishi MK4A Kasei 11 radials
PERFORMANCE: 266 mph maximum speed; 29,365 ft (8,950 m) service ceiling (G4M2); 3,749 mile maximum range
ARMAMENT: 4 x 7.7 mm machine guns; 2 x 20 mm machine gun; 2,205 lb bomb load
TOTAL PRODUCTION: 2,446 of all types
SERVICE DATES: 1940–1945

SUMMARY: The G4M "Betty," as it was known to Allies, was arguably the most important bomber in the Japanese inventory, numerically and strategically. As with many other designs, the G4M lacked heavy armor plating, which when combined with its range meant the "Betty" had to rely on its speed and rather substantial defensive armament. Among its many successes, G4Ms participated in the sinking of the HMS *Repulse* and HMS *Prince of Wales*. It was also notable for a more derisive reason (i.e., its propensity for aerial explosion when hit by enemy fire, due to a lack of self-sealing fuel tanks). In a sense, G4Ms began and ended the Pacific War, participating in the opening combat actions and later carrying the Japanese delegation to the peace talks.

MITSUBISHI KI-21
(Courtesy Art-Tech)

COUNTRY OF ORIGIN: Japan
MANUFACTURER: Mitsubishi Jukogyu K.K.
TYPE: Medium Bomber
CREW: 5–7
DIMENSIONS: Wingspan 73 ft 9.81 in; Length 52 ft 5.90 in; Height 13 ft 3.40 in
LOADED WEIGHT: 16,517 lbs
POWER PLANT: 2 x 850 hp Army Type 97 (Nakajima Ha-5 KAI) radials
PERFORMANCE: 268 mph maximum speed; 28,215 ft (8,600 m) service ceiling; 1,680 mile maximum range
ARMAMENT: 3 x 7.7 mm machine guns; 2,205 lb maximum bomb load
TOTAL PRODUCTION: 2,064 of all types
SERVICE DATES: 1938–1945

SUMMARY: The Ki-21 is most notable for signaling Japanese parity with Western nations in terms of aviation technology. It was the class of the Japanese offensive air forces in the late 1930s, but it was soon obsolescent; this is more a matter of timing than performance measures because the model arrived during the era of the most rapid technological advancement in the Japanese aviation industry. The Ki-21 "Sally" was a reliable aircraft, and it saw extensive use throughout the war as a transport/liaison and second-line ground-support aircraft.

NAKAJIMA B5N
(Courtesy Art-Tech)

COUNTRY OF ORIGIN: Japan
MANUFACTURER: Nakajima Hikoki K.K.
TYPE: Torpedo Bomber, Light Bomber
CREW: 3
DIMENSIONS: Wingspan 50 ft 10.46 in; Length 33 ft 9.5 in; Height 12 ft 1.65 in
LOADED WEIGHT: 8,157 lbs
POWER PLANT: 1 x 770 hp Nakajima Hikari 3 radial
PERFORMANCE: 229 maximum speed; 24,280 ft (7,400 m) service ceiling; 1,404 mile maximum range
ARMAMENT: 1 x 7.7 mm machine gun; 1,764 lb maximum bomb load
TOTAL PRODUCTION: 1,149 of all types
SERVICE DATES: 1938–1945

SUMMARY: The B5N was arguably the world's most effective and modern carrier-borne bomber upon its introduction. It immediately became the front-line torpedo-bomber in the Japanese inventory. In addition to vast participation in the Pearl Harbor strikes, B5Ns are credited with the sinking of no fewer than four American aircraft carriers throughout the war. A recurring theme for Japanese aircraft, however, was their obsolescence because Allied fighters featured superior performance, armor, and armament; for the B5N this meant substantially reduced effectiveness against American naval vessels, and increasingly heavier losses in combat as the war progressed.

NAKAJIMA KI-43
(Courtesy Art-Tech)

COUNTRY OF ORIGIN: Japan
MANUFACTURER: Nakajima Hikoki K.K.
TYPE: Fighter
CREW: 1
DIMENSIONS: Wingspan 35 ft 6.75 in; Length 29 ft 3.31 in; Height 10 ft 8.75 in
LOADED WEIGHT: 5,710 lbs
POWER PLANT: 1 x 1,150 hp Army Type 1 (Nakajima Ha-115) radial
PERFORMANCE: 329 mph maximum speed; 36,750 ft (11,200 m) service ceiling; 1,990 mile maximum range
ARMAMENT: 2 x 12.7 mm machine guns
TOTAL PRODUCTION: 5,919 of all types
SERVICE DATES: 1941–1945

SUMMARY: The Ki-43 Hayabusa ("Peregrine Falcon") was quite similar in appearance to the A6M Zero; in fact, Allied servicemen often misidentified Ki-43s as Zeros. This proved to be advantageous for pilots of later Ki-43 models (–II and –IIIs) because their aircraft featured improved performance—especially a tighter turning radius—than their more famous cousin A6Ms. After a frustratingly long development period (initial designs were solicited in 1937), the Ki-43 became one of the most-produced models in the Japanese inventory. By the time it was mass-produced, however, it was already outperformed by many Allied fighters, making its lack of armor and scant firepower a glaring weakness.

NAKAJIMA KI-84
(Courtesy Art-Tech)

Country of Origin: Japan
Manufacturer: Nakajima Hikoki K.K.
Type: Fighter
Crew: 1
Dimensions: Wingspan 36 ft 10.43 in; Length 32 ft 6.56 in; Height 11 ft 1.25 in
Loaded Weight: 7,955 lbs
Power Plant: 1 x 1,900 hp Army Type 4 (Nakajima Ha-45) radial
Performance: 392 mph maximum speed; 34,450 ft (10,500 m) service ceiling; 1,347 mile maximum range
Armament: 2 x 12.7 mm machine guns; 2 x 20 mm cannon
Total Production: 3,514 of all types
Service Dates: 1944–1945

Summary: The Ki-84 Hayate ("Gale") was the JAAF's most technologically advanced aircraft upon its introduction. Unlike most other Japanese aircraft, the Ki-84 embraced the most modern safety technologies available, including relatively thick armor plating and self-sealing fuel tanks. It was thus arguably the safest aircraft in the Japanese inventory, in addition to being one of the best-performing. Several major problems, however, prevented the Ki-84 from ranking as one of the world's most important aircraft. First, the model arrived too late in the war, with too few capable pilots available, to stem the tide of the Allied counterattack in the Pacific. Second, and equally important, the Ki-84 faced the same frustrating maintenance problems as the Ki-61, severely impacting its usefulness as a front-line fighter.

NIEUPORT-DELAGE NID.29

(Courtesy Art-Tech)

COUNTRY OF ORIGIN: France

MANUFACTURER: Société Anonyme des Établissements Nieuport

TYPE: Fighter

CREW: 1

DIMENSIONS: Wingspan 31 ft 10 in; Length 21 ft 3.5 in; Height 8 ft 4.5 in

LOADED WEIGHT: 2,535 lbs

POWER PLANT: 1 x 300 hp Hispano-Suiza 8Fb V-8

PERFORMANCE: 146 mph maximum speed; 27,887 ft (8,500 m); 360 mile range

ARMAMENT: 2 x 7.7 mm synchronized Vickers machine guns

TOTAL PRODUCTION: 2,048 (including 175 produced by Macchi Nieuport and 608 by Nakajima)

SERVICE DATES: 1922–1933

SUMMARY: Although the prototype of the Nieuport-Delage NiD.29 had been demonstrated in June 1918 and received rave reviews, the end of the First World War on November 11, 1918, resulted in production being delayed until 1921. Unlike previous Nieuports, which had used a sesquiplane layout and rotary motors, Gustave Delage had designed the NiD.29 with a standard biplane configuration and the Hispano-Suiza V-8 inline engine. In addition to serving as France's main fighter until 1928, it was also licensed-produced in Italy and Japan for their air forces. The NiD.29 was also one of the few interwar aircraft to see combat. Whereas the French used it primarily to suppress rebellions in North Africa, it played a key role in Japan's takeover of Manchuria in 1931.

NORTH AMERICAN AT-6 TEXAN/HARVARD
(Courtesy Art-Tech)

COUNTRY OF ORIGIN: United States

MANUFACTURER: North American Aviation, Inc.

TYPE: Trainer

CREW: 2

DIMENSIONS: Wingspan 42 ft 0.25 in.; Length 29 ft 6 in.; Height 11 ft 8.5 in.

LOADED WEIGHT: 5,300 lbs

POWER PLANT: 1 x 600 hp Pratt & Whitney R-1340 radial

PERFORMANCE: 208 mph maximum speed; 21,500 ft (6,550 m) service ceiling; 750 mile range

ARMAMENT: Up to 3 x 0.30 caliber machine guns; optional underwing light bomb rack

TOTAL PRODUCTION: 15,109 of all types

SERVICE DATES: 1936–1958

SUMMARY: By consensus, aviation historians label the Texan as the one most important Allied training aircraft of the war. Production began in April 1935 and ceased in 1945. No fewer than 40 countries operated the AT-6 either during or after the war, even into the 1990s; an additional 2,600 copies of the trainer were produced by Noorduyn in Canada.

NORTH AMERICAN B-25 MITCHELL
(Courtesy Art-Tech)

COUNTRY OF ORIGIN: United States

MANUFACTURER: North American Aviation, Inc.

TYPE: Medium Bomber

CREW: 5–6

DIMENSIONS: Wingspan 67 ft 7 in; Length 52 ft 11 in; Height 15 ft 10 in

LOADED WEIGHT: 36,047 lbs

POWER PLANT: 2 x 1,700 hp Wright R-2600 radials

PERFORMANCE: 272 mph maximum speed; 24,200 ft (7,375 m) service ceiling; 1,275 mile range

ARMAMENT: Up to 10 x .50 caliber machine guns; 8 x 5 in. rockets; 4,000 lb maximum bomb load

TOTAL PRODUCTION: 9,816 of all types

SERVICE DATES: 1940–1959

SUMMARY: The B-25, named for influential Army Air Corps Colonel Billy Mitchell, was developed as a private venture by the North American Aviation company. After a series of impressive flight tests, beginning in January 1939, the USAAC ordered quantity production beginning in September 1939. The –J model was the definitive version of the line, delivered beginning in 1944 yet accounting for more than one half of all B-25 production.

NORTH AMERICAN P-51 MUSTANG

(Courtesy Art-Tech)

COUNTRY OF ORIGIN: United States

MANUFACTURER: North American Aviation, Inc.

TYPE: Fighter-bomber

CREW: 1

DIMENSIONS: Wingspan 37 ft; Length 33 ft 4 in; Height 13 ft 8 in

LOADED WEIGHT: 11,500 lbs

POWER PLANT: 1 x 2,218 hp Packard Merlin vee-type

PERFORMANCE: 487 mph maximum speed; 41,600 ft (12,680 m) service ceiling; 1,160 mile maximum range

ARMAMENT: 6 x .50 caliber machine guns; 10 x 5 in. rockets or 2,000 lb maximum bomb load

TOTAL PRODUCTION: 15,576 of all types

SERVICE DATES: 1941–1953

SUMMARY: The P-51 was truly an incredible air-superiority fighter; indeed, the Truman Committee called it "perfect." The plane was initially designed to meet British specifications, and a preproduction period of just 122 days yielded this remarkable model. Although American interest was slower in coming, production dramatically increased after Pearl Harbor and the Japanese attacks throughout the Pacific; the A6M "Zero" was found to be vastly superior to anything currently in the American inventory, but the Mustang would turn the tide. Approximately 7,956 –D models, considered the quintessential Mustangs, were produced with a more powerful Rolls Royce Merlin engine.

PETLYAKOV PE.2
(Courtesy Art-Tech)

COUNTRY OF ORIGIN: Soviet Union

MANUFACTURER: State Industries; Petlyakov, Tupolev Design Bureau

TYPE: Medium Bomber, Torpedo Bomber

CREW: 3

DIMENSIONS: Wingspan 56 ft 3.5 in; Length 41 ft 6.5 in; Height 11 ft 6 in

LOADED WEIGHT: 18,728 lbs (maximum take off)

POWER PLANT: 2 x 1,300 hp Klimov M-105 vee-type

PERFORMANCE: 360 mph maximum speed; 28,870 ft (8,800 m) service ceiling; 932 mile maximum range

ARMAMENT: 4 x 7.62 mm machine guns; 1 x AG-2 aerial grenade rear-firing launcher; 2,205 (later 6,614) lb maximum bomb load

TOTAL PRODUCTION: Approximately 11,400 of all types

SERVICE DATES: 1940–1945

SUMMARY: The Pe.2's prototype was designed and produced from the gulag; indeed, Petlyakov owed his freedom to his aircraft's impressive top-end performance capabilities. Envisioned as a high-speed escort for the ANT-42 heavy bomber, the Soviet adoption of new air war doctrines led to its deployment instead as a high-speed dive bomber. Twin Klimov M-105 engines, the same power plant as employed in a series of successful Soviet fighters from the era, powered this highly accurate bomber. Due to its reliability in service and in delivering its payload, the Pe.2 became a central part of the Soviet resistance and counterattack along the Eastern Front.

POLIKARPOV I-15
(Courtesy Art-Tech)

COUNTRY OF ORIGIN: Soviet Union

MANUFACTURER: State Industries; Polikarpov, Central Design Bureau (TsKB)

TYPE: Fighter

CREW: 1

DIMENSIONS: Wingspan 31 ft 11.9 in; Length 20 ft; Height 7 ft 7.25 in

LOADED WEIGHT: 3,119 lbs (maximum take-off)

POWER PLANT: 1 x 480 hp M-22 radial

PERFORMANCE: 199 mph maximum speed; 24,670 ft (7,500 m) service ceiling; 297 mile range

ARMAMENT: 2 x 7.62 machine guns; 88 lb maximum bomb load

TOTAL PRODUCTION: Approximately 7,100 of all types (including I-15*bis*, and I-15*ter*)

SERVICE DATES: 1934–1943

SUMMARY: Polikarpov was a pioneer of Soviet-led designs, and produced the greatest fighter of the Soviet biplane era in the I-15. A second-generation of the fighter, the I-15*bis*, could achieve a top speed in excess of 230 mph, maintaining the maneuverability characteristic of biplanes. At the hands of a highly trained pilot, the I-15 proved to be a capable foe for the early monoplane fighters. I-15s served with high distinction on the Republican side of the Spanish Civil War, as well as over China in the Sino-Japanese conflicts, and even into the Winter War phase of World War II. Many were later used as close air support aircraft until the arrival of the Il-2.

POLIKARPOV I-16
(Courtesy Art-Tech)

COUNTRY OF ORIGIN: Soviet Union

MANUFACTURER: State Industries; Polikarpov Design Bureau

TYPE: Fighter

CREW: 1

DIMENSIONS: Wingspan 29 ft 1.25 in; Length 19 ft 9.75 in; Height 7 ft 10.75 in

LOADED WEIGHT: 4,215 lbs

POWER PLANT: 1 x 1,000 hp Shvetsov M-62 radial

PERFORMANCE: 326 mph maximum speed; 31,070 ft (9,470 m) service ceiling; 435 mile maximum range

ARMAMENT: 4 x 7.62 mm machine guns; 6 x RS-82 rockets or 441 maximum bomb load

TOTAL PRODUCTION: Approximately 7,000 of all types

SERVICE DATES: 1935–1943

SUMMARY: The first major Soviet entry into the monoplane era was the I-16. Along with his wildly successful I-15 design, the I-16 helped secure Polikarpov a place of lasting fame in the annals of Soviet aviation history. Thanks to impressive combat performances in the interwar years, perhaps 60 percent of the Soviet fighter inventory of 1941 consisted of I-16s of various types. After the German invasion, the I-16 was reintroduced into production as a stop-gap fighter. It was relatively easy to produce, and could be constructed largely of nonstrategic materials. The model has added symbolic value as one of the types used by Soviet fighter ace A. I. Pokryshkin.

POLIKARPOV U-2
(Courtesy Art-Tech)

COUNTRY OF ORIGIN: Soviet Union

MANUFACTURER: State Industries; Polikarpov Design Bureau

TYPE: Multipurpose

CREW: 2

DIMENSIONS: Wingspan 37 ft 4.75 in; Length 26 ft 9.75 in; Height 10 ft 2 in

LOADED WEIGHT: 1,962 lbs (maximum take-off)

POWER PLANT: 1 x 100 hp Shvetsov M-11 radial

PERFORMANCE: 97 mph maximum speed; 13,125 ft (4,000 m) service ceiling; 3 hours 30 minutes endurance

ARMAMENT: 1 x 7.62 mm machine gun

TOTAL PRODUCTION: Approximately 33,000 of all types

SERVICE DATES: 1928–1952

SUMMARY: The Polikarpov U-2 was a rather simple biplane, most notable for its use as a trainer. It proved to be a sturdy, reliable, and easy-to-fly aircraft. Redesignated the Po.2 after designer N. N. Polikarpov's death in 1944, the U-2 was the perfect trainer for Soviet pilots learning dogfighting tactics. It was quite agile and maneuverable, but well-balanced, thus providing a great deal of in-flight stability for the pilot and instructor. As with most models in the Soviet inventory, many U-2s were retasked as combat aircraft upon the German invasion. In this role, its lack of speed greatly limited its usefulness; nevertheless, U-2s were used for artillery-spotting, close air support, and nighttime bombing runs. Some were also used for psychological warfare, fitted with loudspeakers from which propaganda was broadcast.

POTEZ 63 SERIES
(Courtesy Art-Tech)

COUNTRY OF ORIGIN: France

MANUFACTURER: Etablissements Henry Potez

TYPE: Fighter-Bomber-Reconnaissance

CREW: 2–3

DIMENSIONS: Wingspan 52 ft 6 in; Length 35 ft 10.5 in; Height 10 ft 1.25 in

LOADED WEIGHT: 9,987 lbs

POWER PLANT: 2 x 700 hp Gnome-Rhône 14M radial engines

PERFORMANCE: 264 mph maximum speed; 27,887 ft (8,500 m) ceiling; 932 mile range

ARMAMENT: 5 x 7.5 mm machine guns; 1,323 lb maximum bomb load

TOTAL PRODUCTION: 1,360 of all models, approximately 900 of which were the 63.11 reconnaissance type

SERVICE DATES: 1938–1942

SUMMARY: The Potez 63, designed by Louis Coroller, was similar in design to the Messerschmitt BF-110. It featured an all-metal, cantilever low-wing monoplane, and twin-engine layout. The Potez 63, unfortunately for France, proved to be underpowered and lacked maneuverability. Despite these problems, the French continued to produce them in such numbers that they ultimately became the most numerous French aircraft to serve in the Second World War. This was in part because the French were attempting to use one basic design for multiple purposes. The 630 and 631 were used for fighters, the 633 for ground-attack, the 637 for light bombing, and the 63.11 for reconnaissance. The end result was an aircraft that performed none of these roles very well and that proved extremely vulnerable to German fighters.

PZL P.11 JEDENASTKA
(Courtesy Art-Tech)

COUNTRY OF ORIGIN: Poland

MANUFACTURER: Panstwowe Zaklady Lotnicze

TYPE: Fighter

CREW: 1

DIMENSIONS: Wingspan 35 ft 2 in; Length 24 ft 9.25 in; Height 9 ft 4.25 in

LOADED WEIGHT: 3,968 lbs

POWER PLANT: 1 x 645 hp Bristol Mercury VIS radial engine

PERFORMANCE: 242 mph maximum speed; 26,247 ft (8,000 m) ceiling; 435 mile range

ARMAMENT: 2 x 7.92 mm machine guns; 110 lb maximum bomb load

TOTAL PRODUCTION: 338 (including 80 licensed built by Industria Aeronautica Romana)

SERVICE DATES: 1935–1939

SUMMARY: Based on the earlier PZL P.7 that had been designed by Zygmunt Pulawski, the PZL P.11 Jedenastka was an all-metal, gull-winged parasol monoplane that was one of the fastest and most maneuverable fighters in the world upon its introduction in 1935; however, unfortunately for Poland, its meager resources had been invested in an aircraft design soon to be surpassed by the low-wing cantilever monoplanes that arose in the late 1930s, particularly the Messerschmitt BF-109 they would face with the outbreak of the war in September 1939. Although many PZL P.11s were destroyed on the ground in the initial German Blitzkrieg, outnumbered Polish pilots managed to shoot down 124 German aircraft before Poland collapsed, losing just 114 P.11s in the process.

REPUBLIC P-47 THUNDERBOLT
(Courtesy Art-Tech)

COUNTRY OF ORIGIN: United States

MANUFACTURER: Republic Aviation Corporation

TYPE: Fighter-bomber

CREW: 1

DIMENSIONS: Wingspan 42 ft 7 in; Length 36 ft 1 in; Height 14 ft 8 in

LOADED WEIGHT: 20,700 lbs

POWER PLANT: 1 x 2,300 hp Pratt & Whitney Double Wasp radial

PERFORMANCE: 397 mph maximum speed; 43,000 ft (13,100 m) service ceiling; 800 mile standard range

ARMAMENT: 8 x .50 caliber machine guns; 10 x 5 in. rockets or 2,000 lb maximum bomb load

TOTAL PRODUCTION: 15,683 of all types

SERVICE DATES: 1942–1955

SUMMARY: The P-47 was one of the largest and heaviest single-engine fighters in the World War II era. With external drop tanks that extended its range to up to 2,350 miles, the Thunderbolt made for an ideal escort for B-17s over Germany. The model excelled in this role. It entered combat service in April 1943 and was used throughout the rest of the European air war. P-47s flew a combined 546,000 combat sorties and suffered a loss rate per sortie of less than 0.7 percent.

SAVOIA-MARCHETTI S M.79 SPARVIERO
(Courtesy Art-Tech)

COUNTRY OF ORIGIN: Italy

MANUFACTURER: Societa Idrovolanti Alta Italia / Savoia-Marchetti

TYPE: Medium Bomber, Torpedo Bomber, Reconnaissance

CREW: 4–5

DIMENSIONS: Wingspan 69 ft 6.75 in; Length 51 ft 10 in; Height 14 ft 1.5 in

LOADED WEIGHT: 23,104 lbs

POWER PLANT: 3 x 780 hp Alfa Romeo 126 RC34 radial engines

PERFORMANCE: 267 mph maximum speed; 21,325 ft (6,500 m) ceiling; 1,180 mile range

ARMAMENT: 3 x 12.7 mm machine guns; 2 x 7.7 mm machine guns; 2,755 lb maximum bomb or torpedo load

TOTAL PRODUCTION: 1,370 of all types

SERVICE DATES: 1936–1952

SUMMARY: The S M.79, designed by Alessandro Marchetti to serve as an eight-seat passenger liner, was adopted by the Regia Aeronautica in 1935 and entered service in 1936. The plane combined steel tube, sheet metal alloy, wood, and fabric construction, and quickly proved its worthiness in combat conditions during the Spanish Civil War. The S M.79 was originally used for transporting troops, and was soon adapted for use as a bomber. It assumed new roles for reconnaissance and as a torpedo bomber in the Mediterranean after Italy entered the Second World War. It is ironic that it served on both sides after the Italian surrender in 1943, proving it to be one of the most versatile Italian aircraft during the Second World War. A few remained in service until 1952.

SAVOIA-MARCHETTI S M.81
(Courtesy Art-Tech)

COUNTRY OF ORIGIN: Italy

MANUFACTURER: Societa Idrovolanti Alta Italia / Savoia-Marchetti

TYPE: Medium Bomber and Transport

CREW: 6

DIMENSIONS: Wingspan 78 ft 9 in; Length 58 ft 4.75 in; Height 14 ft 1.5 in

LOADED WEIGHT: 23,040 lbs

POWER PLANT: 3 x 700 hp Piaggio P.X RC35 radial engines

PERFORMANCE: 211 mph maximum speed; 22,966 ft (7,000 m) ceiling; 1,243 mile range

ARMAMENT: 5–6 x 7.7 mm machine guns; 2,205 lb maximum bomb load

TOTAL PRODUCTION: 536

SERVICE DATES: 1935–1944

SUMMARY: The S M.81, introduced in 1935 as a military version of the successful S M.73 civilian transport, used all-metal framing and fabric covering. It arrived in time to serve as both a bomber and transport aircraft during Italy's invasion of Ethiopia. In addition, it played a crucial role in assisting the Nationalist forces during the Spanish Civil War. By the time the Second World War broke out, however, the S M.81 quickly proved to be vulnerable to Allied fighters while operating in daylight. As a result, it was quickly relegated to service as a night bomber and transport duties.

SUPERMARINE SPITFIRE*
(Courtesy Art-Tech)

COUNTRY OF ORIGIN: Great Britain

MANUFACTURER: Supermarine Aviation Works Ltd.

TYPE: Fighter

CREW: 1

DIMENSIONS: Wingspan 36 ft 10 in; Length 32 ft 8 in; Height 12 ft 8 in

LOADED WEIGHT: 8,500 lbs

POWER PLANT: 1 x 2,050 hp Rolls-Royce Griffon 65 V-12

PERFORMANCE: 448 mph maximum speed; 44,500 ft (13,563 m) ceiling; 460 mile normal range, 850 maximum range with drop tanks

ARMAMENT: 2 x 20 mm cannon; 4 x .303 caliber machine guns; 500 lb maximum bomb load

TOTAL PRODUCTION: 20,351

SERVICE DATES: 1938–1954

SUMMARY: Just as the Fokker Dr.I Triplane is the most remembered German fighter of the First World War, the Supermarine Spitfire is the most remembered British fighter of the Second World War. Designed by Reginald J. Mitchell, the Spitfire entered service in 1938 just as the prospect of war in Europe was become closer to a reality. The British Air Ministry

*There were so many models of the Spitfire that the statistics provided here are for the last version, the Spitfire XIV.

312 AIRCRAFT IN ALPHABETICAL ORDER

recognized its potential and moved quickly to expedite production. By the outbreak of the war, the Spitfire comprised 40 percent of Fighter Command's frontline aircraft. Although the Hawker Hurricane actually accounted for more downed German aircraft during the Battle of Britain, this had more to do with the British using the Spitfire to occupy the Messerschmitt BF-109, whereas the Hurricane concentrated on German bombers. The Spitfire, noted from the beginning for its maneuverability and speed—not to mention its firepower—grew increasingly faster as more powerful motors became available, from 355 mph in the 1,030 hp Rolls-Royce Merlin II in the first model to 448 mph in the 2,050 hp Rolls-Royce Griffon 65 V-12 in the last model.

TUPOLEV SB-2
(Courtesy Art-Tech)

COUNTRY OF ORIGIN: Soviet Union

MANUFACTURER: State Industries; Tupolev Design Bureau

TYPE: Light Bomber

CREW: 3

DIMENSIONS: Wingspan 66 ft 8.5 in; Length 66 ft 8.5 in; Height 10 ft 8 in

LOADED WEIGHT: 12,407 lbs (maximum takeoff)

POWER PLANT: 2 x 860 hp Klimov M-100A vee-types

PERFORMANCE: 244 mph maximum speed; 31,400 ft (9,750 m) service ceiling; 777 mile maximum range

ARMAMENT: 4 x 7.62 mm machine guns; 1,332 lb maximum bomb load

TOTAL PRODUCTION: 6,656 of all types

SERVICE DATES: 1936–1943

SUMMARY: The SB-2 was designed to be a fast-moving, quick-strike bomber, thereby representing the modernization of the Soviet bomber fleet. The Tupolev bureau adapted a twin-engine fighter design into a bomber, maintaining impressive speed while affording a generous bomb load capacity. For its time, the SB-2 was arguably among the world's elite bombers. It was used in the Spanish Civil War, as well as the Sino-Japanese conflicts, and saw extensive combat in the Winter War. It sacrificed armor for speed, however; when enemy fighters (especially the Messerschmitt Me-109) could match or surpass the SB-2's speed, the bomber's lack of armor or self-sealing fuel tanks led to numerous terrific midair explosions after taking fire in combat.

TUPOLEV TB-3/ANT-6
(Courtesy Art-Tech)

COUNTRY OF ORIGIN: Soviet Union

MANUFACTURER: State Industries; Tupolev Design Bureau

TYPE: Heavy Bomber, Transport

CREW: 8 (normal), plus 30–35 paratroopers (as transport)

DIMENSIONS: Wingspan 129 ft 7 in; Length 80 ft; Height 20 ft (est.)

LOADED WEIGHT: Approximately 35,366 lbs

POWER PLANT: 4 x 715 hp M-17F vee-types

PERFORMANCE: 122 mph maximum speed; 12,470 ft (3,800 m) service ceiling; 839 mile range

ARMAMENT: 8–10 x 7.62 mm machine guns; 4,409 lb maximum bomb load

TOTAL PRODUCTION: Approximately 818 of all types

SERVICE DATES: 1930–1942

SUMMARY: The TB-3 was a truly massive aircraft for its time, and was one of several early Soviet experiments with extraordi-narily large bombers. Even with its four-engine power plant, the TB-3 produced a top speed only slightly in excess of 120 mph. The plane saw its first real combat action in 1938, and the Soviets recognized that it was ill-suited for use as a bomber in the face of modern enemy fighters. Instead, the TB-3 (also referred to as the ANT-6) was increasingly used as a transport and troop carrier. It is perhaps most important for its use as a paratroop transport, a role for which the model proved extremely adept. In addition to a 30–35 man contingent of paratroopers, the TB-3 could carry loads of equipment, or even small service vehicles on specially fitted external hardpoints. As a transport aircraft, the TB-3/ANT-6 served as the aerial supply line for beleaguered Soviet troops during the siege of Leningrad.

TUPOLEV TU-2

(Courtesy Art-Tech)

COUNTRY OF ORIGIN: Soviet Union

MANUFACTURER: State Industries; Tupolev Design Bureau

TYPE: Medium Bomber

CREW: 4

DIMENSIONS: Wingspan 61 ft 10.5 in; Length 45 ft 3.33 in; Height 14 ft 11 in

LOADED WEIGHT: 16,447 lbs

POWER PLANT: 2 x 1,850 hp ASh-82FNV radials

PERFORMANCE: 342 mph maximum speed; 31,170 ft (9,500 m) service ceiling; 1,250 mile range

ARMAMENT: 2 x 20 mm cannon; 3–5 x 7.62 mm or 12.7 mm machine guns; 8,818 lb maximum bomb load

TOTAL PRODUCTION: Approximately 2,525 of all types

SERVICE DATES: 1944–1961

SUMMARY: The Tu-2 was designed by Andrei Tupolev while incarcerated in the gulag. In addition to winning its designer his freedom, the Tu-2 proved to be a vital part of the Soviet counteroffensive as a modern medium bomber. It combined good high-end speed with reasonable agility, along with a solid package of armor and armament. The model proved extremely durable both in flight and on the ground, making it an ideal front-line bomber. It is rather unique among World War II aircraft in that it remained in service in many Soviet-bloc air forces all the way into the 1960s.

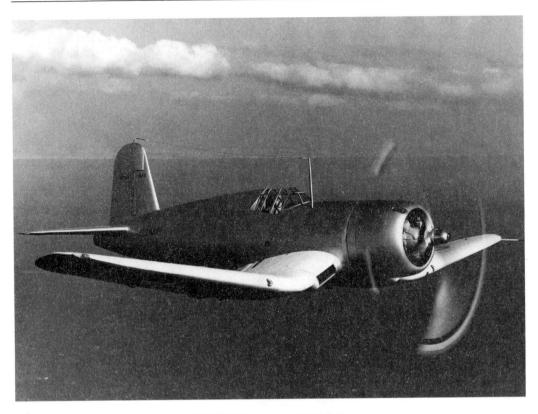

VOUGHT F4U-1 CORSAIR
(Courtesy Art-Tech)

COUNTRY OF ORIGIN: United States

MANUFACTURER: Vought Aircraft Company

TYPE: Fighter

CREW: 1

DIMENSIONS: Wingspan 40 ft 11.75 in; Length 33 ft 8 in; Height 14 ft 9 in

LOADED WEIGHT: 14,670 lbs

POWER PLANT: 2 x 2,100 hp Pratt & Whitney Double Wasp radials

PERFORMANCE: 446 mph maximum speed; 41,500 ft (12,650 m) service ceiling; 1,005 mile range

ARMAMENT: 6 x .50 caliber machine guns; 8 x 5 in. rockets or 2,000 lb maximum bomb load

TOTAL PRODUCTION: 12,571 of all types

SERVICE DATES: 1942–1952

SUMMARY: Although it was the last piston-engine fighter in production, the Corsair was considered by many to be the most capable American fighter of the war. The first prototype, which was developed specifically for use as a carrier-based fighter, flew in May 1940. The Corsair's distinctive gull-wing configuration proved necessary to allow clearance for the aircraft's massive four-blade propeller, a modification made necessary out of the marriage of the smallest possible airframe with the most powerful engine. The design reduced the pilot's view, however, and made carrier landings extremely difficult. As such, Corsairs were initially tasked to Marine squadrons, with carrier groups receiving the aircraft only after more extensive pilot training. Over the course of the war, the F4U scored an 11:1 kill-to-loss ratio, downing 2,140 enemy aircraft in air-to-air combat.

YAKOVLEV YAK-1
(Courtesy Art-Tech)

COUNTRY OF ORIGIN: Soviet Union

MANUFACTURER: State Industries; Yakovlev Design Bureau

TYPE: Fighter

CREW: 1

DIMENSIONS: Wingspan 32 ft 9.67 in; Length 27 ft 9.875 in; Height 8 ft 8 in

LOADED WEIGHT: 6,276 lbs (maximum take-off)

POWER PLANT: 1 x 1,050 hp Klimov M-105P vee-type

PERFORMANCE: 373 mph maximum speed; 32,818 ft (10,000 m) service ceiling; 435 mile maximum range

ARMAMENT: 2 x 7.62 mm machine guns; 1 x 20 mm cannon; 6 x RS-82 rockets or 441 lb maximum bomb load

TOTAL PRODUCTION: Approximately 8,720 of all types

SERVICE DATES: 1940–1945

SUMMARY: Despite an inauspicious start (i.e., its prototype was destroyed during a test flight), the Yak-1 helped bring the Soviet air forces into the modern fighter age. It is one of several models from this era to employ the Klimov M-105 engine. The Yak-1, which was often paired with the Il-2 "tankbuster," had the speed and armament to make it an ideal fighter escort. In the hands of an experienced pilot, the Yak-1 was truly an air-superiority fighter. This was also the model that helped make famous two of the Soviet Union's most accomplished female fighter aces: Valeria Ivanova Khomyakova and "The White Rose of Stalingrad," Lilya Vladimirovna Litvyak (so nicknamed for the white lily painted on the cockpit of her Yak-1).

YAKOVLEV YAK-9
(Courtesy Art-Tech)

COUNTRY OF ORIGIN: Soviet Union

MANUFACTURER: State Industries; Yakovlev Design Bureau

TYPE: Fighter

CREW: 1

DIMENSIONS: Wingspan 31 ft 11 in; Length 28 ft; Height 9 ft 10 in

LOADED WEIGHT: 6,766 lbs (maximum take-off)

POWER PLANT: 1 x 1,360 hp Klimov VK-105PF-3 vee-type

PERFORMANCE: 376 mph maximum speed; 34,768 ft (10,600 m) service ceiling; 881 mile range

ARMAMENT: 1 x 20 mm cannon; 2 x 12.7 mm machine guns; 6 x RS-82 rockets or 440 lb maximum bomb load

TOTAL PRODUCTION: Approximately 14,579 of all types

SERVICE DATES: 1942–1950

SUMMARY: The ultimate development of the Yak-1 series of fighters, the Yak-9 was perhaps the most advanced Soviet fighter of the World War II era. Soviet authorities directed more production capacity toward the Yak-9 than any other fighter in the war's latter stages. In fact, production of the model continued well after the war; almost 16,800 Yak-9s were produced through 1950.

GLOSSARY OF TERMS

Aerofoil A cross-section shape of a wing

Aileron A part of the wing that controls roll left or right

Altitude Conversion Chart

1,000 meters	3,281 feet
2,000 meters	6,562 feet
3,000 meters	9,842 feet
4,000 meters	13,123 feet
5,000 meters	16,404 feet
6,000 meters	19,685 feet
7,000 meters	22,965 feet
8,000 meters	26,247 feet
9,000 meters	29,526 feet
10,000 meters	32,808 feet

Anhedral The downward angle of the tips of the wings in relation to where the wings are attached to the fuselage

Aspect Ratio Division of the wingspan by chord line

Attack Aircraft Aircraft designed to strike small targets at short distance and support ground troops

Autopilot Device that controls an aircraft's flight controls

Bombardier Crew member on bombers who operates the bombsight and controls the aircraft's flight in the moments before dropping a bomb load

Bomber An aircraft designed to drop bombs on distant targets

Camber The degree of curvature of an aerofoil shape; greater camber provides greater lift, but also creates drag

Cannon Armament that is 20 mm or larger

Cantilever Design that uses a solid steel cross-bar running the length of the wings through the fuselage

Chord The width of a wing from the leading edge to the trailing edge

Cockpit The area housing the controls and where the pilot sits, and area for other crew members (observers or tailgunners)

Cowling Covering around the engine to minimize drag

Dihedral   The upward angle from which the tips of the wings are in relation to where the wing attaches to the fuselage

Drag   The aerodynamic forces that resist an aircraft's movement through the air

Elevons   A combination of elevators and ailerons

Elevators   Located on the tail section to set the pitch (up and down motion) of the aircraft

Fighter   An aircraft designed to shoot down other aircraft

Flaps   Extensions on the rear edge of wings that can be lowered to decrease speed; sometimes referred to as air brakes

Fuselage   The long, narrow body of an aircraft, going down its center and housing its engine and cockpit or cockpits

Gap   Distance between the wings

Inline Engine   Stationary engine in which the pistons are set in a straight row

Loaded Weight   The normal loaded weight of an aircraft at takeoff, comprising the aircraft, fuel, crew, and armament

Monocoque   A construction method in which the fuselage is built around wooden hoops, usually using plywood strips, providing for a smooth rounded surface

Nacelle   A shortened fuselage that houses the crew; normally found on twin-engine aircraft or on pushers with the engine being in the rear of the nacelle

Navigator   Crew member in larger aircraft who charts the aircraft's course

Nose   The front section of the fuselage

Observation   Aircraft used within a closer range, usually to assist artillery

Pitch   Movement of the aircraft up and down; controlled by the elevator

Pivot-Mounted Gun   A machine gun mounted on pivot on the side or to the rear of the observer's seat, which allows for the gun to be moved up or down or side-to-side at an opposing plane

Radar   Device that uses reflected radio signals to detect incoming aircraft

Radial Engine   Stationary engine in which pistons are set in a circular or star pattern around the crankshaft

Reconnaissance   Aircraft used for viewing or photographing enemy positions

Retractable Undercarriage   Crank-operated or hydraulic-powered system that allows the undercarriage to be retracted into the fuselage or wings after takeoff

Ring-Mounted Gun   A machine gun mounted on a circular ring around the observer's seat, which allows for a smooth movement and aiming of the gun

Roll   Moving the aircraft on a left or right roll by the ailerons

Rotary Engine   An engine in which the crankshaft is stationary and the engine revolves around it

Rudder   A part of the tail section that moves the aircraft from left to right, generally operated by foot pedals

Service Ceiling   Highest altitude at which an aircraft normally operates

Sesquiplane   Aircraft in which the lower wing is much smaller than the upper wing in either chord or span or both

Slats   Extensions on the leading edge of wings that can be lowered to reduce turbulence and prevent stalls by forcing air over the upper surface of the wings

Slip   Movement whereby the pilot sets the ailerons and rudder in opposite directions so that the aircraft moves forward at an angle; useful for reducing speed quickly by increasing drag

Spin   Caused when an aircraft stalls and begins to spin or rotate around its vertical axis

Stagger   A biplane or triplane in which the wings staggered rather than being in line on the fuselage; the lower wing is normally placed further back

Stall   Caused when an aircraft's angle of attack exceeds its critical angle, resulting in airflow no longer going over the wing, and thus causing the plane to fall

Streamlining   Aircraft design to minimize drag during flight

Supercharger   Device driven mechanically or by turbine propelled by exhaust gases that forces air and fuel into the engine, thereby increasing its capacity and power

Sweptback   When the wings of an aircraft are affixed so that leading edge is at a backward angle rather than a 90 degree angle to the fuselage

Synchronized Gun   A gun that is fixed to the fuselage and equipped with an interrupter gear that is synchronized with the engine so that it will not fire when a bullet would hit the propeller

Tail   The rear section of an airplane that houses the rudder and elevators

Torpedo Bomber   Aircraft armed with torpedoes and used to attack naval ships

Tractor Configuration   An aircraft whose engine and propeller are located in front of the wings

Trainer   Aircraft designed or used to train pilots, sometimes with dual controls for instructor and students

Trim Tab   Tabs on the rudder and elevator that allow the pilot to make adjustments during flight to provide greater stability without having to maintain constant pressure on the controls

Turret   Hydraulically powered machine gun or cannon system placed on larger aircraft for defense against fighters

Variable Pitch Propeller   Manual or automatic system that increases the pitch of propellers to grab more air at higher altitudes, increasing engine efficiency

V-Type Engine   Stationary engine in which the pistons are set in a V-pattern, with two being beside each other

Wingspan   Distance of aircraft from the tips of the longest wing

Yaw   Movement of the aircraft left and right; controlled by the rudder

A SELECTIVE BIBLIOGRAPHY
OF MILITARY AIRCRAFT, 1919–1945

Abate, Rosario. *Aeroplani Caproni: Gianni Caproni and His Aircraft, 1910–1983*. Trento, Italy: Museo Caproni, 1992.

Andrews, Allen. *The Air Marshals: The Air War in Western Europe*. New York: Morrow, 1970.

Andrews, C. F., and E. B. Morgan. *Vickers Aircraft since 1908*. London: Putnam, 1988.

Barnes, C. H. *Bristol Aircraft since 1910*. London: Putnam, 1988.

———. *Handley Page Aircraft since 1907*. London: Putnam, 1987.

Belote, James H., and William Belote. *Titans of the Seas: The Development of the Japanese and American Carrier Task Forces during World War II*. New York: Harper & Row, 1975.

Blanco, Richard L. *The Luftwaffe in World War II: The Rise and Decline of an Air Force*. New York: J. Messner, 1987.

Bowers, Peter M. *Curtiss Aircraft, 1907–1947*. Annapolis, MD: Naval Institute Press, 1979.

Boyle, Andrew. *Trenchard: Man of Vision*. New York: Norton, 1962.

Boyne, Walter J. *Clash of Wings: World War II in the Air*. New York: Simon and Schuster, 1994.

———. *The Influence of Air Power upon History*. Gretna, LA: Pelican Publishing Company, 2003.

Cain, Anthony C. *The Forgotten Air Force: French Air Doctrine in the 1930s.* Washington, DC: Smithsonian Institution Press, 2002.

Catalanotto, Baldassare. *Once Upon a Sky: 70 Years of the Italian Air Force.* Rome: Lizard, 1994.

Christienne, Charles, and Pierre Lissarrague. *A History of French Military Aviation.* Washington: Smithsonian Institution Press, 1986.

Corum, James S. *The Luftwaffe Way of War: German Air Force Doctrine, 1911–1945.* Baltimore: Nautical and Aviation Publications, 1998.

Crane, James S. *Bombs, Cities, and Civilians: American Airpower Strategy in World War II.* Lawrence: University Press of Kansas, 1993.

Deichmann, Paul. *Spearhead for Blitzkrieg: Luftwaffe Operations in Support of the Army, 1939–1945.* London: Greenhill Books, 1996.

Dressel, Joachim. *Bombers of the Luftwaffe.* London: Arms and Armour Press, 1994.

———. *Fighters of the Luftwaffe.* London: Arms and Armour Press, 1993.

Dunning, Chris. *Courage Alone: The Italian Air Force, 1940–1943.* Aldershot, UK: Hikoki Publications, 1998.

Finney, Robert T. *History of the Air Corps Tactical School, 1920–1940.* Washington, DC: Center for Air Force History, 1992.

Francillon, René J. *Japanese Aircraft of the Pacific War.* Annapolis, MD: Naval Institute Press, 1988.

Fredriksen, John C. *International Warbirds: An Illustrated Guide to World Military Aircraft, 1914–2000.* Santa Barbara, CA: ABC-Clio, Inc., 2001.

———. *Warbirds: An Illustrated Guide to U.S. Military Aircraft, 1915–2000.* Santa Barbara, CA: ABC-Clio, Inc., 1999.

Freeman, Roger A. *The Mighty Eighth: A History of the Units, Men, and Machines of the U.S. 8th Air Force.* Osceola, WI: Motorbooks International Publishers, 1991.

Fuchida, Mitsuo, and Masatake Okumiya. *Midway: The Battle that Doomed Japan.* Annapolis, MD: Naval Institute Press, 1955.

Gaston, James C. *Planning the American Air War: Four Men and Nine Days in 1941*. Washington, DC: National Defense University Press, 1982.

Green, William. *Warplanes of the Third Reich*. New York: Galahad Books, 1990.

Gunston, Bill. *Aircraft of the Soviet Union*. London: Osprey, 1983.

Hammel, Eric. *Air War Europa: America's Air War against Germany in Europe and North Africa, Chronology, 1942–1945*. Pacifica, CA: Pacifica Press, 1994.

———. *Air War Pacific: America's Air War against Japan in East Asia and the Pacific, Chronology 1941–1945*. Pacifica, CA: Pacifica Press, 1998.

Hardesty, Von. *Red Phoenix: The Rise of Soviet Air Power, 1941–1945*. Washington, DC: Smithsonian Institution Press, 1982.

Hastings, Max. *Bomber Command*. New York: Dial Press/James Wade, 1979.

Hezlett, Sir Arthur. *Aircraft and Sea Power*. New York: Stein and Day, 1970.

Higham, Robin. *100 Years of Air Power & Aviation*. College Station: Texas A&M University Press, 2003.

Homze, Edward L. *Arming the Luftwaffe: The Reich Air Ministry and the German Aircraft Industry, 1919–1939*. Lincoln: University of Nebraska Press, 1976.

Howson, Gerald. *Aircraft of the Spanish Civil War, 1936–1939*. London: Putnam, 1990.

Hurley, Alfred F. *Billy Mitchell, Crusaders for Air Power*. New York: Franklin Watts, 1964.

Hyde, H. Montgomery. *British Air Policy between the Wars, 1918–1939*. London: Heinemann, 1996.

Jackson, A. J. *De Havilland Aircraft since 1909*. London: Putnam, 1987.

Jackson, Robert. *The Red Falcons: The Soviet Air Force in Action, 1919–1969*. Brighton, UK: Clifton House, 1970.

Jarrett, Philip, ed. *Aircraft of the Second World War: The Development of the Warplane, 1939–45*. Putnam's History of Aircraft Series. London: Putnam, 1997.

———. *Biplane to Monoplane: Aircraft Development, 1919–39*. Putnam's History of Aircraft Series. London: Putnam, 1997.

Jones, Neville. *The Beginnings of Strategic Air Power: A History of the British Bomber Force, 1923–1939*. London: Frank Cass, 1987.

Lee, Asher. *The Soviet Air Force*. New York: John Day, 1962.

Mason, Herbert M., Jr. *The Rise of the Luftwaffe, 1918–1940*. New York: Dial Press, 1973.

Mikesh, Robert C. *Broken Wings of the Samurai: The Destruction of the Japanese Air Force*. Shrewsbury, UK: Airlife, 1993.

Mikesh, Robert C., and Shorzoe Abe. *Japanese Aircraft, 1910–1941*. Annapolis, MD: Naval Institute Press, 1990.

Morison, Samuel Eliot. *History of U.S. Naval Operations in World War II*. Boston: Little, Brown, 1975.

Murray, Williamson. *War in the Air, 1914–45*. London: Cassell Publishers, 1999.

Prange, Gordon W. *At Dawn We Slept: The Untold Story of Pearl Harbor*. New York: McGraw Hill, 1981.

Probert, Henry. *Bomber Harris: His Life and Times*. London: Greenhill Books, 2001.

Proctor, Raymond L. *Hitler's Luftwaffe in the Spanish Civil War*. Westport, CT: Greenwood Press, 1983.

Rimmell, Ray. *R.A.F. between the Wars*. London: Arms and Armour Press, 1985.

Robertson, Scott. *The Development of RAF Strategic Bombing Doctrine, 1919–1939*. Westport, CT: Praeger, 1995.

Saward, Dudley. *Bomber Harris*. Garden City, NY: Doubleday, 1985.

Smith, Malcom. *British Air Strategy between the Wars*. New York: Clarendon Press, 1984.

Spector, Ronald H. *Eagles against the Sun*. New York: Vintage, 1985.

Thetford, Owen. *Aircraft of the Royal Air Force since 1918*. London: Putnam, 1995.

———. *British Naval Aviation since 1912*. London: Putnam, 1977.

Thompson, Jonathan. *Italian Civil and Military Aircraft, 1930–1945*. Los Angeles: Aero Publishers, 1963.

Wilson, Stewart. *Aircraft of WWII*. Fyshwick: Aerospace Publications, 1998.

Wragg, David. *Wings over the Sea: A History of Naval Aviation*. New York: Arco Publishing, Inc., 1979.

INDEX

Aerial combat, media glamorization of, 1–2
Afrika Korps, **52, 53, 184**
Aichi, **222, 227**
Air-to-air rockets, RS-82 (Soviet Union), 31
Air Corps Tactical School (ACTS), **21–22**
Air Force Regulation on the Conduct of the Air War (Wilberg and Wever), **26**
Air power, mobilization of, **73–77,** **73** (table), **74** (table)
    Allied aircraft production, 74 (table), 75–76
    Axis aircraft production, 73 (table), 74–75
Air power, organization of in the interwar period, **20–29**
    France, 26–27
    Germany, 24–26
    Great Britain, 23–24
    Italy, 20–21
    Japan, 28–29
    Soviet Union, 27–28
    United States, 21–23
Air power, use of during the interwar years, **30–34**
Aircraft armament, **18–19**
    air-to-air rockets, 19
    cannon, 19
    machine guns, 18–19

Aircraft carriers (U.S.)
    Lexington, 8
    Saratoga, 8
Aircraft technology, **9**
Aircraft technology (interwar years), **12–20**
    bombsights, 17
    engines, 12, 14, 18
    flaps, 15
    gyroscopes, 16
    hydraulic systems, 15
    impact of on aircraft design, 16
    impact of passenger and freight service on, 12–13
    military-civilian cooperation in, 13
    radio technology, 15–16
    reduction in fuel consumption, 1
    retractable undercarriages, 13
    superchargers, 14
    synchronization gear, 18
    variable pitch propellers, 14–15
Akagi, **68**
Akron, **22**
Alexander, Harold, **52**
Alksnis, Yakov, **28**
Altmark, seizure of by the British, **40,** 77n3
American Expeditionary Force (AEF), **6**
Amoit 143 (France), 27
Antilles Air Task Force, **126**

Arado Flugzeugwerke GmbH, **179**
Arhangelsky, A. A., **156**
Armée de l'Air (France), **27**
    organization of, 41
    role of in the battle for France,
        41, 44
Arnim, Hans Jürgen Dieter von, **53**
Arnold, Henry ("Hap"), **8, 9, 60,
    62, 125**
Atomic bombs, **72–73, 124, 129**
Austria, **31**

Baldwin, Stanley, **18**
Battle of Britain, **5, 11, 17, 19,
    44–49, 58, 59, 79, 89, 132,
    138**
    British casualties from the Blitz,
        48–49
    consequences of, 49
    decision by Hitler to bomb
        London, 47–48
    factors contributing to the RAF's
        early success, 47
    failure of the Blitz, 49
    Luftwaffe losses during, 46–47,
        48, 95
    overestimates of British losses by
        German intelligence, 46–47
    RAF losses during, 47, 48
Beech Aircraft Company, **168**
Belgium, invasion of by Germany,
    41
Belgrade, bombing of by the
    Luftwaffe, **50**
Beriev, Georgii Mikhailovich, **230,
    231**
Berlin, bombing of by the RAF, **47,
    59, 62, 132**
Blackburn, **222**
Bock, Feodor von, **42**
Bockscar, **72, 124, 129**
Boeing 247 (civilian aircraft), **14**
Boeing 307 Stratoliner (civilian
    aircraft), **14**
    weight and wing span of, 14

Boeing 347 Stratoliner (civilian
    aircraft), **14**
Bomber Command (Great Britain),
    58, 59, 62
    shift of from strategic to civilian
        targets, 59
Bombers, **2, 123**
    design of, 16, 17–18
    dive bombers, 17
    myth of as invulnerable, 48
    vulnerability of dive bombers to
        anti-aircraft fire, 17
Bombers (France), **135–138**
    Amiot 143, 136–137, 239
    Breguet 14, 136
    Breguet 19, 136, 248 (photo)
    Breguet 691, 137
    Farman F 221, 137
    Liore de Olivier LeO 20, 136
    Liore de Olivier LeO 451, 138
    Potez 63, 137, 306 (photo)
Bombers (Germany), **138–142**
    Arado Ar 234 Blitz ("Lightning"),
        141–142
    Dornier Do 17, 43, 74, 140
    Dornier Do 217, 97, 140–141,
        262 (photo)
    Heinkel He 111, 17, 33, 37–38,
        43, 46, 74, 139, 181, 276
    Heinkel He 219 Uhu ("Owl"), 97
    Junkers Ju 86, 138–139
    Junkers Ju 87-G, 139–140
    Junkers Ju 87 Stuka, 17, 38, 45,
        46, 74, 96, 139, 279 (photo)
    Junkers Ju 88, 43, 97, 140, 142,
        280 (photo)
    Junkers Ju 188, 141
    Junkers Ju 287, 142
Bombers (Great Britain), **131–135**
    Airco D.H.9, 30
    Armstrong-Whitworth Whitley,
        131–132
    Avro Lancaster, 75, 133, 242
        (photo)
    Bristol Beaufort, 135

Bristol Blenheim, 41, 134
de Havilland DH 98 Mosquito,
    135, 259 (photo)
Fairey Battle, 41, 134, 145
Handley Page Halifax, 75, 133,
    274 (photo)
Handley Page Hampden, 132
Handley Page Heyford, 131
Handley Page V/1000, 30
Hawker Hart, 134
Short Stirling, 132–133
Vickers FB 27 Vimy, 131
Vickers Virginia, 131
Vickers Vildebeest, 134–135
Vickers Wellingtons, 39–40, 132
Bombers (Italy), **142–145**
    Cant Z 1007 Alcione
        ("Kingfisher"), 144
    Caproni Ca 1, 142
    Caproni Ca 5, 142
    Caproni Ca 101, 142–143
    Caproni Ca 310, 144, 253
        (photo)
    Fiat Br 20 Cignona, 17, 143
    Piaggio P 108B, 144–145
    Savio-Marchetti SM 79 Sparviero
        ("Sparrow"), 143–144
    Savio-Marchetti SM 81
        Pipistrello ("Bat"), 143
Bombers (Japan), **145–153**
    Kawasaki Ki-32, 145
    Kawasaki Ki-48, 147, 148
    Kyushu Q1W Tokai ("Eastern
        Sea"), 152
    Mitsubishi G3M, 30, 149–150
    Mitsubishi G3M2, 149
    Mitsubishi G3M3, 149
    Mitsubishi G4M, 30, 69, 150–
        151, 153, 293 (photo)
    Mitsubishi Ki-21, 145–146, 147,
        294 (photo)
    Mitsubishi Ki-67, 148
    Nakajima G5N Shinzan
        ("Mountain Recess"), 151
    Nakajima G5N2, 151

Nakajima Ki-49 Donryu, 148
Tachikawa Ki-36, 146
Tachikawa Ki-55, 146, 186
Yokosuka MXY7 Ohka ("Cherry
    Blossom"), 152–153
Yokosuka P1Y Ginga ("Milky
    Way"), 151–152
Bombers (minor powers), **161–163**
    Commonwealth CA 1 Wirraway
        ("Challenge" [Australia]), 162
    Letov S 328 (Czechoslovakia),
        161–162
    P 37 Los (Poland), 162–163
    PZL P 23 Karas (Poland), 162
Bombers (Soviet Union), **153–161**
    Ilyushin DB-3, 158
    Ilyushin Il-2 Shturmovik, 54, 55,
        56, 95, 116, 158, 277 (photo)
    Ilyushin Il-4, 158
    Kalinin K-7, 155
    Petlyakov ANT-42 prototype, 155
    Petlyakov ANT-42 (later Pe.8),
        155–156, 160
    Petlyakov Pe.2, 160, 302 (photo)
    Petlyakov Pe.3, 54
    Sukhoi Su-2, 157–158
    Sukhoi Su-6, 158
    Tupolev ANT-51, 157
    Tupolev ANT-58, 161
    Tupolev ANT-59, 161
    Tupolev ANT-61 (later Tu-2),
        161, 315 (photo)
    Tupolev SB-2 (ANT-40), 31, 147,
        156–157, 313 (photo)
    Tupolev SB-2bis, 159
    Tupolev TB-1, 153–154
    Tupolev TB-3 (ANT-6), 28, 153,
        154, 314 (photo)
    Yakovlev BB-22, 159
    Yakovlev Yak-2, 159
    Yakovlev Yak-4, 159–160
Bombers (United States), **123–131**
    B-3A, 124–125

Boeing B-17 Flying Fortress, 4,
    17–18, 22, 68, 126–127, 129,
    244 (photo)
Boeing B-29 Superfortress, 70,
    71, 72, 103, 107, 108, 129–
    130, 245 (photo)
Consolidated B-24 Liberators,
    51,103, 109, 127–128, 131,
    254 (photo)
Consolidated B-32 Dominator,
    130–131
Curtiss A-25 Shrike, 202
Douglas A/B-26 Invader, 130
Douglas B-18 Bolo, 125–126
Lockheed B-34 (originally the
    Lockheed PV-1 Ventura), 203
Martin B-10, 16, 17, 22, 125,
    288 (photo)
Martin B-26 Marauder, 128
MB-1, 124
MB-2, 124, 125
North American B-25 Mitchell,
    9, 52, 67, 128, 129, 300
    (photo)
Northrop A-17 Nomad, 125
Bong, Richard, 84
Boyington, Gregory ("Pappy"), 199
Brand, Christopher, 46
British Air Force in France (BAFF),
    41
British Eighth Army, 51
British Expeditionary Force (BEF),
    41, 175
British General Aircraft, 63
Bulgaria, 50
Bush, George H. W., 201
Butts Report, 59

Caproni, Gianni, 3, 142
Casablanca Conference (1943), 60
Cavour, 50, 212
Chamberlain, Neville, 34, 43
Chennault, Claire L., 83
Chetverikov, Igor, 231–232

China, 31, 70, 148, 157, 194,
    219
    Japanese bombing raids on, 147
Chitose, 71
Chiyoda, 71
Chkalov, V. P., 110–111
Churchill, Winston, 10, 30, 40,
    43, 44, 60
Commonwealth Aircraft
    Corporation, 122
Coolidge, Calvin, 8, 9
Command of the Air (Douhet), 4
Coral Sea, Battle of the, 67, 68,
    221
Cornwall, 224
Cot, Pierre, 27, 91, 135
Crete, invasion of by Germany, 50–
    51, 181
Curtiss-Wright Corporation, 196
Czechoslovakia, 34, 64

Daladier, Edouard, 34
Denmark, invasion of by Germany,
    40
DFS (German design firm), 181
Doi, Takeo, 103, 106, 107–108,
    147
Dollfuss, Engelbert, 31
Doolittle, James H. ("Jimmy"), 62,
    128
Dorsetshire, 224
Douglas DC-3 (civilian aircraft),
    14, 192
Douglas DC-4 (civilian aircraft),
    151
Douhet, Giulio, 2, 3–5, 6, 7, 10,
    12, 20–21, 26, 35n1, 49
    court-martial of, 3
    criticism of his superiors, 3
    impact of his theories, 4–5
    offensive theory of air power, 4
    vindication of, 3–4
Dowding, Hugh, 41, 44, 46
Duilio, sinking of, 50, 212
Dunkirk, evacuation of, 43

Dutch Air Force, **43, 120**

Eaker, Ira, **9, 60, 61–62**
Eban Emael fortress, **176, 181**
Eisenhower, Dwight D., **64**
El Alamein, Battle of, **52**
  RAF actions at, 52
Enola Gay, **72, 124, 129**
Enterprise, **68, 69**
Ethiopia, invasion of, **31–32**

Fighters, **2, 79**
  improvements to armaments of,
    18–19
  improvements to engines (for
    greater speed), 18
  night-fighters, 85–86
  "parasite" fighters, 154
Fighters and attack aircraft
    (France), **91–94**
  Blériot-Spad 51, 92
  Blériot-Spad S510, 92–93
  Bloch MB 152, 93
  Dewoitine D 500, 93
  Dewoitine D-510, 260 (photo)
  Dewoitine D 520, 41, 91, 93–94
  Loire-Gourdou-Leseurre LGL 32
    C1, 92
  Morane-Saulnier MS 406, 94
  Nieuport-Delage Ni-D 29, 91–
    92, 298 (photo)
  Potez 25 A2, 92
  Wilbault 72 C1, 92
Fighters and attack aircraft
    (Germany), **94–98**
  Focke Wulf Fw 190 (Germany),
    61, 96–97
  Focke Wulf Ta 154, 97
  Henschel Hs 123, 96
  Junkers Ju 388, 97
  Messerschmitt BF-109, 18, 37,
    38, 40, 43, 45, 47, 52, 61, 89,
    94, 106, 115, 121, 122, 157,
    158, 289 (photo)
  Messerschmitt BF 109E, 106

Messerschmitt BF-109G, 94
Messerschmitt BF-110, 38, 40,
  43, 45, 46, 47, 89, 181, 290
  (photo)
Messerschmitt Me 163, 98
Messerschmitt Me 210, 95
Messerschmitt Me 262 Schwalbe
  ("Swallow"), 42, 61, 62, 64,
  74, 91, 97–98, 291 (photo)
Messerschmitt Me 410 Hornisse
  ("Hornet"), 95–96
Night-fighters, 97, 98
Fighters and attack aircraft (Great
    Britain), **87–91**
Armstrong-Whitworth Siskin
    IIIA, 88
Bristol Beaufighter, 90, 250
    (photo)
Bristol Bulldog, 88, 251 (photo)
Boulton-Paul Defiant, 90
De Havilland Mosquito, 90
Gloster Gauntlet, 88–89
Gloster Gladiator, 41, 88, 89
Gloster Meteor I-III, 91
Gloster Sea Gladiators, 41
Hawker Fury, 88, 97
Hawker Hurricane, 33, 41, 44,
    45, 47, 75, 89, 146
Hawker Hurricane IID, 52–53,
    275 (photo)
Hawker Typhoon, 90–91
Sopwith Camel, 87
Supermarine Spitfire, 18, 33, 43,
    45, 47, 52, 75, 89–90, 106,
    311 (photo)
Fighters and attack aircraft (Italy),
    98–100
Fiat CR 1, 98, 99
Fiat CR 2, 98
Fiat CR 20, 98, 99, 217–218
Fiat CR 32 Chirri, 98, 266
    (photo)
Fiat CR 42 Falco ("Falcon"), 18,
    51, 98, 99, 100

Fiat G 50 Freccia, 99–100, 267
    (photo)
Macchi MC 200 Saetta
    ("Lightning Bolt"), 100
Macchi MC 202 Folgore
    ("Thunderbolt"), 100, 287
    (photo)
Reggiane Re 2000 Falco
    ("Falcon"), 100
Fighters and attack aircraft (Japan),
    101–110
Army Type 91 Fighter, 101
Kawasaki KDA-5 (Type 92
    Fighter), 102
Kawasaki Ki-10, 102, 103
Kawasaki Ki-10-I, 102
Kawasaki Ki-10-II, 102
Kawasaki Ki-38, 103
Kawasaki Ki-44 Shoki ("Devil-
    Queller"), 105–106
Kawasaki Ki-45 KAIc, 104
Kawasaki Ki-45 Toryu ("Dragon
    Killer"), 103–104, 147
Kawasaki Ki-60, 106
Kawasaki Ki-61 Hien
    ("Swallow"), 106–107, 108,
    282 (photo)
Kawasaki Ki-100, 108–109
Kawasaki Ki-102, 108
Kyushu J7W Shinden
    ("Magnificent Lightning"), 110
Mitsubishi A6M Zeros, 30, 65,
    69, 104, 105, 109, 197, 292
    (photo)
Mitsubishi J8M Shusui ("Sword
    Stroke"), 110
Mitsubishi Ki-33, 102
Mitsubishi Ki-39, 103
Mitsubishi Ki-83, 110
Nakajima J1N Gekko
    ("Moonlight"), 109
Nakajima J1N1-S, 109–110
Nakajima Ki-11, 102
Nakajima Ki-27, 18, 102–103
Nakajima Ki-28, 102

Nakajima Ki-38, 103
Nakajima Ki-43 Hayabusa
    ("Peregrine Falcon"), 104–105,
    296 (photo)
Nakajima Ki-84 Hayate ("Gale"),
    107, 297 (photo)
Type Ko 4 Fighter, 101
Fighters and attack aircraft (minor
    powers), **120–122**
Avia B 534 (Czechoslovakia),
    121, 241 (photo)
Avia BH 21 (Czechoslovakia),
    121
CA 12 Boomerang (Australia),
    122
Fokker C V (Netherlands), 120
Fokker D XXI (Netherlands),
    120–121
F.VIII (Netherlands), 13
Fokker G 1 (Netherlands), 121
IAR 80 (Romania), 122
PZL P 7 (Poland), 18, 121
PZL P 11 (Poland), 38, 121, 307
    (photo)
PZL P 37 Los (Poland), 38
Fighters and attack aircraft (Soviet
    Union), **110–119**
Lavochkin LaGG-1, 113
Lavochkin LaGG-3, 11–114, 285
    (photo)
Lavochkin La-5, 114–115, 118
Lavochkin La-5FN, 114, 115
Lavochkin La-7, 115, 284
    (photo)
Lavochkin La-7UTI, 115
Lend-Lease aircraft, 119
Mikoyan-Gurevich MiG-1, 118,
    119
Mikoyan-Gurevich MiG-3, 54,
    119
Polikarpov I-15, 31, 54, 111,
    112, 303 (photo)
Polikarpov I-15bis, 111
Polikarpov I-15ter (I-153), 111

Polikarpov I-16, 18, 31, 54, 99, 112–113, 158, 304 (photo)
Polikarpov I-16 Type 10, 112
Polikarpov I-16 Type 24, 112
Yakovlev Yak-1, 114, 115–116, 317 (photo)
Yakovlev Yak-1B, 115, 116, 117
Yakovlev Yak-1M, 115, 116
Yakovlev Yak-3, 116–117
Yakovlev Yak-7, 117
Yakovlev Yak 9, 54, 114, 117, 318 (photo)
Fighters and attack aircraft (United States), 79–87
Bell P-39 Airacobra, 82–83, 119
Bell P-63 King cobra, 119
Boeing F4B/P-12, 246 (photo)
Boeing P-12E, 81
Boeing P-26 Peashooter, 81, 247 (photo)
Boeing PW-9, 80
Consolidated PB-2A, 81
Curtiss P-1 Hawk, 80
Curtiss P-6E Hawk, 80
Curtiss P-36 Hawk, 82
Curtiss P-40E, 106
Curtiss P-40 Warhawk, 83, 84, 257 (photo)
Curtiss SBC Helldiver, 17
Curtiss Hawk 75A, 41
Curtiss A-3/O-1 Falcon, 86
Curtiss A-8 Shrike, 86
Curtiss PW-8, 80
Douglas A-20 Havoc, 86–87
Douglas P-70 Night Havoc, 85
Lockheed P-38 Lightning, 52, 69, 83–84, 286 (photo)
North American A-36 Apache, 87
North American P-51 Mustang, 72, 84, 85, 87, 106, 301 (photo)
North American P-51B Mustang, 62
Northrop A-17 Nomad, 86

Northrop P-61 Black Widow, 85–86
Republic P-35, 84
Republic P-43
Republic P-47 ("The Jug"), 84–85, 308 (photo)
Seversky P-35, 81–82
Thomas-Morse MB-3, 80
Finland, invasion of by the Soviet Union, **40–41, 49, 157, 194**
Fiske, Bradley, **7**
Flying Tigers, **83**
Foch, Ferdinand, **2**
Focke Wulf Fw 200 Condor (Germany), **57**
Fokker, Anthony, **13, 120**
Fokker Eindecker (Germany), **18**
Ford Trimotor (U.S.), **13, 14**
Formosa, **148**
France, **31, 32, 77n5**
  air power doctrine of, 26–27
  casualties of during the battle for France, 44
  effect of the Great Depression on aircraft production in, 91
  failure of to support Poland militarily, 38
  invasion of by Germany, 41–44
  lack of preparation for war with Germany, 33–34
  nationalization of the aircraft industry, 27
  strength of its air force at the beginning of World War II, 37–38
Franco, Francisco, **33**
Frunze, Mikhail, **27–28**
Fujita, Yuzo, **189**
Fullam, W. F., **7**

George, David Lloyd, **10**
Georges, Alphonse, **41**
German Air Force. See Luftwaffe
German Army
  Army Group A, 43

Army Group B, 42–43
Army Group Center, 53, 54
Army Group North, 53
Army Group South, 53
Fifteenth Panzer Army, 64
Fifth Panzer Army, 64
Seventh Army, 64
Seventh Panzer Division, 43
Sixth Army, defeat of at
    Stalingrad, 55–56
See also Afrika Korps
German Navy, **44**
Germany, **73, 94**
    aircraft production in during
        World War II, 39, 45, 73
        (table), 74
    invasion of Poland by, 34, 38–39
    invasion of Denmark, Sweden,
        and Norway by (Operation
        Weser), 40–41
    invasion of the Netherlands and
        Belgium by, 41–44
    military superiority of over the
        Allies (1940), 42
    private flying clubs in, 179
    rearmament of, 31
    remilitarization of the Rhineland,
        26, 32
    strategic design of for the
        invasion of France, 43
    structure of its air force, 24–26
    World War I aircraft of (Junkers
        C-1 and D-1), 17
Germany, strategic bombing of by
    the Allied forces, **58–63**
    bombing campaign against
        Berlin, 59–60
    bombing of Cologne, 59
    bombing of Dresden, 63–64
    bombing of Schweinfurt ball
        bearing factories, 61
    establishment of Allied air
        superiority, 62–63
    fire bombing of Hamburg, 59
    Luftwaffe response to, 62

total bombing tonnage dropped
    by the Allies, 59, 62–63
Glenn L. Martin Company, **124,
    128**
Goake, Tokuhishiro, **224**
Gorbunov, Vladimir, **113**
Göring, Hermann, **25, 43, 45, 46,
    47**
Gorrell, Edgar, **6**
Great Britain, **31, 32**
    aircraft production in during
        World War II, 39, 74 (table),
        75–76
    assistance of to Greece, 50
    defeat of the Italian Tenth Army
        in North Africa, 51
    lack of preparation for war with
        Germany, 33–34
    See also Battle of Britain
Great Depression, **14, 91, 175**
Greece, invasion of by Italy, **49–50**
    German intervention in, 50
    Greek resistance to, 50
    See also Crete, invasion of by
        Germany
Gromov, M. M., **153, 155, 191,
    193**
Guadalcanal, **69, 70**
Gudkov, Mikhail, **113**
*Guidelines for the Conduct of the
    Operational Air War* (Wilberg),
    25
Guryevich, Mikhail, **118, 119**

Haig, Douglas, **10**
Hamburger Flugzeugbau, **217**
Handley Page Company, **222**
Harris, Arthur, **59**
Hartmann, Erich, **54**
Hashiguchi, Yoshio, **226**
Hassan, Sayyid Muhammad Ibn
    Abdulla, **30**
Hattori, Joji, **185**
Hattori, Rokuro, **152**
Hermes, **224**

Hindenburg, Paul von, **31**
Hirohito (Emperor of Japan), **73**
Hiryu, **68**
Hitler, Adolf, **25, 26, 31, 32, 43, 77n5**
  annexation of Bohemia, Moravia, and the Sudetenland, 34
  blackmail of Great Britain and France with war threats, 33–34
  desire of to attack the Soviet Union, 49
  misjudgment of the British, 44–45
  rationale of for invading Scandinavia, 40
  suicide of, 64
  support of for Franco, 33
Honjo, Sueo, **149, 150**
Horikoshi, Jiro, **219**
Hornet, **67, 224**

Iinuma, Masaaki, **188**
Illustrious, **50, 212**
Ilyushin, Sergei Vladimorovic, **158**
Imashi, Isamu, **145**
Imperial Expeditionary Force (Great Britain), **50**
Imperial Japanese Army (IJA), **28–29**
Imperial Japanese Navy (IJN), **28–29, 70, 104, 109, 149–153, 200, 219–230**
  attack of on Pearl Harbor, 65–66
  modification of Type 93 torpedoes as suicide submarines, 152
Industria Aernautica Romania, **122**
Inoue, Shigeyoshi, **29**
Inskip, Thomas, **23–24**
International Flying Meet (Zurich [1937]), **18**
Ishikawajima, **187**
Italian Tenth Army, defeat of, **51**
Italy, **31–32**
  defeat of at Sidi Barrani, 50, 51
  industrial weakness of, 75
  military commitment of in the Spanish Civil War, 33
  occupation of Albania by, 50
  poor performance of the Italian Army in North Africa, 51
  See also Greece, invasion of by Italy
Itokawa, Hideo, **104**

Jacobs, Hans, **181**
Japan, **28–29**
  aircraft production in, 73 (table), 74–75
  bombing raids on by the United States, 67, 69
  mindset of Japanese soldiers, pilots, and naval personnel, 152–153
  number of frontline aircraft at the beginning of World War II, 74
  use of airpower during the interwar years, 30–31
Japan Air Lines Company (Nippon Koku K.K.), **151**
Japanese Army Air Force (JAAF), **29, 102–109, 145, 147–148, 187, 219, 220**
Japanese Navy Air Force, **29, 109–110, 187**
Jodl, Alfred, **64**
Johnson, Kelly, **83**
Junkers Flugzeug, **17, 180**
Junkers G 38 (Germany), **40**

Kaga, **68**
Kajima, Yoshitaka, **149**
Kalinin, Konstantin Alekseevich, **155**
Kamikaze (Divine Wind) prototype, **188**
Kasserine Pass, Battle of, **52**
Kawanishi, **221, 222, 226, 227**

Kawasaki, **101, 102, 107–108, 187**

Keller, Alfred, **53**

Kesselring, Albert, **45, 53**

Khomyakova, Valeria Ivanova, **116**

Kikahura, Shizuo, 226

Kisaragi, sinking of, **198**

Knauss, Robert, **25**

Kondo, Katsuji, **226**

Kondor Legion (Germany), **33, 38**

Konigsberg, sinking of, **211**

Kono, Kumihiko, **188**

Koyama, Yasushi, **101, 105, 107, 148**

Kozhedub, Ivan, **115**

Kubo, Tomio, **149, 188**

Kusabake, Nobuhiko, **149**

Lavochkin, Semyon, **113, 115**

Leeb, Wilhelm von, **42**

Leigh-Mallory, Trafford, **46**

LeMay, Curtis E., **61, 71, 129**

Lend-Lease Program, **56, 119, 173, 190, 231–232**

Lexington, **224**

Leyte Gulf, Battle of, **198**

Libya, **50, 51**

  Rommel's counteroffensive in, 51

Liddell-Hart, Basil, **2**

Lindbergh, Charles, **12, 84**

Littorio, **50, 212**

Litvyak, Lilya Vladimirovna, **116**

Lockheed Aircraft Company, **83**

  Lockheed Model 14 Super Electra (civilian aircraft), 203

  Lockheed Vega (civilian aircraft), 13

Loening, Grover Cleveland, **205**

Löhr, Alexander, **53**

Ludendorff, Eric, **2**

Luftwaffe, **32, 33, 34, 43, 118, 134, 182**

  assembled forces for Operation Barbarossa, 53–54

  Jagdgeschwader 7, 64

  lack of a long-range bomber, 74

  losses of in the battle for France, 44, 45

  losses of in the Polish Campaign, 39

  Luftflotte 1, 53

  Luftflotte 2, 45, 51, 53, 54

  Luftflotte 3, 45, 46

  Luftflotte 4, 53

  Luftflotte 5, 45, 46–47

  Luftwaffe aces in World War II, 54

  number of frontline aircraft at the Battle of Britain, 45

  number of frontline aircraft at the beginning of World War II, 74, 77n1

  number of frontline aircraft in invasion of France, 41–42

  rebuilding of after the battle for France, 45

  role of in the invasion of Poland (Polish Campaign), 38–39

  strength of at the beginning of World War II, 37–38

Maginot Line, **26, 38, 178**

Malta, **51, 211**

Manchuria, **31**

Manstein, Erich von, **42, 56**

"Marianas Turkey Shoot," **70–71, 148, 198, 225**

Marie, André, **101**

Marshall, George C., **60**

Masuhara, Kozo, **190**

Matsuhara, Hajime, **222**

Matsuo, Kishiro, **227, 228**

McCampbell, David, **198**

McGuire, Tom, **84**

Mein Kampf (Hitler), **49**

Messerschmitt BF 109 (Germany), **19**

Midway, Battle of, **67–69, 75, 221**

Mikoyan, Artem, **118, 119**

Mikuma, **69**

Milch, Erhard, 25–26, 44
Minoru, Genda, 65
Missouri, 79
Mitchell, William ("Billy"), 2, 5–9,
    10, 12, 21, 35n2, 80, 124
  influence of on American air
    power, 9
  insistence of on an independent
    air force, 8
  military career of, 5–6
  outspokenness of, 6–7
  promotion of airpower over naval
    power by, 7–8
  recognition of as America's
    premier airman, 6
  report of predicting war with
    Japan, 8
  service of in World War I, 6
Mitsubishi, 101, 109, 151, 187,
    188, 222
Mitsuzi, Tadano, 151, 152
Mizumo, Shokichi, 188
Moffett, William, 7, 8, 22
Monte Casino, bombing of, 53
Montgomery, Bernard, 52
Morrow, Dwight, 8
Morrow Board, 8–9
Motorenwerke AG, 180
Muashi, sinking of, 71, 200
Munich Conference (1938), 34
Mussolini, Benito, 20, 31, 35n1,
    44
  decision to invade Ethiopia, 31–
    32
  decision to invade Greece, 49–50
  overthrow and subsequent rescue
    of, 53
  underestimation of the tenacity
    of the Greek Army, 50

Nagumo, Chuichi, 29
Nakajima, 101, 109, 151, 187,
    221, 222, 225, 227
  design team of for the Ki-49
    Donryu, 147–148

Nakamura, Katsuji, 109
Naval aircraft, 195
Naval aircraft (France), 214–216
  CAMS 37, 215
  CAMS 55, 215
  Latécoère Laté 298, 215
  Loire 130, 215
  Loire-Nieuport LN 401, 215–216
Naval aircraft (Germany), 216–217
  Arado Ar 196, 216, 240 (photo)
  Blohm und Voss Bv 138, 217
  Dornier Do 18, 217
  Dornier Do 24, 217, 261 (photo)
Naval aircraft (Great Britain), 210–
    214
  bombers
    Blackburn Shark, 212
    Fairey Barracuda, 212–213
    Fairey Swordfish, 50, 202, 212,
      265 (photo)
  fighters and attack aircraft, 210–
    212
    Blackburn Skua, 211
    Fairey Firefly, 211–212
    Fairey Flycatcher, 210–211,
      264 (photo)
    Fairey Fulmar, 211
    Hawker Nimrod, 211
    Hawker Osprey, 134, 211
  flying boats, 213–214
    Felixstowe F5, 213
    Short Sunderland, 57, 214,
      227
    Supermarine Southampton,
      213
    Supermarine Stranraer, 213
    Supermarine Walrus, 214
  reconnaissance and auxiliary
    aircraft, 213
    Fairey IIIF, 213
Naval aircraft (Italy), 218–219
  Cant Z 501 Gabbiano, 218, 252
    (photo)
  Cant Z 506B Airone, 218

Fiat CR 20 (adapted for naval
service), 217–218
Fiat RS 14, 218
Naval aircraft (Japan), **219–230**
bombers, 222–225
Aichi D1A2, 224
Aichi D3As, 65, 68, 224
Aichi D3A2, 224
Aichi D4Y Suisei ("Comet"),
225
Blackburn B2M, 222–223
Nakajima B5N ("Kate"), 65,
66, 68, 223–224, 295 (photo)
Navy Type 99 Carrier Bomber
Model 11, 224
fighters, 219–222
Kawanishi N1K1 Kyofu
("Mighty Wind"), 222, 281
(photo)
Kawanishi N1K1-J Shiden
("Violet Lightning"), 222
Mitsubishi A5M ("Claude"),
18, 30, 219, 220
Mitsubishi A5M1, 219
Mitsubishi A5M3a, 219
Mitsubishi A5M4, 219
Mitsubishi A6M Reisen
("Zero"), 219–221
Nakajima A6M2-N, 221
flying boats
Kawanishi H6K ("Mavis"),
208, 227–228
reconnaissance and auxiliary
aircraft, 225–230
Aichi E13A, 227, 228
Aichi E16A Zuiun ("Auspicious
Cloud"), 229
Kawanishi H6K, 226–227
Kawanishi H8K ("Flying
Porcupine"), 227–228
Kawanishi H8K2-L, 228
Nakajima C6N Saiun ("Painted
Cloud"), 229–230
Nakajima E8N, 225–226

Naval aircraft (Soviet Union), **230–
233**
Beriev KOR-1, 231, 232
Beriev KOR-2, 232
Beriev MBR-2, 230
Beriev MP2bis, 230–231
Chetverikov ARK-3/ARK-4, 231
Chetverikov MDR-6, 231–232
PBY Catalina (from Lend Lease
Program), 231–232, 233, 255
(photo)
Naval aircraft (United States),
195–210
bombers, 201–204
Consolidated PB4Y, 204
Curtiss SB2C Helldiver, 202–
203
Curtiss SBC Helldiver, 17, 201
Douglas SBD Dauntless, 66,
69, 202
Lockheed PBO Hudson, 203
Lockheed PV-1 Ventura, 203
Lockheed PV-2 Harpoon, 203
Martin BM, 201
Northrop BT-1, 202
Northrop BT-2, 202
Vought F3U, 201
Vought SB2U Vindicator, 201–
202
Vought SBU Scout, 17
fighters and attack aircraft, 195–
201
Boeing F2B, 196
Boeing F3B, 196
Brewster F2A Buffalo, 197,
249 (photo)
Curtiss TS-1, 195–196
Douglas DT, 199
Douglas T2D/P2D, 199–200
Douglas TBD Devastator, 200
Grumman F2F, 196–197, 271
(photo)
Grumman F3F, 196–197
Grumman F4F Wildcat, 66,
69, 197–198

Grumman F6F Hellcat, 198, 272 (photo)
Grumman FF ("FiFi"), 196
Grumman TBF/TBM Avenger, 200–201, 273 (photo)
Martin T3M, 199
Vought F4U Corsair, 198–199, 230, 316 (photo)
flying boats, 207–210
    Consolidated P2Y Ranger, 208
    Consolidated PB2Y Coronado, 209
    Consolidated PBY Catalina, 57, 68, 208–209, 231–232, 233, 255 (photo)
    Douglas OA-4/RD, 208
    Douglas OA-4/RD Dolphin, 208
    Grumman JF/J2F Duck, 209
    Grumman JRF Goose, 209
    Hall PH, 208
    Loening OA/OL, 208
    Martin JRM Mars, 210
    Martin PBM Mariner, 209–210
    Naval Aircraft Factory PN-series, 207–208
    Sikorsky XPBS-1, 227
reconnaissance and auxiliary aircraft, 204–207
    Boeing NB, 204
    Consolidated NY, 204
    Curtiss SC Seahawk, 207
    Curtiss SNC Falcon, 205
    Curtiss SO3C Seamew, 206–207
    Curtiss SOC Seagull, 206
    Loening OL, 205
    Naval Aircraft Factory N3N, 204–205
    Timm N2T Tutor, 205
    Vought O2U, 206
    Vought O3U Corsair, 206
    Vought OS2U Kingfisher, 207
    Vought UO, 205–206

Naval Aircraft Factory, **196, 207**
Neosho, 67
Netherlands, invasion of by Germany, **42–43, 120**
    bombing of Rotterdam, 43, 77n4
Norden bombsight, **17**
North Africa, joint British/American landings at (Operation Torch), **52–53**
    aircraft involved in, 52–53
    surrender of the Afrika Korps as a result of, 53
Norway, invasion of by Germany, **40–41**

Ohwada, Shigejiro, **101**
Ohta, Mitsui, **152**
Onishi, Takijiro, **29**
Operation Adlertag, **45, 46**
Operation Barbarossa, **53, 156, 190**
    actions in the Kuban Peninsula, 56
    assault on Moscow, 54–55
    combined German forces assembled for, 53
    decline in German air superiority after the defense of Moscow, 55
    destruction of Russian aircraft on the first day of, 54, 76
    German air power assembled for, 53–54
    German casualties, 54
    inexperience of Russian pilots, 54
    Luftwaffe and Red Air Force losses during, 54, 56
    number of Soviet air sorties in defense of Russia, 55
    relief of Demyansk by the Luftwaffe, 55
    siege of Leningrad, 55, 154
    Soviet casualties, 54
    Soviet counteroffensives, 54, 55

Soviet movement of aircraft production beyond the Urals, 54

tank battle in the Kursk salient, 56

Operation Bodenplatte, **64**

Operation Sea Lion, **45, 48**

Operation Torch, **52–53**

Osipenka, Paulina, **230**

Ota, Shiro, **145**

Owada, Shin, **106**

Ozawa, Jisaboro, **29**

Ozawa, Yasushiro, **228**

Park, Keith, **46**

Patton, George S., **63**

Paulus, Friedrich von, **55, 56**

Pearl Harbor, attack on, **65–66, 74–75, 224**

  casualties of, 66

  failure of to destroy American aircraft carriers, 75

  loss of American aircraft and naval ships, 66

Pershing, John J., **6**

Pétain, Philippe, **44, 77n5**

Petty, G. E., **222**

Petyakov, Vladimir Mikhailovich, **155, 160**

"Phony War" (September, 1939 to April, 1940), **41**

  aircraft losses during, 39–40

Pilots, training of, **19–20**

Pokryshkin, Alexander Ivanovich, **113**

Poland, **31**

  fall of Warsaw to the Germans, 39

  invasion of by Germany, 34, 38–39

  strength of its air force at the beginning of World War II, 37–38

Polikarpov, Nikolai, **110, 118, 191, 231**

Polish Air Force, **38–39, 121**

Polish National Aircraft Company (PZL), **121**

Potez 540 (France), **27**

Prince of Wales, sinking of, **150, 151, 188**

Princeton, **71**

Punitive Expedition (Mexico [1916–1917]), **5**

Raeder, Erich, **40, 44**

Reconnaissance and auxiliary aircraft, **165**

Reconnaissance and auxiliary aircraft (France), **177–178**

  Bloch MB 174, 177, 243 (photo)

  Breguet 19, 178

Reconnaissance and auxiliary aircraft (German), **179–184**

reconnaissance and liaison aircraft, 182–184

  Fieseler Fi 156 Storch, 183, 190, 268 (photo)

  Focke-Wulf Fw 190 Uhu ("Owl"), 183, 269 (photo)

  Focke-Wulf 200 Condor, 183–184, 270 (photo)

  Heinkel He 45, 182

  Heinkel He 46, 182

  Henschel Hs 126, 182

trainers, 178–180

  Arado Ar 66, 179

  Arado Ar 96, 179, 180

  Focke-Wulf Fw 58 Weihe, 180

  Gotha Go 145, 179

  Messerschmitt BF-108 Taifun, 179–180

transports and gliders, 180–182

  DFS 230, 43, 181

  Gotha Go 242, 181

  Junkers Ju 52/3, 33, 40, 43, 45, 50, 120, 180, 181, 278 (photo)

  Messerschmitt 321, 181

Reconnaissance and auxiliary
aircraft (Great Britain), 174–
177
reconnaissance and liaison
aircraft, 177
de Havilland DH9a, 177
Westland Lysander, 177
Westland Wapiti, 177
trainers, 174–175
Airspeed Oxford, 175
Avro Anson, 174–175
Avro Anson Mk.X, 175
de Havilland DH 60T Gypsy
Moth, 174
de Havilland DH 82 Tiger
Moth, 174, 258 (photo)
de Havilland Dominie
(originally the DH 89 Dragon
Rapide), 175
Miles Master, 175
"Queen Bee" drones, 174
transports and gliders, 175–176
Airspeed Horsa, 176, 238
(photo)
Airspeed Horsa Mk.1, 176
Airspeed Horsa Mk.2, 176
Armstrong Whitworth
Albemarle, 176
Bristol Bombay, 175–176
General Aircraft Hamilcar,
133, 176
Reconnaissance and auxiliary
aircraft (Italy), 184–185
Caproni CA 309–316, 184
Fiat CR 20 (two-seat version),
184
Piaggio P 108, 184
Savoia-Marchetti SM 75, 184
Savoia-Marchetti SM 79, 309
(photo)
Savoia-Marchetti SM 81
Pipistrello, 184, 310 (photo)
Savoia-Marchetti SM 82
Canguru, 184–185

Reconnaissance and auxiliary
aircraft (Japan), 185–190
reconnaissance and liaison
aircraft, 187–190
Kawasaki Army Type 88, 187–
188, 283 (photo)
Kokusai Ki-76, 190
Mitsubishi C5M, 188, 189
Mitsubishi C5M1, 189
Mitsubishi C5M2, 189
Mitsubishi Ki-15, 188
Mitsubishi Ki-15-I, 189
Mitsubishi Ki-15-II, 189
Mitsubishi Ki-46, 189–190
Mitsubishi Ki-51, 189
trainers, 185–186
Kyushu K11W, 185
Mitsubishi K3M, 185–186
Mitsubishi K3M3, 185
Tachikawa Ki-55, 186
Yokosuka K5Y, 186
transports, 186–187
Mitsubishi Ki-21 ("Sally"), 186
Mitsubishi Ki-57 ("Topsy"),
186–187
Reconnaissance and auxiliary
aircraft (Soviet Union), 190–
194
reconnaissance and liaison
aircraft, 193–194
Polikarpov R.5, 194
trainers, 190–192
Polikarpov U-2, 191, 194, 305
(photo)
Yakovlev UT-1, 191–192
Yakovlev UT-2, 192
transports, 192–193
Lisunov Li-2, 192
Tupolev ANT-9, 192–193
Tupolev ANT-14, 193
Reconnaissance and auxiliary
aircraft (United States), 165–
174
reconnaissance and liaison
aircraft, 171–174

Curtiss O-52 Owl, 173
Douglas O-2, 172
Douglas O-31, 172
Douglas O-43, 172
Douglas O-46, 172
Grasshopper series, 173–174
North American O-47, 172–173
Piper O-59/L-4, 173
Sperry M-1 Messenger, 171
Stinson L-5, 173
Stinson O-49/L-1 Vigilant, 173
Taylorcraft L-2, 174
Thomas-Morse O-19, 172
trainers, 166–169
Beech AT-10 Wichita, 168
Cessna AT-8, 168
Cessna AT-9 Jeep, 169
Cessna AT-17, 168
Cessna T-50, 168
Cessna UC-78, 168
Consolidated PT-1 ("Trusty"), 166, 256 (photo)
Curtiss AT-9, 169
Curtiss PT-3, 166
Fairchild AT-21 Gunner, 169
Fairchild PT-17, 167
Fairchild PT-19, 167
North American AT-6 Texan, 167, 168, 299 (photo)
North American BT-8 (originally the SEV-3), 167
North American BT-9, 166–167, 168
North American BT-9A, 167
North American BT-9C, 167
North American BT-14, 167
North American P-64, 169
Seversky AT-12, 169
Stearman Kaydet PT-13, 166
Stearman Kaydet PT-17
Stearman Kaydet PT-27
Vultee BT-13 (SNV Valiant), 167–168
transports and gliders, 169–171
Curtiss C-46/R5C, 170–171
Douglas C-1, 169
Douglas C-39/R2D, 169–170
Douglas C-47 Skytrain, 170, 263 (photo)
Douglas C-54/RD2 Skymaster, 170
Waco CG-4 Haig/Hadrian, 171
Red Air Force, **55**
growth in strength of, 56
Red Army (Soviet Union), **27–28**
victory of on the Eastern Front, 56–57
Regia Aeronautica (Italy), **20–21, 32, 211**
number of frontline aircraft at the beginning of World War II, 51, 75
vulnerability of, 51
Reichswehr (Germany), **24**
Reidy, T. H., **230**
Repulse, sinking of, **150, 151, 188**
Richard, Paul-Aimé, **230**
Richthofen, Wolfram von, **39**
Robin, Maxime, **101**
Rommel, Erwin, **43, 53**
actions of in North Africa, 51–52
retreat of from El Alamein, 52
Roosevelt, Franklin Delano, **49, 60**
Royal Air Force (RAF [Great Britain]), **2, 10, 20, 23–24, 30, 62**
action of in North Africa, 51–52
attack of on German naval targets (Wilhelmshaven Raid), 39–40, 59, 60–61, 132
attack/fighter aircraft of, 87–91
Czech and Polish squadrons of, 47
first victory of over the Luftwaffe, 43
losses of in the battle of France, 44, 45
rearmament of, 33

rebuilding of after the battle for France, 45

reorganization of, 23

Squadron 303, 47

strength of at the beginning of World War II, 37–38

use of during the interwar years, 30

Western Desert Force, 52

See also Battle of Britain; Bomber Command (Great Britain)

Royal Canadian Air Force, **213**

Royal Flying Corps (Great Britain), **9–10, 20**

Royal Naval Air Service (Great Britain), **10, 20**

Royal Navy (Great Britain), **24, 44, 48**

attack of on Taranto (Italian naval base), 50

seizure of the *Altmark* by, 40

sinking of German ships at Narvik, 41

Rules for the Use of Aircraft in War (Douhet), **3**

Rundstedt, Gerd von, **42, 43, 443**

Rushing, Roy, **198**

Russian Civil War, **27, 153**

Russo-Finnish War, **88**

Russo-Polish War (1918–1920), **27**

Ryujo, **69**

Saipan, **72, 73**

U.S. invasion of, 70

Saratoga, **69**

Saul, Richard, **46**

SBD Dauntless, **67, 69**

Schlieffen Plan (1914), **42**

Schmid, Josef, **46**

Second Sino-Japanese War, **219, 223**

Seeckt, Hans von, **24–25**

Seversky, Alexander P. De, **167**

Shenandoah, crash of, **8**

Shima, Katsuzo, **150, 219**

Shoho, **67**

Shokaku, **67, 68, 69**

Sicily, **51**

Sidi Barrani, **50, 51**

Sims, William, **7**

Skorzeny, Otto, **53, 181**

Slovakia, **34**

Smith, Herbert, **185, 222**

Smuchkevich, Yakov, **28**

Solomon Islands, Battle of the, **69–70**

Soryu, **68**

Soviet Union, **24, 27–28, 49**

aircraft production in during World War II, 74 (table), 76

introduction of better military aircraft by, 54

invasion of Finland by, 40–41, 49

invasion of by Germany (Operation Barbarossa), 53–58, 76

non-aggression pact with Germany, 34

role of in the Spanish Civil War, 33

use of air power during the interwar years, 31

See also Stalingrad, Battle of

Spaatz, Carl A., **9, 62**

SPAD XIII (France), **19**

Spanish-American War (1898), **5**

Spanish Civil War, **17, 18, 21, 26, 33, 74, 136, 138, 157, 194, 218**

impact of on air power, 33

as a training exercise for Germany's military, 33

Spanish Popular Front, **33**

Speer, Albert, **74**

Sperrle, Hugo, **45**

Sperry, Elmer, **171**

Sperry, Lawrence, **16**

Sperry Aircraft Corporation, **171**

Stalin, Joseph, **28, 33, 34, 60, 161**

Stalingrad, Battle of, **55–56**

STOL (short takeoff and landing), 177, 183
Strategic bombing, 25, 26, 28
    presumed value of, 58–59
Student, Kurt, 43, 50–51
Stumpf, Hans-Jürgen, 45
Sukhoi, Pavel, 157, 158
Sweden, invasion of by Germany, 40
Sykes, Frederick. 10

Tank, Kurt, 96
Taranto, attack of, 50
Tetrarch Mark Mk.IV tank (Great Britain), 63, 176
Thatch Weave flight maneuver, 197
Thomas-Morse Company, 80
Tirpitz, Alfred von, 25
    "risk fleet" theory of, 25
Tirpitz, sinking of, 133, 213
Tizard, Henry, 23
Tobruk, siege of, 51, 52
Todt, Fritz, 74
Tojo, Hisashi, 187
Treaty of Rapollo (1922), 24, 94
Treaty of Versailles, 2, 24, 31
    restrictions of on the Luftwaffe, 94, 178
    restrictions of on the German Navy, 35
Tripolitan War (1911–1912), 3
Trenchard, Hugh, 2, 9–12, 21, 23, 26, 30, 49, 88
    air power doctrine of, 11
    and the budgetary problems of the RAF, 11
    as commander of the Independent Bombing Force, 11
    as commander of the RAF, 10, 11–12
    as commander of the Royal Flying Corps, 10–11
    resistance of to strategic bombing, 10

Trotsky, Leon, 27
Truman, Harry S., 72
Tsukagoshi, Kenji, 188
Tukhachevski, Mikhail, 28
    "deep battle" theory of, 28
Tupolev, Andrei Nikolaevich, 153, 160–161, 192

U-boats, 57–58, 132, 217
Udet, Ernst, 17
Ugaki, Matome, 29
United States, aircraft production of during World War II, 74
    (table), 76
United States Air Force (USAF)
    Eighth Air Force, 60–61, 64
        losses suffered by, 61–62
        raid on Skoda (Czechoslovakia), 64
    Fifteenth Air Force, 53, 61
    Ninth Air Force, 60
    Twentieth Air Force, 72
United States Army Air Corps (USAAC), 9, 16, 21–23, 48, 52, 80, 81–81, 202, 203
    aces of, 84
    attack/fighter aircraft of, 79–87
    bombers of, 123–131
    training program of, 165–166
    use of night-fighters by, 85–86
United States Coast Guard, 208
United States Marine Corps (USMC), 30, 198
    "Black Sheep" squadron of, 198–199
United States Navy (USN), 22–23, 67, 171, 195–210
    training program of, 165–166
United States Strategic Air Forces (USSAF), 59, 60–62
    305th Bombardment Group, 61
    Air War Plans Division (AWPD), 60
    belief of in heavily armed bombers, 60

First Bombardment Wing, 61
reorganization of, 62

Vickers Vernon (Great Britain), **30**
Vickers Victoria (Great Britain), **30**
Vogt, Richard, **187**
Vuillemin, Joseph, **41**

Waco C6–4A Hadrian (United
States), **63**
Wasp, **224**
West Virginia, **153**
Westland Lysanders (Great Britain),
41
Wever, Walther, **26**
Wilberg, Helmuth, **24–25**
Wilhelmshaven Raid, **39–40, 59,
60–61, 132**
*Winged Defense: The Development
and Possibilities of Modern Air
Power—Economic and Military*
(Mitchell), **8**
Winkelman, Gerad, **43**
World War I (the Great War), **1, 5,
19**
aircraft of, 14, 15
effect of on military aircraft, 2
German use of air power in, 25
impact of military aircraft on, 2
Meuse-Argonne Offensive, 6
Nivelle Offensive, 26
Saint-Mihiel Offensive, 6
World War II, **23–24, 153**
Ardennes Offensive, 64
Normandy invasion, 63–64
See also World War II, military
aviation in (European Theater);
World War II, military aviation
in (Pacific Theater)
World War II, military aviation in
(European Theater), **37–38**
opening campaigns, 38–41
role of air power in the Battle of
the Atlantic, 57–58

role of in air power in the Battle
of Britain, 44–49
role of air power in the Battle of
France, 41–44
role of air power on the Eastern
Front, 53–58
role of air power in the
Mediterranean campaigns, 49–
53
role of air power from Normandy
invasion to the German
surrender, 63–64
strategic bombing of Germany,
58–63
World War II, military aviation in
(Pacific Theater), **64–73,
129–130**
Battle of the Coral Sea, 67, 68,
221
Battle of Midway, 67–69, 75, 221
Battle of the Solomon Islands,
69–70
bombing raid on the Marshall
Islands by the United States,
66, 70
campaign to take Iwo Jima from
the Japanese, 72
"Doolittle Raids" on Japan, 67,
69
incendiary bombing of Kobe and
Tokyo by the United States, 71
invasion of Saipan by the United
States, 70
Japanese attack on Australia, 66–
67
Japanese attack on Pearl Harbor,
65–66, 74–75, 224
"Marianas Turkey Shoot," 70–71,
148, 198, 225
ratio of Japanese to American
aircraft at beginning of the war,
66
use of aircraft carriers to project
power rather than battleships,
69

use of atomic bombs against
    Hiroshima and Nagasaki, 72–
    73, 124, 129
Wright Cyclone engines, **14**

Yakovlev, Alexander, **115**, 116–117,
    159–160, 191–192, **193**
Yamamoto, Isoruku, 29, **65**, 66,
    69, 84, 149, 151, 224
    overzealousness of, 67–68, 69
Yamana, Maseo, 151, 152, 224–
    225

Yamato, sinking of, 71, **200**
Yankee Doodle, **60**
Yokosuka, **224–225**
Yorktown, 67, 68, 69, **224**
Yugoslavia, **136**
    invasion of by Germany, 50

Zhukov, Georgi, 31, **55**
Zveno, V. S. Vakhmistrov, **154**
Zuiho, 71
Zuikaku, 67, 68, 71

ABOUT THE AUTHORS

Justin D. Murphy, Ph.D., is Brand Professor of History and director of the Douglas MacArthur Academy of Freedom Honors Program at Howard Payne University, Brownwood, Texas. He is the author of *Military Aircraft, Origins to 1918: An Illustrated History of Their Impact* in the Weapons and Warfare Series. He has published numerous articles and book reviews in scholarly journals and encyclopedias, and has served as associate editor of *The European Powers in the First World War: An Encyclopedia* and *Encyclopedia of American Military History*.

Matthew A. McNiece, M.A., is a graduate of and now assistant professor of history in the Douglas MacArthur Academy of Freedom Honors Program at Howard Payne University in Brownwood, Texas. He has previously contributed to ABC-Clio's Encyclopedias of World War I and II, and is currently working on a dissertation on the social and political rhetoric of American anti-communism for Texas Christian University's American History Ph.D. program.